GU01017971

Jonson, Shakespeare and early modern Virgil

In this wide-ranging and original study, Margaret Tudeau-Clayton
examines how Virgil – the poet as well as his texts – was mediated
in early modern England. She analyses what was at stake in the
reproduction of these mediations of Virgil, focusing, specifically, on
the works of Ben Jonson and on one of Shakespeare's most reson-
antly Virgilian plays, *The Tempest*. She argues that the play offers a
complex model of cultural and socio-political resistance by engag-
ing critically not only with contemporary mediations of Virgil, but
with the ways they were used, especially by Jonson, to reproduce
structures of authority (in relation to nature and language as well as
to the socio-political order). She also shows how instructive comparisons may be drawn between the ways Virgil was constructed
and used in early modern England and the ways Shakespeare has
been constructed and used, especially as national poet, from the
early modern period until our own time.

JONSON,
SHAKESPEARE
AND EARLY MODERN
VIRGIL

MARGARET TUDEAU-CLAYTON

CAMBRIDGE
UNIVERSITY PRESS

CAMBRIDGE UNIVERSITY PRESS
Cambridge, New York, Melbourne, Madrid, Cape Town, Singapore, São Paulo

Cambridge University Press
The Edinburgh Building, Cambridge CB2 2RU, UK

Published in the United States of America by Cambridge University Press, New York

www.cambridge.org
Information on this title: www.cambridge.org/9780521580793

© Margaret Tudeau-Clayton 1998

This publication is in copyright. Subject to statutory exception
and to the provisions of relevant collective licensing agreements,
no reproduction of any part may take place without
the written permission of Cambridge University Press.

First published 1998
This digitally printed first paperback version 2006

A catalogue record for this publication is available from the British Library

Library of Congress Cataloguing in Publication data
Tudeau-Clayton, Margaret, 1952–
Jonson, Shakespeare, and early modern Virgil / Margaret Tudeau-Clayton.
p. cm.
Includes bibliographical references and index.
ISBN 0 521 58079 X (hardback)
1. Jonson, Ben, 1573?–1637 – Political and social views. 2. Literature and society – England
– History – 17th century. 3. Jonson, Ben, 1573?–1637 – Knowledge – Literature.
4. Shakespeare, William, 1564–1616. Tempest. 5. Latin poetry – Appreciation – England.
6. English drama – Roman influences. 7. Social classes in literature. 8. Rome –
In literature. 9. Virgil – Influence.
I. Title.
PR2642.S58T84 1998
822.3'09351 – dc21 97–4226 CIP

ISBN-13 978-0-521-58079-3 hardback
ISBN-10 0-521-58079-X hardback

ISBN-13 978-0-521-03274-2 paperback
ISBN-10 0-521-03274-1 paperback

To my parents,
Bobs and Jean-François,
for their difference and mine.

'. . . this strange institution called literature . . . at once wild and institutional'

Jacques Derrida, *Acts of Literature*

Contents

Illustrations

Preface

This book has its origins in a childhood privileged by the benevolent presence of two outstanding classicists, my father Fred Clayton, and my godfather, Jackson Knight. To the former I owe the gift of love for language, literature and the life of the mind.

To Tony Tanner of King's College, Cambridge, a brilliant critic and inspiring teacher, I owe thanks for first showing me how to pay attention to a literary text, and to John Barrell and David Simpson for introducing me to the question of the relation of the literary text to history and politics. I have benefited too from the exceptional erudition of the late Robert Bolgar and the critical acumen of Frank Kermode. Constructive dialogue with my thesis examiners, Anne Barton and the late James Smith, pointed me in the direction of a book, which has since grown out of various, more and less direct conversations with scholars and critics the world over. Colleagues and students at the Universities of Geneva and Lausanne have provided a stimulating and supportive environment over the past several years; special thanks to Gregory Polletta and Rick Waswo (Geneva), and Neil Forsyth and Peter Halter (Lausanne). The readers for Cambridge University Press were constructive in their critical comments, especially Ian Donaldson, whose insights have been particularly valuable. Pippa Berry of King's College, Cambridge has been a precious friend, supplying me with an on-going exciting intellectual exchange as well as with important help with the final draft. Josie Dixon of Cambridge University Press has been a steady support throughout. The staff in various libraries, notably the staff of the rare books room at Cambridge University Library, are to be thanked for their efficient, friendly service. My thanks too to the authorities of the University of Lausanne for the term's leave they gave me to work on the book, and for their contribution towards the cost of its publication.

Special mention must be made of Lisa Jardine, without whose

ix

informed advice and consistent, energetic encouragement this book would probably not have seen the light of day.

Finally, my deepest thanks to Jean-François, sometimes almost, but, mercifully, not often 'the wife', for his stoic patience, and *haute cuisine*; and to 'the girls' for the sweet irony of their absolute indifference to my labours.

Bibliographical note

Citations and quotations from Virgil will be taken from the Loeb edition by H. Rushton Fairclough, unless otherwise indicated. Translations will be mine, again unless otherwise indicated. In quoting from early modern texts I have normalised i/j and u/v spellings, and silently expanded abbreviated forms. The native form of the proper name is given where it is recognisably related to the Latinised form (for example, Eritreo). The Latinised form is otherwise retained (for example, Pontanus rather than Spanmüller), as it is also retained when it is the more commonly used form (for example, Ramus).

Introduction

This book is not about authors and texts but 'authors' and 'texts', not definitive meanings but finite mediations, the *figures* produced and circulated in the discourses of a historically and culturally specific universe. What is at stake in the production and circulation of these figures? How do they come to be contested, erased? And what is at stake in their contestation and erasure?

My case study will be the multivalent figure of Virgil in early modern England, which I shall compare, briefly here, and occasionally throughout, with the case of Shakespeare(s). Though necessarily different in many important ways, there are likenesses between the two, which go beyond the multiformity Chris Baswell suggests is characteristic of the reception of 'central' figures in the various layers and media, popular as well as learned, of a given culture.[1] This is indicated, if unwittingly, by historical critics from the eighteenth century on, who, seeking 'to discover a modern face under the classical mask' of the *dramatis persona* of Virgil in Ben Jonson's play *Poetaster* (first performed 1601), have come to the very unhistorical conclusion that this face is none other than the face of Shakespeare.[2] Indeed, 'Mr William Poel dressed "Virgil" as Shakespeare' for a performance of the play produced in London on 26 April 1916 (*H&S*, vol. 1, p. 432, note 1), at the height, that is, of the massive tercentenary celebrations mobilising the figure of Shakespeare – at once universal and specifically English – in affirmation of 'an Anglo-centric

---

[1] Christopher C. Baswell, *Virgil in Medieval England: Figuring the 'Aeneid' from the Twelfth Century to Chaucer* (Cambridge University Press, 1995), p. 16 and p. 31. Baswell suggests twentieth-century Shakespeare and Freud as examples comparable to medieval Virgil.

[2] *Ben Jonson*, edited by C. H. Herford, Percy and Evelyn Simpson, 11 vols. (Oxford: Clarendon Press, 1925–52), vol. 1, p. 432. I refer to this edition throughout using the abbreviation *H&S* with the volume and page numbers, modernising titles. On the identification of Jonson's Virgil with Shakespeare see also Ben Jonson, *Poetaster*, edited by Tom Cain (Manchester University Press, 1995), p. 217.

universe'[3] at a moment of international as well as national political and ideological crisis.

This identification of Jonson's *dramatis persona* with Shakespeare, which might, I imagine, have offended the author of *Poetaster*, if not the author of the prefatory poem to the first folio (discussed below), is a function of an ideological equivalence in the 'system of representations' informing the discourses constituting a certain form, or level, of cultural consciousness.[4] Within this system, that is, Virgil stands for what Shakespeare stands for: an ideal, absolute paradigm of the national poet; a repository of universal human wisdom;[5] a stable, monolithic and sacred object of reverential attention at the centre of a homogeneous community of educated readers/spectators.

Idealist and essentialist, suppressing the differences and discontinuities of history, this equivalence has come to be confined to the discourses of the academy, as Virgil has become virtually unrecognisable as a currency of signification outside them (and the equivalence consequently meaningless). Within the academy, the equivalence has been produced by, and has served to reproduce the system of representations informing the discourse of traditional literary history, consisting in the master authors – or great books – of the canon. What is ultimately at stake in the reproduction of this equivalence is thus the common ground, or shared 'body', which has traditionally given a sense of collective identity to the academic community in English studies. The current crisis, largely articulated around the question of the canon, is, amongst other things, a crisis of collective identity; it has become increasingly problematic to use 'we' and to assume shared objects – purposes as well as texts.[6]

---

[3] Malcolm Evans, 'Deconstructing Shakespeare's Comedies', in John Drakakis, ed., *Alternative Shakespeares* (London and New York: Methuen, 1985), p. 84.

[4] The term 'ideological' is used in the sense, derived from Althusser, which Kavanagh expounds, the phrase 'system of representations' being Althusserian. See James H. Kavanagh, 'Ideology', in Frank Lentricchia and Thomas McLaughlin, eds., *Critical Terms for Literary Study* (University of Chicago Press, 1990), p. 310. Kavanagh's example of a contemporary 'cultural icon', though dealing with a very different form of cultural consciousness, nevertheless shows, as I try to do, how authors are turned into figures (or icons) and *used*. For this use of the term 'ideology', see also Jonathan Dollimore, 'Introduction', in Jonathan Dollimore and Alan Sinfield, eds., *Political Shakespeare* (Manchester University Press, 1985), pp. 6–7; Howard Felperin, 'Political Criticism at the Crossroads: The Utopian Historicism of *The Tempest*', in Nigel Wood, ed., *The Tempest. Theory in Practice* (Milton Keynes and Philadelphia: Open University Press, 1995), pp. 35–7.

[5] Compare Gollancz, in 1916, on Shakespeare's 'power to instil in men's hearts his manifold observations on the myriad problems of life and eternity' (quoted in Evans, 'Deconstructing Shakespeare's Comedies', p. 84) with 'Tibullus' on Virgil (in *Poetaster*): '. . . could a man remember but his lines, / He should not touch at any serious point, / But he might breathe his spirit out of him.' (v.i.121–3) See Jonson, *Poetaster*, edited by Cain, p. 217 and below chapter 5, pp. 171–2.

[6] See further Jonathan Culler, 'English in the Age of Cultural Studies', *Bulletin de la société des anglicistes de l'enseignement supérieur* 40 (1996), p. 8, and the forum on 'relations between cultural studies and the literary', *PMLA* 112:2 (March 1997), pp. 257–86.

Though still occasionally wheeled out, as, for example, in Louis Zukofsky's self-declared 'eccentric study', the specific identification of Jonson's *dramatis persona* with Shakespeare, which Herford and Simpson quite rightly dismissed as anachronistic, is itself no longer an object of collective attention within the academy.[7] Nevertheless, as we shall see in chapter 6, when we look at critical discussion of the intertextual relation of *The Tempest* to the *Aeneid*, the ideological equivalence of Shakespeare and Virgil has largely been maintained. For this intertextual relation has usually been construed in terms of source, echo, allusion or analogue, terms, that is, which foreground likeness, although more recently it has been construed in terms of 'transvaluation' (Bono) 'transformative imitation' (Miola) 'responding' (Wiltenburg), and 'rewriting' (Hamilton and Felperin).[8] These are terms which allow for difference(s) within a construction of the relationship which nevertheless remains non-contestatory. Virgil and Shakespeare continue, that is, to be 'idolized' as figures of equal, absolute value, and the structure of literary history they serve to reproduce is confirmed.[9]

Confined today to the discourses of the academy, the equivalence of these two figures appears to have been first inscribed, significantly enough, on the base of the monument to Shakespeare at Stratford, 'erected between 1616 and 1623'.[10]

> Judicio Pylium, genio Socratem, arte Maronem:
> Terra tegit, populus maeret, Olympus habet.
> (In judgement a Nestor, in genius a Socrates, in art a Virgil:
> The earth covers him, the people mourn him, Olympus has him.)
> (Halliday's translation)

[7] Louis Zukofsky, *Bottom: On Shakespeare* (University of California Press, 1987), p. 13. For the case against this identification see *H&S*, vol. 1, pp. 432–3.

[8] Barbara J. Bono, *Literary Transvaluation: From Vergilian Epic to Shakespearean Tragicomedy* (University of California Press, 1984); Robert S. Miola, 'Vergil in Shakespeare: From Allusion to Imitation', in John D. Bernard, ed., *Vergil at 2000* (New York: AMS Press, 1986), p. 225; Robert Wiltenburg, 'The *Aeneid* and *The Tempest*', *Shakespeare Survey* 39 (1987), p. 159; Donna B. Hamilton, *Virgil and The Tempest: The Politics of Imitation* (Columbus: Ohio State University Press, 1990), p. xii; Felperin, 'Political Criticism', p. 54. See further chapter 6, pp. 194–6.

[9] The word 'idolized' is used by Gary Taylor in his review of Bono's book, 'Licit and Illicit Quests', *Times Literary Supplement*, 16 August 1985. Hamilton, apparently quite unselfconsciously, closes: 'The closing language . . . invokes the authority of Virgil, which Shakespeare has made his own.' (Hamilton, *Virgil and The Tempest*, p. 137) A welcome exception to this tendency, though one about which I have other reservations (see note 38 below), is provided by the recent work of Heather James, who has followed up an article on *Titus Andronicus* as a subversive Ovidian critique of the Virgilian model with a book on Shakespeare's Troy including a chapter on *The Tempest*. See Heather James 'Cultural Disintegration in *Titus Andronicus*: Mutilating Titus, Vergil and Rome', *Themes in Drama* 13 (1991), pp. 123–40, and *Shakespeare's Troy: Drama, Politics and the Translation of Empire* (Cambridge University Press, 1997). I am grateful to Heather James for allowing me to see chapters of her book prior to their publication.

[10] F. E. Halliday, *A Shakespeare Companion 1550-1950*, reprint (London: Duckworth, 1955), p. 420.

Not 'arte Nasonem' (in art an Ovid) as earlier representations might have led us to expect,[11] but 'arte Maronem' (in art a Virgil). This may be a trace of the presence of Virgil in the last, or late, play *The Tempest*, although, as I shall argue, there is a questioning of, as well as a quest for, this presence, and the relationship is not simply one of likeness. The phrase 'arte Maronem' might recall, in particular, the natural philosopher and magician Prospero, who bears traces of received figures of Virgil, as we shall see, and through whose art the eponymous tempest is raised, which evokes, if it also interrogates, the opening event of the *Aeneid*. Be that as it may, the inscription marks the boundary between the material, temporally confined life of Shakespeare and the after-life of 'Shakespeare', the culturally constructed figure of the ideal, absolute poet, the English/British equivalent to the received paradigm of Virgil. At the same time it marks the monument (and by extension Stratford) as a privileged site of presence, a metonymy of the cultural figure, and thus prepares the ground for the turning of the site (monument and town) into a place of pilgrimage.

Thus begun, the cultural processing – the turning of the body of Shakespeare into the body of 'Shakespeare' – is subsequently elaborated by the publication in 1623 of the 'works', as they are described by Heminge and Condell in their preface to readers, and, more insistently, by Digges in his prefatory poem, in imitation, like Jonson's publication of his 'works' seven years earlier, of the *Opera* of the classical authors.[12] Specifically, Shakespeare's 'works' are divided into three 'kinds', which, in their progression from a light, or 'lesser' kind through a middle, or more serious kind to the highest, and most serious, echo the received threefold hierarchical division – *humilis, medius, grandiloquus* – of the Virgilian *Opera*, a cultural career model which was consciously followed, by Spenser amongst others, and which here serves to stabilise the playing over and subversion of generic boundaries within the corpus.[13]

---

11 See Jonathan Bate, *Shakespeare and Ovid*, 2nd edn (Oxford: Clarendon Press, 1994), pp. 2–3, 21, 83–4, and further below chapter 5, p. 158.

12 See *The Riverside Shakespeare*, edited by G. Blakemore Evans et al. (Boston: Houghton Mifflin Co., 1974), pp. 63, 71; David Riggs, *Ben Jonson: A Life* (Cambridge, Mass. and London: Harvard University Press, 1989), pp. 220–6, 239.

13 On Spenser see Richard Helgerson, *Self-Crowned Laureates: Spenser, Jonson and the Literary System* (University of California Press, 1983), pp. 63, 82. Compare Riggs on the 'shape' Jonson imposes on his works, which 'marks his passage from the lesser genre of comedy to the greater one of tragedy' (Riggs, *Ben Jonson*, p. 225). The marking of the specifically Virgilian shape of Shakespeare's 'works' is underscored by an article which argues for deep parallels between the two middle kinds – Virgil's *Georgics* and Shakespeare's Histories. James C. Bulman, 'Shakespeare's Georgic Histories', *Shakespeare Survey* 38 (1985), pp. 37–47. Bulman of course simply assumes the equivalence which the first folio aspires to establish, working as Magreta de Grazia puts it

A contribution to this formation of 'Shakespeare' is furnished by Jonson's prefatory poem (*H&S*, vol. 8, pp. 390–2): unlike the famously flawed Shakespeare of *Timber*, and the conversations with Drummond, who 'lacks art',[14] this Shakespeare is the ideal paradigm of the (art-ful) poet. As such he does indeed resemble the Virgil of *Poetaster*. For, like this Virgil, he is 'not of an age, but for all time!' (line 43), an absolute and universal figure who stands above history, a position which in each case is represented by an image of celestial prominence and permanence: while Virgil in *Poetaster* is compared to 'a right heavenly bodie' (v.i.105), Shakespeare is addressed as 'thou Starre of *Poets*' (line 77).[15]

But if this Shakespeare is, like the figure of Virgil, universal and 'for all time', he is also emphatically British (and this is the crucial differentiating feature). The lines immediately preceding the claim to universality are these:

> Triumph, my *Britaine*, thou hast one to showe,
> To whom all Scenes of *Europe* homage owe.
>
> (lines 41–2)

While Virgil in *Poetaster* stands as the revered, unifying centre of a homogeneous community of 'learned heads' (v.i.53), as we shall see, 'Shakespeare' here stands as the revered, unifying centre of 'Britain', dynastically inscribed, but in need of an imaginary as well as a legal identity.[16] Indeed, we shall see in chapter 4 that Jonson mobilises 'Virgil' to promote this new/ancient national identity, as he mobilises Shakespeare here, specifically in order to represent Britain as the revered unified centre and apex of an (undifferentiated) rest of Europe.[17]

'performatively rather than referentially'. Magreta de Grazia, *Shakespeare Verbatim: The Reproduction of Authenticity and the 1790 Apparatus* (Oxford: Clarendon Press, 1991), p. 41. This comment comes in her brilliant comparative analysis of the two collections of 'works' (Shakespeare's and Jonson's) (pp. 29–42), which points up their differences as well as their shared aim of announcing 'the content . . . of enduring significance, meriting preservation' (p. 32).

[14] See *H&S*, vol. 8, pp. 583–4, and *H&S*, vol. 1, pp. 133, 138.

[15] On the classical derivation, and contemporary political implications of the 'stellification' of Shakespeare see James, *Shakespeare's Troy* (forthcoming), chapter 1.

[16] See William Ferguson, *Scotland's Relations with England: A Survey to 1707* (Edinburgh: John Donald 1977), pp. 97–106; Roger Lockyer, *The Early Stuarts: A Political History of England 1603–1642* (London and New York: Longman, 1989), pp. 158–68.

[17] See chapter 4, pp. 128–9. Jonson's 'my' slipped in here – 'my *Britaine*' – (as in 'My *Shakespeare*' (line 19)) makes a claim for a share in the authorship of 'Britaine' (and of 'Shakespeare') – one of many appropriating moves in this poem. See de Grazia, *Shakespeare Verbatim*, p. 22. James treats English and British as interchangeable terms (e.g. 'the England that Jonson lovingly celebrates as "my Britain"') and so misses the specificity of the political agenda Shakespeare is made to serve in this poem. James, *Shakespeare's Troy*, chapter 1.

This twofold function – as guarantor, on the one hand, of a national identity and unity and, on the other, of the *differentiating superiority* of that identity, a function which authorises both British nationalism and British imperialism – sets the agenda for the career of the figure of Shakespeare, especially from the eighteenth century through to the twentieth when, still absolute and universal, Shakespeare has become a 'monumental signifier of "Englishness"'.[18] 'The ideological mode of the Shakespeare industry is', as Terence Hawkes has remarked (about Stratford in particular but the comment has a more general relevance), 'centripetal, integrating', although it is, of course, at the same time, alienating and oppressive.[19] Articulated through a range of discourses at different levels of cultural consciousness, outside as well as inside the educational institutions, this ideology is nowhere writ so large as at Stratford (as Holderness as well as Hawkes has pointed out[20]). Already marked by the monument mentioned above as a privileged metonymy, this site has been turned into a centre of pilgrimage, the fetishised object of millions of tourists in quest of 'roots', if they are American,[21] or of the essence of what it is to be English, which continues to be bound up, if contradictorily, with what it is to be human through the continued insistence on the universality of Shakespeare.

Though in another ideological universe 'learned Maro's golden tomb' is similarly fetishised as a privileged site of presence by a character admittedly prone to fetishism, Christopher Marlowe's Dr Faustus.[22] The scene opens with Wagner (the Chorus in the B-text) telling how '(l)earnèd Faustus' (III, Chorus, line 1) has turned from reading 'the secrets of astronomy' '(g)raven in the book of Jove's high firmament' (lines 2 and 3) to 'cosmography' (line 7) – a reading/writing of/on the

---

[18] Evans, 'Deconstructing Shakespeare's Comedies', p. 86. Note the not insignificant *glissement* from Britishness to Englishness; even Shakespeare could not hold Britain together. On the career of 'Shakespeare' see most substantially de Grazia, *Shakespeare Verbatim*; and Christopher Norris, 'Post-Structuralist Shakespeare: Text and Ideology', in John Drakakis, ed., *Alternative Shakespeares*, pp. 47–66.

[19] Terence Hawkes, *That Shakespeherian Rag: Essays on a Critical Process* (London and New York: Methuen, 1986), p. 14; David Margolies, 'Teaching the Handsaw to fly: Shakespeare as Hegemonic Instrument', in Graham Holderness, ed., *The Shakespeare Myth* (Manchester University Press, 1988), pp. 42–53; Malcolm Evans, *Signifying Nothing: Truth's True Contents in Shakespeare's Text* (Brighton: Harvester, 1986), p. 64.

[20] Graham Holderness, 'Bardolotry: Or the Cultural Materialist's Guide to Stratford-upon-Avon', in Holderness, ed., *The Shakespeare Myth*, pp. 2–15.

[21] Evans, *Signifying Nothing*, p. 4, citing L. Marder, *His Exits and Entrances: The Story of Shakespeare's Reputation* (London: J. Murray, 1964), p. 233.

[22] References are to the A-text (1604) in Christopher Marlowe, *Dr Faustus*, edited by David Bevington and Eric Rasmussen (Manchester University Press, 1993).

earth which he then performs on his entrance by tracing a map of
Europe.

> Having now, my good Mephistopheles,
> Passed with delight the stately town of Trier,
> . . .
> From Paris next, coasting the realm of France,
> We saw the river Maine fall into Rhine,
> . . .
> Then up to Naples, rich Campania,
> . . .
> There saw we learnèd Maro's golden tomb,
> The way he cut, an English mile in length
> Thorough a rock of stone in one night's space.
> From thence to Venice, Padua and the rest,
>
> (iii.i.1-2, 6-7, 9, 13-16)

It is, of course, specifically appropriate that the tomb of the magician
Virgil should feature as a landmark in a cultural tour of Europe conduc-
ted by the magician Faustus. The relation between them is, however,
underscored by the epithet 'learnèd', which is used of both Faustus and
Virgil, and which is not used of Virgil in the source text.

There is, however, a more general point to be made about the use of
this epithet, namely, that practices of Virgil as mage/magician were
regularly associated with the erudition of Virgil the poet until the early
seventeenth century when the figure of Virgil as mage/magician was
first made an object of historical enquiry, as we shall see in chapter 3.
This is important, because the separation of the figure of Virgil as
mage/magician from the figure of Virgil as learned poet and the
classification of the former as popular in origin and provenance acquired the status of virtual fact with the publication, in 1872, of Comparetti's *Virgilio nel medio evo*, which is articulated around this division.[23]
Although Comparetti has not been without his critics, as we shall see,
this monument to nineteenth-century nationalism and historical positiv-
ism, and the divisions it inscribes have not lost their hold; Baswell, for
example, accepts as given the 'popular' character of Virgil as magician
and excludes this figure from his otherwise wide-ranging study of Virgil

[23] D. Comparetti, *Virgilio nel medio evo*, 2 vols. (Livorno: Francesco Vigo, 1872), published in English as *Vergil in the Middle Ages*, trans. E. F. M. Benecke (London: Swan Sonnenschein; New York: MacMillan, 1895). There is a more recent edition of the Italian text by Giorgio Pasquali, 2 vols. (Florence: La Nuova Italia, 1937–41), and a new edition of the English translation by Jan Ziolkowski (Princeton University Press, 1997).

in medieval England.[24] Further, critics to date have failed to address the particular blindspot of such a study, perhaps because it is characteristic of traditional historicism even as it continues to be practised today. It is a blindspot that may be summarised here as the blindness of traditional historicism to the historical character of its own discourse and method, a discourse and method which began to emerge precisely during the early modern period. By ignoring its own historicity, that is, traditional historicism becomes its own worst enemy.

What I shall try to show is how the figure of Virgil the mage/magician was bound up with a figure of Virgil as natural philosopher and how both were bound up with mediations of specific Virgilian texts as natural philosophical discourse, and, more generally, with a mediation of the formal structure of Virgilian verse as a form of knowledge. In part one I shall consider the canonical status of these mediations and their place in early modern English culture. Belonging, at least initially, to what I have called the more esoteric learned man's Virgils, we shall see how these objects came to be more widely circulated, and, more importantly, how they came to be interrogated, as the map of the universe/nature they imply came under pressure with what I have called the Protestant turn. As I shall show in chapter 1, this turn entailed the dismantling of an institutionalised structure of authority analogous to the structure of the Catholic Church, which tended, as it was used, to reproduce in early modern English culture, a hierarchy of privilege between insiders and outsiders. It is a turn which, more specifically, tended to dismantle a universe in which Virgil the poet inhabited with both Virgil the natural philosopher and Virgil the mage/magician – figures which ceased subsequently to exist other than as objects of a sceptical, historical mode of enquiry which itself belonged to this turn. In this connection it is no coincidence that the 'book of Jove's high firmament' described by the Chorus in the speech from *Dr Faustus* quoted above is the 'book' we will meet again in mediations of Virgil as mage/magician and in mediations of his texts and verse as knowledge of nature, the 'secrets' of nature and of the text constituting, as this image implies, a single system of knowledge.[25]

To return again, briefly, to the comparison with Shakespeare. In both

---

[24] See Baswell, *Virgil in Medieval England*, p. 16. This is unfortunate because it is in texts from this period that the first written traces of this figure of Virgil are to be found, as we shall see. See Margaret Tudeau-Clayton, 'Competing for Virgil: From the Courtroom to the Marketplace', *International Journal of the Classical Tradition* 4:4 (Spring 1998).

[25] See Michel Foucault, *Les mots et les choses* (Paris: Gallimard, 1966), pp. 48–9.

cases the place of burial, and the figure for which it is a privileged metonymy, serve as landmarks, marks, that is, invested with signifying value within a system of marks written on to the land. In the case of 'Shakespeare' the land is, as I have already indicated, England, a map, both material and imaginary in which the figure of Shakespeare serves to stand for a national collective identity, as 'our' 'common' heritage, and even as 'our' capital (the image of Shakespeare has adorned National Westminster Bank cheque cards and the £20 note[26]). And it is this unified, grounded England which is at stake in the continued production and circulation of this figure of Shakespeare. There have, of course, been attempts to deconstruct this figure and what it serves to underwrite. Indeed, such deconstructions have been designated 'a modish topic' and, more importantly, have provoked a reaction reductive and trivialising to the point of parody.[27] Nevertheless, in England at least, certainly outside the academy and to an extent within it, there has been no effective displacement of 'Shakespeare'. Indeed, the attempts at deconstruction of received interpretations seem often, rather, attempts at *appropriation*, precisely *Alternative Shakespeares*, and not, as any effective change would require, alternatives *to* 'Shakespeares'. The analogy that comes to mind is that of a disputed holy site; it is not the holiness of the ground that is contested, merely who, and whose construction of the world will occupy it. Actually to effect a displacement of 'Shakespeare' in English culture, certainly outside the academy and probably inside too, would require little short of a cultural and ideological revolution.

It is as a site of cultural and ideological contestation at a pre-revolutionary moment that I shall situate *The Tempest*. This contestation is articulated, specifically, through the intertextual relation to received figures of Virgil and specific mediations of his texts, which are evoked only to be interrogated and displaced. There is, first, the figure, mentioned above, of Virgil as natural philosopher/mage and magician, which is evoked through the figure of the mage/magician Prospero, who, through his art, produces not only the eponymous tempest, but also a masque setting forth the total, closed and enchanted universe implied in these received mediations of Virgil, as we shall see. With the

[26] Graham Holderness, 'Preface: "All This"', in Holderness, ed., *The Shakespeare Myth*, pp. xi–xii.
[27] Alison Shell, 'Picking the Critical First Eleven', *The Times Higher Education Supplement*, 23 November 1990; Richard Levin, 'The Poetics and Politics of Bardicide', *PMLA* 105:3 (1990), pp. 491–504. For a lucid, comparative analysis of what is at stake in England and the States respectively, see Don E. Wayne, 'Power, Politics and the Shakespearean Text: Recent Criticism in England and the United States', in Jean H. Howard and Marion F. O'Connor, eds., *Shakespeare Reproduced: The Text in History and Ideology* (New York and London: Methuen, 1987).

disturbance of the masque this universe is confronted and interrogated by another universe, and universe of otherness – a 'new world' – and displaced as the past. It is a moment of dis-rupture that is anticipated in the opening scene, which stages a confrontation between what we might call the seaman's grammar of nature (adapting the title of the handbook cited by Frank Kermode – John Smith's *Sea Grammar*) and the Virgilian grammar, which is again dis-placed.[28] Through these two moments, in particular, the play articulates what I have called the 'Protestant turn', interrogating and dis-placing the received Virgilian mediations as groundless fictions of the past, and at the same time dis-mantling the structure of authority and the hierarchy of privilege – in short, the politics – implied in their production and circulation as knowledge.

This is not, however, the only figure of Virgil that is brought into (the) play and interrogated. For Prospero is not only natural philosopher/ mage/magician, but stick-wielding 'schoolmaster' (I.ii.172) and father, who 'informs', and so forms within the subjectivity of his daughter – 'Tis time / I should inform thee farther' (I.ii.22–3) – as he once attempted, with Miranda, to form the savage Caliban – 'You taught me *language*' (I.ii.365) – who, however, resisted 'any *print* of goodness' (I.ii.354; my emphasis), remaining 'as disproportion'd in his manners / As in his shape' (v.i.290–1).[29] The figures of Virgil in play here are what I have called the less esoteric English schoolboy's 'Virgils' – Virgil as example and figure of normative – 'proper' – formal and moral discourses, in the vernacular as well as in Latin, which, as we shall see in part one, were acquired through education in early modern England. What I shall argue is that these discourses, acquired in particular through imitation and translation exercises, constituted a form of property and power, which we might usefully call the 'Father tongue', and which served doubly to reproduce the hierarchy between high and low born, gentle-man and commoner. We shall see too how this figure of Virgil came to be more and less radically contested with the Protestant turn, and, in

---

[28] See William Shakespeare, *The Tempest*, edited by Frank Kermode, 6th edn, reprint (London and New York: Routledge, 1994), pp. 3–7. I quote from this edition throughout. I have hyphenated words with the prefix 'dis' here, and throughout, in anticipation of my argument in chapter 6, which will show how the play uses such words in relation to 'dusky Dis' (IV.i.89) – a personifica-tion of the negative or privative prefix.

[29] Note the word-play 'farther' (I.ii.23) 'father' (I.ii.21), which is underscored by repetition of the words throughout the scene: 'father' and 'farther' (or 'further') are each used four times, three times at the end of a line. For Miranda to be (in)formed further is to be (in)formed as a 'copy' of her father, 'By him *imprinted*' as Theseus remarks of the father daughter relation in *A Midsummer Night's Dream* (I.i.50; my emphasis). All quotations from plays other than *The Tempest* are from *The Riverside Shakespeare*.

chapter 6, how this turn is dramatised in *The Tempest* through its 'noise-makers' (including a representative commoner as well as the native Caliban) and through the 'noise' with which the play, like the isle, is 'full' (III.ii.133). Through this contestatory noise the turn is made at once against the Virgilian model of 'Language' and, more radically, against containment by and within the binary structures of symbolic forms. The play, that is, stages the 'discovery' of a radical and irreducible alterity – a 'dis' or 'confused noise' – within nature, history and the human subject, a discovery which, with the dis-enchantment of nature to which it is linked, marks the onset of the modern era.[30]

In staging the Protestant turn at both more and less radical levels the play engages not only with received figures of Virgil but with the uses made of them in early modern English culture in general and in the Jonsonian corpus in particular. I shall consequently introduce this intertextual relation into my discussion of Jonson's representation and use of Virgil, in chapters 4 and 5. At once extensive (covering the corpus) and intensive (closely analysing key texts), these chapters will show, at the most general level, how Jonson's use both of the learned man's Virgils and of the schoolboy's worked to (re)produce a hierarchy of privilege, whether between the learned and the ignorant, or between the virtuous who speak 'Language' and the vicious who speak no-language or noise. In *Poetaster* the hierarchies come together in the representation of Virgil's stage audience as a privileged, learned and virtuous elite who speak the play's normative 'Language' at the centre of power, the court. Unique in English drama, as far as I know, for its representation of Virgil on stage, *Poetaster* will occupy much of our attention, especially in chapter 5, where I will show how the Virgilian scenes explicitly promote, with this hierarchy of privilege, what might be described as a bourgeois ethos and ideology, which are, however, contained within a structure of absolute political authority. Indeed, the relationship which Virgil – a learned and virtuous poet, as we are reminded, of unprivileged origins – enjoys with the absolute sovereign is precisely the relationship which the learned voice of Virgil is used to promote for an aspiring authorial 'self' in *The King's Entertainment* and particular court masques (chapter 4). Specifically, the more esoteric objects of the learned man's Virgils are used not only to (re)produce a hierarchy of privilege between the learned and the ignorant, but to ground at once Jonson's own

---

[30] See Anthony Cascardi, *The Subject of Modernity*, reprint (Cambridge University Press, 1994), especially pp. 16–71.

learned voice/self and the socio-political order under James which this voice celebrates.

In using Virgil to do this ideological work at once of underwriting his own voice and 'the king', and of (re)producing a hierarchy of privilege, Jonson often draws on the traditional structure of hermeneutic authority, which I compare in chapter 1 with the structure of the Catholic Church. His Virgil might, for this reason, be described as 'Catholic'. It is Catholic too in the more straightforward sense that the edition of the *Opera* which he owned, and which he used so scrupulously that we may identify with some precision at what point it was in his possession, was produced by a Jesuit scholar.[31] The same description might be used too of Jonson's habitual practice in translating Virgil, since he consistently (if not necessarily consciously) follows the principles advocated and practised by the authors of the first Catholic translation of the Bible into English (1582), always 'very precise and religious in folowing (his) copie', even to the point of using words which 'seeme strange' in English.[32] There is to such 'religious' translations a reverence which is characteristic of Jonson's relation both to Virgilian Language/Life (the schoolboy's Virgils) and to Virgilian knowledge (the learned man's Virgils) throughout the corpus. Expressed explicitly, it is also implied, not only in this 'religious' mode of translation, but, more generally, in the mode of the intertextual relation, which is always a relation of likeness, indeed of legitimation in likeness.

By contrast, *The Tempest* in its non-reverential, interrogatory – and Protestant – mode asserts rather its own difference as well as the difference of history and nature to the Virgilian model. Dis-placing this model it simultaneously invalidates the use of it as a legitimising ground to underwrite the structures of authority and privilege in place – the use

---

[31] *Symbolarum libri XVII*, edited by J. Pontanus (Augsburg, 1599), described by Stephen Orgel in an introductory note to the Garland reprint as 'the greatest of the Renaissance Virgils', *The Renaissance and the Gods*, no. 18, 3 vols. (New York and London: Garland, 1976), vol. 1, n. pag. For Jonson's copy see D. McPherson, 'Ben Jonson's Library and Marginalia. An Annotated Catalogue', *Studies in Philology* 71:5 (1974), p. 96. Whether a gift or a purchase this very expensive edition is itself indicative of more than the simply 'conventionally high' 'estimation of Virgil' Maus attributes to Jonson, thus dismissing the Latin poet from Jonson's 'favorite' authors. Katherine E. Maus, *Ben Jonson and the Roman Frame of Mind* (Princeton University Press, 1984), p. 4. Jonson's regular and precise use of Virgil calls for more than such cursory attention.

[32] I quote from the foreword to the Rheims Bible, as this is given in Manfred Görlach, *Introduction to Early Modern English*, reprint (Cambridge University Press, 1993), pp. 265–8 (quotation from p. 267). Interestingly, this is a very early, if not the first, instance of the use of 'religious' of translation practices, here, of course, without the pejorative inflection it has since acquired. The use of the term here, and the subsequent transformation of its value, tell us a great deal about the history, and ideology of translation practices in Europe.

made of it, that is, both in early modern English culture generally and in the Jonsonian corpus in particular.[33] Indeed, in its description of the eponymous performed tempest as 'roaring war' (v.i.44) *The Tempest* announces the logic of its own – and the Protestant – turn, a turn which tends at once to the dismantling of received figures and structures of authority, and, more generally, to the discovery of the 'confused noise' or 'roaring' of an irreducible alterity within nature, history and the human subject. This logic is recognised some fifty years later in the Restoration version, which, as we shall see, treats the play overtly as an anticipation of the civil war. But, by what we may call a Catholic re-turn (and one of the authors, John Dryden, was, of course, like Jonson, a convert to Catholicism), the play is revised as a critique of Protestant/ Puritan ideology and, more particularly, of attempts in the New World to construct a socio-political order on this ideological ground. Amongst the specific strategies of this revision is the reworking of the intertextual relation to Virgil. Effectively erased from the play proper this is rein-serted in the form of a closing masque (by Thomas Shadwell), which, like and with the play proper, endorses an authoritarian form of govern-ment and a politics of repression. The relation between the Virgilian and Shakespearean texts is thus turned into a relation of likeness, both texts serving to underwrite the newly restored monarchy. Indeed, the figure of Shakespeare, 'the ultimate patriarchalist authority figure',[34] is explicitly mobilised in the prologue to the play where we are told, 'Shakespear's power is sacred as a King's'.[35] Put 'Virgil' in the place of

[33] Compare Kavanagh's note on the politics of the Catholic and Protestant positions: 'The Catholic position was associated with attempts to support a traditional conception of social hierarchy ... while the Protestant position was associated with a "levelling" tendency ... King James's watchword, "No bishops, no king" succinctly captured the fear of radical Protestantism and the intensifying ideological bind in which the English monarchy found itself as a result of Henry VIII's actions in tying the fate of the institution to the developing Reformation'. Kavanagh, 'Shakespeare in Ideology', in Drakakis, ed., *Alternative Shakespeares* (quotation from p. 233, note 6). What I want to show is how these positions are implied in intertextual relations to a central figure of elite culture, the politics of imitation in a broad sense. Indeed, what I have described as Jonson's 'Catholic' relation to Virgil illustrates his commitment to the 'principle of hierarchy' which David Norbrook has identified as the basic tenet of Jonson's political beliefs. David Norbrook, *Poetry and Politics in the English Renaissance* (London, Boston, Melbourne and Henley: Routledge and Kegan Paul, 1984), pp. 175–94. Ironically, of course, though a 'Catholic' position tended – ideologically – to support the hierarchical structure of authority in place, to identify oneself as a Catholic in England under James was, for Jonson as for others, to occupy a potentially dangerous, and marginal, socio-political position. See Peter Womack, *Ben Jonson* (Oxford: Basil Blackwell, 1986), p. 25.
[34] Katherine E. Maus, 'Arcadia Lost: Politics and Revision in the Restoration *Tempest*', *Renaissance Drama* NS 18 (1982), p. 205.
[35] 'Prologue', in John Dryden, *The Works*, edited by H. T. Swedenberg, Jr, 19 vols. (University of California Press, 1956–79), vol. 1, p. 6, line 24.

'Shakespeare' here and the line exactly paraphrases Jonson's representation and use of Virgil, especially in *Poetaster*: in both texts the poet is an absolute, ideal and transcendent figure of authority serving to underwrite the political structure in place. By a supreme irony of history, that is, Shakespeare has been turned, strategically, into a figure, like and equivalent to the figure(s) of Virgil which *The Tempest* interrogates and dismantles.

This figure of Shakespeare belongs, of course, to the cultural processing I outlined above, which makes 'Shakespeare' equivalent to 'Virgil', and which produces the unhistorical identification of the *dramatis persona* in *Poetaster* with Shakespeare. There *is* a relationship here, a relationship, moreover, of likeness. But the likeness is not so much between the poets and texts 'as they are' or 'were' but as they have been constructed – turned into figures – and *used*.

Thus to insist on authors and their texts as relative, historically embedded objects is to renounce the essence on which the traditional humanist project is predicated. It is to focus, rather, on what for the historical critic, working within the assumptions of this project, are accretions, deformations even, as in the following representative, if perhaps particularly unsophisticated example from the opening of a survey of Virgil in sixteenth-century France.

L'œuvre d'un grand écrivain est ... soumise moins ... aux vicissitudes du temps. Manifestation de ce que l'âme a de permanent et absolu, créée en dehors de lois qui régissent la vie organique et sociale, elle est une réalité inaltérable. Les générations ... l'interprètent ... la déforment, mais ne peuvent atteindre à ce qui fait son essence même.[36]

This is striking, not so much for its particularly explicit essentialism and idealism, as for their contradiction in what follows. For Hulubei goes on to foreground the differences of specific interpretations and representations, the 'deformations' in circulation in early modern France; the essence is nowhere to be discerned or is, rather, always somewhere else. Much the same may be said of the monumental survey by Comparetti I mentioned earlier and of the work of those who expressly follow in his wake: the assumption of 'essence' is consistently contradicted by the foregrounding of 'accidents'.[37] It is a contradiction like the contradiction informing the practices of traditional textual criticism (historically and methodologically related to traditional historicism): the ostensible end/

[36] A. Hulubei, 'Virgile en France au seizième siècle', *Revue du seizième siècle* 18 (1931), p. 1.
[37] For example, Merrit Y. Hughes, *Virgil and Spenser* (University of California Press, 1929).

object – the authentic, essential text – being thrust to an infinite distance by the logic of procedures which foreground differences, deformations.

In the discourses of what might be called poststructuralist humanism the traditional historicist's 'deformations' have been turned into the plurality and openness of a 'classic'.[38] They become, that is, the defining qualities of a permanent, transcendent object, the 'essence' being proved by (or immanent in) the 'accidents'. A secular return to the sacred figure of the Many in the One, which, as we shall see, was used of the single/plural Virgil, this move permits change, or difference, to be recuperated into permanence, historical contingencies into transcendence. But it tends again to evacuate the specificities of the historical dimension – the conditions and stakes of the production of particular mediations, in particular socio-cultural environments.

It is this dimension that is missing from Thomas Greene's otherwise exemplary work on imitation in the Renaissance.[39] Like Cave before him, Greene makes the 'poststructuralist turn', including, in his proposed taxonomy, the categories of heuristic and dialectical imitation, categories which formalise the differential, conflictual and anxious dimension to the intertextual relation.[40] It is indeed as a heuristic/dialectical imitation that we might describe the intertextual relation of *The Tempest* to Virgil, since, as my summary will have indicated, it 'involves a passage from one semiotic universe to another' as well as 'a conflict between two *mundi significantes*'.[41] Moreover, Greene's contrastive category of 'sacramental imitation' might well serve to point up Jonson's reverential treatment of Virgil throughout the corpus, and especially in

[38] Frank Kermode, *The Classic* (London: Faber and Faber; New York: Viking, 1975). In the wake of new historicism, this plurality and openness have been translated, in terms of the marketplace, as competing interpretations. Both Baswell and James organise their work around the idea of 'competing versions', whether of the *Aeneid* (Baswell) or of the Troy legend (James). Both are deft close readers, but their work betrays the limits, both from the political and from the historical point of view, of the use of the language of the marketplace, as the universal condition of cultural production, and the absolute critical criterion defining the value of the 'classics' of the canon. Indeed James bestows on Virgil the privilege of setting the competitive ball rolling with his figure of Fama (in *Aeneid* 4), 'who becomes a champion for later authors to challenge the truth and ethics of the Troy legend', and so in effect restores to Virgil the prestige and 'original' authority that elsewhere she argues is contested. James, *Shakespeare's Troy*, chapter 1. See further Tudeau-Clayton, 'Competing for Virgil: From the Courtroom to the Marketplace'.
[39] Thomas Greene, *The Light in Troy: Imitation and Discovery in Renaissance Poetry* (New Haven and London: Yale University Press, 1982). Harold Bloom insightfully describes Greene as 'may be our very last Renaissance Humanist' in Harold Bloom, ed., *Ben Jonson. Modern Critical Views* (New York, New Haven and Philadelphia: Chelsea House Publishers, 1987), p. 5.
[40] Compare Terence Cave, *The Cornucopian Text: Problems of Writing in the French Renaissance* (Oxford University Press, 1979), especially pp. 35–72.
[41] From the definitions, respectively, of heuristic and dialectical imitation in Greene, *The Light in Troy*, p. 46.

Poetaster, which precisely 'celebrates an enshrined primary text, by rehearsing it liturgically, as though no other form of celebration could be worthy of its dignity' (p. 38). But, though Greene writes eloquently about the individual author's sense of historical distance and difference from the classical model, he does not finally avoid the denial of history, which is the trap of formalism (whether new critical or poststructuralist): the texts and authors he reads float as permanent, transcendent objects, Virgil, in particular, being treated throughout as a monolithic figure of pre-Christian repose. The stakes of imitation are, consequently, limited to the psychological, private and individual. By bringing a relative, historical and ideological perspective to bear on the objects of imitation, here, specifically, Virgil, we may go beyond the recuperative individualism of such work to explore *what else* was at stake, in, for example, the dialectical imitation staged by *The Tempest* and the sacramental imitation staged in *Poetaster*.

In what follows I have myself drawn on the work of poststructuralist thinkers, both in my use of specific concepts and in my reading practices. I have, however, used these practices and concepts only in so far as they have served a historical understanding for today of the stakes of particular intertextual relations.[42] This book should, consequently, be taken as a contribution, in the first instance, to the 'larger history' Mario di Cesare has outlined as the project entailed in '(s)eeking the Renaissance Vergil', a project which would, he suggests, 'try to assess fully the place and impact of Vergil on Renaissance education', 'on politics', 'on social history' '*and* the effect which changing contexts' 'for instance, because of the Reformation' 'had on the study of Vergil'.[43] Bar the implicit essentialism this could almost serve to sum up what I have tried to do by exploring the relation between figures of Virgil and the discursive environments in and by which they are produced and circulated in early modern England, and, in particular, the interrogations and contestations of what I have called the Protestant turn. This has

---

[42] I use 'for today' advisedly, to underscore that the history we write is necessarily bound to the present, that it is possible now to proceed only 'as if' there were stable objects to recuperate and describe. What follows should be read under the sign of this 'as if'.

[43] Mario A. di Cesare, 'Seeking the Renaissance Vergil', in Lotte Hellinga and John Goldfinch, eds., *Bibliography and the Study of Fifteenth-Century Civilisation* (London: British Library, 1987), pp. 187–8. Ten years later Theodore Ziolkowski laments the piecemeal character of work on Virgil's *Nachleben* and calls for more large scale work. Theodore Ziolkowski, 'Vergil's *Nachleben*: From Monograph to Mélange', *International Journal of the Classical Tradition*, 4:1 (Summer 1997). A comprehensive survey of work done in the 1980s is provided in Craig Kallendorf, 'Introduction: Recent Trends in the Study of Vergilian Influences', in Craig Kallendorf, ed., *Vergil. The Classical Heritage* (New York and London: Garland 1993), pp. 1–20.

allowed me, I hope, subsequently to do something to turn Shakespeare from a collaborator in cultural and social hegemony, which is one way we might describe Jonson's Virgil, into a member of the resistance, more of a Caliban than a Prospero, as it were. This is not only to turn Shakespeare against 'himself' but also, I hope, to enable students to hear a contemporary, liberating dimension to *The Tempest*'s historically specific thrust, to hear it say, as in an important sense I believe it does, 'What cares these roarers for the *name* of Shakespeare?'[44]

[44] In thus making explicit, 'the political implications for the present and future as well as for the past' of my work, I share the position of Howard Felperin, amongst others (Felperin, 'Political Criticism', p. 59), although I differ from him in my reading of *The Tempest*, the intertextual relation to Virgil, and its present as well as past political implications.

PART ONE

Figures of Virgil and their place in early modern England

CHAPTER I

English readers' Virgils

Between the publication of the *editio princeps* (Rome 1469?) and 1600 at least 275 editions of the Virgilian *Opera* were published.[1] Of these only nine were produced in England and eight of these nine within the last three decades of the sixteenth century.[2] Further, these eight English editions all draw on editions published on the continent.[3] It was thus either directly, like Ben Jonson, or indirectly, from the continent that readers and writers in early modern England received their Virgils, not only the material objects – the books – but also what I have called the figures of Virgil – the mediations of the texts, and of the poet, produced by the various forms of commentary supplied in the different editions.

For the Virgilian texts were much more often than not published with some form of commentary. Most obviously, there is the material formal-

---

[1] For my statistics I have used mainly G. Mambelli, *Gli annali delle edizioni vergiliane* (Florence: Leo S. Olschki, 1954), though as a rough guide to general trends only. As others have pointed out, Mambelli is inaccurate; indeed, his 'error and omission rate' has been put at over 20 per cent by Craig Kallendorf who, nevertheless, acknowledges his usefulness as the 'basic bibliographical guide' (Kallendorf, 'Recent Trends', p. 5). For a more accurate picture we must await the annotated list of sixteenth-century commentaries being prepared by Professor G. N. Knauer for E. F. Cranz and P. O. Kristeller, eds., *Catalogus translationum et commentariorum* (Washington: The Catholic University Press, 1960–). Professor Knauer has underscored (privately) the inadequacies of Mambelli's work; see too di Cesare, 'Seeking the Renaissance Vergil', pp. 188–90. Specifically, Mambelli gives only two of the editions of the *Opera* published in England and misplaces one of these under editions of the *Eclogues* (see next note).

[2] According to the *Short Title Catalogue* the publishers and dates of these editions, which were all published in London, are: Pynson *c*. 1515 (Mambelli, no. 279, misidentified as an edition of the *Eclogues* published *c*. 1550); Bynneman, 1570; Bynneman, 1572; J. Kyngston, 1576 (Mambelli, no. 246, dated 1577); Middleton, 1580; Middleton, 1583; Middleton, 1584; Orwin, 1593; F. Kingston, 1597. See *STC*, 2nd edn, vol. 2, nos. 24787–91.

[3] The editions published by Bynneman contain notes by the Italian scholar Paolo Manuzio, first published, according to Mambelli, in the Venice Aldine edition of 1558 (Mambelli, no. 218). The editions published by J. Kyngston and F. Kingston give, with these, the textual 'observationes' of the German scholar G. Fabricius (Goldschmidt), first published with Manuzio's notes by Plantin in Antwerp in 1556 (Mambelli, no. 231). The same material is provided by Middleton. Orwin gives the notes by the Geneva based French Protestant scholar and publisher H. Stephanus (Estienne) first published by him in Geneva *c*. 1576 (Mambelli, no. 245). As Mambelli points out the notes by Manuzio and by Stephanus are largely drawn from the ancient commentary by Servius, a widespread dependence I shall discuss later.

ly identified by titles as commentary: of the 275 editions of the *Opera* mentioned above no less than 162 are described as 'with commentary'. This is how fifty-six of the eighty-seven editions of the *Eclogues* published between 1470 (*editio princeps*) and 1600, and thirty-one of the thirty-eight editions of the *Georgics* published between 1486 and 1600 are described too.[4] Local confirmation that the Virgilian texts circulating in early modern England tended to be 'with commentary' is provided by the sixteenth-century copies of Virgil in the libraries of Cambridge – there are twice as many with commentary as there are without – and by extant records of institutional and private book collections.[5] Of the seventy-eight copies of Virgil mentioned in the 150 lists dating from 1500 to 1600 that I have looked at, there are three times as many described as 'cum commento' (sometimes with more specific information) as there are described as 'sine commento'. That the category 'sine commento' is used at all suggests, moreover, that the most frequently used category – 'Virgilius' simply – is as likely to refer to a copy with a commentary as it is to one without.

To this material formally categorised as commentary, supplementary, uncategorised forms of commentary, such as prefatory addresses (to readers, patrons etc.) and illustrations, should be added.[6] Of particular importance are the woodcuts designed by Sebastian Brant with an explicitly didactic purpose for the first illustrated edition of the *Opera* (Strasbourg, 1502).[7] That the Virgilian texts are 'shaped' by these illus-

[4] All the editions of the *Georgics* were published on the continent. Four editions of the *Eclogues* were published in London by W. de Worde in 1512, 1514, 1522 and 1529 (*STC*, 2nd edn. vol. 2, 24813–15; Mambelli gives 1512, 1516 and 1533). A commentary is supplied, which seems to be adapted (and not as Mambelli says merely copied) from the commentary by Hermannus Torrentinus (= van Beeck), first published according to Mambelli in Deventer in 1492. Eighteen editions of the *Eclogues* with the *Georgics* were published between 1475 and 1600, all on the continent, seven with commentary.

[5] The records are mainly those listed in Sears Jayne, *Library Catalogues of the English Renaissance* (University of California Press, 1956), pp. 93–133. But I have also looked at records from the Cambridge University Inventories not listed by him. I am grateful to Elisabeth Leedham-Green for access to these prior to their publication in Elisabeth Leedham-Green, *Books in Cambridge Inventories: Book-Lists from Vice-Chancellor's Court Probate Inventories in the Tudor and Stuart Periods*, 2 vols. (Cambridge University Press, 1986). Two lists are given in Lisa Jardine, 'Humanism and the Sixteenth-Century Arts Course', *History of Education* 4 (1975), pp. 16–31; see also Margery Smith, 'Some Humanist Libraries in Early Tudor Cambridge', *Sixteenth Century Journal* 5 (1974), pp. 15–34. For the sixteenth-century copies of Virgil in Cambridge libraries see H. M. Adams, *Catalogue of Books Printed on the Continent of Europe 1501–1600 in Cambridge Libraries* (Cambridge University Press, 1967), vol. 2, pp. 316–20.

[6] Compare di Cesare, 'Seeking the Renaissance Vergil', p. 186.

[7] For Brant's didactic purpose and the scope of his influence on later illustrations, see, amongst others, T. K. Rabb, 'Sebastian Brant and the First Illustrated Edition of Vergil', *Princeton University Library Chronicle* 21:4 (1960), pp. 187–99; Anna Cox Brinton, *Descensus Averno: Fourteen Woodcut Reprints Reproduced from Sebastian Brant's Virgil* (Stanford University Press, 1930). Further bibliographical references are given in Kallendorf, 'Recent Trends', p. 6, note 13.

trations is vividly demonstrated by the two to which I shall pay particular attention, the illustration to *Georgics* 1, lines 231–51 (figure 4) and the illustration to the tempest in *Aeneid* 1 (figure 1). In the first the passage in the *Georgics* is mediated as cosmographical discourse – a disclosure of the actual order of the universe – and Virgil implicitly figured as natural philosopher, 'poeta naturae ipsius conscius' (a poet conversant with very nature).[8] As the citation, from Macrobius, indicates, this mediation was inherited from the ancient commentaries, commentaries which enjoyed canonical status in the early modern world, as we shall see. In early modern England, specifically, it was a mediation that belonged to what I have called the learned man's Virgils. In chapter 3 we shall see how this mediation came under pressure with the discovery of the New World, and, more generally, with the 'discovery' of a new order of nature, and how the Virgilian order, consequently, came to be categorised as art, not truth, and as the past. This entailed the interrogation of the authority not only of Virgil as natural philosopher but also of the ancient commentaries, which supplied the 'ground' of Virgil's authority, as we shall see. Their canonical status and the institutionalised structure of authority implied in the Virgilian text were thus undermined.

It is in relation to discoveries in the New World that the tempest in *Aeneid* 1 is shaped in the second of Brant's illustrations that I shall look at. As Anna Cox Brinton showed many years ago (in a little read but useful article), this illustration alludes overtly to the first illustrated edition of the letter of Columbus on the discovery of America (Basle, 1493).[9] *The Tempest* too alludes to, or, to invoke the sense of the Latin *alludere*, plays New World narratives and discourses over the ground of the Old, the play being set on the geographical, more precisely, the topographical site, as well as the textual *locus*, of the tempest in *Aeneid* 1. But while Brant's illustration tends merely to assert likeness, *The Tempest* advertises the dis-location – what Derrida calls 'le jeu' – between the two worlds, the difference that history makes to geography/topography: 'This Tunis, sir, was Carthage' (II.i.80).[10] As we shall see in chapter 6, it is not only the difference of the Virgilian topography that the play foregrounds but also the difference of the Virgilian cosmography, or

---

[8] Ambrosius Theodosius Macrobius, *Commentarii in Somnium Scipionis*, edited by J. Willis (Leipzig: Teubner, 1970), p. 65. See further below, chapter 3.

[9] Anna Cox Brinton, 'The Ships of Columbus in Brant's Virgil', *Art and Archaeology* (September 1928), pp. 83–6, 94.

[10] Jacques Derrida, *Acts of Literature*, edited by Derek Attridge (New York and London: Routledge, 1992), p. 64. Heather James sees the relation between the two worlds and discourses as a 'strained yoking' but does not link this to the historicisation of Virgil (James, *Shakespeare's Troy*, forthcoming, chapter 6).

Figure 1   Sebastian Brant's woodcut illustration to the tempest in *Aeneid* 1 in *Publii Virgilii Maronis opera*, Strasbourg, 1502

grammar of nature, both being dis-located in the other place of the past.

As widely circulated as Brant's illustrations, if not more so, was the thirteenth book to the *Aeneid*, a 'supplement' completed in 1428 by the Italian humanist Maffeo Vegio (1407-1458) (published in Venice in 1471 and furnished with illustrations by Brant in 1502). Actually entitled *Supplementum* – Derridean well *avant la lettre* – this 'completion' of the *Aeneid* was included in at least twenty-three editions of the *Opera* published on the continent before 1600 and in three of the editions published in London (by H. Middleton).[11] More significantly still for the English context, this 'supplement' was included in the translation into Scots by Gavin Douglas (completed in 1513, first published in London in 1553), and the translation into English by Thomas Phaer and Thomas Twyne (London, 1584). Pointing up what the *Supplementum* supplies, other, that is, than a linear, narrative fulfilment and closure, these translations point up how the *Supplementum* generically belongs to, and even specifically resembles early modern commentaries, in particular the elaborate allegorical commentary (?Florence, ?1480) by the Italian Neoplatonist Cristoforo Landino.[12] This is important, because of the suggested likeness in relation to a 'primary' text of an 'imitation'[13] and a

[11] Three other attempts at a thirteenth book were made between the fifteenth and the seventeenth centuries, but they were not included in editions of the *Opera*. See Anna Cox Brinton, *Maphaeus Vegius and his Thirteenth Book of the Aeneid: A Chapter on Virgil in the Renaissance* (Stanford University Press, 1930), p. 2. For my statistics on the circulation of Vegio's text I have again used Mambelli, though he does not note its inclusion in the editions by Middleton. For the success and importance of Vegio's 'supplement' see Vladimiro Zabughin, *Vergilio nel rinascimento italiano* (Bologna: Zanichelli, 1923), vol. 1, p. 282; di Cesare, 'Seeking the Renaissance Vergil', p. 186; Craig Kallendorf, 'Maffeo Vegio's Book XIII and the *Aeneid* of Early Italian Humanism', in Anne Reynolds, ed., *Altro Polo: The Classical Continuum in Italian Thought and Letters, A Volume of Italian Studies* (University of Sydney, 1984), pp. 47–56; Charles S. Ross, 'Maffeo Vegio's "schort Cristyn wark", with a Note on the Thirteenth Book in Early Editions of Virgil', in *Modern Philology: A Journal devoted to Research in Medieval and Renaissance Literature* 78:3 (1981), pp. 215–226.

[12] I discuss these relations in 'Supplementing the *Aeneid* in Early Modern England: Translation, Imitation, Commentary', *International Journal of the Classical Tradition* (forthcoming). The intertextual relation of Landino's commentary to Vegio's supplement is not included in what is otherwise a comprehensive account of where Landino follows, and where he departs from other interpretations, in Craig Kallendorf, 'Cristoforo Landino's *Aeneid* and the Humanist Critical Tradition', *Renaissance Quarterly* 36 (1983), pp. 519–46 (a full bibliography of relevant critical material is given in notes 1 and 10). Invaluable access to Landino's interpretation for English-speaking scholars is provided in Don Cameron Allen, *Mysteriously Meant: The Rediscovery of Pagan Symbolism and Allegorical Interpretation in the Renaissance* (Baltimore and London: Johns Hopkins University Press, 1970) and T. H. Stahel, 'Cristoforo Landino's Allegorization of the *Aeneid*: Books III and IV of the Camoldese Disputations', PhD dissertation, Johns Hopkins University, 1968, which gives a good translation and introduction.

[13] Twyne calls Vegio a 'happie imitatour' in Thomas Phaer and Thomas Twyne, *The xiii bookes of Æneidos. The thirteenth [sic] the supplement of Maphæus Vegius* (London, 1584), n. pag.

commentary. Echoing the Virgilian text throughout, the *Supplementum* (to adapt Derrida) supplies a lack it simultaneously fills, exactly like the commentaries in the editions 'with commentary', indeed, we might add, exactly like any commentator, or imitator.[14]

The lack specifically supplied by Landino and Vegio consists in what, for the sake of convenience, we may call 'moral matter', although their moral discourses cannot be separated from spiritual and political discourses. 'Moral matter' was supplied too, in the English context, by the grammar school teacher, whose function was, like that of the commentator, to mediate the Virgilian text as morally edifying discourse – discourse, that is, to in-form the moral subjectivities, and 'manners' of schoolboys. Virgil as figure of a normative moral discourse, a *norma vivendi*, with Virgil as figure, and model, of formal excellence, a *norma loquendi* (another figure inherited from the ancient commentaries, as we shall see) are the two (problematically related) figures that constituted what I have called the 'less esoteric' schoolboys' Virgils. Together with the 'more esoteric' learned man's Virgils these figures recur in uses made of the Virgilian texts and in representations of the poet that we shall look at in the Jonsonian corpus (chapters 4 and 5). And in *The Tempest* it is not only the Virgilian topography and cosmography and the figure of Virgil as natural philosopher that come under interrogation but the schoolboys' model and example of normative moral and formal discourses.

The 'moral matter' supplied by these early modern commentators/ imitators/schoolteachers supplements what is supplied by the earliest extant commentaries on Virgil by 'Servius'[15]and Macrobius, commentaries which, as I have indicated, enjoyed canonical status in the early

---

[14] Some of Vegio's Virgilian echoes are exhaustively catalogued in *Das Aeneissupplement des Maffeo Vegio*, edited by Bernd Schneider (Weinheim: Acta Humanoria der VCH Verlagsgesellschaft, 1985). See also B. L. Hijmans, Jr, '*Aeneia Virtus*: Vegio's *Supplementum* to the *Aeneid*', *The Classical Journal* 67 (1971–2), pp. 144–55; and W. S. Maguiness, 'Maffeo Vegio continuatore dell'Eneide', *Aevum*, 42 (1968), pp. 478–85; Craig Kallendorf, *In Praise of Aeneas. Virgil and Epideictic Rhetoric in the Early Italian Renaissance* (Hanover, N. H. and London: University Press of New England, 1989), pp. 100–28.

[15] I use inverted commas (and 'name' below) advisedly; modern scholarship has raised the difficult question of the authentic Servius, comprehensively discussed in G. P. Goold, 'Servius and the Helen Episode', *Harvard Studies in Classical Philology* 74 (1970), pp. 101–68. For this reason I do not refer to modern editions of Servius but to a relatively accessible sixteenth-century edition of the Virgilian *Opera*, which gives what we may call the early modern Servius: *Opera ... cum XI commentariis* (Venice, 1544) reprinted in *The Renaissance and the Gods*, 2 vols. (New York and London: Garland, 1976). As the debates about Macrobius do not concern the content of the commentary, I shall refer throughout to Ambrosius Theodosius Macrobius, *Saturnalia*, edited by J. Willis (Leipzig: Teubner, 1970). For a good translation see Macrobius, *The Saturnalia*, translated by P. V. Davies (New York and London: Columbia University Press, 1969).

modern world.[16] The name of Servius appears more often than any other in the titles of editions 'with commentary', and at least five editions of the commentary without the complete Virgilian text were published before 1600.[17] The commentary by Macrobius (in the *Saturnalia*) was published thirty-four times between 1472 and 1600, which is in marked contrast to the mere fifteen times since.[18] There are marked contrasts of attitude too: while a nineteenth-century scholar like Comparetti treats Macrobius dismissively, an early modern scholar and translator like Gavin Douglas is respectfully, even reverentially deferential.[19] That such deference, towards Servius as well as towards Macrobius, is general is demonstrated by the largely, if not absolutely, uncritical use made of their commentaries in small and large editions. Local examples of the point are provided by the editions printed in London by Bynneman and Orwin (see note 2): as Mambelli has pointed out, the notes by Manuzio reproduced by Bynneman and the notes by Stephanus reproduced by Orwin are largely taken from Servius.

But though largely uncritical, the notes are sometimes (and sometimes of necessity) selective. In the English context we shall see how, partly on account of these selections, the different objects produced by

[16] Though 'canonical' is a term used of interpretations, it tends to be used quite casually, without any explicit attempt to theorise, or explore the stakes of the constitution and preservation (and contestation) of canonical interpretations. The critic whose work most nearly approaches such theorisation is Frank Kermode. See especially, 'Institutional Control of Interpretation', in *Essays in Fiction 1971–82* (London, Melbourne and Henley: Routledge and Kegan Paul, 1979), where, although 'canonical' is not explicitly used, it is certainly implied. With regard specifically to 'Servius' in early modern Europe, the phrase 'quasi-canonique' has been used, though again casually, by Jean-Claude Margolin. Jean-Claude Margolin, 'Erasme, lecteur et exégète de Virgile', in R. Chevallier, ed., *Présence de Virgile* (Paris: Les Belles Lettres, 1978), p. 293. Baswell notes the 'extraordinary diffusion' of Servius in the medieval period and the continuation of this into the early modern world (Baswell, *Virgil in Medieval England*, pp. 49, 81). Zabughin points out local and more wholesale attacks on Servius made by early modern Italian humanists, which inflicted damage without, however, dismantling the commentary's canonical status, Zabughin, *Virgilio nel rinascimento*, vol. 1, p. 44, and vol. 2, pp. 8–9, 78–9. Further examples of critical responses to Servius are given in M. L. Lord, 'The Use of Macrobius and Boethius in some Fourteenth-Century Commentaries on Virgil', *International Journal of the Classical Tradition*, 3:1 (1996), pp. 7–8.   [17] Mambelli, *Gli annali*, nos. 4, 5, 9, 10 and 54.

[18] *I Saturnali di Macrobio Teodosio*, edited by N. Marinone (Turin: Unione Tipografico-Editrice Torinese, 1967), pp. 83–4. The significant influence of Macrobius on fourteenth-century commentators has been underscored by Lord, 'The Use of Macrobius and Boethius', pp. 3–8. More locally, the *Saturnalia* is mentioned in the recollections of reading done at Cambridge in 1617–19 by Simond D'Ewes, quoted in Rosemary O'Day, *Education and Society 1500–1800* (London and New York: Longman, 1982), p. 114.

[19] Comparetti, *Virgilio nel medio evo*, vol. 1, pp. 84–92; for the deference of Douglas to Macrobius, which he shows towards Servius too, see chapter 2, pp. 50–1. See also Lord, 'The Use of Macrobius and Boethius', p. 14. For an excellent discussion of changes in attitudes towards Servius and a reassessment of his commentary on the *Eclogues* see Annabel Patterson, *Pastoral and Ideology: Virgil to Valéry* (Oxford: Clarendon Press, 1988), pp. 30–42.

the different interpretative discourses within the canonical commentaries circulated unequally and so constituted what I have called more and less esoteric objects. We shall see too how both more and less esoteric objects came under interrogation and, consequently, the canonical status of the ancient commentaries which produced them.

Something of the authority of these canonical commentaries and of what is at stake in such an interrogation may be gauged from the portrayal of Servius and Virgil on the frontispiece to Petrarch's manuscript copy of the *Opera* (figure 2), a frontispiece which was designed by Simone Martini in collaboration with Petrarch.[20] On the one hand, Virgil is represented 'in a pose often assigned to biblical prophets, or evangelists',[21] that is, as a *vates* whose texts are divinely inspired (note the heavenward orientation of the writing instrument), and so derive their authorship, and authority, from an absolute, transcendent 'other' place. On the other hand, Servius, whose commentary is given with the Virgilian text,[22] is represented as a priest-like mediator, who stands between the divinely inspired text and those the text both addresses and represents. Written under the figures of Servius and Virgil is an inscription, probably composed by Petrarch himself, which underwrites their significance: 'Servius altiloqui retegens archana maronis, / Ut pateant ducibus pastoribus atque colonis'. (Servius unfolding the sacred mysteries of the sublime Maro that they may be visible to leaders, shepherds and farmers.)[23] The religious register of 'archana' here confirms the sacred origin and character of the poet's utterances and the priest-like function of Servius, while the syntax of the phrase articulates the authority and control exercised by the latter, visually represented on the frontispiece by the commentator's central position and by his directive gesture (the pointing finger). What is figured on the frontispiece is then a double displacement of the origin – authority as well as authorship – of the poet's utterances. On the one hand, there is the transcendent, divine

[20] See Victor Massena, Prince D'Essling and Eugène Muentz, *Petrarque ses études d'art, son influence sur les artistes, ses portraits et ceux de laure. L'illustration de ses écrits* (Paris: Gazette des Beaux Arts, 1902), p. 13; for an analysis of the twentieth-century reception of the painting, see Patterson, *Pastoral and Ideology*, pp. 19–30.

[21] Greene, *The Light in Troy*, p. 35; see Patterson, *Pastoral and Ideology*, p. 23.

[22] Pierre de Nolhac, *Pétrarque et l'humanisme* (Paris: Champion, 1907), vol. I, p. 141. Lord has shown that Petrarch was also 'an especially avid reader of Macrobius', and mentions twenty-five notes in his copy of Virgil 'copied from Macrobius or referring to him'. Lord, 'The Use of Macrobius and Boethius', pp. 3–7, 14–22. See also de Nolhac, *Pétrarque*, vol. I, pp. 149, 157–60.

[23] For Petrarch's composition of these lines see de Nolhac, *Pétrarque*, vol. I, pp. 141–2. I am puzzled by Greene's uncertainty about the identity of the pointing figure ('possibly Servius'); the inscription is quite unambiguous.

Figure 2   Frontispiece to Petrarch's 'Ambrosian Virgil'

place 'above', and, on the other, the adjacent and yet central, privileged place of the canonical commentary – a privileged place that Robert Kaster has argued belongs to the 'implicit self-image' of Servius, his 'sense of his own authority'.[24]

This displacement of authority on to the commentator is arguably a recurring feature of commentary, an aspect of the 'double', even duplicitous character of its deictic project – directing attention at once away from itself to the poet (Servius's pointing finger) and towards itself (his commanding gaze). Likewise general and recurring is the supplementary character of the commentary's relation to the 'primary' text: supplying a lack it simultaneously fills, or, to use the figure provided by the frontispiece, folding (or im-plying) in the text that which it simultaneously unfolds (ex-plicates), the commentary renders the poet's utterances at once opaque and transparent ('retegens ... archana ... pateant'). What distinguishes a canonical commentary, and especially the canonical commentaries of Servius and Macrobius in the early modern world, is the privileged status bestowed on their authority by the institutions which mediate and transmit the 'primary' text. An institutionalised structure of authority is thus folded into the text and preserved through the production and circulation of the canonical commentaries as canonical. It is a structure which, as I have indicated, is analogous to the structure of authority in the Catholic Church, a structure architecturally figured in the division between chancel and nave. In this structure the canonical commentary occupies the place of the priest in the chancel, who mediates the sacred word to those Frank Kermode has called 'outsiders'.[25] The structure in turn serves to guarantee the secret and sacred character of the text – 'full' of a latent, or transcendent meaning accessible only via the mediation of these canonical commentaries – and, at the same time, sets strict limits to interpretation. For, although, as I have indicated, there are various kinds of interpretative discourse within the canonical commentaries on Virgil and the objects produced are plural, yet this plurality is limited, the limits being those set by the discursive boundaries of the commentaries. To interrogate these objects is, thus, to interrogate the institutionalised structure of authority

---

[24] Robert Kaster, *Guardians of Language: The Grammarian and Society in Late Antiquity* (University of California Press, 1988), p. 171. His superb analysis points up how this authority is exerted in particular to regulate linguistic usage, to maintain, that is, the figure of Virgil as a normative model of 'proper language', a figure which will be central to what follows.

[25] Frank Kermode, 'Institutional Control', where the analogy between religious institutions and the institution of the literary academy is most thoroughly explored. Where I depart from Kermode is in my insistence on the difference made by what I have called the Protestant turn.

implied in them, and to dismantle the limits to interpretation it sets. This is precisely to make the Protestant turn – a turn architecturally figured in the dismantling of the divide between chancel and nave. It is a turn which, as we shall see in what follows, is made in relation to specific Virgilian objects produced by the canonical commentaries, and dramatised in *The Tempest*.

To return to the material production and circulation of these Virgilian objects in early modern England: the copies of the *Opera* mentioned above belonged mainly to a small, but (from the 1540s) rapidly growing minority from the propertied classes who received some form of education beyond basic literacy.[26] Within this minority the different objects produced by the different interpretative discourses within the canonical commentaries constituted more and less esoteric objects – the learned man's 'Virgils' and the schoolboys' 'Virgils'. The difference between those in possession of the more esoteric objects, and those in possession of the less was thus largely a difference within the basic social division between a privileged minority and an unprivileged majority.[27] The production and circulation of both objects thus tended to underwrite this basic division, as we shall see, specifically and precisely in what follows. But we shall also see, when we look at Ben Jonson's use of Virgil, that to the extent – the very limited extent – that a few of unprivileged social origins – such as Jonson himself – enjoyed access to learning in general and to Virgil in particular, these objects could be turned to promote a bourgeois ideology and ethos. Working in the interests of Jonson's own upward social mobility, as his critics were quick to point out, this ideology is potentially in tension with, but ultimately contained by the political structure of an absolute monarchy. Jonson's Virgil, that is, always serves 'the king'. More specifically, in his use of the learned man's Virgil Jonson draws on the traditional 'Catholic' structure of hermeneutic authority implied in the production and circulation of the

---

[26] For developments in education see Lawrence Stone, 'The Educational Revolution in England 1560–1640', *Past and Present* 28 (1964), pp. 41–80; K. Charlton, *Education in Renaissance England* (London: Routledge and Kegan Paul, 1965); F. Caspari, *Humanism and the Social Order in Tudor England* (University of Chicago Press, 1954). Stone's case has of course been qualified, for example, by Rosemary O'Day, who shows how the grammar schools still served primarily the privileged elite and, more importantly (for my purposes), how they served as agents of social control rather than of revolution. O'Day, *Education and Society*, especially pp. 25–42.

[27] This is the diagram given in Lawrence Stone, 'Social Mobility in England 1500–1700', *Past and Present* 33 (1966), pp. 16–55. In her detailed analysis of the university and grammar school populations Rosemary O'Day concludes that few of the unprivileged majority had access to formal education. O'Day, *Education and Society*, pp. 38, 105.

received canonical mediations of Virgil. What we may call a 'Catholic' hermeneutic and traditional structure of authority thus cohabit with a more egalitarian bourgeois ethos and ideology in Jonson's use and representation of Virgil, indeed, I think we may say, in his writing generally.

In order to specify the character of the more and less esoteric objects which constituted English readers' Virgils we need now to look more closely at the interpretative discourses of the canonical mediations. Like so much Western writing about writing, these discourses are informed by the basic category division between 'res' (matter) and 'verba' (words); indeed, in a comparison of Homeric and Virgilian passages Macrobius explicitly uses the phrase 'verborum et rerum copia' (Macrobius, *Saturnalia*, p. 297). The same phrase is used as the title to the seminal, and widely circulated, early modern handbook on composition by Erasmus: *De copia verborum ac rerum* (London, 1512).[28] More specifically, Macrobius is quoted by Erasmus at the outset as authority and authorisation for the representation of Virgil as model of the two categories of verbal style – brevity and copiousness (indeed Erasmus takes from Macrobius not only the Virgilian examples but, with very slight modifications, the comments on them).[29] The quotation serves to reinscribe that authority and to confirm Macrobius as canonical commentator. Further, Virgilian texts are quoted, or cited, in both parts of the Erasmian text, as they are throughout the canonical commentary of Macrobius, as examples of both 'verba' and 'res'.

This practice, in both texts, tends to the reproduction of Virgil as plural objects. At the same time the poet is implicitly represented by Erasmus in this opening passage, as he is throughout by Macrobius, as the example of a writing which *incorporates*, in a single, unified whole, both 'words' and 'matter'. This contradiction, between the representation of Virgil as single, unified whole and the reproduction of different plural objects – 'Virgils' – through exegetical (and pedagogical) practices, is a recurring feature of early modern Virgil. Its traces are visible, for

[28] The importance of this text has been repeatedly demonstrated; see, for example, R. Bolgar, *The Classical Heritage and its Beneficiaries* (Cambridge University Press, 1954), pp. 273–5, Cave, *The Cornucopian Text*, especially p. 9, note 14 where other bibliographical references are given, and pp. 17–18. References will be to Desiderius Erasmus, *De duplici copia verborum ac rerum Commentarii duo*, edited by Betty I. Knott, in *Opera omnia*, vol. 1-6 (Amsterdam, New York, etc.: North-Holland, 1988). There is a good translation in *Literary and Educational Writings 2*, edited by Craig R. Thomson, in *Collected Works of Erasmus* (Toronto University Press, 1974–), vol. 24, pp. 279–659.
[29] Erasmus, *De copia*, chapter 3, pp. 28–30; Macrobius, *Saturnalia*, p. 241.

example, in Jonson's portrayal of Virgil in *Poetaster*. But it is a contradiction that has persisted in the humanist tradition, as any of the more elaborate editions of Shakespeare will exemplify. Indeed, the move made by what I called in the introduction poststructuralist humanism – the move which turns plurality into a sign of immanence and transcendence – is both an attempt to figure a way out of (or to trans-figure) this contradiction, and a secular return to the figure of the One in the Many, the figure of God/Nature used explicitly by Macrobius (and implicitly by Erasmus) of the single and plural Virgil.[30]

The figure of *copia* has, of course, been superbly deconstructed by Terence Cave, who points up its 'essential duplicity', especially in the Erasmian text, its tendency to turn 'words' and 'things' into '"word-things"' (Cave, *The Cornucopian Text*, p. 34). It is, however, important to recognise that there are differences between the 'word-things' produced under each of the categories 'verba' and 'res', and that these differences are a *function* of the discursive category division. Specifically, each category produces different Virgilian objects. The same is true of the categories of the Macrobian commentary, though the objects produced as 'matter' ('res') by Macrobius are not the same as the objects produced as 'matter' by Erasmus, as we shall see in more detail below. The determining relationship between the discursive category of the interpretative discourse and the Virgilian object is even advertised by the structure of the Macrobian text, divided as it is between different speakers at a Platonic Symposium, each an expert in a particular field, who turn Virgil into a figure of their own expertise.[31]

These exegetical discourses constitute sub-divisions within the basic category division between 'words' and 'matter'. If we take Servius as well as Macrobius, there are, within the category of 'words', on the one hand, 'explanations' of specific terms or phrases. Principally supplied by the Servian commentary it is these explanations that are selected, if rather arbitrarily, for inclusion in the notes to smaller early modern editions, like the editions published in London by Bynneman and Orwin (see note 2), and like the editions recommended for use in the

[30] Macrobius comments: 'vis autem videre quem ad modum haec quattuor genera dicendi Vergilius ipse permisceat et faciat unum quoddam ex omni diversitate pulcherrimum temperamentum?' (Macrobius, *Saturnalia*, p. 242) ('You may wish, then, to see how Vergil actually blends these four styles and from completely diverse elements produces a beautifully balanced combination?' (Davies, *The Saturnalia*, p. 284)). The Virgilian text is then compared to the work of God in Nature as a work of unity in multiplicity (Macrobius, *Saturnalia*, p. 243).

[31] Landino similarly structures his allegorical commentary in this form, thus implicitly acknowledging the authority of Macrobius, though the form is not so obviously a figure of the One in the Many.

English grammar schools by John Brinsley (see chapter 2). As well as these explanations, the smaller editions choose, on the other hand, classifications of terms and phrases according to formal systems of analysis, notably the system of rhetoric. As we shall see in the next chapter, formal analyses of phrases and passages are reproduced from Servius and Macrobius in the small editions specifically recommended for use in English grammar schools. The implied figure of Virgil as orator and of his texts as rhetorical schemes is, moreover, reinforced through recommended pedagogical practices informed by the Erasmian text with its (revised) system of rhetoric (see next paragraph). Virgil as orator, the model and example of eloquence – a *norma loquendi* – was, indeed, the first object acquired by English schoolboys. To the extent that it is reproduced from Servius and Macrobius the canonical status of these commentaries and the structure of authority implied in the text are confirmed.

But if the figure of Virgil as *norma loquendi* is reiterated, the system his texts exemplify or figure is itself redefined, and this redefinition entails a change in specific formal analyses if not in the representation of the poet. At its simplest this redefinition limits rhetoric to figures of speech and assigns to logic, or dialectic, the 'invention' and ordering of arguments (which Macrobius, for example, assigns to rhetoric).[32] Effected mainly, though not wholly, through the reforms of Ramus and his followers,[33] this redefinition of the notoriously unstable, but crucial boundary between rhetoric and logic was claimed by later Ramists such as Gabriel Harvey to have been followed by Erasmus, whose division between 'verba' and 'res' is also a division between figures of speech ('verba') and the ordering of kinds, or modes of arguments ('res').[34] This turning of 'words' into 'matter' tends of course to point up the instability and permeability of the boundary between the two (and of the boundary between rhetoric and logic) and so to support Cave's argument. Yet the turn effects a change in the status or function both of the formal moves categorised under 'res' and of the objects they produce, logic, or dialectic providing, as de Man says, 'traditionally, as well as substantially' the link between the 'field of language' and 'knowledge of the world'.[35] That

[32] See W. S. Howell, *Logic and Rhetoric in England 1500–1700* (Princeton University Press, 1956), pp. 146–72.

[33] Lisa Jardine, *Francis Bacon: Discovery and the Art of Discourse* (Cambridge University Press, 1974), especially pp. 17–58.

[34] Gabriel Harvey, *Ciceronianus*, introduced by H. S. Wilson and translated by C. L. Forbes (Lincoln: University of Nebraska Press, 1945), pp. 82-3. See also Howell, *Logic and Rhetoric*, p. 252.

[35] Paul de Man, *The Resistance to Theory* (Minneapolis: University of Minnesota Press, 1986), p. 13.

is, the invention and ordering of arguments are invested with an epistemological (and referential) function and the objects produced by these formal moves, including the Virgilian examples, are invested with truth value.

In the Erasmian text this truth is primarily moral. In chapter 2 we shall see how, despite Harvey's claim, this moral orientation produces, in *De ratione studii* (another pedagogic handbook), an interpretation of a specific Virgilian text which is quite different from an interpretation of the same text produced by the system of Ramist logic. As in the second part of the *De copia*, the implied figure of Virgil is that of moral authority, a *norma vivendi*. We shall see too how the separation between this Virgil as *norma vivendi* and Virgil as *norma loquendi* – an effect of the dualistic structure of *De copia* – is underscored by the absence of formal analysis in this and other mediations of Virgilian texts as moral discourse. It is a separation in contradiction with the representation of Virgil as single, unified whole, and yet necessarily produced by the teaching practices Erasmus's texts institute. It is a separation that is a function of a more general separation between formal and moral orders – eloquence and virtue – a separation which haunts the educated consciousness of the early modern world informed by it.

In the texts of Ramus and his followers the truth disclosed by logic is not limited to moral truth, logic being conceived as the most general and comprehensive of disciplines. As far as the production and circulation of 'Virgils' in early modern England is concerned the importance of these texts and the practices they institute is twofold. On the one hand, a tendency to prefer biblical to secular examples poses a radical challenge to the mediation of Virgilian texts as useful knowledge (and Ramism was, of course, linked in England to radical Puritanism).[36] On the other hand, in Ramist texts which retain examples from Virgil, and in the edition of the *Georgics* produced by Ramus, which was recommended for use in English grammar schools, the Virgilian text is mediated as natural philosophy, which is how it is mediated by the canonical commentaries, and illustrated by Brant, as we saw at the outset of this chapter. As we shall see, Ramist treatments tend to turn this more esoteric object of the canonical mediations into a less, and so to undo the hierarchy implied in the divide. More importantly, in their orientation towards formal rationalisation and practical use they tend to expose Virgil's knowledge of nature to those whose first objective is experienced control in the

---

[36] See Hugh Kearney, *Scholars and Gentlemen: Universities and Society in Pre-Industrial Britain 1500–1700* (London: Faber and Faber, 1979), pp. 46–70, especially pp. 51, 61.

natural world, and so contribute to the interrogation of this Virgilian object and to the dismantling of the structure of authority, and hierarchy of privilege, implied in its production and circulation.

The subversive thrust of Ramism was, however, strictly relative, in so far as the Ramist system, like the more traditional systems, was available only to those with some form of education beyond basic literacy. More radical still than the Ramists who expose Virgil's knowledge of nature to interrogation, or who jettison Virgil for the Bible, are the sectarians who challenge the teaching of the Ramist system of logic, especially to future ministers, on the grounds that 'the people which have not learned logicke are shut out and discouraged from talking, pleading and mutual edifying in the church meeting'.[37] What is condemned here is the effect of social differentiation and exclusion which the practice of the discourse of logic produces in the community. For others, as we shall see, the (re)production of the social hierarchy through the use of normative discourses – whether Ramist or more traditional – is rather to be promoted. In his recommendations to university students 'not with intention to make Scholarship their profession', the Cambridge tutor Holdsworth, for example, represents the desired end of university education as: 'to gett such learning as may serve for delight and ornament and such as the want wherof would speak a defect of breeding'.[38] The discourses acquired through university education, in particular here the forms of rhetoric ('ornament'), are represented as a material sign, like other forms of property, which serve to mark, and make, a 'gentleman', 'the most fundamental' social category in early modern England, as Stone says, but also the most notoriously 'vague and volatile'.[39]

Where the use of such discourses significantly makes/marks this difference is in places where social life is represented, negotiated and regulated: the church (as the quotation from Browne above indicates), the law courts, and the sites of cultural production. John Brinsley, the pedagogue whose handbooks will be studied in the next chapter, specifi-

---

[37] Robert Browne as quoted in Kearney, *Scholars*, p. 75. For the impact of Ramism on the discourses used in sermons, see O'Day, *Education and Society*, pp. 127–8.

[38] Quoted in Harris F. Fletcher, *The Intellectual Development of John Milton*, 2 vols. (Urbana: University of Illinois Press, 1956 and 1961), vol. 2, p. 647. Compare Gabriel Harvey (in 1583) on learning as 'one of the fairest and goodliest ornaments that a gentleman can beautify and commend himself withal' (quoted in O'Day, *Education and Society*, p. 126).

[39] Stone, 'Social Mobility', p. 17, and Stone, 'The Educational Revolution', p. 58. See also Kearney, *Scholars*, pp. 26–7, L. Montrose, 'Of Gentlemen and Shepherds: The Politics of Elizabethan Pastoral Form', *English Literary History* 50 (1983), p. 428 and Peter Laslett, *The World we have lost; England before the Industrial Age*, 2nd edn. (New York: Charles Scribner's Sons, 1971), p. 27. That the language acquired through the formal apparatus of an education in the humanities served as a sign of social status is ironically advertised in *The Merchant of Venice* (see chapter 6, note 27).

cally links the schoolboys' acquisition of 'the puritie and perfection of the Latine tongue' and the same 'in our owne English tongue' to their being 'fitted for divinite, lawe, or what other calling or faculty soever they shall bee after imployed in'.[40] We shall see too how this 'pure' English was acquired by translation and imitation of classical authors, including centrally Virgil, whose texts exemplify the normative, proper Language to be taught to, and deployed by future gentlemen, preachers and lawyers. Indeed, in his Ramist handbook for lawyers, *The Lawiers Logike* (1588), we shall see that Abraham Fraunce uses Virgilian examples alongside common law examples to illustrate the precepts of logic. As paradigmatic example of a normative, 'proper Language', constituting at once a form of property and power, Virgil may then be described as a figure of the 'Father tongue', the Language used by the few with education, property, wealth and power, whose use of these discourses served to underwrite their difference and power.

It is in terms of an acquisition of the 'Father tongue' that I shall consider the formation of the schoolboy and the place of Virgil in this formation in the next chapter. Specifically, I shall consider the place of translation and imitation exercises and shall suggest that, far from being always necessarily subversive, as Christopher Hill, following Conley, argued,[41] translations, at least translations of Virgil, could rather serve attempts at stabilising the vernacular and, with it, the social hierarchy, the 'Language' of the 'gentleman' being distinguished as his 'proper' property.

Such a use of Virgil points up what is at stake in the more radical move of the sectarians, who seek to throw out the normative discourses

---

[40] 'The Contents' in John Brinsley, *Ludus literarius* (London, 1612), reprinted in *English Linguistics 1500–1800*, no. 62 (Menston: The Scholar Press, 1968), points 31 and 32 (n. pag.). The orientation of reading and writing towards public life has been emphasised in recent work; see, for example, William Sherman, *John Dee. The Politics of Reading and Writing in the English Renaissance*. (Amherst: University of Massachusetts Press, 1995), especially pp. 59–65. Rosemary O'Day shows how both grammar school and university education for the well born were 'geared closely to their vocation or profession as gentlemen'. O'Day, *Education and Society*, p. 95 (see also her comments on Brinsley, p. 50).

[41] Christopher Hill, *Intellectual Origins of the English Revolution* (Oxford University Press, 1965), pp. 28–33; C. H. Conley, *The First English Translators of the Classics* (New Haven: Yale University Press; Oxford University Press, 1927), *passim*. A (very imprecisely conceived) relationship between politics and early translations, of Virgil specifically, has been asserted more recently in William Frost, 'Translating Virgil, Douglas to Dryden: Some General Considerations', in George de Forest Lord and Maynard Mack, eds., *Poetic Traditions of the English Renaissance* (New Haven and London: Yale University Press, 1982), pp. 271–86. The weakness of these arguments is their tendency to consider not the *practice* of translation, but rather circumstantial biographical evidence. Indeed, in the case of Phaer, Conley, who argues for a link between translation and Protestantism, is obliged to fly in the face of the most patent evidence – Phaer's dedication of the first edition of the translation (of seven books) (1558) to Queen Mary.

the Virgilian texts exemplify. For to seek to throw out these discourses –
this 'Language' – was to seek to throw out a means and form of
socio-political differentiation, in order to inscribe a new, and revolutionary, form – of 'godliness' marked by 'plainness' of discourse (and
dress).[42] A turn from one criterion of social differentiation to another,
the turn to 'plainness' is also, specifically, a turn away from the system of
rhetoric, 'ornament' being, of course, the standard trope for this system
(as, for example, in Holdsworth's description of the object of university
education quoted above, and as in Puttenham's chapter, 'Of Ornament', discussed in chapter 2). In its alignment of godliness and plainness, that is, this turn registers the failure of the humanist alignment of
formal and moral orders, eloquence and virtue, a failure analysed,
though in very different ways, by Richard Waswo, and by Anthony
Grafton and Lisa Jardine.[43] These scholars point out, on the one hand,
the early modern humanists' insistence on this equation of eloquence
and virtue (inherited from the ancients) and, on the other, how, despite
this insistence (or, as Waswo argues, a reason for it), the forms of
eloquence were acquired quite independently of any moral formation.

One of the texts quoted by Grafton and Jardine to illustrate the
'severing' of 'the virtuous man from the accomplished public speaker' –
Gabriel Harvey's annotations to book 12 of his Quintilian – features
Virgil as example and model of the orator who is 'Great Statesman'
rather than good man.

Omnes fere Megalandri, egregij erant vel natura, vel arte Oratores. Quales sub
rege Henrico ... [here follows a list of recent and contemporary examples] ...
Quot aulici, urbiciq(ue), Cicerones, et Virgilii: Columbi et Sfortiae!

(Well-nigh all the greatest men were outstanding Orators either by nature or by
art. As under King Henry VIII ... How many courtiers and civic figures,
Ciceros and Virgils, Columbuses and Sforzas!)[44]

---

[42] See Kearney, *Scholars*, especially p. 76.
[43] R. Waswo, *Language and Meaning in the Renaissance* (Princeton University Press, 1987); A. Grafton
and L. Jardine, *From Humanism to the Humanities* (Cambridge, Mass.: Harvard University Press,
1986). There is a chronological dimension to Grafton and Jardine's account, which is less
marked in Waswo's account. This treats the equation of eloquence and virtue as one of the
'mechanisms of control' deployed against 'the power of words to constitute meanings', a power,
he argues, that was glimpsed during the Renaissance (Waswo, *Language and Meaning*, p. 197).
Interestingly, the persistence of the eloquence/virtue equation (with slight modifications) in
humanism's self-representations is noted in both books (Waswo, *Language and Meaning*, p. 191,
Grafton and Jardine, *Humanism to Humanities*, p. 23). On the failure of 'Renaissance Humanism'
see also Montrose, 'Of Gentlemen', p. 438.
[44] Grafton and Jardine, *Humanism to Humanities*, p. 193; they quote from V. F. Stern, *Gabriel Harvey:
his Life, Marginalia and Library* (Oxford: Clarendon Press, 1979), p. 153.

Virgil here is a figure of the eloquence proper to, and the property of, an elite whose status and power are thus marked, in short a figure of what I suggested above we might call the Father tongue. There is no suggestion, as the humanists insist in their representation of the poet, but in their pedagogical practices contradict, and as Ben Jonson, in particular, insists in his representation of Virgil throughout the corpus and especially in *Poetaster*, that the forms of Virgilian eloquence are necessarily related to virtue, that (in Jonson's terms) 'Language' and 'Life' constitute a single, transcendent order.

Recognition of, and anxiety about the separation of eloquence from virtue, indeed, more generally, about the separation of symbolic forms from any order other than their own (their 'vanity' in every sense of the word), may be glimpsed in early modern writings of various kinds. In this book I shall only look at examples specifically linked to the figure of Virgil. And of the several examples of eloquent and vicious characters in the Shakespearean corpus I shall discuss only Antonio in *The Tempest*. Duplicitous double and supplanting supplement to a figure with distinctly Virgilian features, as we shall see, Antonio is a skilful orator who conjures possible worlds through the language of his 'strong imagination' (*The Tempest*, ii.i.202), and who succeeds, specifically, in generating, by virtue of this eloquence, what René Girard has called 'désir mimétique', acting as both model and mediation to produce an imitation by Sebastian of his own prior act of supplantation.[45] The strategic eloquence of this statesman-courtier serves not only as a sign of social difference, his 'noble' estate, but as a cover, or dissimulation, of viciousness – his 'base' moral condition. This 'confusion' of the categories of 'high' and 'low' is one of several 'confusions' of traditional analogical structures that the play performs. Specifically, it illustrates the separation of the formal order from the moral, eloquence from virtue, which the practices of imitation produce, and so tends to endorse the 'Protestant' suspicion of 'ornament'. More generally, the suspicion of symbolic forms and their imitation, which emerges with the 'Protestant turn', is underscored through Antonio and his imitator Sebastian: for imitation is shown not only to run to imitation, but, more importantly, to tend to the evacuation of symbolic forms. Indeed, Antonio and Sebastian together produce an example and image of language as itself a hollow, self-echoing – 'vain' – imitation of nature.

---

[45] René Girard, *Shakespeare: les feux de l'envie* (Paris: Benard Grasset, 1990), pp. 429–30.

The 'Protestant' scepticism about symbolic forms and their imitation, as well as the failure of the Renaissance and Old World humanist ideal, are pointed up by the failure of the discourses of Gonzalo to 'work'. Embodying the humanist ideal of the virtuous and eloquent statesman Gonzalo is, as we shall see, specifically associated with Virgilian figures of the ideal (from *Aeneid* 1). Together with the Virgilian model this ideal is dis-located as the past by the irony of other voices, especially the voices of Antonio and Sebastian, the shadows, as I shall call them, of imitation/commentary.

But the play's critical thrust goes beyond the authority of Virgil – whether as formal model or as natural philosopher – to engage with the uses to which this authority is put, in particular in the Jonsonian corpus. For the Boatswain's derisory imperative 'use your authority' (I.i.24) recalls not only the Virgilian *locus* of the tempest in *Aeneid* 1, but the closing scene of *Poetaster* when Augustus uses the same imperative – 'use your authoritie' (v.iii.398) to invest Virgil (earlier portrayed in terms of the same Virgilian *locus*) with power to oversee the judgement of the poetasters, especially their language. It is indeed throughout the Jonsonian corpus that Virgil is thus used as a normative, regulatory figure of authority – whether the schoolboys' Virgil, as here, or the learned man's. In either case, his use of Virgil tends to (re)produce a hierarchy of privilege, whether between the 'learned' and the 'ignorant', or between those who speak 'Language' and those who speak 'no-Language', or what is represented, especially in the anti-masques, as 'noise'. In *Poetaster*, these hierarchies come together as a hierarchy precisely between Virgil's stage audience – a privileged elite of virtuous and 'learned heads' (v.i.52), who speak the play's normative Language at the centre of power, the court – and the vicious and ignorant majority of 'common men' (v.i.103) and women, who speak multiple, particular 'languages'. The interrogation and contestation articulated in *The Tempest* are thus directed both at the authority of Virgil – as natural philosopher and as model of a normative 'proper' Language – and at the uses made of these figures to reproduce the difference between high and low, nobles/gentles and common men.

In the Jonsonian corpus, it is above all in *Poetaster* and *Timber* that the schoolboys' figure of Virgil as model of a normative 'proper' Language is reproduced. There are two passages in *Timber* in particular, which will be considered in more detail in chapter 5, but which furnish here a useful transition to chapter 2, as their pedagogic register and purpose are overt.[46] In both passages, practices recommended (mainly) by Quintilian for the instruction of Roman schoolboys are translated into the contemporary context, the overt aim being instruction in 'Language', a normative ideal standard for the vernacular as for Latin, which Virgilian practice exemplifies and represents – a standard of 'proper' English (as well as 'proper' Latin) serving to distinguish the 'gentleman' or, as Jonson – in his recommendations for the education of a *noble* man's son – calls him, 'man'.

In the first passage, translating Quintilian's advice (from book two of the *Institutio*) as to which authors schoolboys should read first, Jonson writes:

As *Livy* before *Salust*, *Sydney* before *Donne*: and beware of letting them taste *Gower*, or *Chaucer* at first, lest falling too much in love with Antiquity ... they grow rough and barren in language onely ... *Spenser*, in affecting the Ancients, writ no Language: Yet I would have him read for his matter; but as *Virgil* read *Ennius*. The reading of *Homer* and *Virgil* is counsell'd by *Quintilian*, as the best way of informing youth, and confirming man. (*H&S*, vol. 8, p. 618)

Here Quintilian's examples of ancient authors (Cato and the Gracchi) have been replaced by contemporary equivalents (Gower and Chaucer) so that the 'rough and barren' style of the Roman schoolboy exposed to the former becomes that of the English schoolboy, and writer, exposed to the latter and, like Spenser, 'affecting the Ancients'. In what is an addition to the passage from Quintilian, Virgilian practice is given as exemplary of the normative standard – the 'Language' – from which Spenserian practice is a departure, a 'deformation'. To read Virgil for such 'Language' is, moreover, explicitly recommended as the practice which will in-form – give subjective shape, and muscles to – the civilised human subject, 'man'.

Nearly two hundred lines later Virgilian practice is again cited as example and figure of a normative standard of 'Language', and again as a corrective to contemporary practice in the use of archaisms.

Custome is the most certaine Mistresse of Language, as the publicke stampe makes the current money. But wee must not be too frequent with the mint, every day coyning. Nor fetch words from the extreme and utmost ages ... the eldest of the present, and newest of the past Language is best. For what was the ancient Language, which some men so doate upon, but the ancient Custome?

---

[46] The passages (*H&S*, vol. 8, pp. 618, 622) belong to those treating the education of a noble man's son, which appear to have been prepared specifically for the Earl of Newcastle (see *H&S*, vol. 11, p. 260). See further chapter 5, pp. 179–82.

Yet when I name Custome I understand not the vulgar Custome: For that were a precept no lesse dangerous to Language, then life, if wee should speake or live after the manners of the vulgar: But that I call Custome of speech, which is the consent of the Learned; as Custome of life, which is the consent of the good. *Virgill* was most loving of Antiquity; yet how rarely doth hee insert *aquai*, and *pictai! Lucretius* is scabrous and rough in these; hee seekes 'hem: As some doe *Chaucerismes* with us, which were better expung'd and banish'd. (p. 622)

Explicitly characterised by the monetary analogy (from Quintilian) as a form of property, the ideal normative discourse – 'Language' – to be acquired is associated here, as in the earlier passage, specifically with restraint in the use of archaisms, a restraint which is said (by Jonson though not, as we shall see in chapter 5, by Quintilian) to have been Virgil's practice. Spenserian practice is thus condemned again as at once 'no Language' and not-Virgilian; the two phrases are indeed virtual synonyms.

In the terms 'expung'd' and 'banish'd' in the second passage a purification of the language, by means of, and to produce 'Language', is envisaged. In *Poetaster*, such a purification is staged: the poetaster Crispinus is judged, like Spenser, to produce 'no Language' and receives a purge, which (like the judgement) is overseen by Virgil, figure once again of the normative economy of 'Language'. Indeed, the parallel is more specific; for, once purged, Crispinus is 'prescrib'd' (v.iii.560) a 'dyet' (line 536) of recommended authors and practices by Virgil, and amongst these prescriptions is, 'Shun ... old ENNIUS' (line 542), which is to say, shun the use of archaisms.

In both *Timber* and *Poetaster*, that is, Virgil is mobilised as example and figure of a 'pure' economy of 'Language', which works so as to produce itself in the (thereby) 'purified' vernacular. It is similarly as a normative, 'pure' Language that Virgil is taught to schoolboys, and imitated in cultural productions of the elite, as we shall see in the next chapter. Invested with absolute value as 'pure' – above the corruption of change – this Language – (re)produced especially through translation and imitation exercises – tends, as we shall see, to regulate and stabilise not only the (rapidly expanding) vernacular, but also gestures of the body (which it encodes), and, with these, the structure of the social order doubly inscribed both within and by this exclusive economy. More specifically, the economy of pure 'Language' Jonson's Virgil represents is characterised by what is described, metonymically, as Virgil's 'chaste... eare' (*Poetaster*, v.i.108), a phrase (derived from J. C. Scaliger) which draws linguistic and moral/sexual orders into a single economy, marked by habitual restraint – precisely such restraint as, in the second passage from *Timber* quoted above, Jonson attributes to Virgil in the representation of his 'loving' but restrained practice in the use of archaisms.

Like the representation of Virgilian 'Language' as 'pure' in pedagogical discourses we shall look at in the next chapter, Jonson's more specific representation tends to reassert the humanist alignment of eloquence and virtue, to close the separation between 'words' and 'moral matter', which exegetical and pedagogical practices produce. Such idealisations of its object(s), as of those in possession of these objects as the guardians of 'Language' and 'Life' (as in the second passage from *Timber* above), recur in representations of the practices and purposes of a humanist education (or education in the humanities), the term 'discipline', for example, doing much the same ideological work as Jonson's phrase 'chaste ... eare', bringing together formal and moral economies, 'Language' and 'Life', 'Language' *as* 'Life' in a single, strenuous and, we might add, strenuously masculine ethos.[47] What such idealisations (a matter of faith finally) cover are, on the one hand, the separations – the different objects produced in practice – and, on the other hand, the ideological work of inclusion/exclusion that is done by the production and circulation of these different objects. In the case of early modern Virgil, this work is done by the production and circulation both of the schoolboys' Virgil(s), and of the 'learned' man's Virgil(s). In the case of the former, to which we now turn, the idealisation of Virgil as example and figure of Language and Life reinforces the exclusion produced by their production and circulation. For these Virgilian objects are invested with universal meaning and value, while those in possession of them are identified as the privileged guardians of what 'makes'/marks the civilised human subject, which implicitly or explicitly denies what is civilised, indeed what is human to those without access to these objects – those who, in *Poetaster*, are called 'common men' (v.i.103) and above whom Virgil and his circle of 'gentle' and 'learned' heads are placed as beings of a different and superior 'human' 'kind'.[48]

---

[47] See Grafton and Jardine, *Humanism to Humanities*, pp. 137–8, and David Birch, *Language. Literature and Critical Practice* (London and New York: Routledge, 1989), pp. 62–3.

[48] For an expert summary of the relevant tradition of thought see Robert Kaster's (significantly titled) chapter 'The Guardian and His Burden' and its review of 'the oldest article of faith in the literary culture, extending back to Isocrates, repeated through the Renaissance and beyond. The eloquent man was nothing less than a distinct and artificial species': 'as superior to the uneducated as they are to cattle'. Robert A. Kaster, *Guardians of Language*, pp. 15–31 (quotation from p. 17).

CHAPTER 2

Informing youth, and confirming man: an English schoolboy's Virgils

The reading of . . . *Virgil* is counsell'd by *Quintilian*, as the best way of informing youth, and confirming man.

> Jonson, *Timber, H&S*, vol. 8, p. 618

> Tis time
> I should inform thee farther.
>
> Shakespeare, *The Tempest*, 1.ii.22–3

From early modern records of grammar school curricula and educational handbooks it has been established that, by the middle of the sixteenth century, boys who attended grammar schools in England probably read, as prescribed texts, Virgil's *Eclogues* and the *Georgics* in the fourth year, and the *Aeneid* in the fifth.[1] Like the curriculum, recommended teaching practices appear to have remained relatively stable, a point which will be specifically illustrated by the handbooks I shall focus on in this chapter, John Brinsley's *Ludus literarius* (1612) and *A Consolation for our Grammar Schooles* (1622).[2] These handbooks are particularly useful not only because recommended teaching practices are described in great detail (especially in *Ludus*), but also because specific editions of the prescribed authors, including Virgil, are recommended.[3] Together with

---

[1] T. W. Baldwin, *William Shakespere's Small Latine and Lesse Greeke*, 2 vols. (Urbana: University of Illinois Press, 1944), vol. 1, pp. 305–6; according to Baldwin the grammar school curriculum attained a more or less definitive form under Edward VI. M. L. Clarke comments that if Virgil is 'almost universally included'. in extant curricula, there is 'some evidence' that the *Georgics* may have been omitted. M. L. Clarke, 'Virgil in English Education since the Sixteenth Century', *Virgil Society Lecture Summaries* 39 (1957), p. 2; see also M. L. Clarke, *Classical Education in Britain 1500–1900* (Cambridge University Press, 1959), p. 11. It is, however, only the *Georgics* that more radical Protestant and Ramist educators recommend, as we shall see.

[2] Throughout I use the edition of *Ludus* cited in chapter 1, and John Brinsley, *A Consolation for Our Grammar Schooles* (London 1622), reprinted in *The English Experience*, no. 203 (Amsterdam and New York: Da Capo Press, 1969).

[3] 'For short comments and annotations of *Virgil*, there may be used *Ramus* upon the Eclogues and Georgicks. Also the Virgils printed with H. Stephens annotations; and with Melancthons . . .

other descriptions of teaching practices these texts allow us to trace the contours, and the significant modifications to the contours of the early modern English schoolboy's Virgils.

The recommended teaching practices in *Ludus* and *A Consolation* – and the contours of the Virgilian objects they produce – are recognisably Erasmian. Not only are textbooks by Erasmus recommended but the pedagogic discourse is informed by the same discursive category division between 'words' and moral 'matter'. Despite, that is, Brinsley's Puritanism and Ramism he remains humanist in his practices, and, specifically, does not make the turn away from Virgil made by those English Ramists who preferred biblical to classical examples.[4] The turn he makes is rather towards the promotion of increased access to the more esoteric objects of the canonical commentaries. For, while *Ludus* recommends three small editions of the *Opera*, as well as Ramus's edition of the *Eclogues* and *Georgics*, *A Consolation* recommends an in-folio edition with the 'large' commentaries of Servius and Donatus by G. Fabricius (i.e. Goldschmidt) (Basle, 1551) as well as two smaller, but still relatively large editions, one an Aldine edition by J. Meyen (Venice, 1576), the other a newly published edition by F. Taubmann (Wittenberg, 1618) (see note 3). These three editions all include 'matter' from the canonical commentaries (Macrobius as well as Servius) which is not included in the small editions recommended in *Ludus*, editions which draw on Servius very heavily, and on Macrobius (less heavily), but only for explanations and formal analyses of 'words'. Brinsley's modifications to

---

Virgils printed with *Erythraus* Index', Brinsley, *Ludus*, pp. 123, 196; 'Commentaries for them who desire their helpe ... For *Virgil*, besides the large Commentary of *Servius* and *Donate*, with the Annotations of sundry other, set out by *Frabricius* [*sic*]: see, The Analysis of *Ramus* on the *Eclogues* and *Georgicks* ... *Meins* Annotations on *Virgil* ... *Taubman* on *Virgil*, a very profitable worke.' Brinsley, *A Consolation*, p. 66; Ramus is recommended again, *A Consolation*, p. 70. Place and date of first publication of these recommended editions, according to Mambelli: *Bucolica*, edited by P. Ramus (Paris, 1556); *Georgica*, edited by P. Ramus (Paris, 1556); *Opera*, edited by H. Stephanus (= Estienne) (Geneva, 1576?); *Opera*, edited by P. Melancthon (Hagenau, 1530); *Opera*, edited by N. Erythraeus (= Eritreo) (Venice, 1539); *Opera*, edited by G. Fabricius (= Goldschmidt) (Basle, 1551); *Opera*, edited by J. Meyen (Venice, 1576); *Opera*, edited by F. Taubmann (Wittenberg, 1618). For the editions consulted see the bibliography. References throughout will be modernised with an abbreviated title and 'edited by'. Ramus and Estienne are described by Hulubei as 'les plus grands éditeurs du poète, pendant la deuxième moitié du XVIe siècle' (Hulubei, 'Virgile en France', p. 17), although France is her specific focus. About a fifth of the editions of Virgil listed by Adams are editions recommended by Brinsley, which suggests the extent to which these recommendations represented current practice (Adams, *Catalogue*, vol. 2, pp. 316–20).

4 See further below, pp. 93–4. For Brinsley's Puritanism see T. C. Pollock's introduction to John Brinsley, *A Consolation for our Grammar Schooles* (New York: Scholars Facsimiles and Reprints, 1943), pp. iii–iv.

his recommendations thus tend to the wider circulation of this 'matter', which consequently becomes 'less esoteric'.[5]

More importantly, in the most up-to-date of the editions recommended in *A Consolation* – by Frederick Taubmann – the mediation as natural philosophy of the Virgilian map of the universe in *Georgics* i – a mediation received from the canonical commentaries and not included in the smaller editions – is explicitly challenged as contrary to what has been learnt from contemporary navigational experience.[6] It is thus not only that the mediation of the Virgilian texts as natural philosophy and of Virgil as natural philosopher is more widely circulated, but that the specific challenge to this mediation, which emerges with the elaboration of new maps of the world, is circulated with it.

It is a challenge that, as we shall see in the next chapter, is similarly explicit in Ramus's commentary on the *Georgics*, which Brinsley recommends in *Ludus* as well as in *A Consolation*. How far schoolboys were exposed to this challenge depended, however, on the extent to which logic was taught in the grammar schools, a curricular question that, it appears from *Ludus*, was under debate. For Brinsley argues (surprisingly perhaps given his recommendations of Ramus) that 'disputations in Logick' belong to the specific 'Priviledges' of the universities and should be confined to them (Brinsley, *Ludus*, pp. 206-7). The argument itself implies that such careful preservation of privileges was not always practised and this is borne out by an earlier handbook (published 1588) by William Kempe (fl. 1590), the Ramist master at Plymouth, who recommends that for 'learning and handling good authors', including '*Virgils Aeneis*' the boys should be taught logic as well as grammar and rhetoric.[7]

The exposure, interrogation and erasure of mediations of the Virgilian texts as natural philosophy and the implied figure of Virgil as natural philosopher, including the effects of Ramism, will be examined in the following chapter, where I shall also consider the relation of this

---

[5] That the recommendations in *A Consolation* represent a general innovation in practices is suggested when Brinsley mentions the recent increased availability of 'helpes', which he would like to encourage by making his recommendations (Brinsley, *A Consolation*, p. 59; see also p. 29). With regard to the Servian commentary given by Fabricius it is not significantly different from that given in the more accessible sixteenth-century edition from which I quote (see chapter 1, note 14). Mambelli comments: 'Il Fabricius non si è servito ... di nuovi manoscritti, ma ha riveduto accuratamente il testo di Servio e di Tiberio Cl. Donato' (Mambelli, *Gli annali*, p. 72).

[6] *Opera omnia*, edited by F. Taubmann, (Wittenberg, 1618), p. 142. See further chapter 3, p. 89

[7] William Kempe, *The Education of Children in Learning* (1588), reprinted in *Four Tudor Books on Education*, edited by Robert D. Pepper (Gainesville, Fla.: Scholars Facsimiles and Reprints, 1966), pp. 232-3. See also Howell, *Logic and Rhetoric*, p. 260.

figure to the figure of Virgil as mage/magician, which found its way into the grammar schools through a translation of the *Eclogues*. These figures and mediations belong, finally, to both chapters, their wider circulation effecting a modification to the contours of the schoolboy's Virgil, which otherwise remained a relatively stable object from Erasmus through to Brinsley. It is with this relatively stable object that the rest of this chapter will be concerned.

THE SCHOOLBOY'S VIRGILS: FORMAL MODEL AND MORAL GUIDE

Informed by the dualism between 'words' and 'matter' pedagogic discourses from Erasmus through to Brinsley produce a twofold figure of Virgil – Virgil as formal model (a *norma loquendi*) and Virgil as moral guide (a *norma vivendi*). This twofold figure – a function of the more general separation between moral and formal discourses we considered above – is also reproduced by the notes in the smaller editions of Virgil recommended in *Ludus*, although the formal model is much more prominent. It is indeed this Virgil, as *norma loquendi*, that Brinsley's recommended pedagogic practices tend to produce as prior to, and as separate from, Virgil as moral guide, though at a later stage an attempt is made to bring them together in imitation exercises. In what follows I shall look, first, at how this separation is produced and at how the normative discourses Virgil exemplified, especially Virgilian 'eloquence', served to mark/make a gentleman, and, then, at how the forms of Virgilian eloquence fall under the shadow of the Protestant turn from 'ornament' to 'plainnesse and simplicite'.[8] In this (sceptical) view of figurative discourse, Virgilian eloquence appears as a strategic dissimulation of a will to power. It is a view that grows out of, or, as I shall prefer to put it, shadows the practices of the humanist education it turns against.

I have suggested we might call the normative discourses exemplified by Virgil the 'Father tongue', a description which is intended at once to evoke and to modify Walter Ong's well-known argument about the study and acquisition of Latin as a Renaissance puberty rite – a *rite de passage* from the world of women and ignorance (the home) to the world

---

[8] From a passage discussed below, in George Puttenham, *The Arte of English Poesie*, edited by G. D. Willcock and A. Walker, reprint (Cambridge University Press, 1970), p. 154.

outside of men and wisdom.[9] Though valuable, Ong's argument, in its deployment of the generalising paradigms of an anthropological discourse, fails to take into account the relation of this *rite de passage* to specific socio-political structures, fails, at its simplest, to take into account that in early modern England it was not only most women who were excluded by this rite, but also most men. The world into which the English schoolboy was initiated through the acquisition of the 'Father tongue' was not so much the world of 'men', as opposed to 'women', as the world of a select few men, mainly those who belonged to the privileged minority by virtue of property, wealth and power. Indeed, the 'Father tongue' is itself another form of property and power. It is important to emphasise this, because the categories of Ong's anthropological argument tend, finally, to echo the universalising idealism of humanist representations of humanist education, like Jonson's representation of Quintilian's advice, quoted at the head of this chapter, that the reading of Virgil is 'the best way of informing youth and confirming *man*' (my emphasis).

Thus to idealise and universalise such discourses as the discourses which make/mark a 'man', which is to say a 'civilised' human subject, or 'gentleman', is of course to authorise the representation, and repression, of those without access to these discourses, as those inferior to and less than the ideal norm – less than 'man', less than 'civilised', less, finally, than 'human'. In Sidney's *Arcadia*, for example, we shall see how the formal system of (Ramist) rhetoric (illustrated in Fraunce's *Arcadian Rhetorike* by Virgil alongside Sidney) furnishes strategies of differential representation, the base-born being distinguished from the high-born as those whose language and gestures authorise the contempt with which they are treated. More immediately important is the authorisation such an idealisation furnishes in *A Consolation* for the colonisation and subjection of 'all ruder countries and places; namely ... *Ireland, Wales, Virginia, with the Sommer Ilands*' (Brinsley, *A Consolation*, title-page), '*a principall meanes to reduce a barbarous people to civilitie,*' being '*schooles of learning*' (ibid., 'The Epistle Dedicatorie'), and, in particular, the 'attaining of our *English tongue ...*, *that all may speake one and the same Language*' (ibid., title-page), '*the verie savage... whether* Irish *or* Indian' (ibid. 'The Epistle Dedicatorie'). Sponsored by the Virginia Company to promote the establishment of a school in Virginia, *A Consolation* turns the teaching programme of *Ludus* into a programme for the 'reduction' of 'barbarous' 'savages' to 'civilitie', specifically through the teaching of 'one and the

[9] W. Ong, 'Latin Language Study as a Renaissance Puberty Rite', in *Rhetoric, Romance and Technology* (Ithaca and London: Cornell University Press, 1971), pp. 113–41.

same Language'.[10] As we shall see, Brinsley's 'Language' is a normative ideal, which makes/marks the civilised human subject, and which is acquired, specifically, through the translation and imitation of classical authors including, centrally, Virgil, figure of the 'civilised' and 'civilising' Language, in the vernacular as well as in Latin, which serves to 'reduce' and 'subject' the 'uncivilised', 'wild' and 'barbarous'.

This is one of the figures of Virgil brought into play in *The Tempest*. Father and 'schoolmaster' (i.ii.172) to Miranda, Prospero seeks to 'inform' her 'farther' (i.ii.23), which, as the echo of 'father' (line 21) suggests, is to form her within as a 'copy' of her father' just as Jonson's schoolboy is 'informed' by the reading of the paradigm of the Father tongue, 'Virgil' (see introduction, note 29). Hers is, indeed, a humanist education, which has always consisted in in-formation by, and memory of Father(s). It is an education that, as we shall see, tends to suppress the memory of the 'mother tongue' – not only the native popular vernacular(s) (and their culture(s)), which return in the 'noise' of the commoners, but also the maternal voice/body, which returns in the 'noise' of nature, especially in the roaring of the sea *('la mer(e)')* to which, as we shall hear, the imitative language of the play aspires.

It is at this level, in the 'noise' of her language, that we shall detect traces of a resistance in Miranda to in-formation by her father (and his Language). For the only (negatively expressed) resistance that she shows, at least initially – the only possible form of resistance, perhaps, under such double subjection to father and schoolmaster – is the withdrawal of attention to which Prospero alludes with paternal and schoolmasterly irritation (i.ii.78, 87, 106). More explicit resistance is expressed by her own pupil, the 'savage' Caliban, to whom Miranda 'taught' 'language' (i.ii.368), as she herself reminds him in a speech which not only recapitulates his education, but also chastises his recalcitrance (i.ii.353-64). As a teacher, Miranda here sounds just like the father by whom she has been in-formed, so much so that editors have frequently followed the revisionary move made in the Restoration version of the play, which attributes the speech to Prospero.[11] This is, of course, to erase the point

---

[10] For the sponsorship of *A Consolation* see Pollock's introduction to Brinsley, *A Consolation*, p. iii. The verb 'reduce' is used in the sense 'To lead or bring back from error in action, conduct or belief, *esp.* in matters of morality or religion: to restore to the truth or the right faith' (*OED*, ii.8.a) but carries too the sense 'To bring ... under control or authority, to subdue, conquer' (ibid., iii.20.b).

[11] See Kermode's footnote to i.ii.353. The revision may be symptomatic of a recoil from the combination of (feminine) virginal innocence and (masculine) authority in a woman. On the other hand, the likeness of Miranda's speech to Prospero's discourse, in a speech which not only describes the teaching of language but, in its teacherly, even authoritarian mode, reproduces a pedagogic *style*, reminds women teachers that they have always had to 'sound like' Father in order to be recognised as speaking with authority.

that humanist education in-forms within as a 'copy' of the Father (tongue), suppressing the relation to the Mother (tongue), which, in Miranda's case, returns, as we shall hear, under the pressure of sexual desire.

Caliban's resistance is not only expressed explicitly, but in the 'noise' to which his language particularly aspires, and in his 'disproportion'd' gestures (v.i.290). This resistance, I shall argue, may be taken not only as the resistance of the 'verie savage . . . Irish or Indian' to the colonisation of land, mind and body by the 'Language' of the colonisers, but also as the resistance of a 'verie savage' – a radical alterity – within nature, history and the 'self', a resistance marked by 'noise' as well as by other 'noise-makers'. It is, finally, I shall argue, an 'original' resistance both more generally and radically to symbolic forms, and, more specifically, to the Virgilian model of 'Language', 'the perfect instrument' not only 'of empire', but of the in-formation – and regulation – of 'subjects' at home.[12]

'VIRGILL . . . FLUDE OF ELOQUENS'[13]

This figure of Virgil as a standard of eloquence – a *norma loquendi* – originates long before and endures long after the early modern period.[14] The treatment of the Virgilian texts as hortatory discourse in the *Saturnalia* provided one authoritative source of reference for the early modern world.[15] This is signalled by Gavin Douglas who, in the opening prologue to his translation, invokes Macrobius as an authority, who 'writis . . . sans faill / in his gret volume clepit Saturnaill'.[16] The defer-

---

[12] The quotation, from the Bishop of Avila, 'in his presentation of the first grammar of a modern European vernacular to Queen Isabella of Castilla in 1492', has become, as Felperin notes, 'something of a *leitmotif* in revisionist readings of *The Tempest*. Felperin, 'Political Criticism', p. 46.

[13] Gavin Douglas, *Virgil's 'Aeneid' translated into Scottish Verse*, edited by David F. C. Coldwell, Scottish Text Society, 4 vols. (Edinburgh and London: Blackwood, 1957-64), vol. 2, p. 3.

[14] For its later life see, for example, L. Proudfoot, *Dryden's 'Aeneid' and its Seventeenth-Century Predecessors* (Manchester University Press, 1960), p. 116.

[15] The relevant section of the *Saturnalia* is fragmented and it is not clear whether we have two parts of one exposition by the figure of 'Eusebius', or the conclusion to an exposition by this figure (book 5, section I) plus part of a different exposition by the figure of 'Symmachus' on rhetorical devices (the six extant chapters of book 4, which are without introduction or conclusion). Marinone tends towards the former view (Macrobius, *I Saturnali*), Davis to the latter (Macrobius, *The Saturnalia*). For my purposes the question is not of major importance since the passage in book 5 is too short to indicate distinct criteria and the readings reproduced by early modern editors are those in book 4.

[16] Douglas, *Virgil's 'Aeneid'*, vol. 2, p. 4. Priscilla Bawcutt points out that in following lines Douglas virtually translates from the *Saturnalia*. Priscilla Bawcutt, *Gavin Douglas: A Critical Study* (Edinburgh

ence of 'sans faill' (flawlessly) and 'gret', which suggests intellectual as
well as physical weight, underscores the authority of the canonical
commentary even as it is invoked to underwrite the representation,
which follows, of Virgil's 'eloquens', '(s)o inventive of rhethorik flowris
sweit' (p. 5). Then, the editor of one of the small editions recommended
in *Ludus* (Eritreo) reproduces almost all of Macrobius's specific analyses
alongside the relevant passages in the text.[17] In another of the recommended small editions, by Melancthon, Macrobius's system of rhetoric
is implied in the classification of 'places' of argument according to the
criterion of 'pathos', though sometimes the Erasmian criterion of 'amplification' is preferred.[18] These reproductions of the Macrobian analyses, or system, at once ground the figure of Virgil as orator and
reinscribe the canonical status of the commentary. In specific instances
of analysis this canonical status may have been mildly interrogated by
Ramist teachers (like Brinsley) for whom 'places' of argument belonged
to logic rather than rhetoric, as we saw in chapter 1. But the figure of
Virgil as orator is never put into question either by the editions Brinsley
recommends or by the pedagogical practices he promotes.

In Brinsley's programme, the reading of poetry, beginning with
Virgil's *Eclogues*, coincides with the learning of the (Ramist) system of
rhetoric, which furnishes both the formal apparatus for reading and its
end, poetry being studied 'for ornament ... the main matter to be
regarded in it, is the puritie of phrase, and of stile' (Brinsley, *Ludus*, p.
191). Poetical and rhetorical are implicitly interchangeable terms, as
they are explicitly in the representation of the practice of using 'Grammatical translations' to turn 'every verse into the Grammatical order,
like as it is in the translation; after into the Poeticall ... For the making of
a verse, is nothing but the turning of words forth of the Grammatical
order into the Rhetoricall, in some kind of metre' (p. 192).

How this practice turned the Virgilian text is suggested by Brinsley's
own 'grammatical translation' of the *Eclogues* (figure 3).[19] At the centre in
large print there is a translation covered with various marks directing
the reader to one of three columns of notes: in one there is a paraphrase

University Press, 1976), p. 86. Servius, to whom Douglas is similarly deferential, is likewise
virtually translated, in the prologue to book 6 (Douglas, *Virgil's 'Aeneid'*, vol. 3, pp. 1–2).
[17] Virgil, *Bucolica, Georgica et Aeneis*, edited by N. Eritreo (Venice, 1555).
[18] Virgil, *Opera*, edited by P. Melancthon (Lyon, 1537).
[19] John Brinsley, *Virgils Eclogues, with his booke De Apibus* (London, 1633). Patterson dismisses this
translation as pedestrian (Patterson, *Pastoral and Ideology*, pp. 164–5), a dismissal that stems from
the view that '(t)he stronger the philological or pedagogical motives... the weaker became the
genre as a vehicle of cultural information' (ibid., p. 61), a view my arguments implicitly contest.

Grammatically tranflated.   3

THE FIRST
ECLOGVE,
which is called
(1) *Tityrus.*

[The fpeakers are]
(2) *Melibeus and Tityrus.*

Melibeus.

a In this Eclogue (as was fhewed in the Argument) *Melibeus* laments his owne calamity, & the eftate of the reft of the townf-men of *Mantua*, by comparing their mifery with the fortunate eftate of *Tityrus*, which he admireth with a fecret indignation: That he mightly at his eafe under the fhade, and play his country ditties upon his pipe.

a Tityrus, thou * lying all along under the (3) covert of * the (4) broade (5) beech tree, Doeft * || devife a wood-land (6) fong *upon a flender (7) oaten pipe.

b When they contrarily were enforced to leave their country and pleafant fields: And glad to flie their native foile, yet he lying at his eafe under the cool fhade, might fing his fongs in praife of his love faire *Ama-ryl,* to caufe the very woods with their eccho to refound the fame,

b Wee || leave the * bounds of our countrey and [our] || fweet (8) fields: We || flie || our countrey: [but] *thou (Tityrus)* lying fecurely in the * fhade,

B2 ||Teach-

1 *Tityrus* a fained name of a fhepheard, moft expert in country muficke (as was faid,) here fignifieth *Virgil* the famous Poet, et reftored to his poffeffions by the commandement of *Auguftus.*
* *Lying downe*[viz. lying at thy eafe or refting quietly.]
* *Covert* [viz fhade or fhadow.
The beech tree fpreading largely, [viz. with great armes or branches.]
* *Meditate.*
|| *Tune.*
|| *A fong fit to bee fung in the woods* [or a rurall or countrey fong, or a beard-mans or fheepheards ditty.
With a fmall oate.
||*Forfake, or are driven to leave or for-got.*
* *Ends or coafts.*
||*Pleafant grounds or lands.*
|| *Flie from, or are driven out and ba-nifhed from our native foyle.*
* *Tityrus, thou be-ing fluggifh* [viz.fo-cure or lying at thy reft, or idle and careleffe.

2 *Melibeus* a heard-man fo called ὅτι με-λει αυτῶ τῶ βοῶν, be-caufe he had care of cattell,reprefenting a townfman of *Mantua,* caft out of his poffef-fions by the Roman fouldiers, to whom their lands were gi-ven.
3 *Tegmen*]q.tegimen à tegendo.Synecd.gen.
4 *Patule*]à patendo.
5 *Fagi.*]Syn.fpec.
6 *Mufam*] Metonimia efficientis.
7 *Avena*] Metalepfit, an oate for a pipe made of oaten ftraw, Met. materia, & Met. adjunchi,and taken for any pipe,Syn.fpec.
8 *Arvum ab aranda,* fuch a field properly as is ready to be fown, now plowed or tilled, Syn.fpec.
* *Shadow.*

Figure 3   John Brinsley, *Vergils Eclogues, with his booke De Apibus*, London, 1633, p. 3

in English, in a second, 'explanations' in English of words and phrases (often translated from the Servian commentary), in a third, what Brinsley calls 'the Poeticall phrases ... set in the margents' which, in the process of learning to turn verses, the boys are 'to give ... to our English phrases' (Brinsley, *Ludus*, p. 192). In this column, we find, for example, 'musam', from the second line of the first eclogue, classified as 'Metonimia [*sic*] efficientis' (metonymy of efficient cause). The English phrase in the translation to which this is linked (by the number 6) is 'song', which translates not the Virgilian 'musam', but 'rusticum carmen', the gloss which Servius gives to 'silvestrem musam'.[20] Such a translation (and there are examples throughout) confirms not only the canonical authority of Servius, but, as I suggested in chapter 1, the displacement of authority implied in such a commentary. What is a supplement in the margins in the editions has become, in the translation, the centre, while the original centre has become a supplement, an 'ornament' or 'poeticall phrase', literally 'in the margents'. Here in the margins, the Latin phrase is glossed in terms of the system of Ramist rhetoric, or, we might say, it is *grafted* on to that system, a graft which turns 'musam' in effect into a metonymy of 'Metonimia efficientis'.

This grafting of the Virgilian texts on to the system of rhetoric is reinforced by the practice of learning by heart the rules of rhetoric from the *Rhetorica* of Omer Talon (A. Talaeus) or Charles Butler's *Rhetoricae libri duo*, together with a few of the examples provided, 'so that they can give the word or words, wherein the force of the rule is'.[21] Virgilian examples abound in both textbooks: fragments from the original text they are grafted on to the system of rhetoric and invested through repetition with the 'force of the rule' they illustrate. Specific Virgilian words and phrases are thus turned into metonymies of particular forms, and Virgil is confirmed as a model of the normative system of rhetoric which is the object of these exercises.

The object of the study of Virgil, the system of rhetoric also furnishes the categories for the identification and subsequent construction of 'poetical/rhetorical' phrases in the exercise of 'contracting', a rudimentary form of imitation which requires the boys to turn 'seaven or eight verses into fowre or five: yet still labouring to expresse the whole matter of their Author ... *with all significant Metaphors, and other tropes and phrases,* so much as they can' (Brinsley, *Ludus*, p. 194; my emphasis).

Thus they may proceed ... from the lowest kind of verse in the Eclogues, to somthing a loftier in the Georgicks; and so to the stateliest kind in the Æneids: wherein they may be tasked to go through some booke of the Æneids, every day

---

[20] Virgil, *Opera*, vol. 1, fo. 1r; the Servian gloss is echoed again in the explanation in the second column: 'A song fit to bee sung in the woods or a rurall or country song ...'. Fairclough stays closer to Virgil by translating 'silvestrem ... musam', 'the woodland Muse'.

[21] Brinsley, *Ludus*, p. 203; see Howell, *Logic and Rhetoric*, pp. 262–9.

contracting a certaine number ... those who take a delight in Poetry ... will in a short time attaine to that ripenesse, as that they who know not the places which they imitate, shall hardly discerne in many verses, whether the verse bee Virgils verse or the schollars. (ibid.)

Traced here is an ideal, hierarchically organised career through the school which retraces the 'career' of Virgil from *humilis* (the 'lowest kind') through *medius* ('something a loftier') to *grandiloquus* ('the stateliest kind'), a career assiduously followed by Spenser, amongst others, and echoed in the first folio organisation of the Shakespearean corpus. The paradigm of such a career, Virgil is also the model at every stage of it, the highest achievement being to produce a text which is so like the model as to be indistinguishable from it. It is, in other words, likeness, not originality or difference that is the criterion of judgement, and it is a likeness that is judged according to the system of rhetoric through, and for which Virgil is studied, model and figure of the ideal of civilised eloquence.

THE ELOQUENCE OF THE CIVILISED SUBJECT: VOICE AND GESTURE

In the Ramist system, this ideal of civilised eloquence includes the proper use of voice and gesture. In a chapter entitled 'Of pronouncing naturally and sweetly, without vaine affectation' Brinsley stresses the importance that the mastery of these forms has for the future social roles of the boys, who will thus be equipped for communication, either at the universities, or as 'Gentlemen who goe to travell, Factors for Marchants [*sic*] and the like' (Brinsley, *Ludus*, p. 211). That these forms serve to differentiate a privileged elite is signalled by his use of the word 'grace' (p. 212), while the adverb 'naturally' in the title indicates that they are, at the same time, somehow universal, permanent forms.

The same is suggested by the recommendation of Talon's textbook for classroom exercises:

that they may doe every thing according to the very nature; acquaint them to pronounce some speciall examples, set downe in Talaeus Rhetoricke as pathetically as they can. (p. 213)

As in the first part of the textbook, which treats figures of style, there are examples from Virgil in the second part, which treats delivery. Here too the examples are fragments grafted on to the system of rhetoric and turned into metonymies of specific forms, here specific paralinguistic modes and their significance. Thus Dido's plea to Aeneas, which begins 'Mene fugis?' (*Aeneid* 4, lines 314-30), is grafted on to the mode of a gentle, meek tone of voice, which signifies the desire to mollify.[22] To render (and to acquire) this significance required a simple dramatisation of the passage, an acting out with the prescribed (which Brinsley calls 'natural') 'voice'. The Virgilian fragments thus become performance texts through which paralinguistic modes are acquired, invested with normative value through the representation of them as 'natural'. It is through such performances that the voices and gestures of the boys are regulated, in-formed by the universal 'natural' modes to which they are thus given access.

It is not, however, only performances of fragments that are suggested by Brinsley. Substantial portions of the Virgilian texts are to be performed in the course of being studied.

> when they shall come to Virgils Eclogues, cause them yet still more lively, in saying without booke, to express the affections and persons of sheepeheards; or whose speech soever else, which they are to imitate. Of which sort are the Prosopopeyes of . . . Juno, Neptune, Æolus, Æneas, Venus, Dido, etc. . . . Virgils Æneids. (Brinsley, *Ludus*, p. 213)

Though furnishing specific confirmation of the point, made by others, that schoolboys' training in delivery constituted a form of theatrical training,[23] the interest here is rather in the second example – the scenes which open the *Aeneid* – which suggests that intermediary school performances of the Virgilian tempest may bear on the intertextual relation of *The Tempest* to the Virgilian *locus*. Certainly, as we shall see, it is one of these scenes of 'prosopopeia' – the scene of Neptune's speech of rebuke to the winds of Aeolus – that is ironically evoked in *The Tempest*, specifically through the figure of Neptune's 'dread trident', a metonymy, as I shall show, for the ideal normative Language exemplified by the Virgilian model.

If such performances in schools provided theatrical training, their primary function was (as the earlier quotation indicates) a training for public life, an in-forming with modes of voice and gesture at once 'civilised' and 'natural'. This lends further particular significance to the resistance of Caliban to in-formation by the colonist, schoolmaster and father Prospero. For Caliban's resistance is marked not only in his

---

[22] Omer Talon (A. Talaeus), *Rhetorica, e Petri Rami . . . praelectionibus observata* (Paris, 1577), pp. 68-9.
[23] B. L. Joseph, *Elizabethan Acting*, rev. edn (Oxford University Press, 1964), *passim*, and Andrew Gurr, *The Shakespearean Stage 1574-1642*, 3rd edn, (Cambridge University Press, 1992), pp. 95-103. Gurr mentions Brinsley though inexplicably calls him Richard (ibid., p. 96).

language, but in his body, as the adjective 'deformed' in the 'Names of the Actors' indicates, and as Prospero's description of him 'as dispropor- tioned in his manners / As in his shape' (v.i.290–1) underscores. Provid- ing, as Kermode points out, a criterion within the play by which 'civilised' characters are measured, Caliban, more radically, furnishes a measure and critique of the universalising of proportioned 'forms of behaviour' (Orgel's gloss on 'manners') as 'natural'.[24] His resistance, I shall argue, is the resistance of a radical alterity/(in)difference within the self as well as within nature and history to the normative discourses which the 'civilised' 'natural' forms of Virgilian eloquence represent, a radical resistance, that is, to in-formation by the 'proper' (and 'propor- tioned') gestures of the body as well as by the 'proper' language, of the 'Father tongue'.

VIRGIL AS *NORMA LOQUENDI*: FROM LATIN TO ENGLISH

Caliban's resistance is, of course, a resistance to the realisation of the ideal 'Father tongue' in the vernacular. That the normative system represented by Virgil should be deployed to inform schoolboys with 'proper' English as well as with 'proper' Latin is indicated by the general statement of objectives in *Ludus*, which, moreover, explicitly links the acquisition of 'proprietie and puritie' 'in our owne English tongue' to the public roles the boys are to fill (Brinsley, *Ludus*, 'The Contents', points 31 and 32). As I have indicated, use of such a 'pure' and 'proper' language necessarily tended to the (re)production of social differences. Here it is worth adding that the representation of this language as 'pure' invests it with value as an absolute ideal, immune from the corruption of change, like the *sermo Latinus* of Virgil.

It is, indeed, through the use of 'grammatical translations', like Brinsley's of the *Eclogues*, that this 'pure' vernacular is to be acquired. For one of the declared purposes of their use is 'growth in our English tongue together with the Latin' (Brinsley, *Virgils Eclogues*, fo. A3v), 'to proceed as well in our English tonge as in the Latine' 'to attaine variety and copie of English words', '(a)nd so in time, to come to proprietie, choise, and puritie, as well in our English as in the Latine' (Brinsley, *Ludus*, pp. 106–7). The ideal vernacular is here characterised in the terms

---

[24] Frank Kermode, 'Introduction', *The Tempest*, p. xxxviii; Shakespeare, *The Tempest*, edited by Stephen Orgel (Oxford University Press, 1994), p. 203. This critique is reinforced by what Felperin calls the 'discursive disturbance' surrounding Caliban, the play's multiple and contra- dictory descriptions of him. Felperin, 'Political Criticism', p. 49.

used, on the one hand, of the object of Ramist rhetoric ('puritie' and 'proprietie') and, on the other, of the object of the Erasmian system ('variety and copie'). It is, in short, through the systems through which the ideal normative discourse in Latin is mediated and acquired that the equivalent vernacular discourse is to be acquired. And it is 'Virgil translated' that exemplifies and figures this ideal of a 'pure' vernacular, the 'proper' property of the educated minority.

What Brinsley calls 'proprietie' the putative author of *The Arte of English Poesie* (1589), George Puttenham, calls 'decencie' or 'decorum' in the third book – 'Of Ornament'. As Derek Attridge has shown, this normative, regulatory principle of decorum is contradictory and un-stable, at once rule-bound (art) and natural, universal and accessible only to a privileged elite, just like Brinsley's principle of propriety (for which the same argument could indeed be made).[25] Of particular importance, for our purposes, is Puttenham's application of decorum as a critical criterion to the language used by Douglas and Stanyhurst in their translations of the opening of the *Aeneid*. For, as we shall see, his practice works to inscribe and police boundaries within the vernacular, which tend to the reproduction of the socio-political structure. First, however, I want to look at an earlier example of Virgil translated, where decorum is mobilised to handle a particularly prominent contradiction in Puttenham's own discourse, to do, that is, some policing at another level. This contradiction has to do with the use of figures. What is particularly important is that the paradigmatic example of Virgilian practice falls under the shadow of a sceptical, ironic view of figurative discourse as dissimulation, becomes, that is, the example of a poetics of duplicity, or of what Montrose calls the 'ironic poetics' of Puttenham's text, which 'registers the failure of Renaissance Humanism: the impossi-ble union between eloquence and virtue, the inevitable collusion be-tween scholarship and power' (Montrose, 'Of Gentlemen', pp. 438–9). What is more, the Virgilian paradigm is represented in a way which clearly suggests how this Protestant turn against 'ornament' is a function (or 'shadow') of the humanist practices it turns against.

Initially, Puttenham gives rather the humanist view, characterising the use of figures as that which differentiates poetic discourse, 'disguising it no litle from the ordinary and accustomed: neverthelesse making it nothing the more unseemely or misbecomming, but rather decenter and

---

[25] Derek Attridge, 'Puttenham's Perplexity: Nature, Art and the Supplement in Renaissance Poetic Theory', in Patricia Parker and David Quint, eds., *Literary Theory / Renaissance Texts* (Baltimore and London: Johns Hopkins University Press, 1986), pp. 257–79.

more agreeable to any civill eare and understanding' (Puttenham, *The Arte*, p. 137). 'Ornament' here is the distinguishing mark of a discourse shared by those who thereby recognise their own inclusion amongst the community of the 'civill'. Later, however, such departures from 'common utterance' are represented as transgressive 'abuses':

As figures be the instruments of ornament in every language, so be they also in a sorte abuses or rather trespasses in speach, because they passe the ordinary limits of common utterance, and be occupied of purpose to deceive the eare and also the minde, drawing it from plainnesse and simplicitie to a certaine doublenesse, whereby our talke is the more guilefull & abusing, for what els is your *Metaphor* but an inversion of sence by transport; your *allegorie* by a duplicite of meaning or dissimulation under covert and darke intendments ... (p. 154)

This representation of figures as manipulative dissimulation is contained, on the one hand, by the drawing of boundaries between kinds, or modes of discourse, and, specifically, by the drawing of a boundary around the discourse of 'the poetical science' through the characterisation of it as play,[26] on the other, by the mobilisation of decorum as the principle regulating these boundaries and the use of figures within them. But the sceptical, ironic view returns to haunt definitions of specific figures, most notably the definition of allegory, which is indeed where Montrose detects most explicitly the 'ironic poetics' of Puttenham's text (Montrose, 'Of Gentlemen', p. 439). And amongst the examples of this 'Figure of false semblant' is the closing line of Virgil's third eclogue.

Not only do 'dissimulation' and 'duplicite' return in the representation of this figure, but the boundary between 'poeticall' and other discourses, which is drawn earlier to dispel anxieties about the use of figures, is explicitly dismantled. All discourses are acknowledged, if ambivalently, to be permeated by this figure, especially the discourses of the court where, as Montrose suggests, this 'Courtly figure' functions as a form, or mode of negotiation in relations of power.

the Courtly figure *Allegoria* ... is when we speake one thing and thinke another ... The use of this figure is so large, and his vertue of so great efficacie as it is supposed no man can pleasantly utter and perswade without it ... in somuch as not onely every common Courtier, but also the gravest Counsellour, yea and the most noble and wisest Prince of them all are many times enforced to use it, by example (say they) of the great Emperour who had it usually in his mouth to say, *Qui nescit dissimulare nescit regnare.* Of this figure therefore which for his

---

[26] See Daniel Javitch, *Poetry and Courtliness in Renaissance England* (Princeton University Press, 1978), p. 91.

duplicitie we call the figure of [*false semblant or dissimulation*] we will speake first as of the chief ringleader ... either in the Poeticall or oratorie science.

And ... we may dissemble ... in earnest aswell as in sport, under covert and darke termes ... But properly & in his principall vertue *Allegoria* is when we do speake in sence translative ... neverthelesse ... having much conveniencie ... *Virgill* in his shepeherdly poemes called *Eglogues* used as rusticall but fit *allegorie* for the purpose thus:

> *Claudite iam rivos pueri sat prata biberunt.*

Which I English thus:

> *Stop up your streames (my lads) the medes have*
> *drunk their fill.*

As much to say, leave of now, yee have talked of the matter inough: for the shepheards guise in many places is by opening certaine sluces to water their pastures, so as when they are wet inough they shut them againe: this application is full Allegoricke. (Puttenham, *The Arte*, pp. 186–7)

The unsettled and unsettling ambivalences of the first paragraph, suggested in the distancing moves ('as it is supposed', 'yea', 'are enforced', 'say they'), are brought under control in the second, once again through the mobilisation of decorum ('properly' 'having much conveniencie'), which continues into the representation of the ('fit') example from Virgil. Nevertheless, this strategy of containment does not entirely dispel the shadow of dissimulation, particularly if we recall Puttenham's earlier characterisation of the Virgilian eclogues as *generically* duplicitous:

the Poet devised the *eglogue* ... not of purpose to counterfait or represent the rusticall manner of loves and communication: but under the vaile of homely persons, and in rude speeches to insinuate and glaunce at greater matters, and such as perchance had not been safe to have been disclosed in any other sort, which may be perceived by the Eglogues of *Virgill*, in which are treated by figure matters of greater importance then the loves of *Titirus* and *Corydon*. (p. 38)

For Montrose, this representation of the Virgilian eclogue may be generalised to other forms of the pastoral mode, both as represented and as practised, which epitomize Puttenham's 'ironic poetics'. But it is important that there is nothing original, or unique about Puttenham's representation of Virgilian practice, which is, as Annabel Patterson succinctly puts it, 'an updating of the Servian hermeneutic'.[27] More importantly, perhaps, the example of allegory from Virgil's third eclogue, which Puttenham later gives, is lifted straight out of Servius.[28] As

---

[27] Patterson, *Pastoral and Ideology*, p. 128; compare the visual representation on the Petrarchan frontispiece, figure 2 and the discussion in chapter 1, pp. 28–30.

[28] 'allegoricos hoc dicit, iam cantare desinite: satiati enim audiendo sumus.' (This is spoken allegorically for have done with your singing we've had our fill) (Virgil, *Opera*, vol. 1, fo. 23v).

in Brinsley's translation of the *Eclogues*, the Servian comment supplies the ground of the Virgilian text, which becomes an ornament, or supplement. Again too, the canonical status of the commentary and the structure of authority folded into the Virgilian text are confirmed. But here the shadow of the sceptical view of figures turns the structure of authority into a structure of duplicity, a covert mode of manipulative control such as characterises the discourse of those who negotiate relations of power in and around the centre, at court. As in Harvey's annotations to Quintilian discussed in chapter 1, Virgil is here a figure of the eloquence proper to the statesman, though Harvey will not suggest, as Puttenham does, that such eloquence is necessarily duplicitous, a deliberate concealment of 'covert and darke intendments'. Further, Puttenham's specific Virgilian example of such duplicitous eloquence confirms what I suggested in relation to Harvey's comment – that the duplicitous model shadows the logic of exegetical and pedagogical practices, which produce Virgilian 'words' and 'matter' as separate objects.

That the (re)production of such Virgilian eloquence could serve as a mode or form of control is illustrated by Ben Jonson's use of Puttenham's Virgilian example to close an early play for the public playhouse – *Every Man In His Humour* (first performed in the Curtain theatre in 1598, published 1601 (*H&S*, vol. 3, pp. 191–289)). That the 'meaning' of the line from the third eclogue, quoted untranslated by Judge Clement in the Quarto version, lies in the Servian mediation of it as an allegory of closure is clear from the Folio version of the play which, we shall see in chapter 5, replaces Virgil's Latin with a vernacular version of the Servian mediation. This is one of several modifications made to the Quarto text (others include the removal of another Virgilian quotation), which I shall discuss there. What I want to point out here is simply that, in the place of the play's first production as performance, the Virgilian quotation constituted a relatively esoteric object, which worked to differentiate insiders from outsiders, a learned community from the rest. More precisely, the structure of authority folded into the Virgilian text through the mediation of the canonical commentary, is mobilised to produce a hierarchy between a privileged, learned elite and an un-privileged, ignorant majority. The structure of authority serves, in short, precisely as a covert or dissimulated mode of control, as the context of the Virgilian example in Puttenham's text suggests it might. Jonson's use of the example may indeed have been coloured by this context, for in his personal copy of Puttenham's *Arte* the definition of allegory – 'which is when we speake one thing and thinke another' – has been underlined.[29] It points up what we shall see in detail later, that Jonson's use of more and less esoteric Virgilian objects as a mode of dissimulated control works essentially as *irony*.[30]

It is as a mode of dissimulated control that the voice of Virgil is used throughout the Jonsonian corpus. Not that such a use could have been represented by either Puttenham or Jonson as a strategic dissimulation of a will to control by inclusion/exclusion. Indeed, this ideological work is covered in their texts by an idealising humanist discourse, as in the passage from Puttenham I quoted earlier, which approves the use of figures, as a differentiating mark of the civilised subject. It is such ideological work – of inclusion/exclusion – that always tends to be concealed by ideal representations of the normative, civilising Language Virgil and 'Virgil translated' represent, as, more generally, such work has continued to be concealed by ideal representations of the objects of an education in the humanities.

It is in terms of 'a dialectic of inclusion and exclusion' that Louis Montrose has analysed the politics of Elizabethan pastoral (Montrose, 'Of Gentlemen', p. 448). His work gave a vital new turn to critical discussion, which has since been brilliantly expanded in Annabel Patterson's work on pastoral and ideology. But neither critic recognises how the ideological work – of exclusion/inclusion – is done at the level of the selection of forms, especially the selection of 'rustic' forms. For, while Patterson does not enter into specific questions of form, Montrose simply comments in passing that the 'sort of pastoral' used by the Elizabethan courtiers is 'rustic in its imagery and personae (and, sometimes, in its diction)' (p. 440).[31] That the establishment of the formal character of 'rustic' discourse in the vernacular entailed tensions and contradictions is indicated in Puttenham's representation of the Virgilian example of allegory as 'rustic but fit'. The 'but' here articulates the

---

[29] George Puttenham, *The Arte of English Poesie* (London, 1589), reprinted in *English Linguistics 1500–1800* (Menston: The Scholar Press, 1968), p. 155. See McPherson, 'Ben Jonson's Library', pp. 79–80.

[30] Irony is linked to allegory by Abraham Fraunce, who comments that the trope of irony 'continued maketh a most sweet allegorie'. Abraham Fraunce, *The Arcadian Rhetorike* (London, 1588), edited by Ethel Seaton (Oxford: Basil Blackwell, 1950), p. 10.

[31] Although the character of pastoral forms has been treated in the large body of critical material on the genre, the ideology of these forms has not usually been discussed. See, for example, Jean Hubaux, *Le réalisme dans les Bucoliques de Virgile* (Paris: Champion, 1927); Thomas G. Rosenmayer, *The Green Cabinet: Theocriticus and the European Pastoral Lyric* (University of California Press, 1969), pp. 247–82. And where the ideology of the pastoral mode is discussed, there has been little specific attention to details of form, as in the work of Montrose and Patterson and in the seminal work of Raymond Williams – *The Country and the City* (London: Granada, 1975).

tension of a system of representation that seeks to include those it simultaneously excludes. Again it is the principle of decorum that is to determine and to police the boundary, this time the boundary, on the one hand, between the formalised or figured rustic and the actual rustic (who without access to the system decorum represents is necessarily excluded), and, on the other, the boundary, within the system of representation, between the figure of the 'rustic' and the figure of the gentleman. It is, specifically, through the designation of 'proper' forms to each class of figure that the practice of decorum will do this work, and so tend to inscribe these boundaries *on* the vernacular. It is such a twofold inscription of the division between low (the rustic) and high (the gentle/noble), both within and by a normative system of representation, that a 'fit' translation of Virgil will serve.

This is exactly the ideological thrust of Puttenham's criticism of Richard Stanyhurst's and Gavin Douglas's efforts at rendering the first lines of the *Aeneid*. Appearing as they do amongst examples drawn primarily 'from incidents in court life' (Attridge, 'Puttenham's Perplexity', p. 270), which are given to illustrate the regulatory, normative system decorum represents, these examples underscore that, as model of this system, 'Virgil translated', like the system itself, is the property of those who move in the places of power. This is pointed up by the preceding discussion of decorum, which, as Attridge has shown, reveals, on the one hand, that the system decorum represents is not finally reducible to a determinate set of rules (hence the examples), and so is apparently 'natural', but, on the other, that being explicitly identified as the property of a socio-political elite with education and court experience, 'the "naturalness" of decorum ... is an ideological product, a sixteenth-century equivalent of one of Barthes's modern *myths*, whereby a historically specific class attitude is promoted and perceived as natural' (p. 269).

In the criticism of Richard Stanyhurst's translation what is promoted as 'natural' through the mobilisation of decorum is, specifically, a correspondence between linguistic and social orders, a hierarchy of 'termes' which corresponds to (and so underwrites) the socio-political hierarchy of 'estates'.

And yet in speaking or writing of a Princes affaires & fortunes there is a certaine *Decorum*, that we may not use the same termes in their busines, as we might very wel doe in a meaner persons, the case being all one, such reverence is due to their estates. As for example, if an Historiographer shal write of an Emperor or King, how such a day hee joyned battel with his enemie, and being over-laide ranne out of the field, and tooke his heeles, or put spurre to his horse and fled as fast as hee could: the termes be not decent, but of a meane souldier or captaine it were not undecently spoken. And as one, who translating certaine bookes of *Virgils Æneidos* into English meetre, said that *Æneas* was fayne to trudge out of Troy: which terme became better to be spoken of a beggar, or of a rogue, or a lackey: for so wee use to say to such maner of people, be trudging hence ...

The same translatour when he came to these wordes: *Insignem pietate virum, tot volvere casus tot adire labores compulit* [*sic*]. Hee turned it thus, what moved *Juno* to tugge so great a captaine as *Æneas*, which word tugge spoken in this case is so undecent as none other coulde have bene devised, and tooke his first originall from the cart, because it signifieth the pull or draught of the oxen or horses, and therefore the leathers that beare the chiefe stresse of the draught, the cartars call them tugges, and so wee use to say that shrewd boyes tugge each other by the eares, for pull. (Puttenham, *The Arte*, pp. 273–4)[32]

Although readers today might well agree with Puttenham's judgement on Stanyhurst's translation, and might even have recourse to a criterion of appropriateness, their opinion would be based not on connotations of social class, but on the mode or kind of action each word denotes in the system of meanings which are current usage in standard English, in particular given the generic category of the Latin text.[33] Puttenham too has recourse to usage in each case ('wee use to say'), as well as to a (spurious) etymology in the second, but these are secondary criteria mobilised to endorse as 'natural' the socio-political boundaries drawn within, and on to the vernacular through the application of the first

---

[32] Puttenham is clearly working from memory: in the second example he misquotes the Virgilian lines, which read 'impulerit' (*Aeneid* 1, line 11), not 'compulit' (nowhere recorded as an alternative); and Stanyhurst's translation, which runs 'What grudge or what furye kindled / Of Gods thee Princesse ... / With sharp sundrye perils too tugge so famous a captayne.' Richard Stanyhurst, *Translation of the First Four Books of the Aeneis* (Leyden, 1582), edited by E. Arber (London: The English Scholars' Library, 1880), p. 17. Editors of *The Arte* have not noted these misquotations. Puttenham's first example refers to Stanyhurst's rendering of the opening lines 'I blaze thee captayne first from Troy cittye repairing, / Like wandring pilgrim too famosed Italie trudging ...' (ibid.).

[33] The *OED*'s early modern examples of the uses of 'trudge' and 'tug' do not suggest the social connotations projected by Puttenham. Indeed, one of the examples of the use of 'tug' is from Milton's representation of his biblical/epic hero Samson. In the Shakespearean corpus, the (four) instances of 'tug' do not imply these connotations. On the other hand, they are implied in the (six) instances of 'trudge', which is used always of, or to, low-born characters, often servants.

The problems of literary translation, though formulated differently, have of course not been solved; contemporary theories have not yet come up with anything more satisfactory than provisional working criteria. See Susan Bassnett-McGuire, *Translation Studies*, reprint (London and New York: Routledge, 1988), especially pp. 76–132.

criterion of decorum. An ideal translation of the *Aeneid* is thus projected, which by inscribing the socio-political hierarchy on to the vernacular would serve to regulate and stabilise social boundaries, together with lexical/semantic boundaries, both of which were, of course, changing with exceptional rapidity.[34]

Testimony to the shifting character of semantic boundaries is furnished even as the attempt to fix them is made in the example taken from Gavin Douglas's translation, which comes between the two examples from Stanyhurst's translation.[35] Puttenham's objection here is to Douglas's translation of Virgil's opening description of Aeneas 'fato profugus' 'by fate a fugitive'. Invoking again the criterion of decorum he criticises the term 'fugitive' as 'undecently spoken' not only because it does not correspond to the 'estate' of Aeneas (it is 'a notable indignity offred to that princely person' (p. 274)), but also (and principally) because it does not correspond to his moral character. Taking as the ground of his case the 'Authours intent' (p. 273) (still a criterion of criticism in discussion of literary translations[36]), Puttenham argues that Virgil intended 'to avaunce' Aeneas 'above all other men ... for vertue and magnanimitie' (pp. 273-4), echoing a recurring politico-moral interpretation of Aeneas as model of the ideal, virtuous prince, which we shall meet again (in editions of the *Opera*, for example, and in one of Jonson's masques), and which here furnishes a contrast with the cowardly 'historical' king who flees the field of battle (in the passage quoted above). By outlawing 'fugitive' as in contradiction to this moral meaning Puttenham entirely fails to recognise the historical distance between Douglas's text and his own, and the modification to the word's semantic boundaries which has occurred, specifically the erasure of the morally

[34] 'The period 1530–1660 exhibits the fastest growth of the vocabulary in the history of the English language' (Görlach, *Introduction to Early Modern English*, p. 136); see also Charles Barber, *Early Modern English* (London: André Deutsch, 1976), pp. 166–95. Görlach points out that there were 'no dictionaries or academies to curb the number of new words' (p. 138), i.e. no official, institutionalised agents of control. Virgil, as used by Puttenham here, Sidney (below) and by Jonson might be described precisely as an unofficial agent of control. In parallel with the expansion of the vocabulary, 'the period 1560–1640 was an exceptionally mobile one' (Stone, 'Social Mobility' p. 36). See also L. Stone, *The Crisis of the Aristocracy 1558-1641* (Oxford: Clarendon Press, 1965), p. 36.

[35] Puttenham appears to have confused the two translators, for having quoted Douglas, after Stanyhurst, he proceeds to introduce the second example from Stanyhurst with 'The same translatour' (in the passage quoted above). Again editors of *The Arte* have not recorded this confusion.

[36] See, for example, Bassnett-McGuire, *Translation Studies*, p. 91 and the argument against such a criterion in Barbara Belyea, 'The Notion of "Equivalence": The Relevance of Current Translation Theory to the Edition of Literary Texts', in Jacques Flamand and Arlette Thomas, eds., *La traduction: l'universitaire et le practicien* (University of Ottawa Press, 1984), pp. 43-7.

neutral sense the word carries in Douglas's translation.[37] Thus, even as he seeks to fix boundaries within and on the vernacular – and with them the social order – Puttenham unwittingly confirms their movement in time. The arbitrary changes of history are affirmed by the very turn which seeks to establish a language – a 'Language' – which transcends them.

That vernacular eloquence has achieved the same kind of transcendent permanence achieved by Virgil in Latin (and Homer in Greek) is the implicit claim of *The Arcadian Rhetorike* (1588), Abraham Fraunce's vernacular version of Ramist rhetoric. For, while he faithfully translates the definitions from both parts of Omer Talon's handbook, Fraunce consistently departs from it in his examples, in every case giving, after (untranslated) quotations from Homer and Virgil (some of which are taken from Talon), a quotation from Philip Sidney's *Arcadia* (first published 1590), followed by (untranslated) quotations from contemporary European writers. The European vernaculars are thus collectively celebrated as equal to the normative standard of the *sermo Latinus* of Virgil's Latin, while English is placed as the *primus inter pares* and Sidney as the English equivalent to Virgil, the figure and model of vernacular eloquence.

That this eloquence is the property of a socio-political elite is indicated by the examples chosen from the *Arcadia*. In the first part, the examples of figures of speech are taken, in all but two instances, from speeches by the high-born gentles and nobles, and from the discourse of the (implicitly high-born) narrator, while, in the second part, the examples of voice and gesture are all taken from the narrator's descriptions of the high-born. Apart from the two exceptions (discussed below), there are no examples from the speeches of the base-born characters – principally comprising the family Damoetas, Miso and Mopsa – or from descriptions of their voices and gestures. Yet they are far from reticent; Damoetas, for instance, in what is clearly an ironic understatement, is described as 'a man of no fewe wordes',[38] and their voices and gestures are frequently described.

It is indeed the narrator's descriptions of the modes of voice and gesture used by base-born characters that suggest that Fraunce's selec-

---

[37] See *OED*, s.v. 'fugitive' sense 2 ('exiled'); the last example of this sense given in the *OED* is dated 1598. Interestingly, Sidney uses it of Aeneas, perhaps recalling Douglas's opening lines in his *Defence of Poesie*. Philip Sidney, *The Complete Works*, edited by A. Feuillerat, 4 vols. (Cambridge University Press, 1912–26), vol. 3, p. 25. Stanyhurst gives 'Like wandring pilgrim', which might have inspired Puttenham's proposed alternative, 'a wanderer' (p. 274).

[38] Sidney, *The Complete Works*, vol. 4, p. 225.

tion of examples was determined by a prior strategy of differential representation in the *Arcadia* itself. For these descriptions resemble descriptions by Fraunce of the modes of voice and gesture that are *contrary* to those prescribed by the Ramist system. For example, Fraunce (following Talon freely) advises against 'continuall straining without intermission. To brawle in the beginning with a shriking [*sic*] voyce is rude and unmannerly', which we may compare with this description by Sidney's narrator of how Damoetas 'came swearing to the place . . . with a voyce like him, that playes *Hercules* . . . The first worde he spake after his rayling oathes was, Am not I *Dametas*? Why, am not I *Dametas*?'[39] Again Fraunce (following Talon) comments,

Stand Upright and straight as nature hath appoynted: much wavering and overcurious and nice motion is verie ridiculous . . . The countenance must turn with the bodie . . . a moderation is to be had in the gesture of the hand . . . that it rather follow than goe before and expresse the words. (Fraunce, *The Arcadian Rhetorike*, pp. 120, 122, 126)

Compare:

Mopsa . . . stoode all this while with her hande some tyme before her face, but Comonly (with a certeyne speciall grace, of her owne) wagging her Lippes, and grenning, in stede of smyling: But all the wordes hee coulde gett of her was (wrying her waste) . . . (Sidney, *The Complete Works*, vol. 4, pp. 95–6)

These examples suggest that the system of Ramist rhetoric furnishes a strategy of differential representation which works, essentially through irony, so as to include and simultaneously exclude those (base-born, or rustic) without access to it. The boundary between high and low, gentle and rustic is drawn both within and by means of the system, as in Puttenham's deployment of decorum. Again this is done through the assigning of the forms 'proper' to each class of figure, the forms 'proper' to the base-born being contrary, 'improper' and even (in Brinsley's sense of the word) 'unnatural' forms. These forms are not only linguistic but paralinguistic and gestural, the difference of the rustic being marked in the representation of his 'contrary' modes of voice and gesture as well as in the representation of his 'rusticall but fit' discourse.

   That this strategy of differential representation follows Virgilian practice in the *Eclogues*, especially the third, is implicitly claimed, on the one hand, by the names Damoetas and Mopsa, and, on the other, by the imitation of the third eclogue given amongst the *Arcadia*'s own *Eclogues*

---

[39] Fraunce, *The Arcadian Rhetorike*, p. 106; Sidney, *The Complete Works*, vol. 4, p. 28.

at the end of the second book.[40] Mopsa is a feminised form of Mopsus, the name of one of the shepherds who participates in the singing match in Virgil's fifth eclogue, and Damoetas is the name (taken from Theocritus) of one of the shepherds who participates in the singing contest in the third eclogue, and who, not insignificantly, is described as 'indocte' (line 26).[41] And, although Sidney's Damoetas does not participate in the singing match which imitates *Eclogue* 3, those who do are represented in the ironic mode which is used throughout of the base-born family, and which is the mode through which the strategy of differential representation is characteristically articulated. Indeed, it is from this imitation (as well as from a description of Mopsa's gestures and an example of her speech) that Fraunce's only examples from the discourses of base-born characters are taken. What is more the first example is given (with the description of Mopsa) to illustrate, precisely, 'Ironia' – defined as 'perceived by ... contrarietie' – while the second is given to illustrate 'derision' – one of the effects of the exclamatory mode which is explicitly linked to irony (Fraunce, *The Arcadian Rhetorike*, pp. 10, 69). The irony and derision are, in both instances, double, being directed not only by the characters against each other (as in the next quotation), but also against the characters by the 'gentle' narrator and his implied 'gentle' readers.

This is apparent if we look at the narrator's introductory frame to the imitation of Virgil's third eclogue. For, drawing attention to the kind of forms – the 'maner' – used by the base-born speakers, the narrator's ironic mode identifies these as contrary to proper forms.

Owte startes a Jolly yonker, his name was *Nico:* whose tungue had borne a very ytching silence all this whyle, and having spyed one *Pas* a Mate of his, as madd as hym self, bothe (in deede) Laddes to clyme up any Tree in the worlde, hee bestowed this maner of Salutatyon uppon hym, and was with like reverence requyted.

Nico. *And are you there oulde* Pas? *in trouthe I ever thoughte,*
   Amongst us all wee should fynde oute some thing of noughte.

Pas. *And I am here the same, so mote I thryving bee,*
   Dispayrde, in all this flock, to fynde a knave, but thee,
             (Sidney, *The Complete Works*, vol. 4, p. 134)

[40] In the first version of the *Arcadia* in Sidney, *The Complete Works*, vol. 4, pp. 134–8; in the revised version, ibid., vol. 1, pp. 344–8. I quote from the first.
[41] Fairclough translates 'Master Dunce'. A deliberate insult on the part of the other contestant Menalcas, 'indocte' is exactly how Sidney's Damoetas is represented. (The name of Damoetas is also used in Virgil's second and fifth eclogues, while Mopsus is used again in the eighth.)

Of the few critics who have bestowed attention on this imitation, William Ringler treats it as a not particularly successful 'parody', while Merrit Y. Hughes considers it a 'burlesque', and, extraordinarily, an 'irresponsible imitation'!⁴² But such judgements assume, as given, boundaries within the vernacular which have remained problematic for translators of the third eclogue to this day, the problem being, specifically, how to produce a mode, or forms, equivalent to the Virgilian forms characterised, indeed criticised, as 'rustic'.⁴³ For, as Hubaux points out, these forms (themselves imitations of Theocritus's use of Dorian dialect) were 'interdites par la grammaire classique' (Hubaux, *Le réalisme*, p. 98), and were even attacked as 'not-Latin' by an early critic – an attack which is recorded, if only to be condemned, in the life of Virgil given in larger sixteenth-century editions.⁴⁴ Sidney's poem is not so much a distortion of the Virgilian model (i.e. parody or burlesque) as an attempt to produce within the vernacular such 'rustic' de-formations – at the levels of diction, imagery, syntax and versification – which are not only in contrast, but contrary to the forms of eloquence used by the high-born, as the ironic thrust of the framing introduction (which Ringler and Hughes do not consider) emphasises. It should, in short, be taken as part of the strategy of differential representation in the *Arcadia* as a whole, which, like Puttenham's deployment of decorum in his criticism of the translations of the *Aeneid*, works to inscribe on the vernacular boundaries between high and low – gentle and rustic – forms. Indeed one of the terms Puttenham condemns as fitting for the base-born but unfitting for Aeneas – the verb 'trudge' – is used by Pas,⁴⁵

---

⁴² Philip Sidney, *The Poems*, edited by William A. Ringler, Jr (Oxford: Clarendon Press, 1962), p. 399; Hughes, *Virgil and Spenser*, pp. 275, 274.

⁴³ See, for example, Day Lewis's attempt: 'Watch it! What right have you to lecture a chap?' (for 'Parcius ista viris tamen obicienda memento' (line 7)); 'I bet' for 'credo' (line 10) and 'You amateur' for 'indocte' (line 26). *The Eclogues, Georgics and Aeneid of Virgil*, translated by C. Day Lewis (Oxford University Press, 1966), pp. 10–11. Thirty years later these phrases suggest not 'rustic' discourse but the hearty, male discourse of Oxbridge commonroom or army mess – versions of pastoral, perhaps, for Day Lewis.

⁴⁴ 'Nec Virgilius qui columen linguae Latinae fuit, caruit obtrectatoribus. In Bucolicis enim ... sed insulsissime ... quidem deridet ... Dic mihi Damoeta cuium pecus? an ne Latinum?' (Virgil, *Opera*, vol. 1, fo. iiv) (Even Virgil the pillar of the Latin language was not without his detractors. One critic ridiculously derided as not-Latin 'Dic mihi Damoeta cuium pecus?') The quoted criticism specifically derides the use of 'cuium' 'une forme archaique de l'interrogatif ... encore employée à la campagne' (Hubaux, *Le réalisme*, p. 99). In a more recent, comprehensive discussion, Jeffrey Wills suggests the form recalls the comedies of Plautus and Terence as well as Theocritus. Jeffrey Wills, 'Virgil's *cuium*', *Vergilius* 39 (1993), pp. 3–11. (My thanks to John A. Dutra for this material.) We might compare the question 'is it Latin' ('an ne Latinum?') with Jonson's condemnation of Spenser's use of archaisms as at once 'no Language' and not-Virgilian.

⁴⁵ 'Lalus ... *with shame did trudge*,' (Sidney, *The Complete Works*, vol. 4, p. 135); see above, pp. 63–4 and

a useful, if slight, coincidence, which underscores the similar ideological work being done through criticism of translations of Virgil by one, and through an imitation of Virgil by the other.

This ideological work emerges to virtual explicitness in a preface to a translation of *Aeneid* 4 published in the 1630s. For the translator, Sir Robert Stapylton (?–1669), claims that '(i)n Englishing *Vergil*' he has used 'a Language, not *so low* as to bring downe his *Aeneis* to his *Eclogues*, and levell the expressions of his Princes with his Shepheards: nor *so high*, that he should not be intelligent to the Unlearned, as if he still spake *Latin*.'[46] This definition of the object of translation as a language which includes the unlearned without levelling (!) the distinction between high and low, social as well as linguistic, categories, could hardly point up more clearly the ideological work being done by Sidney's imitation, and Puttenham's criticism of translations of Virgil. Drawing boundaries which at once include and doubly exclude those without access to the system which represents them, both criticism and imitation tend, we might say, to the enclosure (and appropriation) of the 'common ground' of the vernacular and thereby to the dispossession of those who speak/ live in it.[47]

Corroboration for this analysis of Sidney's imitation of Virgil's third eclogue is furnished by Abraham Fraunce's other handbook, *The Lawiers Logike* (1588), which, as the title indicates, seeks to reform the practice of the law according to the system of Ramist logic.[48] For, in a departure from the *Dialecticae* (to which, as to the *Rhetorica* in *The Arcadian Rhetorike* he is usually faithful), Fraunce gives the Virgilian shepherds' repetition of 'Dic, quibus in terris' at the end of the singing match (lines 104 and 106) as an example of 'an unorderly confusion', as, that is, a form which is contrary to the general rule of formal debate: 'In every syllogisticall conflict and controversie, there is a defendant and an opponent. The

---

note 33.

[46] Robert Stapylton, *Dido and Aeneas. The fourth booke of Virgils Aeneis* (London, 1634?), as quoted in Görlach, *Introduction to Early Modern English*, p. 273.

[47] I have adapted my terms here to recall the point made by Raymond Williams: 'What has been lent to shepherds, and at what rates of interest, is much more in question. It is not easy to forget that Sidney's *Arcadia*, which gives a continuing title to English neo-pastoral, was written in a park which had been made by enclosing a whole village and evicting the tenants. The elegant game was then only at arm's length – a rough arm's length – from a visible reality of country life.' (Williams, *The Country and the City*, p. 33) More than merely analogous, the *Arcadia*'s differential system of representation furnishes a pre-text for such 'rough' treatment, and is itself a form of violence.

[48] References will be to Abraham Fraunce, *The Lawiers Logike, exemplifying the praecepts of Logike by the practise of the Common Lawe* (London, 1588), reprinted in *English Linguistics 1500–1800*, no.174, edited by R. C. Alston (Menston: The Scholar Press, 1969).

first is to urge, prove, conclude; the other to repell, avoyd, and drive backe.'

The disputation being once begon [*sic*], it is an unorderly confusion for the same man sometimes to aunswere, sometimes to reply ... much like the two clownes in *Virgill*, which, when they could not aunswere what was propounded, begin [*sic*] a freshe with a new doubt on the necke of the olde: *Dic, quibus in terris*, quoth the one, and *Dic, quibus in terris*, quoth the other, Areede me a riddle, sayth *Damaetas*: and Areede me a riddle replyeth *Menalcas*, thincking it a faire conquest, to have taken and given blowe for blowe, as Bakers and Butchers use to doe, who never care for any curious wardes [*sic*], but lay on loade like good fellowes, one for one, till both begin to stagger, with their valiant blood about their brused pates. I have therefore in a word or two, layd downe some generall instructions and directions for orderly disputations. (Fraunce, *The Lawiers Logike*, fo. 101r)[49]

Here it is not only Virgil's shepherds that are represented by the system of logic as outside it and consequently as deserving of contempt ('clownes'), but figures from contemporary English society taken to be their equivalent, 'Bakers and Butchers', whose exclusion from the forms of 'civilised' exchange is further underscored by the representation of the degeneration from verbal quarrel to physical brawl. As in the *Arcadia*, there is at once an inclusion and exclusion of those without access to the system by which they are represented. As in the *Arcadia* too, this is articulated through an ironic mode ('curious wardes', 'good fellowes', and, especially, 'their valiant blood about their brused pates'); indeed, whether a conscious recollection or not, Fraunce here sounds remarkably like Sidney's narrator. And the violence is the same.

This tends to belie the inclusiveness projected in the prefatory address to lawyers: 'Coblers be men, why therefore not Logicians? and Carters have reason, why therefore not Logike?' (n. pag.) It is belied too by the closing argument in favour of a generalised application of logic, its use not only 'in reading or writing, but in every civill assembly or meeting':

[49] The Virgilian lines are given in the *Dialecticae*, but as an example of the refutation of like by like, not of unorderly confusion. See P. Ramus, *Dialecticae libri duo, Audomari Talei praelectionibus illustrati* (Paris, 1556), p. 79 and P. Ramus, *Dialectique* (1555), edited by Michel Dassonville (Geneva: Droz, 1964), p. 82. There may be some influence from the Servian gloss to an earlier line (line 10): 'Et rustice et naturaliter respondet. non enim ante purgat obiecta, sed alia obiicit. Ita enim irati facere consueuerunt [*sic*], cum aut non potuerint, aut noluerint obiecta dissoluere.' Virgil, *Opera*, vol. 1, fo. 17r (He replies in a way that is both rustic and natural. For he doesn't first deal with [compare Fraunce's 'repell'] the accusations, but instead makes new accusations. This is the habitual behaviour [compare Fraunce's 'use to doe'] of angry men who either cannot or will not refute accusations.) The register of the gloss is forensic; like Fraunce, Servius is talking about formal disputations to which the 'rustic and natural' mode of the shepherds does not conform.

Neyther let any man thinke, that because in common meetings and assemblies the wordes and tearmes of Logike bee not named, therefore the force and operation of Logike is not there used and apparant ... although in common conference wee never name ... woords of art, yet doo we secretly practise them in our disputations, the vertue whereof is, to make our discourses seeme true to the simple, and probable to the wise. (fo. 120r)

The public discourses informed by the system of logic are here acknowledged to work covertly, differently perceived and judged by those with access to the system and those without. That those without access cannot enter such discourses is the reason the sectarian Robert Browne gives for logic not to be used in church meetings (see chapter 1, p. 36). To be thus excluded 'in common meetings and assemblies' is indeed to be dispossessed, and disempowered.

Thus, though the practical orientation and relative facility of access of the Ramist system of logic did contribute to the exposure and interrogation of specific received mediations of Virgilian texts, what the quotations from Fraunce's handbook point up is the strictly relative character of this access. Whether confined, as Brinsley recommends, to the universities, or more widely taught in schools, as Kempe recommends, the system of logic remained, like the system of rhetoric, a normative system of representation for the vernacular as well as for Latin confined to a socio-political elite whose use of discourses informed by these systems served to mark their difference and confirm their power.

That Virgil and Virgil translated (and imitated) exemplify and figure these discourses is, finally, illustrated by the examples of logical analyses which Fraunce gives immediately after the closing argument quoted above.

I have, for examples sake, put downe a Logicall Analysis of the second *Aegloge* in *Virgill*, of the *Earle of Northumberlands* case in Maister *Plowdens* reportes, and of Sir *William Stamfords* crowne plees. (fos. 120r–120v)

The Latin text of Virgil's eclogue and a translation by Fraunce are followed by an analysis in diagrammatic form, which divides the text into places or modes of argument according to the Ramist system (fos. 120v–124r), just as Plowden's report of the case of the Earl of Northumberland (a case involving the establishment of royal prerogatives over mineral wealth) is analysed (fos. 125r–139r). Thus turned to illustrate the system a legal case is shown to illustrate, Virgil becomes, almost literally, a figure of the Law.

'EVERY VERTU BELANGAND A NOBILL MAN':[50] VIRGIL AS
MORAL AUTHORITY

Produced with, but distinct from Virgil as formal model was Virgil as moral authority – a *norma vivendi*. For, even if the normative formal systems the Virgilian texts exemplify are invested, at the level of representation, with moral value through the use of terms such as 'pure' and 'proper', pedagogic and exegetic practices tended always to produce separate objects. This is suggested, in *Ludus*, in Brinsley's representation of general aims: the boys should learn, he comments,

> to make right use of the matter of their Authours, *besides* the Latin . . . To help to furnish them, with varietie of the best morall matter, and with understanding wisedome and precepts of vertue, as they growe; *and withall* to imprint the Latine so in their minds thereby, as hardly to be forgotten. (Brinsley, *Ludus*, 'The Contents', point 24; my emphasis)

These pedagogic aims and practices are recognisably Erasmian. The relation is indeed explicit and specific: in *Ludus* the *De copia* is recommended as a source of style and the companion text, the *Adagia*, as a source of moral matter, while in *A Consolation* Erasmus is one of Brinsley's acknowledged authorities.[51]

Brinsley's specific recommendations of these Erasmian texts point up and perpetuate the separation between 'words' and 'matter' produced by the practices the texts institute. As we saw earlier, it is a separation articulated in the structural division of the *De Copia* between the categories of 'verba' and 'res', which, specifically, produce different Virgilian objects. We saw too that the canonical commentaries are likewise structured by this division, although the Virgilian 'matter' they produce is not primarily moral as it is, predominantly, in the Erasmian text. This moral orientation, as well as the division between 'words' and 'matter', is illustrated too in *De ratione studii* (first published, according to Margolin, in 1514[52]). A seminal pedagogic textbook of general importance because, as Baldwin has pointed out, its methods and practices were followed in English grammar schools throughout

---

[50] Douglas, *Virgil's 'Aeneid'*, vol. 2, p. 12.
[51] Brinsley, *Ludus*, pp. 172–90, especially, pp. 183 (error for p. 182), 189; Brinsley, *A Consolation*, p. 24; see Baldwin, *William Shakespere's Small Latine*, vol. 1, pp. 450–1.
[52] Margolin, 'Erasme', p. 290. References are to Erasmus, *De ratione studii*, edited by J.-C. Margolin, in *Opera Omnia*, vol. 1-2 (Amsterdam: North Holland, 1971), pp. 111–51.

the sixteenth century, this text is of particular importance here, because Erasmus gives, as one of his examples, a model lesson on Virgil's second eclogue.[53]

What Erasmus requires of the teacher is that he assume the position of a commentator, providing the supplementary 'ground' or pretext through which the text is to be mediated. In this case, specifically, the mediation is to come between, and effectively to erase the interpretation of the second eclogue as a celebration of homosexual love in general, and as an allusion to Virgil's paedophilia in particular, an interpretation which carried the authority of the Servian commentary.[54] The boys' minds are to be protected beforehand ('praemuniat') with an introduction ('praefatio'), which consists in a binary structure of oppositional precepts – that friendship can be created only where there is likeness and that unlikeness breeds hatred and distrust (Erasmus, *De ratione*, pp. 139–40). This is to be reinforced by proverbs and adages drawn from other authors. The second eclogue may then be treated as an illustration of the second precept (pp. 140–2). Consequently, Erasmus affirms, nothing base or sordid will enter their minds – 'nihil ... turpe veniet in mentem'.[55] As Margolin has observed, this is strange enough to modern readers; we might contrast, in particular, a recent editor's analysis, which structures the poem according to its 'violent and abrupt changes of mood' and which foregrounds the homosexuality Erasmus seeks so diligently to have repressed.[56] More significant, perhaps, is the contrast with the analysis of the same eclogue by Abraham Fraunce, which is probably no less strange to modern readers. For, despite Gabriel Harvey's claim that Erasmus anticipated the Ramist reforms in his divisions, we see here how the moral orientation of Erasmian practice produces, in a specific instance, an object quite different from

[53] Baldwin, *William Shakespere's Small Latine*, vol. 1, p. 75; Erasmus, *De ratione*, pp. 139–42. See Margolin, 'Erasme', p. 294, and Anthony Grafton, 'Renaissance Readers and Ancient Texts: Comments on some Commentaries', *Renaissance Quarterly* 38 (1985), pp. 637–9.
[54] 'Virgilius dicitur in pueros habuisse amorem: nec enim turpiter eum diligebat.' (Virgil is said to have been fond of boys; not that there was anything base in his love.) Virgil, *Opera*, vol. 1, fo. 10r. The comment is echoed in the gloss to Spenser's January eclogue. Edmund Spenser, *Poetical Works*, edited by J. C. Smith and E. de Selincourt (Oxford University Press, 1970), pp. 422–3.
[55] Erasmus, *De ratione*, p. 142. In 'turpe' here is the return of the 'turpiter' of the repressed Servian gloss, quoted in the previous note, which is precisely what is to be kept out of the schoolboys' minds.
[56] Margolin, 'Erasme', p. 294; *Vergil: Eclogues*, edited by R. Coleman (Cambridge University Press, 1977), pp. 108–9.

the object produced by the practice of the Ramist system of logic.[57]

In the second part of the *De copia*, it is not the arguments that furnish the moral colour so much as the examples, including examples from Virgil. The golden bough in *Aeneid* 6, for instance, is said to figure 'wisdom set apart in a hidden place and found only by a few',[58] an allegorical reading which is to be found elsewhere in the Erasmian corpus, and which is echoed in a marginal note in Thomas Phaer's translation, and implied in one of Jonson's poems, where itself 'hidden wisdom' it serves, like the Servian mediation of the last line of the third eclogue in *Every Man In*, as a dissimulated form of control, working to separate the ('wise') few from the many.[59]

There are, however, exceptions to the general tendency of the second part of the *De copia* to illustrate formal strategies of argumentation with moral examples, the most notable being the long section on descriptions (Erasmus, *De copia*, pp. 202–16), which includes the example of a tempest, illustrated by recommended *loci* from Ovid (*Metamorphoses* 11) and from Virgil (*Aeneid* 1) (p. 204), which, as we shall see, the opening scene of *The Tempest* appears to recall. This section reinforces the tendency of the structural division of *De copia* to separate moral and formal orders, and so works against the contrary tendency of the moral content of the examples. This is underscored by the companion text, the *Adagiorum collectanea* (1500), revised as *Chiliades* (1505), a collection of comments on sententious expressions, including fourteen from Virgil, which gives no formal analysis.[60] That the *Adagia* provides moral edification rather than

[57] See chapter 1, pp. 34–5 and above, p. 71. It is worth remarking that the structure of moral precepts recommended to the teacher of Virgil's second eclogue expands, in the examples from other authors, into a much more general – and divinely ordained – principle of organisation, which structures the natural world as well as the human and moral. It is a principle we find again in the *De copia* and the *Methodus* as the principle (*ratio*) of selection and organisation to be used in gathering 'matter' from authors (and specifically the Bible in the *Methodus*). See Grafton and Jardine, *Humanism to Humanities*, pp. 147–8. This is to be done 'according to similars and opposites', that is, according to a principle which, in the *De ratione*, is turned as a moral principle illustrated by Virgil's second eclogue. Erasmus, *Literary and Educational Writings 2*, edited by Craig R. Thomson, p. 636.

[58] Ibid., p. 612, translating 'sapientam in abdito sepositam paucisque deprehensam' (Erasmus, *De copia*, p. 236).

[59] See Margolin, 'Erasme', pp. 298–301 (Margolin argues that such moral allegorising shows how Erasmus read Virgil through a transfiguring Christian humanism and specifically through a 'philosophia Christi'); Thomas Phaer, *The Nyne Fyrst Bookes of the Eneidos of Virgil converted into Englishe vearse* (London, 1562), n. pag.; chapter 5, p. 193.

[60] Erasmus, *Adagiorum chilias tertia*, edited by F. Heinemann and E. Kienzle, in *Opera omnia*, vols. II-5, II-6 (Amsterdam and Oxford: North Holland, 1981). See T. C. Appelt, *Studies in the Contents and Sources of Erasmus' Adagia, with Particular Reference to the First Edition and the Edition of 1526* (University of Chicago Press, 1942); M. M. Phillips, *The Adages of Erasmus: A Study with Translations* (Cambridge University Press, 1964).

eloquence is pointed up by Brinsley's recommendation of it as a source of moral matter, while *De copia* is recommended as a source rather of 'stile' (see above, p. 72).

That the schoolteacher-commentator did tend to choose either moral matter or formal analysis is illustrated by a schoolboy's notes on the *Georgics* dictated by Christopher Johnson, master of Winchester during the 1560s.[61] Baldwin has commented that the quotations are 'models of construction, whether they helped the moral defects of the boys or not' (p. 332). But there is no trace of formal analysis in these notes; like Erasmus's model teacher in the *De ratione*, Johnson turns the Virgilian lines into edifying moral and political precepts. While the description of the bees is given as an example of the well run state, what is bad for the land is turned as a figure of what is bad for the state, and when it is not the 'culture' of the state, it is the moral 'culture' of the boys that the lines are turned to illustrate and inform.[62]

The two objects – Virgil as *norma loquendi* and Virgil as *norma vivendi* – are produced too by the notes to the small editions recommended by Brinsley in *Ludus*. For, although most consist in either explanations of words and phrases, or formal classifications, some do give brief, moral or politico-moral comments, such as, 'Describit principem non tam sui, quam suorum curam agere' (He describes a prince who is concerned not so much for himself as for his men).[63] A comment on Aeneas as he scans the horizon for signs of his companions' ships after the tempest in *Aeneid* I, this note represents his conduct in terms of the contemporary politico-moral ideal of the prince who puts his public duties before his private

---

[61] BL MS, Add. 4379. See Baldwin, *William Shakespere's Small Latine*, vol. 1, pp. 321–39.

[62] BL MS, Add. 4379, fos. 128r, 83v; fos. 80v, 97v and 129v. Such mediations 'prepare the ground' for the use of agricultural figures to represent the political order, as in the Shakespearean corpus; indeed, parallels between Virgil's *Georgics* and Shakespeare's history plays have been suggested, although sixteenth-century mediations of the *Georgics* are not taken into account (Bulman, 'Shakespeare's Georgic Histories'). These mediations are no more taken into account in Anthony Low, *The Georgic Revolution* (Princeton University Press, 1985). Working from the premise that 'the poem is pre-eminently about the value of hard and incessant labor' (p. 8) Low argues that because of the denigration of such labour and the prevalence of aristocratic ideals the georgic 'was not congenial' (p. 18), a point he supports by citing Johnson's initial comment that agriculture is not to be despised. But, as the rest of Johnson's commentary shows, and as we shall see in the next chapter, this was not how Virgil's poem was mediated in the sixteenth century. When not mediated as formal model or moral matter it was mediated rather as knowledge of nature. A useful corrective to Low's rather fixed view of the genre is provided in Alistair Fowler, 'The Beginnings of English Georgic', in Barbara K. Lewalski, ed., *Renaissance Genres: Essays on Theory, History and Interpretation* (Harvard University Press, 1986).

[63] Virgil, *Bucolica, Georgica et Aeneis*, edited by N. Eritreo, p. 117; and Virgil, *Opera*, edited by P. Melancthon, p. 119.

interests.[64] A more specific version of the commonplace mediation of
Aeneas as model of the ideal prince, which we have already met in
Puttenham and which we will meet again in a masque by Jonson, the
comment remains isolated, surrounded as it is by notes explaining words
and phrases and classifying formal features. A more thorough elaboration of this mediation would require the more extended commentary
of a schoolteacher like Johnson.

In Brinsley's programme, this effect of separation between Virgilian
'matter' and 'words' is countered at a later stage by the use of the
Poetarum flores for exercises in verse composition. For the *Flores* is an
anthology of passages from the classical poets, especially Virgil and
Ovid, selected and grouped according to their moral content.[65] Brinsley
recommends that the teacher select a theme and specific passages, 'to
see how they can turne the same *ex tempore* into other verses, to the very
same purpose; either by imitation, or contraction ... or ... how they can
make other verses of their own like unto them' (Brinsley, *Ludus*, p. 195).
Theoretically, such exercises would inform the boys with morally
edifying matter as well as with 'eloquence'. And they certainly left traces
on habits of composition; Ben Jonson, for example, conflates *loci* from
different authors on the same moral theme in his own collection, called
Timber.[66] More interesting, because more specifically Virgilian, is the
trace of such exercises in the speech given by Gonzalo on the shores of
Prospero's island after the tempest (*The Tempest*, ii.i.1–9). For announcing itself as on the 'theme of woe' (line 6), the speech incorporates
Mirandula's general classification of Aeneas's speech on the shores of
Carthage after the tempest in *Aeneid* i – 'De Afflictione' (Mirandula,
Flores, p. 33) – a classification as a commonplace on woe to which the
earlier assertion 'Our hint of woe / Is common' (lines 3–4) may also
allude. This inclusion, in an imitation, of the frame – the formal system
of classification through which the model is mediated – tends, of course,
to alienate the discourse from itself and from the speaker. It points up, in
short, how such exercises in imitation tend, in practice, not so much to

[64] E. H. Kantorowicz, *The King's Two Bodies: A Study in Medieval Political Theology* (Princeton University Press, 1957), pp. 95–6.
[65] 'Sunt haec ex sylva poetarum scitissime decerpta, quibus aut sententia moralis naturalisve, aut laus virtutis, aut censoria morum castigatio, aut praecepta saluberrima continentur'. (These are skilfully selected excerpts from the wealth of matter supplied by the poets, which contain moral or natural wisdom, praise of virtue, severe reproof of (bad) behaviour, or wholesome precepts.) Octavianus Mirandula, *Illustrium poetarum flores* (Leyden, 1555), title-page, verso.
[66] For an example see Margaret Clayton, 'Ben Jonson "in travaile with expression of another": His Use of John of Salisbury's *Policraticus* in *Timber*', *The Review of English Studies* NS 30, no.120 (1979), p. 401.

integrate moral matter and eloquence as to turn moral 'matter' into mere form – hollow and ineffective 'words, words, words'. Gonzalo's speech is indeed ineffective, failing in its consolatory purpose – a purpose which again it shares with the Virgilian model, mediated in the *Flores* as 'Afflictorum consolatio illustris' (ibid.). It is a failure that is pointed up by the ironic commentary of Antonio and Sebastian, the shadows of imitation/commentary through whom, as we shall see, the Protestant scepticism towards imitation – specifically imitation of Virgilian forms of eloquence – is articulated.

CHAPTER 3

Secrets of nature and culture: the learned man's Virgils

ita suo more velut aliud agendo implet arcana.
Thus, as is his wont, Virgil discloses sacred mysteries while appearing to do something else.   Macrobius, *Saturnalia*, p. 171

... the most learned of poets, *Virgil*, when he would write a Poeme
of the beginnings, and hidden nature of things, with other great
Antiquities, attributed the parts of disputing them to *Silenus* . . .
          Jonson, *Oberon, The Fairy Prince* (*H&S*, vol. 7, p. 343, note c)

The quotation from Macrobius comes from the first complete extant
exposition in the *Saturnalia*, which is given by the figure of Praetextatus,
who expounds Virgilian lines (mostly from the *Aeneid*) in terms of ancient
civil and religious ritual practices.[1] That this is at once secret and sacred
knowledge is signalled by the word 'arcana', which anticipates the
phrase 'archana maronis' used in the representation of Servius and
Virgil on the Petrarchan frontispiece.[2] Here too there is a displacement
of authority on to the commentator, who, supplying a lack he simultaneously fills, lays claim to the ground within or behind the original, or
primary text, which becomes a supplement, something else ('aliud').[3]
This claim is ratified, for both Macrobius and Servius, by the canonical
status which, as we have seen, they enjoyed in the early modern world,
and which served to fold an institutionalised structure of authority into
the Virgilian text, analogous to the structure of the Catholic Church.

[1] Macrobius, *Saturnalia*, pp. 161–92. On the historical Praetextatus see A. Cameron, 'The date and identity of Macrobius', *Journal of Roman Studies* 56 (1966), p. 28.
[2] See figure 2 and chapter 1, pp. 28–30. Turk points out that 'arcana' is used more generally in the introduction to the *Saturnalia* claiming for it the status of 'le maître mot' in Macrobius's treatment of Virgil. E. Turk, 'Les *Saturnales* de Macrobe: Source de Servius Danielis', *Revue des études latines* 41 (1963), p. 341. Baswell points out, in addition, that Virgil's poetry is 'figured by Macrobius as a holy place, like a temple' (Baswell, *Virgil in Medieval England*, p. 93).
[3] Citing Robert Kaster's characterisation of the relation between commentator and Virgilian text as narcissistically reflecting on the commentator, Baswell notes the latter's power without entering into the question of the implied control of interpretation (Baswell, *Virgil in Medieval England*, pp. 91–4).

The specific information given by Praetextatus immediately before the comment quoted above, as well as other information of the same kind, is supplied in the translation of the first four books of the *Aeneid* by the Anglo-Irish Catholic convert Richard Stanyhurst, who, however, uses a strategy of minimal indication, which works so as to preserve its character as 'arcana' together with the implied structure of authority.[4] The same strategy is used to reveal/conceal what Stanyhurst calls 'secretes of Nature' in a dedicatory letter, where, in his own inimitable idiom, he makes much the same point about these 'secrets' as Praetextatus makes about the secrets of ancient culture, claiming that Virgil 'doth laboure, in telling as yt were a *Cantorburye tale*, too ferret owt the secretes of Nature'.[5] What this implies, of course, is that as Virgil has ferreted out the secrets of nature, so the reader must ferret out these secrets in the Virgilian text; they belong, that is, to a single hermeneutic and system of knowledge.[6]

It is these two forms, or modes of secret knowledge that constitute the more esoteric objects of the learned man's Virgils. In the case of the secrets of ancient culture, I shall show how the institutionalised structure of authority folded into the Virgilian text was reproduced and the canonical status of the ancient commentaries confirmed, and introduce the ideological work done by this more esoteric object in the corpus of writings by Ben Jonson, who was, of course, like Stanyhurst, a convert to Catholicism. In the case of the secrets of nature, with which this chapter is chiefly concerned, I shall show how the institutionalised structure of authority folded into the Virgilian text was both reproduced, and, increasingly, challenged, as the map or grammar of nature furnished by the canonical commentaries came under pressure from what I have called the Protestant turn. The logic of this turn is a logic at once of dis-enchantment and of dis-rupture, tending at the same time to the dismantling of the structures of authority which the production and

---

[4] See Margaret Clayton, '"Tempests, and such like Drolleries": Jonson, Shakespeare and the Figure of Vergil' (PhD thesis, University of Cambridge, 1986), pp. 77–9.
[5] Stanyhurst, *Translation of the First Four Books of the Aeneis*, p. 4. The allusion to the native tradition of poetry is discussed below, pp. 106–7.
[6] See introduction, p. 8. Baswell points out that in his commentary on the dream of Scipio (discussed below) Macrobius 'never fully distinguishes' between 'natural and textual secrets' (Baswell, *Virgil in Medieval England*, p. 98). The continued hold exercised by this system is signalled in a letter from Galileo to Kepler (19 August 1610) in which he criticises university teachers who seek to read nature as they read Virgil or Homer: 'cette espèce d'hommes se figure que la philosophie est un livre comme l'*Enéide* ou l'*Odysée*, et que la verité ne doit pas être recherché dans l'univers ou dans la nature, mais ... dans la comparaison des textes' (as cited in G. Gusdorf, *La révolution galiléene*, 2 vols. (Paris: Payot, 1969), vol. 1, p. 92).

circulation of this grammar of nature served to underwrite.[7] It is a grammar that informs not only canonical mediations of particular Virgilian passages, but also mediations of Virgil's practices as natural philosopher and as magician, and mediations of the structure of his verse as a form of knowledge, like music. While Jonson draws on this grammar in his use of specific Virgilian texts, it is invoked, in *The Tempest*, with its Virgilian inflections, only to be interrogated and displaced as the past by the play's staging of the Protestant turn. It is indeed to the universe of this grammar of nature, a universe of a certain mode and form of relation/religion, as well as a form of knowledge, that, I would suggest, the play bids farewell, rather than to the theatre, as critics have tended to think.

'ARCHANA MARONIS': THE SECRETS OF ANCIENT CULTURE

What Chris Baswell has said of Servius – that he wrote 'at a crucial moment at the end of the fourth century' when there was 'a considerable need to recuperate a fading Virgilian language and world' – might be said of Macrobius too, who was writing, according to Cameron, 'not ... very long after 431', although, as Cameron suggests, 'the pagan past' may be not so much recuperated as 'idealized', an idealisation nowhere more apparent than in the care with which the ancient civil and religious ritual practices informing the *Aeneid* are expounded through the figure of Praetextatus.[8] In the early modern world, however, this recuperated/idealised Virgilian world tended to petrification, fixed by and within the ancient commentaries, which, by virtue of their relative proximity to Virgil, acquired canonical authority as the privileged means of access to the anterior Virgilian world.

In the case of Macrobius, this canonical status is indicated not only by the frequency of publication during the early modern period, which I mentioned in chapter 1, but, more specifically, by the recourse which early modern editors and scholars had to the exposition by Praetextatus. Passages are quoted or summarised, for example, by J. Badius Ascensius

---

[7] The investment of the Catholic Church in maintaining traditional forms of knowledge is signalled by explicit moves made by the Council of Trent (the crucial agent of the counter-reformation) to preserve them. See F. Lestringant, *L'atelier du cosmographe ou l'image du monde à la Renaissance* (Paris: Albin Michel, 1991), especially p. 42.

[8] Baswell, *Virgil in Medieval England*, p. 49; Cameron, 'The Date and Identity of Macrobius', p. 37. Whether idealised because, as Turk argues, it was pagan (Turk, 'Les *Saturnales*'), or because, as Cameron prefers, it was past, idealisation of the ancient world was ideologically, and politically loaded in the fourth century, as Patterson points out (Patterson, *Pastoral and Ideology*, p. 41).

(1462–1535), the continental scholar, editor and publisher whose commentary appeared in at least fifteen large editions of the *Opera* before 1600 (published mostly during the first half of the century), and whose edition of 1501 (with his commentary) has been shown to have been used by Gavin Douglas.[9] Meyen and Taubmann do the same as Ascensius in their smaller, but still relatively large editions (published 1576 and 1618 respectively), recommended by Brinsley in *A Consolation*, while almost the whole exposition is incorporated into the notes in the large editions by Jacobus Pontanus (first published 1599) and J. de la Cerda (first published 1608-13). Further, in the introductions to these editions, Virgil is explicitly represented as an expert on ancient rites, Macrobius being cited by de la Cerda as the authoritative source of reference.[10]

By contrast, the notes in the small editions which Brinsley first recommends in *Ludus* do not supply this information: Eritreo (whose edition was first published in 1539) gives references to the relevant passages in the Macrobian commentary (which is itself an indication of its authority), but for the reader without access to the text thus cited, the matter it expounds remains literally 'elsewhere', a hidden, mysterious object, *arcana* indeed.[11] This presence/absence of the Macrobian commentary in these early modern editions tends, on the one hand, to show how the claim made by Praetextatus to the ground of meaning behind the Virgilian text is confirmed, and, on the other, to suggest how this hidden meaning remained effectively *arcana* for schoolboys, until they had access to larger editions such as Brinsley recommends in his later handbook.[12]

Much the same may be said of the notes in the Servian commentary which supply information of this kind. For they are not included in the notes to the small editions recommended by Brinsley, which, as we have

---

[9] Hulubei, 'Virgile en France', pp. 7–13; Bawcutt, *Gavin Douglas*, pp. 111–26.

[10] Virgil, *Symbolarum libri XVII, quibus . . . Bucolica, Georgica, Aeneis . . . declarantur*, edited by J. Pontanus (Augsburg, 1599), p. 22; Virgil, *Opera omnia*, edited by J. de la Cerda (Leyden, 1612–19), chapter 3. See too Landino's comments in Virgil, *Opera*, vol. 1, n. pag. For Petrarch's incorporation of some of these comments in notes to his copy of Virgil, see Lord, 'The Use of Macrobius and Boethius', pp. 3–6.

[11] Ramus quotes from this exposition but only twice, as most of the lines (seventy-nine) are from the *Aeneid* (fourteen only are from the *Eclogues* and the *Georgics*).

[12] In 1660 the pedagogue Charles Hoole will recommend that Servius and de la Cerda be made available for consultation by schoolboys (see Baldwin, *William Shakespere's Small Latine*, vol. 2, p. 397). Further, de la Cerda is mentioned in the catalogues of two schools, Merchant Taylors' (in 1662) and Hawkeshead Grammar School (in 1679). See R. T. D. Sayle, 'Annals of Merchant Taylors' School Library', *The Library*, 4th series, no. 15 (1934–5), p. 459; R. C. Christie, *The Old Church and School Libraries of Lancashire*, Chetham Society, 2nd series, 7 (Manchester: Charles Simms, 1885), pp. 145–62.

seen, draw heavily on Servius, but primarily for explanations and formal analyses of 'words'.[13] They too thus constituted *arcana* for the schoolboy until he had access to larger editions which included them. Where this information did circulate, apart from the large editions, was in encyclopedias and specialist studies by antiquarian scholars, like Barnaby Brisson and John Selden, who sought, in their turn, to recuperate for the early modern world the ancient world, and who in so doing drew on both Macrobius and Servius, and, in particular, regularly quoted from Servius when quoting from Virgil.[14] These quotations again confirm the authority of the commentaries as the privileged means of access to the ground of the Virgilian text and to the ancient world from which it came.

It is from such specialised studies as well as from his copy of the edition of the *Opera* by Pontanus that Ben Jonson took esoteric Virgilian matter of this kind to use in particular court masques (notably *Hymenaei*) and in his contribution to *The King's Entertainment*. As in Stanyhurst's translation, these Virgilian objects are used in such a way as to preserve their character as *arcana* and to (re)produce the implied structure of authority – and hierarchy of privilege – between learned insiders and ignorant outsiders. More specifically, they furnish a ground – authoritative and authorising origin – both for an authorial master self/voice and for the order it names, especially the new order of 'Britain' under the new king James. In *The King's Entertainment*, in particular, an ancient rite of foundation evoked by Virgil in *Aeneid* 5 is turned so as to furnish both London and James with a 'ground', which, in the published version, is itself grounded in notes (taken from Pontanus) revealing/ concealing at once Virgil's and Jonson's learning. Such 'learning', whether in the place of performance or in the published version, tends, as we shall see, to the obfuscation of the origins and history it ostensibly celebrates. The 'archana Maronis', which the ancient commentaries (and the texts of early modern scholars such as Brisson and Selden) disclose in order to recuperate and preserve (if also to idealise) a past world, is turned, in this (con)text, to cover – underwrite as well as

---

[13] Many, if not all of these notes emerged with the discovery of the so-called 'Servius Danielis', or 'Servius Auctus' in 1600 (see Goold, 'Servius', pp. 102–12). For our purposes what is important is that the discovered material cannot be regarded as belonging to early modern Servius; indeed, it constituted, in a peculiarly literal way, *arcana*, not only for the schoolboy, but, more generally, for the early modern world.

[14] Barnaby Brisson, *De ritu nuptiarum . . . De iure connubiorum* (Paris, 1564), *passim*; Barnaby Brisson, *De formulis et sollemnibus populi Romani verbis, Libri VIII* (Frankfurt, 1592), *passim*; John Selden, *De dis syris, syntagmata II*, 2nd edn. (Leyden, 1629), pp. 66, 190, 197.

conceal – both the immediate past and the present. History is, in short, used to cover history. And, as Thomas Dekker points out, such obfuscation serves at once Jonson's self-fashioning as learned, national poet and the (re)production of a hierarchy of privilege between learned insiders and ignorant outsiders.

'ARCHANA MARONIS': SECRETS OF NATURE

In a very long introduction, Macrobius anticipates both the exposition by Praetextatus, and another exposition, which, though subsequently lost, was evidently given first, and which, as the anticipations indicate, consisted in the mediation of lines from Virgil (especially *Georgics* 1) in terms of 'astrologia' and 'philosophia'.[15] Though lost, it is possible to glean something of what this exposition supplied from the other extant work by Macrobius, the *Commentary on the Dream of Scipio* (henceforth *Somnium*), which was, as Baswell points out, 'enormously influential' in the medieval period, and which was published as often as the *Saturnalia* before 1600.[16] In this discussion of a Ciceronian fragment according to Neoplatonic cosmology, Virgilian texts are quoted throughout, in particular *Georgics* 1 and *Aeneid* 6, and the poet is explicitly represented as conversant with the actual order of nature, 'poeta naturae ipsius conscius' (*Somnium*, p. 65). It is this figure of Virgil – as natural philosopher, especially skilled in mathematics and astronomy/astrology – together with the implied Neoplatonic map, or grammar of nature that was both reproduced and, increasingly, challenged in the early modern world. And it is with this figure, and with this grammar of nature, that the figure of Virgil as magician was bound up, 'la forme magique' being, as Foucault succinctly put it, 'inhérente à la manière de connaître' (Foucault, *Les mots*, p. 48).

In the central section, which is on cosmology (*Somnium*, pp. 55–124), two passages from Virgil are recurrently cited: Anchises' speech to Aeneas on the creation of the universe in *Aeneid* 6 (lines 724–51), and the description of the universe in *Georgics* 1 (lines 231–51). According to Macrobius, Anchises' phrase 'spiritus intus alit' (line 726) refers to the World Soul, while 'mens agitat molem' (line 727) refers to the Divine

---

[15] Macrobius, *Saturnalia*, pp. 6–132, especially, pp. 11, 75–6, 131.
[16] Baswell, *Virgil in Medieval England*, p. 97; Macrobius, *Commentary on the Dream of Scipio*, translated and introduced by W. H. Stahl (New York: Columbia University Press, 1952), pp. 61–2. For Petrarch's incorporation of notes from the *Somnium* into his Virgil, see Lord, 'The Use of Macrobius and Boethius', pp. 5–7.

Mind which, emanating as the World Soul, binds all things together in the golden chain described by Homer (*Somnium*, pp. 57–8). Later, the phrase 'magno se corpore miscet' (line 727) is quoted in affirmation of the representation of the universe as a single 'body' (p. 67), and, finally, the description of the diverse creatures of the world (lines 728–9) is quoted in a passage on the nature and effects of music which, as James Hutton has shown, 'had an effect on the tradition' of representations of the art 'that can hardly be exaggerated', and which, as he points out, Lorenzo's discourse on music in *The Merchant of Venice* echoes:[17] through the harmony of music extraordinary control over men (body and mind), as well as over animals, may be exercised, since the World Soul and the inhabitants of the material world it inspires – comprehended in Virgil's lines – are, thereby, drawn to the Divine Mind which consists in such harmony (*Somnium*, p. 106).

This universe is evoked not only by Lorenzo's discourse on music, but by *The Tempest*, which both dramatises and, in a speech by Ariel which clearly echoes Lorenzo's (iv.i.175–181), describes the Macrobian representation of the character and effect of music. 'No Shakespeare play calls for more music', comments Stephen Orgel,[18] and in no play is music so explicitly represented as a form, or function of knowledge of nature, notably through Ariel, figure of 'the aeriel spirit' through whose agency, in Ficino's account, for example, music works (Hutton, 'Some English Poems', p. 21). It is indeed through Ariel's 'sweet air' (i.ii.396) and 'airy charm' (v.i.54) that the natural philosopher Prospero exercises the kind of control described by Macrobius.[19] At the same time, as David Lindley has pointed out, another, different model of music – 'as an outburst of individual feeling' – is also represented in the play.[20] This interrogation of the model of music as knowledge by a model of music as individual expression exemplifies and epitomises the play's interrogation of an 'old world' (and specifically Virgilian) grammar of nature – a grammar inflected by likeness and 'sympathy' – by a 'new world' grammar inflected by difference. It is an interrogation that is staged too in relation to 'proportioned' forms of verse and dance, both construed within the

[17] James Hutton, 'Some English Poems in Praise of Music', *English Miscellany* 2 (1951), pp. 11–13, 34–8.

[18] Shakespeare, *The Tempest*, edited by Stephen Orgel, p. 220.

[19] Frank Kermode notes 'the underpinning of technical "natural philosophy"' 'in all that concerns Ariel' (Shakespeare, *The Tempest*, edited by Frank Kermode, p. 143). On the concept of 'air' see further below note 39.

[20] David Lindley, 'Music, Masque and Meaning in *The Tempest*', in David Lindley, ed., *The Court Masque* (Manchester University Press, 1984), p. 48.

'sympathetic' grammar of nature as forms of knowledge. In staging these interrogations the play exposes the limits of the relation of these forms both to nature and to human minds/bodies, and so the limits of their efficacy as forms of control, forms, that is, which serve to 'temper and order', as the gloss to 'charme' in Spenser's October eclogue puts it.[21]

To return to the canonical mediations of Anchises' speech in *Aeneid* 6. Servius reproduces the same grammar of nature as Macrobius: the universe is a single whole made up of the four elements and God, all things ('universa') being generated by the emanation of God as divine spirit through the elements, man, an epitome of creation, being made up of the soul (divine spirit) imprisoned by the body (four elements) until the release of death (Virgil, *Opera*, vol. 2, fo. 353v). Indeed, the Virgilian underworld is treated by both Servius and Macrobius (in an earlier section of the *Somnium* on the origin and descent of souls) entirely in terms of this universe, Tartarus, specifically, being interpreted by Servius as a figure for earth, the lowest of the spheres, from which the souls of an elect are allowed to escape.[22] In the *Somnium*, the lower regions are interpreted as a figure both of the body and of the region subject to corruption between the moon and the earth, while the Virgilian representation of after-life punishments is interpreted in terms of the sufferings of material existence (*Somnium*, pp. 42–6). As Pierre Courcelle has shown, the Neoplatonic universe supplied by Macrobius and Servius was, though frequently and variously modified, effectively endorsed by the Church Fathers, its monotheism being relatively easy to accommodate within a Christian theology.[23] With the canonical authority of the early commentaries endorsed by the Church, the speech of Anchises (and the whole of *Aeneid* 6) continued to be treated as natural philosophy by editors in the early modern world, at least by editors of the larger editions, such as Pontanus, de la Cerda, Taubmann and Meyen, who in their comments on the speech all mention Macrobius and summarise his representation of the Virgilian universe. In the smaller editions recommended in *Ludus* there is, on the other hand, at most a terse classification of Anchises' speech as 'Locus philosophicus' (by Melan-

---

[21] Spenser, *Poetical Works*, p. 459. See too the note on the 'secret working of Musick' (ibid., p. 458), which summarises the sympathetic model I outline here.
[22] Virgil, *Opera*, vol. 2, fo. 340v. Compare Macrobius, *Somnium*, pp. 40–55. See J. W. Jones, Jr, 'Allegorical Interpretation in Servius', *Classical Journal* 56 (1960–61), pp. 220–1; J. W. Jones, Jr, 'The Allegorical Traditions of the *Aeneid*', in J. D. Bernard, ed., *Vergil at 2000. Commemorative Essays on the Poet and his Influence* (New York: AMS Press, 1986), p. 112.
[23] Pierre Courcelle, 'Les Pères de l'Eglise devant les enfers virgiliens', *Archives d'histoire doctrinale et littéraire du Moyen Age* 22 (1955), pp. 40–57, 68–9.

cthon) or a citation of book and chapter in the *Somnium* (by Eritreo).[24] Like the secrets of ancient culture, this grammar of nature thus appears to have remained for English schoolboys effectively *arcana* until access to larger editions was instituted.

That for early modern natural philosophers the text of Anchises' speech constituted, by contrast, a commonplace description of the universe is indicated by citations in the work of some of the more prominent. Ficino, Agrippa, Campanella and Bruno all quote or allude to the passage in their representations of the universe, while Bruno appears to have used it in the defence of his unorthodox ideas before the Venetian inquisitors (and the endorsement of the Church Fathers may have helped here). The phrase 'mens agitat molem' was, moreover, the motto chosen in 1587 by the founders of the Academia degli Uranici, a centre for Neoplatonic thought.[25] As the work of Walker and Yates has shown, and as the titles of these natural philosophers' texts indicate, the form, or mode of knowledge understood to be concealed/revealed in the Virgilian text was the secret and sacred form of knowledge believed to enable man to exercise the extraordinary control of the material world called natural magic.[26] It is indeed the limits of this control – on the one hand, the boundary between what is possible and what is not, and, on the other, the boundary between what is legitimate and what is not – that set the terms of Gabriel Naudé's 'apologie', or defence of Virgil, amongst other great men (including Agrippa), against the accusation that they practised (black) magic, as we shall see. And it is in terms of the boundary between what is legitimate and what is not that a similar 'apologie' is formulated by the major English natural philosopher John Dee.

The Neoplatonic universe – of material elements animated by divine spirit/mind – is the universe evoked in *The Tempest*, especially through the figure of the Virgilian natural philosopher and mage/magician, Prospero. But this universe informs too representations of Virgil in the Jonsonian corpus. While, at a general level, Jonson attributes to this 'the most learned of poets' knowledge of nature (in the quotation at the head of the chapter), at a more specific level, in *Poetaster* and *Hymenaei*, he draws on the canonical mediation, as Neoplatonic natural philosophy,

---

[24] Virgil, *Opera*, edited by P. Melancthon, p. 272; Virgil, *Bucolica, Georgica et Aeneis*, edited by N. Eritreo, p. 267.

[25] See D. P. Walker, *Spiritual and Demonic Magic from Ficino to Campanella*, Studies of the Warburg Institute 22 (London: Warburg Institute, 1958), pp. 13, 128; Francis Yates, *Giordano Bruno and the Hermetic Tradition* (London: Routledge and Kegan Paul, 1964), pp. 69, 137, 350, 365, 380.

[26] These titles are: *De occulta philosophia* (Agrippa), *Theologia libro primo* (Campanella) and *De magia* (Ficino).

of the scene of Juno's presence at the 'union' of Dido and Aeneas in
Aeneid 4 (a scene which Prospero's betrothal masque evokes too). More
specifically relevant here is the use he makes of the canonical mediation,
as Neoplatonic natural philosophy, of the descent into Hades, in a local
version – a descent into the 'underworld' of Fleet Ditch – in the last of
his collection of epigrams. For the canonical mediation of the Virgilian
descent furnishes a ground – or master text – which allows the learned
reader to understand, and so to 'escape' into the place of a learned and
virtuous elect, represented, in *Every Man In His Humour*, precisely as those
whom just Jove loves, that is, those few said by the Sibyl to escape
Tartarus/Dis to regain the 'upper air' (*Aeneid* 6, lines 129–30). It is,
moreover, as a member of this elect that Virgil is represented in *Poetaster*,
in a place above the change/corruption, moral as well as material,
inherent, in a Neoplatonic universe, in the 'underworld' of matter. It is
this place – a place immune from the contingencies of temporal and
material existence – that, in what I take to be self-conscious contrast, the
Virgilian Prospero, 'troubled' (*The Tempest*, IV.i.159) rather, and '*dis-
tempered*' (line 145) by noise from the underworld – 'dusky *Dis*' (line 89)
– is not allowed to occupy.

To return to the *Somnium*, and the second of the recurrently cited
Virgilian texts – *Georgics* 1, especially the description of the universe (lines
231–51) and the signs of good and bad weather which follow (lines 252–8,
335–7, 351–464). It is with reference to this description that Macrobius
represents Virgil as conversant with the order of nature, 'poeta naturae
ipsius conscius' (Macrobius, *Somnium*, p. 65). Servius likewise treats the
passage as a description of the actual order of nature, while Fulgentius,
the slightly later commentator on the *Aeneid*, whose commentary also
enjoyed a measure of authority in early modern Europe,[27] declares that
Georgics 1 consists entirely in a disclosure of the order of the universe:
'Primus vero georgicorum est omnis astrologus'.[28]

That the description of the universe in *Georgics* 1, 'excerpted and
anthologized' and 'heavily annotated' through the medieval period
(Baswell, *Virgil in Medieval England*, pp. 315–16), continued to be treated as
natural philosophy in the early modern world is vividly signalled by the

---

[27] *Fulgentius the Mythographer*, translated by Leslie G. Whitbread (University of Ohio Press, 1971), pp. 24–31.
[28] Fabius Planciades Fulgentius V.C., *Opera*, edited by R. Helm, rev. edn. by J. Préaux (Stuttgart: Teubner, 1970), p. 84. 'astrologus' here, as in the description of Virgil's knowledge in the introduction to the *Saturnalia*, is not (*pace* Whitbread) 'astrology' as distinct from 'astronomy'. The distinction between the two was a function of the revision of the grammar of nature in the early modern world. See Gusdorf, *La révolution galiléene*, vol. 1, p. 77.

Figure 4   Sebastian Brant's woodcut illustration to Virgil's description of the universe
in *Georgics* I, lines 231–51 in *Publii Virgilii Maronis opera*, Strasbourg, 1502

woodcut illustration in the first major illustrated edition of the *Opera* by
Sebastian Brant (Strasbourg, 1502; figure 4), which belongs generically
to illustrations given in editions of the *Somnium* and in editions of the
standard text on cosmography and astro-nomy/logy, the *Sphaera mundi*
by John Holywood.[29] Further, in one of the larger editions recommen-

---

[29] See Ruth Mortimer, 'Vergil in the Light of the Sixteenth Century: Selected Illustrations', in
John Bernard, ed., *Vergil at 2000*, p. 162.

ded by Brinsley – by John Meyen – this generic alignment is underscored by a citation (though no more) of the *Somnium* and the *Sphaera* alongside the passage.[30] Pontanus and de la Cerda cite the *Somnium* too in their discussions of the passage as a description of the universe. By contrast, the smaller editions recommended by Brinsley in *Ludus* refer to neither; indeed, if the practice of the master at Winchester discussed in the previous chapter was typical, the natural philosophy must have been omitted, or glossed over in favour of moral mediations, unless, that is, the edition of the *Georgics* by Ramus, which Brinsley also recommends and in both handbooks, was used.

For Ramus treats the *Georgics* as natural philosophy, a disclosure of 'almost everything about nature which the necessities of human life require that we know' ('res fere naturales omnes, quarum cognitionem necessitas humanae vitae desiderat'), the formal principles of logic being deployed to unfold this necessary and useful knowledge.[31] However, in his comment on the description of the universe in *Georgics* 1, Ramus refers neither to Macrobius nor to Holywood, and, most importantly, emphasises the 'error' made by Virgil in representing as 'torrida' and uninhabitable the middle 'zone', which is now known to be perfectly temperate ('hodie temperies ibi summa pernoscitur' (p. 77)). The same point is made by de la Cerda, while in the one seventeenth-century edition recommended by Brinsley, Frederick Taubmann declares that contemporary experiences in navigation ('hodiernae navigationes et experientia') have proved that the region below the equator is so pleasant to live in as to be like an earthly paradise ('tanquam in terrestri Paradiso').[32] An instance of the general turn made by contemporary cosmographers against the ancients,[33] this turn against the Virgilian map is made not only by such explicit comments, but also, more implicitly, by the citation of textual sources and analogues (by Pontanus, de la Cerda and Ramus, for example). For such intertextual citations tend silently to recategorise the text as primarily a textual, even a 'poetic' or 'literary' *locus* rather than as 'natural philosophy', which is to say, as 'knowledge'. It is a tendency which finds its logical end in a modern editor's comment that, to the

[30] Virgil, *Opera*, edited by J. Meyen, p. 47.
[31] Virgil, *Georgica*, edited by P. Ramus, pp. 15–16. Compare Richard Willes's briefer 'vera praecepta de re rustica', translated by Fowler, 'true precepts about husbandry'. Richard Willes, *De re poetica* (1573), translated by A. D. S Fowler (Oxford: Basil Blackwell, 1958), p. 100.
[32] Virgil, *Opera omnia*, edited by F. Taubmann, p. 142.
[33] The French cosmographer André Thevet, for example, gives over a chapter to a criticism of the ancients, including their representation of the torrid zone, which he claims is rather 'plus salubre à la vie humaine que nulle des autres' (as quoted in F. Lestringant, *L'atelier du cosmographe*, p. 48).

question posed by 'the difficulty in precisely accounting for Virgil's system' (i.e. its coherence as a representation of the universe), 'the answer is a literary one', 'Virgil's primary concern is to recall precisely a number of authors.'[34] The turning of the Virgilian passage from 'natural philosophy' into 'literature' is thus made definitive.[35]

The description of the universe is linked to what precedes – the seasons for sowing – by 'idcirco' (to this end (line 231)) and to what follows – the weather signs – by 'hinc' (hence (line 252)). Ramus elaborates these links in terms of the necessity ('necessitas'), which is at once a formal proposition ('proposita') and a natural law, the formalised system of determining relations between the heavens and the earth which is 'astrologia' – the science which makes prediction possible ('per astrologiam licet . . . praediscere').[36] Despite, that is, his comment on the description of the universe and its implicit recategorisation, Ramus treats what precedes and what follows, as in his preface he treats the *Georgics* as a whole, as useful knowledge of nature, specifically as 'astrologia' – the term used by Macrobius and Fulgentius. In this his treatment is like earlier non-Ramist treatments, such as Thomas Elyot's in his educational treatise *The Governor* (1531).

> Is there any astronomer / that more exactly setteth out the ordre and course of the celestial bodies: or that more truely dothe devine in his prognostications of the tymes of the yere / in their qualities / with the future astate [*sic*] of all things provided by husbandry / than Virgile doth recite in that warke?[37]

More important still than such general representations is the inclusion of Virgil's signs in works on weather prediction. Lynn Thorndike mentions three examples – one from the fourteenth century and two from the sixteenth[38] – to which we might add a fourth, *Signorum prognos-*

---

[34] *Virgi: Georgics*, edited by Richard F. Thomas, 2 vols. (Cambridge University Press, 1988), vol. 1, p. 107.

[35] What may be an idiosyncratic re-turn is registered in a recent study, which asserts that '(r)eal science is the beginning of the poem', although no mention of the description of the universe is made in the pages which follow. David O. Ross, Jr, *Virgil's Elements: Physics and Poetry in The Georgics* (Princeton University Press, 1987), p. ix.

[36] Virgil, *Georgica*, edited by P. Ramus, p. 79.

[37] Thomas Elyot, *The Book named The Governor* (1531), reprinted in *English Linguistics 1500–1800* (Menston: The Scholar Press, 1970), fo. 33r. Elyot's opening description of the poem as a 'paradise' has been indignantly dismissed by L. P. Wilkinson – a dismissal which is a measure of the gap between sixteenth- and twentieth-century readers. L. P. Wilkinson, *The Georgics of Virgil. A Critical Survey* (Cambridge University Press, 1969), pp. 294–5; Low, who cites Wilkinson with sympathy, suggests Elyot's description illustrates a tendency to transform the georgic into pastoral idyll. Low, *The Georgic Revolution*, p. 31.

[38] Lynn Thorndike, *A History of Magic and Experimental Science*, 8 vols. (New York and London: MacMillan, 1923–58), vol. 3, p. 143; vol. 5, pp. 296–7; vol. 6, p. 486.

ticorum de tempestatibus aeris physica explicatio, by J. Willich (1501–55), a text which is based entirely on the signs in *Georgics* 1.[39] A copy of this, bound with Willich's commentary on the *Georgics*, was owned by the English natural philosopher John Dee,[40] who, in his important preface to Billingsley's translation of Euclid, likewise (and perhaps partly for this reason), treats the *Georgics* as a disclosure of the order of nature, and the 'signs' in, *Georgics* 1 as a revelation of actual relations and so as a source of practical knowledge through which men (especially navigators) might gain a more efficient control of their environment. First, in the section on 'Cosmographie', he recommends that a man should learn 'the Risinges and Settinges of Sterres (of *Virgill* in his *Georgikes*: of *Hesiod*: of *Hippocrates* … of *Diocles* … and of other famous *Philosophers* prescribed) a thing necessary, for due manuring of the earth, for *Navigation*, for the Alteration of man's body'.[41] Then, in an elaboration of the science of Navigation, he advises, more specifically, the would-be Navigator to learn 'more evident tokens in Sonne and Mone' 'such as (the Philosophicall Poete) *Virgilius* teacheth, in hys *Georgikes*', and, quoting the signs given by the sun, especially the signs of a tempest (*Georgics* 1, lines 438–9, 450–60, 463–4), adds, '(a)nd so of Mone, Sterres, Water, Ayre, Fire, Wood, Stones, Birdes, and Beastes' 'a certaine Sympathicall forewarnyng may be had: sometymes to great pleasure and proffit, both on Sea and Land' (fos. diiiiv–A1r). A predictive relation of signification – *x* means *y* will happen – is here a function of the relations of affinity – of 'sympathy' – which obtain in the Neoplatonic universe of heavenly (active) agents and (passive) material elements.[42] Although, as Peter

[39] I have consulted a copy bound with Willich's commentary on the *Georgics* (first published, according to Mambelli, Basle, 1539). I have not established if/when the text on weather prediction was published separately. The title is almost impossible to translate: in particular it is important to stress the point made by Betty Dobbs about the notion of 'air': 'Air is the medium through which the powers are conveyed; it is an air far removed conceptually from an atomistic atmosphere, much vaster in extent and richer in function.' Betty J. T. Dobbs, *The Foundation of Newton's Alchemy or 'The hunting of the Greene Lyon'* (Cambridge University Press, 1975), p. 38. Equally complex is the word 'tempestates', which covers at once notions of time, seasonal changes, and particular meteorological phenomena, notably storms, or tempests. That it is in the 'circle' of the air that weather changes and especially storms were thought to be engendered is indicated in Brant's woodcut (fig. 4). Bearing this in mind we might render the title: 'A physical explanation of the signs related to weather changes produced in and by the air'. It is worth recalling too that the production of the tempest by Prospero (like his production of music) is done through the 'airy spirit' Ariel – another indication of the 'technical "natural philosophy"' (Kermode) underpinning this figure (see note 19).
[40] R. J. Roberts and A. N. Watson, *John Dee's Library Catalogue* (London: The Bibliographical Society, 1990), item no. 1193.
[41] John Dee, *The Elements of Geometrie … translated by H. Billingsley with a very fruitfull Preface made by M. I. Dee* (London, 1570), fo. biiir.
[42] See Foucault, *Les mots*, pp. 38–9.

French has argued, Dee may have been relatively exclusive about much of his work, which he shared with a small group of initiates, his Preface is generally agreed to have been addressed to a broad audience of non-university men, including merchants and artisans as well as navigators.[43] Moreover, these recommendations by 'England's leading expert on applied astrology and astronomy' (Sherman, *John Dee*, p. 98) are echoed in *The Booke of the Sea Carte*, a still more emphatically use-orientated handbook for seamen, which names Virgil, amongst 'other naturalle philosophers', for '(p)ronostycacion'.[44] Such recommendations constituted a significant exposure of the Virgilian text, and the implied grammar of nature, to those outside the universities whose first objective was experienced control in the physical world, and especially at sea. Such an exposure necessarily tended to the interrogation and dismantling of this grammar of nature, as well as of the mediation of the Virgilian texts as natural philosophy and of Virgil as natural philosopher, 'poeta naturae ipsius conscius'.

This exposure was accelerated in the English context by the Protestant university men and Ramists who made more radical moves within what I have called the Protestant turn. For, if a Virgilian text is retained at all by these scholars and educators, it is the *Georgics*. For example, in his educational treatise *The Nobles, or of Nobility* (1563), which promotes the primacy of the Bible, Christ as the model of true nobility, and godliness as the crucial socio-political criterion, the Protestant don Lawrence Humphrey recommends the *Georgics*, but not the *Aeneid*, though he does not (*pace* Kearney) explicitly reject the latter. Similarly, at Trinity College Dublin, 'a Ramist foundation' for 'the first thirty years of its existence (1591–1620)', the arts course, which 'seems to have been drawn up almost exclusively with the Bible in mind', retains only the *Georgics*, here, specifically, as we might expect, 'with Ramus as a guide'.[45] As we have seen, it is 'with Ramus as a guide' that the *Georgics* are at once mediated and interrogated as knowledge of nature. For, while the text as a whole and the weather signs in particular are treated as natural philosophy, the description of the universe in *Georgics* 1 is

---

[43] Peter French, *John Dee: The World of an Elizabethan Magus* (London: Routledge and Kegan Paul, 1972), pp. 160–87; see Sherman, *John Dee*, p. 22. Sherman has revised the view of Dee (espoused by French, for example) as a retired scholar/mage, by pointing up his active involvement in business and politics, and in the theory and practice of navigation (pp. 148–81).

[44] As quoted in A. F. Falconer, *Shakespeare and the Sea* (London: Constable, 1964), p. 140.

[45] Kearney, *Scholars*, pp. 67, 69. Kearney cites the student notebook of James Usher, later Archbishop of Armagh, whose later sermons will illustrate the likeness of Usher's ideology to Humphrey's (p. 52).

exposed as incorrect, and tacitly recategorised as not-knowledge and so, we might say, as 'useless'.

A radical conception of the useful and necessary in the English context is illustrated by Dudley Fenner who, in his vernacular Ramist handbook (1584), replaces all the classical examples with biblical (although the text is, admittedly, addressed specifically to ministers as a guide to the writing of sermons).[46] Though likewise preferring biblical to classical examples, the Scottish Ramist Roland MacIlmaine retains some of Ramus's secular examples in his treatise (1574), including examples from Virgil, which he translates into the vernacular as Ramus does in his *Dialectique* (1555). Notable amongst these is the use of the *Georgics* to illustrate the *method* of logic – defined as progression from the most general to the most particular. For it (re)produces the mediation of the poem as useful knowledge, and of *Georgics* 1 in particular as knowledge of the actual relations that obtain in the universe.

... the poetes, orators and all sort of writers how oft soever they purpose to teach there (sic) auditor, doo alwayes follow this order of methode ... Virg. in his Georgicks parted his matter ... into fower partes: and in the first booke he intreateth of common and generall thinges, as of Astrologie, and thinges engendered in the ayer, and of cornes and there manuring, which is the first part of his work ...[47]

Of particular interest here is the phrase 'of Astrologie, and thinges engendered in the ayer' (translating 'ut Astrologiam, Meteorologiam'), which recalls not only the classification of *Georgics* 1 as 'astrologia' by the early commentators, but also the specific elaborations of the weather signs in terms of the region of the air – agent as well as site of changes – 'de tempestatibus aeris' (see above, especially note 39). Like Ramus's comment on the weather signs, MacIlmaine's comment turns the Virgilian order of nature into a rationalised, formal order disclosed by the system of Ramist dialectic.

This rational formalisation of the relations that obtain in nature is more overt still in the Virgilian example which Abraham Fraunce takes from the *Dialecticae* to illustrate the argument from 'adjuncts' in *The Lawiers Logike*.

[46] Dudley Fenner, *The Artes of Logike and Rhetorike set foorth in the English tounge* (London, 1584). See Howell, *Logic and Rhetoric*, pp. 219–21, 255–6.
[47] Roland MacIlmaine, *The Logike of the Most Excellent Philosopher P. Ramus Martyr, translated by Roland MacIlmaine* (London, 1574) edited by C. M. Dunn (Northridge, Calif.: San Fernando Valley State College, 1969), pp. 56–7. See Ramus, *Dialecticae*, pp. 251–2; Ramus, *Dialectique*, pp. 147–8.

Natural Philosophers, Phisitians, Astronomers, and other professors use much this place: as when they dispute of chaunge of weather, diversitie of causes and occasions of diseases, signes of stormes and tempestes, as, *vento rubet aurea Phoebe*, when the Moone is red, she betokeneth wind.[48]

Translating 'de aëris affectionibus' 'chaunge of weather' Fraunce moves away from the notion of air as the site and agent of weather change. More importantly, although he represents the Virgilian example of a weather sign (*Georgics* 1, line 431), like Dee, as an example of predictive signification (compare Fraunce's 'betokeneth' with Dee's 'tokens'), the predictive relation which, in Dee's *Preface*, is a function of the 'sympathy' inherent in nature, is formalised and rationalised as a relation which is not given so much as proposed, a hypothesis open to rational 'dispute', subject to debate like the relation of cause and effect which Fraunce (if not Ramus) classifies similarly as a relation of 'adjuncts'.

It is in its tendency to formalise and rationalise the order of nature, to open this order to 'dispute', as well as in its orientation towards the useful and necessary, and its relative facility of access that Ramism contributed to the interrogation and eventual erasure of the figure of Virgil as natural philosopher, the poet whose knowledge allows prediction of weather change and, in particular, prediction of tempests at sea. For, like Dee's *Preface*, Ramist mediations tended to expose the Virgilian grammar of nature to 'dispute', or dialogue, with those whose first objective was experienced control in the material world, especially seamen and navigators.

'CHARMES WERE WONT TO BE MADE BY VERSES':[49] VIRGIL AND MAGIC

It is in relation to the figure of Virgil as natural philosopher, the mediation of *Georgics* as natural philosophy and the conditions of their erasure that I want to look again at the figure of Virgil as magician. What we shall see bears out Michel Foucault's point that magic was inherent to the form or mode of knowledge – the epistemic structure – that prevailed until the early seventeenth century. For practices of Virgil the magician are mediated in terms of the Neoplatonic universe of active celestial agents and passive material elements, the universe, that is, which informs mediations of Virgilian texts, especially the *Georgics*, as

---

[48] Fraunce, *The Lawiers Logike*, fo. 43v. The Latin text, from the gloss by Talon, runs: 'Sic Astrologi de pluvia, tempestate, serenitate, et caeteris aëris affectionibus augurantur, ut: – *Vento rubet aurea Phoebe*.' Ramus, *Dialecticae*, p. 59.

[49] The gloss to 'charme' in Spenser's October eclogue. Spenser, *Poetical Works*, p. 459.

natural philosophy. It is, moreover, within this Neoplatonic universe that the French scholar Gabriel Naudé (1600–53) undertakes what is the first attempt to collect systematically, and to investigate critically the relevant material, in the final chapter of his *Apologie pour tous les grands personnages qui ont esté faussement soupçonnez de magie* (Paris, 1625).[50] This has been effectively ignored by later, nineteenth- and twentieth-century critics, who follow Naudé, but only where they recognise their own procedures, or what we may call their own epistemic structure.[51] There is, indeed, a turn within Naudé's text towards what we may recognise as a scientific historical method, but this turn is made within what remains a traditional epistemic structure. To fail to recognise this is to fail to take into account the historicity both of Naudé's text and of the turn that it makes. It is, ultimately, as I indicated in my introduction, the failure of traditional historicism to take account of the historical character of its own origins.

The turn to scientific historical method (and so the appeal to later critics) is apparent, first, in Naudé's initial declared intention of establishing the general causes that lead someone to be suspected of practising magic ('les causes generales que l'on a peu avoir de ce soupçon' (Naudé, *Apologie*, preface, n. pag.)); second, in his avowed espousal of objective neutrality in the search for truth ('cette indifference qui doit tousjours porter le flambeau en cette recherche de la verité' (p. 6)). Then, in the chapter on Virgil, the texts which mention Virgil's practices as a magician are listed, though critical inquiry is limited, initially at least, to a dismissal of these accounts as contrary to common sense, reason and probability (pp. 607, 620). More attention is given to the account of the bronze fly made by Virgil to ward off flies from Naples, which is given by the twelfth-century humanist John of Salisbury, on the one hand, because John is an author(ity) Naudé clearly respects and, on the other, because this particular story raises the question as to whether it is possible to harness supernatural power in such objects (talismans). To determine this point Naudé cites an anecdote told by Scaliger, 'lequel ayant faict une petite platine gravée de diverses figures et caracteres sous une certaine constellation pour l'employer à cet effet, il ne l'eut pas si tost placée sur les fenestres qu'il y a eut une mouche plus hardie que les autres qui la vint estrener de son ordure' (p. 624). Here

[50] On Naudé see Gusdorf, *La révolution galiléene*, vol. 1, pp. 69–70
[51] Comparetti, *Virgilio nel medio evo*; J. W. Spargo, *Virgil the Necromancer: Studies in Virgilian Legends* (Cambridge, Mass.: Harvard University Press, 1934); J. Céard, 'Virgile, un grand homme soupçonné du magie', in R. Chevallier, ed,. *Présence de Virgile* (Paris: Les Belles Lettres, 1978).

experiment and observation expose as illusory (and derisory) faith in a
specific form of control: the 'effect' of harnessing supernatural power by
making such objects under a particular formation of the celestial agents
('sous une certaine constellation') cannot be thus achieved.

That the universe within which this demonstration of the limits of
what is possible is given remains the traditional Neoplatonic universe of
active celestial agents and passive material elements is clear both from
the specific argument about Virgil and from the more general arguments of the earlier chapters (which later critics have invariably ignored). In the case of Virgil, Naudé's explanation for 'la premiere cause et
origine de ce soupçon' that Virgil was a magician is:

la cognoissance des Mathematiques, en laquelle Virgile avoit tellement penetré,
suivant le rapport de Macrobe, Donatus, Lacerda, et le commun consentement
de tous les Autheurs, que nonobstant qu'il fust excellent Philosophe et tres
experimenté Medecin, l'on peut toutefois dire avec verité que la premiere de ses
perfections après la Poesie, estoit ce qu'il sçavoit en l'Astronomie et autres
parties des Mathematiques, lesquelles ayans tousjours ésté plus subjettes à être
soupçonées de Magie ... (p. 631)

The generalising move of the final clause here recalls an earlier chapter
which deals with the 'general causes' one may be suspected of being a
magician – the knowledge and practice of mathematics (chapter 5) –
and with the distinction between '(l)a Magie permise et celle qui est
defenduë et illicite' (p. 25), which is fundamental to Naudé's argument,
but which nineteenth- and twentieth-century critics have either ignored
(Comparetti) or passed over (Céard, 'Virgile, un grand homme', p. 278).
This distinction underpins both the argument about 'general' causes
and the individual cases. For it is the retirement and detachment
necessary for the practice of the fourth kind of magic, which Naudé calls
natural, that, he argues, provokes suspicion of illicit practices amongst
the populace.

Defining this kind of magic, he explains that a man may exercise his
reason by limiting himself to common knowledge, or rather

pour s'eslever à des speculations plus eminentes et relevées, se tirer de la presse,
s'escarter du commun, prendre l'essor, et se guinder à tire d'aisles à ces voutes
asurées du plus pur de nostre ame, à ce Paradis terrestre de la contemplation
des causes, ... cette Magie, que les Perses nommoient anciennement Sagesse,
les Grecs Philosophie, les Juifs Cabale, les Pythagoriciens Science de nombres
formels, et les Platoniciens souverain Remede, qui donne à l'ame une parfaicte
tranquillité, et au corps une bonne habitude, par la vertu qu'il a de pouvoir
conjoindre les effets passibles aux vertus agentes, et d'approcher les choses

elementaires d'icy bas aux actions des estoilles et corps celestes, ou plutost des intelligences ... (pp. 42–3)

It is to this earthly paradise of a contemplative knowledge of nature that those who practise natural philosophy/magic aspire. And it is the retirement necessary to achieve such knowledge that Naudé gives both as a general and as a particular cause for suspicion of illicit practices. Thus it is on account of his retirement to acquire such knowledge that Virgil is claimed by Naudé to have raised the suspicion of the people of Naples, who began to circulate rumours of diabolic practices (pp. 629–34). This conclusion, which has since acquired the status of virtual fact, was adopted by Comparetti, who ignored its articulation in Naudé's text as an effect of the retirement necessary to achieve the natural philosopher's/magician's contemplative knowledge of nature. Equally, he failed to recognise that the universe within which this argument is made remains the traditional Neoplatonic universe of the canonical early commentaries, as the explicit reference to Macrobius in the first passage quoted above signals.

Comparetti's separation of the 'popular' narratives of Virgil the magician from the 'learned' traditions of Virgil the poet continues to exert its hold, although his work has not been without its critics. Pasquali, for example, queried some time ago precisely 'la distinzione comparettiana fra tradizione dotte e tradizione popolare', while Fabio Stok has more recently declared that Comparetti's 'hypothesis' may be 'decisively rejected'.[52] Though Stok's own hypothesis – that the narratives reflect socio-cultural realities of the medieval world in which they emerged – is not an entirely satisfying alternative, it is less important here than his point that the earliest records of the narratives appear in 'serious medieval literature' (p.19), that is, in discourses of knowledge. This is corroborated by citations from this 'serious literature' given by Céard, which show that the practices of Virgil as magician were consistently associated with his learning, especially in natural philosophy and, once again, mathematics.[53] Céard does not, however, see the link with mediations of Virgilian texts, no doubt because these mediations have been erased. It is perhaps for the same reason that Stok sees no link

---

[52] Comparetti, *Virgilio nel medio evo*, edited by Giorgio Pasquali, p. xxx. Fabio Stok, 'Virgil between the Middle Ages and the Renaissance', *International Journal of the Classical Tradition* 1:2 (1994), p. 18.

[53] Céard, 'Virgile, un grand homme', pp. 271–2. This is not to deny that versions of the narratives develop away from these associations in various media, more and less 'popular'. See the examples gathered by Comparetti, *Virgilio nel medio evo*, vol. 2. For the tradition of portraits of Virgil as magician in the visual arts, see Nigel Llewellyn, 'Virgil and the Visual Arts', in Charles Martindale, ed. *Virgil and his Influence* (Bristol Classical Press, 1984), pp. 118–19.

either, although he recognises, in a general way, the close connection between the textual and biographical traditions.

And yet this link is made explicitly and specifically in a later text, from the end of the fifteenth century, which is cited neither by Naudé nor by later critics (who tend to follow his selection of material as well as features of his method and conclusion). A formal defence of astrology addressed to Charles VIII by Simon de Phares, an eminent and well travelled French astrologer and biologist condemned by the authorities for illegitimate practices, this names Virgil amongst other examples of distinguished astrologers.

Cestui Virgille montre bien en ses euvres et, par especial en ses *Georgiques*, mesmement ou Ier et IId livre, là où il entrejecte en ses vers quelque chose de la disposicion de l'air et là il monstre assez à quoi sert icelle partie de astrologie qui est des ellections, quant partout il commande observer la disposicion des corps celestes. A icelui Virgille fut donnée la seigneurie de Naples pour sa grande science. Il fist trente deux merveilles les plus grandes . . .[54]

This is the universe to which other mediations of the *Georgics* as natural philosophy, and especially as 'astrologia', and Naudé's type of natural philosopher/mage, exemplified by Virgil, belong. It is, moreover, in terms of this universe that de Phares goes on to describe Virgil's making of marvellous objects, the first being a bronze fly, which, having been made under a particular constellation, '. . . eslevée en l'air touit toutes mouches à certaines distances d'elle' (p. 114). It is of course precisely the making of this object and objects like it that Naudé claims observation shows to lie outside the domain of the possible. The other limit that Naudé and de Phares are equally concerned to establish is the limit of what is possible without diabolic assistance, the limit, that is, of the lawful. For de Phares, as for later natural philosophers, the definition of this limit was of course urgent, being a matter of life and death.

It is both with, and without diabolic assistance that Virgil is said to have performed marvellous feats in the first independent narrative, the so-called romance of Virgil, which, despite the criticism of Comparetti's work, has never been treated as other than popular literature.[55] As a

---

[54] Simon de Phares, *Recueil des plus celebres astrologues et quelques hommes doctes*, edited by Ernest Wickersheimer (Paris: Champion, 1929), p. 114. A student at Paris, Simon de Phares spent three years in Oxford and travelled in Ireland and Scotland during the 1470s. See de Phares, *Recueil*, pp. vi–vii, and Thorndike, *A History of Magic*, vol. 4, pp. 553–6.

[55] First published in French at the beginning of the sixteenth century this was published in English in Holland (?1518) and in London (?1550). See *STC* 2nd edn, vol. 2, nos. 24828–29; Comparetti, *Virgilio nel medio evo*, vol. 2, pp. 150–9; Spargo, *Virgil, the Necromancer*, pp. 67, 236–53. References will be to: *This boke treateth of the lyfe of Virgil, and of his death, and many other marvayles that he did in his lyfe tyme by witchecrafte and nygromancy, through the develles of hell* (London?, 1550?) (henceforth *Lyf*).

result, intertextual relations with the learned tradition have not been recognised, beyond the parallel Comparetti himself points out between the opening chapters of the *Lyf* – in which Virgil loses land and goes to Rome to seek its restoration from the emperor – and the mediations of the first and ninth eclogues as allegories of Virgil's life, summarised by Servius, 'Perdito . . . agro Virgilius Romam venit'.[56] The Virgil of the *Lyf*, for example, is, like Naudé's Virgil, an extraordinarily learned scholar who pursues his studies in retirement – a retirement which, in the *Lyf*, if not in Naudé's narrative, leads to the seizure of his (neglected) lands by greedy kinsmen.

Still more significant is the relation between mediations of Virgilian texts, in particular the *Georgics*, as natural philosophy/'astrologia', and the representation in the *Lyf* of the marvellous feats Virgil performs when, unlike the Virgil of the allegorical mediations, he does not have his land restored. For these feats, performed against the assembled forces of the emperor and Virgil's kinsmen, are represented in terms of the 'disposition' of the 'air', controlled sometimes with, and sometimes without diabolic assistance.

Virgil by nygromancy did cast the ayre over al his fruyte and corne of his landes . . . and he caused it to be gathered and brought into his houses . . . As the enemies of Virgill came to take hym he closed the aire that they had no myght to goe forward nor back warde but stode still, of the which the [*sic*] marvailed . . . (A banquet is set before the enemies but) . . . the might have none thereof, but the smoke or reke. For they of the hoste were clothed with the aire. (*Lyf*, fos. Biiv–n. pag.)

While the representation of Virgil's mode of control here recalls medi-ations of the *Georgics* as natural philosophy, specific details look forward to the figure of Prospero, the natural philosopher/magician, who through the 'disposition' of Ariel, the spirit of the air he controls, performs extraordinary feats, including a disappearing banquet, against those who have seized the dukedom he 'neglected' in order to acquire the knowledge permitting such control. More important here, however, is another intertextual relation, between the narrative of the *Lyf*, and one of Virgil's texts, *Eclogue* 8. For the first feat performed by Virgil in the passsage quoted above – the supernatural transportation of corn – is one of the feats Alphesiboeus claims to have seen performed by Moeris (line 99). Servius comments that such practices by 'magical arts' had led to legislation, which is no doubt the reason it was taken seriously as a

---

[56] Having lost his land Virgil made his way to Rome. Virgil, *Opera*, vol. 1, fo. 1r; Comparetti, *Virgilio nel medio evo*, vol. 2, p. 153.

possible form of control by some early modern editors.[57] Of these Badius Ascensius is the most significant, for he not only treats the poem as about what can actually be achieved by 'carmina' – 'charms' – but adds an allegorical interpretation according to which Alphesiboeus stands for Virgil, the incantation for an appeal to Augustus for his lost lands (Virgil, *Opera*, vol. 1, fo. 40v). The magical feats which Alphesiboeus describes, including the transportation of corn, are thus brought within the narrative framework which the opening of the *Lyf* shares with the allegorical mediations of *Eclogues* 1 and 9.

This has a particular importance for the English context, because Abraham Fleming uses Ascensius in his translation of the *Eclogues* and *Georgics* for schoolboys (1589).[58] 'Touching the person of *Alphesibey* [*sic*]' he writes in 'The Argument' to *Eclogue* 8, 'beeing a shepherd, you must note that it is allegoricall, and offereth us this sense or meaning, even the poets seeking of *Agustus* [*sic*] his favour for the recoverie and having againe of his lands and cattel' (p. 22). Still translating Ascensius he goes on,

> Now because sorcerie or magicall art did alwaies offend the Romans, and that they could in no wise away with it, and was therfore flatly forbidden to be used; the poet therfore followeth a fine fansie of his owne, desiring heere of the muses a charme of *Alphesibey*, as if himselfe had been utterly ignorant of such practices.

The last clause invites the reader to understand a concealed knowledge of magical practices within a narrative of the pursuit of lost lands, which certainly suggests, if it does not directly recall, the *Lyf*. Indeed, the 'poetical' practices here are represented as 'covering' the magical, Virgil the poet, Virgil the magician, both deployers of 'carmina' – songs/ charms – to recover what has been lost.

To the difficult question this raises as to how the *Lyf* was read, and by whom, a specific answer is suggested by its inclusion in John Dee's 'living library'.[59] How Dee, and his numerous visitors, might have read such a text is suggested by another section in the preface to Billingsley's translation of Euclid, on 'Thaumaturgike', defined as the making of

---

[57] Virgil, *Opera*, vol. 1, fo. 44v. This is mentioned by Macbeth as a feat performed by witches (*Macbeth*, IV.i.55).

[58] Abraham Fleming, *The Bucoliks of Publius Vergilius Maro, Together with his Georgiks. All newly translated into English verse* (London, 1589).

[59] Sherman, *John Dee*, pp. 29–52. Roberts and Watson, *John Dee's Library Catalogue*, item no. 1729. Dee's manuscripts include one on the philosopher's stone by 'Vergilius' (ibid., M35). It is specifically the 'secrets' of the system of alchemical knowledge that are revealed/concealed by Richard Stanyhurst, who was himself engaged in alchemical practices. See Clayton, '"Tempests, and such like Drolleries"', pp. 73–7; J. M. Dryoff, 'Approaches to the Study of Richard Stanyhurst's translation of Virgil's *Aeneid*' (PhD dissertation, University of Boston, 1971), p. 67; and on Virgil as alchemist, Spargo, *Virgil the Necromancer*, p. 21.

'straunge workes, of the sense to be perceived, and of men greatly to be wondred at', marvels, which, as Ian Calder has pointed out, could be thought by Dee only in terms of the Neoplatonic universe of spiritually animated elements, the universe, that is, of 'sympathicall' relations which 'the Philosophicall Poet' discloses in his *Georgics*.[60] It is as such a 'disposing' of the material world through the agency of, and in the 'air' that we may suppose he read the narrative of marvels in the *Lyf*.

That diabolic assistance was necessary to achieve such marvels would, of course, have been denied by Dee, officially at least. Indeed, this section in the preface is immediately followed by 'A Digression Apologeticall', one of Dee's more prominent pieces of 'self-advertisement' (Sherman, *John Dee*, pp. 10–11), which seeks, like the 'apologies' of de Phares and Naudé (indeed we are dealing here with a discursive genre), to claim as within the limits of the 'natural' and the lawful, certain practices, and to argue, as Naudé will argue for Virgil, that the ignorant populace is responsible for rumours of contact with diabolic forces. It is, similarly, as within the limits of the natural and lawful that, in his edition of the Virgilian *Opera* (published 1608–13), de la Cerda represents Virgil as 'ingeniosissimus rerum ARTIFEX', giving, as examples, two of the marvellous objects mentioned in the *Lyf* and claiming that diabolic assistance is not necessary for their construction.[61] Less than twenty years later Gabriel Naudé (who cites de la Cerda in the passage quoted above) will seek to determine the limits of the natural not only according to what does and does not require such assistance (the distinction between black and white magic), but also according to what observation and experience show to be possible. In making this turn, though within a traditional Neoplatonic universe, he will begin, but only begin, to turn away from the universe in which magic is inherent to the form of knowledge, the universe which Virgil as the maker of marvellous objects inhabits with Virgil the natural philosopher and both with Virgil the poet.

'CHARMES WERE WONT TO BE MADE BY VERSES': VIRGIL AND 'THEE TRUE MAKING OF VERSES'[62]

To this same universe belongs a representation of the quantitative form of Virgil's verse as a form of knowledge, like music. Concurrent with this

---

[60] Dee, *The Elements of Geometrie*, fo. A1r; I. R. F. Calder, 'John Dee Studied as an English Neoplatonist' (PhD thesis, The Warburg Institute, University of London, 1952), p. 479. See too Sherman, *John Dee*, pp. 97, 99.

[61] Virgil, *Opera*, edited by J. de la Cerda, vol. 1, chapter 3.

[62] Spenser, *Poetical Works*, p. 459: Stanyhurst, *Translation of the First Four Books of the Aeneis*, p. 10.

was a representation of it as a form of expression and persuasion, as, that is, a form of rhetoric. While the first attributes a meaning to the form which can only be apprehended by an act of intellectual faith, the second attributes to it a meaning which may be heard by the ear, and, with the turn to individual sense experience, comes to prevail. Linked to the 'untuning of the sky' in representations of forms of music,[63] the undoing of the representation of quantitative form as knowledge removed a vital impulse from the effort to institute principles according to which the form might be imitated in the vernacular – the effort which modern scholars have called the 'quantitative movement'.

In a chapter on 'causes', in what is still the most thorough critical discussion of the movement to date, Derek Attridge quotes a passage from Richard Willes's *De re poetica* (1573), which reproduces this representation of quantitative form as knowledge.[64] More than merely the commonplace 'comparison of the artist's creation of harmony with God's creation of the universe', as Attridge suggests (p. 115), this *identifies* metric form with the measure, or proportion with which the order of the universe was created by God and is sustained,[65] all things being, as John Dee, quoting Boethius, puts it, '(f)ormed by the reason of Numbers'.[66] Metrical form thus belongs to the form of knowledge called natural magic by Naudé, who, in his syncretic sweep, includes under this heading the Pythagoreans' 'Science des nombres formels' (see above, p. 96). And it is in the science of number that, as we have seen, Virgil the natural philosopher was said to be particularly skilled.

The centrality of Virgil to the 'quantitative movement' in early modern England is indicated by the frequency with which examples of translations of his texts are used, or references made to his practice. Thus, in 1570, Roger Ascham, an early advocate of quantitative metre in the vernacular, criticises Henry Howard's translation of the fourth

---

[63] John Hollander, *The Untuning of the Sky: Ideas of Music in English Poetry 1500–1700* (Princeton University Press, 1961); see also Lindley, 'Music, Masque and Meaning in *The Tempest*', p. 57.

[64] Derek Attridge, *Well-Weighed Syllables: Elizabethan Verse in Classical Metres* (Cambridge University Press, 1974), pp. 114–24.

[65] 'Metri origo a Deo opt. max. est, quippe qui hunc mundum & quaecunque eius ambitu continentur, certa ratione, quasi metro composuit, usque adeo ut harmoniam in coelestibus terrenisque rebus Pythagoras confirmarit. quo enim pacto mundus consisteret, nisi certa ratione ac definitis numeris ageretur?' (The origin of metre is from almighty God inasmuch as He created this world and all that is contained in its sphere according to a definite form, in metre as it were. Pythagoras indeed has claimed that there is a harmony in heavenly and earthly things. For how could the world cohere unless moved by a definite form and fixed numbers?) Willes, *De re poetica* (1573), p. 62 (Fowler's translation modified). The phrase 'certa ratione' is difficult to translate, since 'ratio' covers ideas of reason and language as well as of design and proportion.

[66] Dee, *The Elements of Geometrie*, fo. 1r.

book of the *Aeneid* for its feet 'not distinct by trew quantitie of sillables', a criticism echoed in 1586 by William Webbe, who claims that the translation by Thomas Phaer (completed by Thomas Twyne) conforms more closely to 'a ryght Heroicall verse', which he goes on to exemplify with his own translation of the first two eclogues.[67] As in most discussions of the form, both underscore the learning and knowledge it requires. That these are understood to comprehend more than merely technical skills is indicated in Webbe's opening sketch of the origins of poetry, which attributes to 'this measurable or tunable speaking' of quantitative verse (note the association with music) an ordering and civilising 'force' such 'that *Plato* affirmeth therein to be contained . . . an inchauntment'.[68]

More specifically linked to Virgilian practice is a passage in Sidney's *Defence of Poesie* which represents the 'divine force' inherent in the 'exquisite observing of number and measure in the words' 'propper to the Poet'. Considering, like Webbe, the early treatment of poets and poetry, Sidney comments, specifically, on the title of *vates* which the Romans attributed to the poet.

so heavenly a title did that excellent people bestowe uppon this hart-ravishing knowledge, and so farre were they carried into the admiration thereof, that they thought in the chanceable hitting uppon any of such verses, great foretokens of their following fortunes were placed. Whereupon grew the word of *Sortes Vergilianæ*, when by suddaine opening *Virgils* booke, they lighted uppon some verse of his . . . although it were a verie vaine and godlesse superstition, as also it was, to thinke spirits were commaunded by such verses, whereupon this word *Charmes*, derived of *Carmina*, commeth: so yet serveth it to shew the great reverence those wittes were helde in, and altogither not without ground, since both by the Oracles of *Delphos* and *Sybillas* prophesies, were wholly delivered in verses, for that same exquisite observing of number and measure in the words, and that high flying libertie of conceit propper to the Poet, did seeme to have some divine force in it.[69]

The dismissal as illusory and illegitimate ('vaine and godlesse') of specific

---

[67] Roger Ascham, *The Scholemaster* (1570) in G. Gregory Smith, *Elizabethan Critical Essays*, 2 vols, reprint (Oxford University Press, 1964), vol. 1, p. 32; William Webbe, *A Discourse of English Poetrie* in Smith, *Elizabethan Critical Essays*, vol. 1, pp. 256, 283–4. The full text of the translation is given in William Webbe, *A Discourse of English Poetrie*, edited by E. Arber (London: The English Scholars' Library, 1870), pp. 73–9. See Attridge, *Well-Weighed Syllables*, pp. 98–9 (Ascham), pp. 256–62 (Webbe). Twentieth-century critical opinion has reversed these judgements; Henry Howard's translation in particular has been generally hailed as a major contribution 'to the formation of the great English style'. H. B. Lathrop, *Translations from the Classics into English. From Caxton to Chapman 1477-1620* (Madison: University of Wisconsin Press, 1933), p. 101.

[68] Webbe, *A Discourse*, in Smith, *Elizabethan Critical Essays*, vol. 1, p. 231.

[69] Sidney, *The Complete Works*, vol. 3, p. 6.

practices with regard to the Virgilian texts – the treatment of them as prophetic (the *Sortes Vergilianae* practised from the second century on[70]), on the one hand, and as exercising supernatural control (an allusion presumably to Virgil as magician), on the other – is checked ('so yet ... altogither not without ground') by the suggestion that these are illegitimate developments of a legitimate representation of poetry as 'knowledge', and, specifically, prophecy, a function explicitly associated with the form of quantitative metre, which, if not granted control over spirits, is nevertheless allowed, if tentatively, to be linked to a 'divine force'.

That Sidney's persistent attempts at quantitative verse in the vernacular were motivated, at least in part, by a faith in its relation to a divine order of things is corroborated by what is known about his friendships, on the one hand, with Richard Stanyhurst and, on the other, with John Dee.[71] In particular, Peter French has suggested the affinity between Sidney's and Dee's conceptions of quantitative verse, defined, like music, in terms of the Neoplatonic universe of celestial agents and passive material elements. Such indeed was Dee's faith in the value of the form as knowledge that, like his fellow Neoplatonist Giordano Bruno, and like Sidney, he made attempts at quantitative verse himself (French, *John Dee*, pp. 147–53).

But perhaps the most interesting trace of this representation of quantitative form is to be found in a curiously incoherent passage in the discussion of metre in the second book – 'Of Proportion Poeticall' – in *The Arte of English Poesie*. Indeed, the whole discussion is of some interest, since it carries traces of the two representations mentioned at the outset, though tending to prefer the representation of metre as a form of expression. Having opened, rather like Willes, with 'God made the world by number, measure and weight' and having linked poetical and musical proportion, Puttenham subsequently treats the '*simpathie*' of 'musicall numerositie' as a relation 'with th'eare' only, without reference to the order of the universe (Puttenham, *The Arte*, pp. 64, 69). More significantly still, in the chapter with which we are immediately concerned – dealing with how 'the use of the Greeke and Latine feete might be brought into our vulgar Poesie' (p. 112) – tentative initial approbation of Stanyhurst's translation of the *Aeneid* gives way to unqualified con-

[70] Helen A. Loane, 'The *Sortes Vergilianae*', *The Classical Weekly* 21:24 (1928), pp. 185–9.

[71] On Sidney's friendships, with Stanyhurst see Dryoff, 'Stanyhurst's Translation of the *Aeneid*', p. 61; with Dee, French, *John Dee*, pp. 126–60, and F. G. Robinson, *The Shape of Things Known: Sidney's 'Apology' in its Philosophical Tradition* (Cambridge, Mass.: Harvard University Press, 1972), pp. 121–2, 126–7. The quantitative verse is collected in Sidney, *The Poems*, edited by Ringler, and analysed in Attridge, *Well-Weighed Syllables*, pp. 173–87.

demnation of '*his exameters dactilicke* and *spondaicke*' 'such as for a great number of them my stomacke can hardly digest for the illshapen sound of many of his wordes *polisillable* and also his copulation of *monosillables*' (pp. 117–18). The criterion of criticism here is the pleasure (or lack of it) experienced by the ear of the individual reader, the criterion, that is, of metre as a form of expression rather than as a form of knowledge.

Proceeding to discuss how to determine the length of syllables, the major problem for the would-be imitator in the vernacular, which, for the ancients, was done, in many instances, 'by preelection in the first Poetes,' (p. 118), Puttenham sketches, by way of illustration, how Virgil was 'driven of necessitie' (p. 119) to accept the received quantities of the words he used to write the first line of the *Aeneid*, the 'reason' being 'bare tradition'.

Such as the *Cabalists* avouch in their mysticall constructions Theologicall and others, saying that they receaved the same from hand to hand from the first parent *Adam*, *Abraham* and others, which I will give them leave alone both to say and beleeve for me, thinking rather that they have bene the idel occupations, or perchaunce the malitious and craftie constructions of the *Talmudists*, and others of the Hebrue clerks to bring the world into admiration of their lawes and Religion. (p. 119)

The comparison here is at once incoherent and strangely excessive. Carried away by his sceptical dismissal of the claims of the Cabalists (and by his anti-Semitism) Puttenham undermines rather than confirms the point he is trying to make – that Virgil received the quantities of words by tradition. What this suggests is interference from some un-stated relation between the Cabalists' 'mysticall constructions' and Virgil's 'observing of number and measure' according to tradition, that is, from a representation of such observation as itself a form of received, secret and sacred knowledge, which, for Naudé, we should recall, includes not only Pythagorean 'Science de nombres formels' but also Cabala (see above, p. 96). Indeed, exactly contemporary with *The Arte of English Poesie* is the *Hebdomades, sive septem de septenario libri* (Venice, 1589), a commentary by the Italian humanist Fabio Paulino, which is construc-ted around a line on the number seven from the sixth book of the *Aeneid* (line 646), and which makes of Virgil 'un Virgile cabaliste'.[72] It is such a figure of Virgil and such a representation of Virgilian quantitative form

---

[72] Céard, 'Virgile, un grand homme', p. 276. Paulino's text is quoted by Pontanus in a chapter of his introduction which Jonson appears to have drawn on for his eulogies of Virgil in *Poetaster*. See chapter 5, pp. 172–3

as sacred, received knowledge that Puttenham's urbane, Protestant and pragmatic scepticism cannot admit.

In contrast, the Anglo-Irish Catholic Richard Stanyhurst represents Virgilian metre as a form of sacred, received knowledge in the closing lines of the dedicatory letter to his translation of the *Aeneid*, 'of the extended experiments in quantitative metre' 'the most thoroughgoing', destined to become the focus of contemporary debates about the form.[73]

Good God what a frye of such *wooden rythmours* dooth swarme in stacioners shops, who neaver enstructed in any grammar schoole, not atayning too thee paringes of thee Latin or Greeke tongue, yeet lyke blynd bayards rush on forward, fostring theyre vayne conceites wyth such overweening silly follyes, as they reck not to bee condemned of thee learned for ignorant, so they bee commended of thee ignorant for learned. Thee reddyest way therefore too flap theese droanes from the sweete senting hives of *Poëtrye*, is for the learned too applye theym selves wholye ... to thee true making of verses in such wise as the *Greekes* and *Latins*, thee fathers of knowledge, have doone; and too leave too these doltish coystrels theyre rude rythming and balducktoom ballads. (Stanyhurst, *Translation of the First Four Books of the Aeneis*, p. 10)

Using a figure of stupidity from the medieval period ('blynd bayards') to represent those who write native accentual verse ('*wooden rythmours*') and a figure of divinely inspired wisdom and eloquence from the classical period ('sweete senting hives') to represent 'true' (quantitative) poetry, Stanyhurst explicitly turns the specific into a more general opposition with the terms 'learned' and 'ignorant'.[74] That the practice of the 'true making of verses' belongs to the wisdom inherited by the 'learned' from the ancients is signalled not only by the (inherited) figure of the bee, but also by the representation of the ancients as the 'fathers of knowledge'. The form of Virgil's poetry belongs for Stanyhurst, that is, to the 'secretes of Nature' which, in the quotation given at the outset of this chapter, he claims Virgil has 'sealde up' for the learned, while 'telling, as yt were a *Cantorburye tale*', a figure which anticipates the opposition in this

---

[73] Attridge, *Well-Weighed Syllables*, p. 166. See Gabriel Harvey's praise, in Smith, *Elizabethan Critical Essays*, vol. 2, p. 231, and Nashe's rejoinder, in ibid., p. 240. Compare the comments in *The Arte* quoted above.

[74] The figure of the bee to represent the poet's divinely inspired wisdom and eloquence recurs from Plato's *Ion* on. For some examples, from the classical and early modern period, see Greene, *The Light in Troy*, p. 62 (Cicero), p. 68 (Horace), pp. 73–4 (Seneca the younger), p. 84 (Macrobius), pp. 98–9 (Petrarch), pp. 199–200 (Ronsard), p. 275 (Jonson). The figure is also used by Nashe, and specifically of the 'profitable knowledge' that may be 'sucked' from Virgil's poetry. Thomas Nashe, *The Works*, edited by R. B. McKerrow, rev. edn. by F. P. Wilson, 5 vols. (Oxford University Press, 1966), vol. 1, pp. 29–30. Compare Ariel: 'Where the bee sucks, there suck I' (*The Tempest*, v.i.88).

passage between the native tradition and the classical, the fathers of superficial tales for the ignorant, and the 'fathers of knowledge' for the learned.

This representation of Virgilian quantitative form appears not to have circulated in the grammar schools where the English schoolboy's learning of metre was very much a question of learning definitions and rules, especially rules for the determination of quantities (Attridge, *Well-Weighed Syllables*, pp. 41–68). When significance is attributed to metric patterns the implied model is, moreover, that of metre as a form of expression. Thus, in a preface to the edition of the *Opera* which Brinsley specifically recommends for its '*Index*' 'for Authorities and uses of all words' (i.e. for the learning of quantities) (Brinsley, *Ludus*, p. 196), Virgil's skill in metre is represented as 'summi Vatis artificium' and the ancient oracles' use of the form rehearsed.[75] But the relation of the form to the prophetic function is not elaborated in what follows, which is dominated by definitions and rules, and where meaning is attributed to the metric pattern it is meaning as expression. A series of dactyls is said, for instance, to be suitable for the expression of strong wishes (fo. biiiv), and a series of spondees for the speeches of venerable characters whose mode of speaking is influenced by their age (n. pag.; compare the use of spondees in the speeches of Gonzalo in *The Tempest*). It is this kind of meaning too that is attributed to the (few) examples of descriptions of nature: spondees alone (perhaps with the exception of the fifth foot) are to be used 'cum et mora et colluctatio alicuius rei *exprimenda est*, ut in Tempestatibus' (fo. biiiiv; my emphasis).[76] Here the natural phenomenon of a tempest and the formal pattern of spondees are represented in terms of a slow, ponderous movement ('mora') and clashing effect ('colluctatio'), their relation as a relation of mimetic expression, which the onomatopoeic (and spondaic) character of 'colluctatio' itself echoes. It is an imitative effect we might be prepared to recognise in, for example, Miranda's description of the tempest (*The Tempest*, 1.ii.1–13), a description in which spondaic patterns work with patterns of sound to imitate the 'noises' of nature.

Less obvious for modern readers, though still invoking metre as expression, is the praise of Virgil's description of the beginning of autumn in *Georgics* 2, 'prima vel autumni sub frigora, cum rapidus Sol' (line 321; or nigh to autumn's first chills, when the fierce Sun), on the grounds that the temperate combination of the opposite qualities of hot

---

[75] Virgil, *Bucolica, Georgica et Aeneis*, edited by N. Eritreo, fo. aiiiv and n. pag.

[76] Examples follow: *Aeneid* 1 (line 53), *Georgics* 2 (lines 310–11); *Georgics* 1 (line 311), *Georgics* 3 (line 151).

and cold, which constitutes the mean climate of autumn, is expressed in the temperate combination of dactyls and spondees ('Spondei et Dactyli temperatura' (n. pag.)). To hear this relation of course requires the prior mediation of the season of autumn as a temperate combination of hot and cold, a requirement which, together with the mediation of metric form in such terms, makes it less obviously recognisable to modern (and especially North European) readers.

Through such examples as these, the English schoolboy may have learnt to hear relations between natural phenomena and Virgilian metric patterns. But these relations would have been those of metre as mimetic expression. The representation of Virgilian metric form as a form of knowledge, specifically, knowledge of the 'reason of Numbers' (Dee) by which God made and sustained the universe remained a more esoteric object, like the 'secrets of Nature' to which indeed it belonged.

THE VEIL IS TORN: PROFANATION OF 'ARCHANA MARONIS' AND HISTORICAL CHANGE

It is for its aspiration to preserve the knowledge of nature as *arcana* – a secret and sacred 'body' received from the ancients, including Virgil – that I want to look briefly at *Mythomystes*, a treatise on the art of poetry by the confirmed Neoplatonist Henry Reynolds, published in 1632, though perhaps written earlier.[77] Condemning modern poets as pretenders to the art, in contrast and in opposition to the ancients, Reynolds identifies three features which characterise the latter and so the 'true poet': first, a neglect of material for spiritual reality (pp. 15–27); second, the practice of concealment from the vulgar majority (pp. 27–44); third, an understanding of nature's secrets (pp. 44–82). The last two are particularly closely related inasmuch as it is the secrets of nature that the ancients deliberately concealed from the vulgar majority. Fixed and absolute truths, these secrets were handed down by the learned from the Egyptians to the Greeks and hence to the Latins.

Of which beades, the ingenious *Ovid* has made a curious and excellent chaine; though perhaps hee understood not their depth; as our wisest Naturalists doubt not to affirme, his other Contreymen *Lucretius*, and that more learned Scholler

---

[77] Henry Reynolds, *Mythomystes* (1632), reprint (Menston: The Scholar Press, 1972). Little is known of Reynolds other than that he was a friend of Michael Drayton, who addressed a verse-letter to him, 'Of Poets and Poesie'. Michael Drayton, *The Works*, edited by W. J. Hebel, 5 vols., reprint (Oxford University Press, 1961), vol. 3, pp. 226–31. In the notes Reynold's date of baptism is given as 1581 (ibid., vol. 5, pp. 216–17).

(I meane Imitater) of *Hesiod,* the singular *Virgil* did; and which are the sinewes and marrow, no lesse than starres and ornamants of his incomparable Poems: And still by them, as by their masters before them, preserved with equall care from the mischiefe of divulgation, or Prophanation. (pp. 37–8)

Reynold's type of the true poet and his particular representation of Virgil echo Naudé's type of natural philosopher and his representation of the example of Virgil. A 'learned Scholler' above historical change, Virgil transmits to the learned the permanent secrets of nature through his texts, here, specifically again the *Georgics.* The figures used to represent these secrets suggest, if cryptically, the canonical Neoplatonic mediations of the Virgilian universe as a single 'body' composed of active celestial agents and passive material elements, the universe, that is, of a certain form of knowledge which, as we have seen, Virgil the poet inhabits with Virgil the natural philosopher, and Virgil the magician.

For Reynolds, as for Naudé, the secret and sacred character of this form of knowledge requires withdrawal from the vulgar majority. For Reynolds, profanation by the vulgar is, in addition, a function of history. In his opening pages, the opposition between the fixed absolute truths of nature transmitted by the learned, and the opinions of the vulgar majority is projected as a degenerative version of history: a former, healthful 'knowledge of the Truth of things' (p. 2) has given way to a degenerate, present state of multiple, conflicting opinions, because of a general relaxation of restraints and, in particular, an indiscriminate exposure of the secrets concealed by the ancients to the ignorant multitude (pp. 1–3). The dissolution attendant upon such exposure is figured in metaphors of rape and fragmentation ('deflowred:' 'broke in pieces'), which suggests again a vision of nature as a single, whole (and female) 'body', a vision now broken up, irreversibly contaminated by the shifting, multiple and heterogeneous perspectives of the vulgar majority, bringers and embodiments of historical change.

The argument that divulgation of inherited knowledge constituted a profanation was, of course, itself inherited, a commonplace argument, which, as Betty Dobbs has pointed out, was addressed by Robert Boyle as late as 1655, in his appeal for the 'free communication' of 'alchemical as well as medical secrets', and which, she shows, was bound up with socio-political reform.[78] It is, in this respect, no coincidence that *Mythomystes* is addressed to a future 'ardent royalist', Lord

---

[78] Dobbs, *The Foundation of Newton's Alchemy*, pp. 68–9. See, more generally, Hill, *Intellectual Origins of the English Revolution, passim.*

Matravers.[79] For what is at stake in the argument against profanation is an institutionalised structure of authority tending to underwrite analogous structures in both church and state.[80]

This point is dramatised by Ben Jonson in *The Alchemist* (*H&S*, vol. 5, pp. 273–408), which, consequently, provides us with a useful transition to part two. Like Reynolds, Jonson uses the figure of a woman's body made common by multiple violations to represent the profanation of the secrets of nature inherited from the ancients, specifically the secrets of alchemy. But this figure – Doll Common – is also invested with political significance, as a figure of 'your *republique*' (i.i.10), the system of government of the 'venter *tripartite*' (i.i.135), constructed on the ideological ground of 'All things in common' 'Without prioritie' (i.i.135, 136). This is later recalled by Face, whose appeal to the 'common cause' (iv.iii.76) echoes Subtle's earlier citation of the 'common cause' of the Puritans (iii.ii.71), an echo which underlines the (ironic) likeness between the two anti-hierarchical ideologies and socio-political systems. Then, in the (again ironic) rehearsal of the argument against the profanation of the secret and sacred knowledge of nature received from the ancients, Mammon (!) asserts that Sisyphus was damned 'To roule the ceaseless stone, onely, because / He would have made ours common' (lines 209–10), at which point 'Doll is seene' (SD to line 210). Not merely a 'neat theatrical joke', as Mares suggests,[81] this invites recognition of the key (indeed common) figure in the analogous spheres, representing the making common which characterises, and works to produce the dismantling of mutually reinforcing hierarchical structures of authority, which I have called the Protestant turn. Indeed, like *The Tempest*, *The Alchemist* announces the logic of this turn, for the equal partners of the 'venter tripartite' begin and end by quarrelling and this quarrelling is likened by Doll to the 'undoing' of 'civill warre' (i.ii.82).[82]

[79] See Kinney's introductory note to Reynolds, *Mythomystes*, n. pag.

[80] The first is succinctly comprehended in a line from the seventeenth-century English poet John Collop quoted by Hill in his argument that there were 'links between science, Puritanism and the Parliamentary cause': 'Vile men would, prelate-like, have knowledge hid.' (Hill, *Intellectual Origins of the English Revolution*, pp. 72, 29.) The second is equally succinctly comprehended in James's well known watchword, 'No bishops, no king' (quoted in Kavanagh, 'Shakespeare in Ideology', p. 23, note 6).

[81] Ben Jonson, *The Alchemist*, edited by F. H. Mares, reprint (Manchester University Press, 1979), p. 72.

[82] The association of 'making common' with political collapse is explicitly made in the *Book of Homilies* too. See Kearney, *Scholars*, p. 36. Annabel Patterson usefully identifies 'making common' as a key 'ideologeme' in a tradition of radical discourse, though she does not include knowledge as one of its objects. Annabel Patterson, *Shakespeare and the Popular Voice* (Oxford and Cambridge, Mass.: Basil Blackwell, 1989), pp. 41–7.

Though the secrets of alchemy are not specifically associated with Virgil by Jonson, as they are by others (see note 59), the poet is represented, in the quotation at the head of this chapter, as 'the most learned of poets' revealing/concealing secrets of nature. More importantly, Jonson draws on canonical mediations of particular Virgilian texts as Neoplatonic natural philosophy, and so mobilises the received structure of authority to (re)produce by inclusion/exclusion the hierarchy of insiders/outsiders – the priesthood/the laity – that *Poetaster* stages as the opposition between Virgil's elite, learned, virtuous and eloquent audience at the centre of power, the court, and the common men outside who, as in *Mythomystes*, are associated with multiple, false opinions. The reading by Virgil of a passage which reveals/conceals 'secrets of nature' is, moreover, staged as a closed, secret and sacred ceremony, its interruption by one of the common men, as a profanation. This interruption anticipates, if in inverted form, the pivot of the binary anti-masque/main masque structure which the court masque acquires with Jonson, and which is informed by a system of oppositions like that which informs *Poetaster*. For the universe of the anti-masque is a universe of multiple, particular heterogeneous voices – Reynold's world of vulgar opinion – opposite and opposed to the total, closed and monovocal world of the main masque, the world of truth and unity which the anti-masque figures threaten to disturb and profane.[83]

In *The Tempest*, the total and closed universe of the Jonsonian main masque is interrogated through the disturbance of a betrothal masque brought about by a figure that, in *Bartholomew Fair*, Jonson identifies as an emblem of *The Tempest*'s hybrid character – the '*Servant-monster*' Caliban.[84] Indeed, the use made by Jonson and Reynolds of the figure of the violated body of a woman to represent the profanation of the ancients' secret and sacred knowledge of nature suggests that Caliban's attempted rape of Miranda may be taken, at one level, as a pre-figuring of his dis-turbance of the masque. For it is the paradisiacal, enchanted (indeed wonder-ful), total and closed order of nature inherited from the ancients, in particular from the learned poet/mage Virgil, that is em-

[83] The figure of profanation is linked by Greene to the first stage of the Jonsonian masque, which he analyses in terms of what he sees as the double gesture of the humanist imagination – the plunge into chaos (disinterment) and the construction of order (resurrection) (Greene, *The Light in Troy*, pp. 220–41). But he does not see that the chaos, and the profanation to which it is linked, are consistently associated with the multiple, particular heterogeneities of the vulgar and ignorant multitude, every man in his humour.

[84] In 'The Induction' (*H&S*, vol. 6, p. 16). See further Clayton, '"Tempests, and such like Drolleries"', p. 274, and Margaret Tudeau-Clayton, '"I do not know my selfe": The Topography and Politics of Self-knowledge in *Bartholomew Fair*' (forthcoming).

bodied in the masque. Specifically, it evokes not only the first and fourth books of the *Aeneid*, but mediations of the *Georgics* and of Virgil's 'proportioned' verse as knowledge, which, as we have seen, were central to the (re)production of Virgil as natural philosopher/magician. What the dis-turbance of the masque stages is, then, the dialogical interrogation, or 'dispute' to which these mediations were exposed, in part, as we have seen, with the discovery of the New World – a discovery with which Caliban is obviously associated. It is a 'dispute' anticipated in the opening scene by another moment of dis-rupture, when the Virgilian grammar of nature is evoked only to be derided by a character who belongs to the very social group – of unprivileged seamen – to whom Virgil as natural philosopher, and, especially, as foreseer of tempests was particularly exposed. It is above all, though not exclusively, at these two moments that the Virgilian grammar of nature, inflected in relations of likeness, is interrogated by a different universe and universe of difference and dis-placed as the 'groundless' art of the past by the play's staging of the Protestant turn, which, at the same time, dis-allows the uses made of this grammar, and of Virgil, to underwrite – ground – structures of privilege and power.

PART TWO

Jonson, Shakespeare and figures of Virgil

CHAPTER 4

'the most learned of poets': Jonson's use of Virgilian authority

Ben Jonson appears to have acquired his copy of the expensive in-folio edition of the Virgilian *Opera* by the German Jesuit scholar Jakob Spanmüller (called Pontanus) sometime between its publication (Augsburg, 1599) and the writing of *Poetaster*, performed in 1601.[1] For the formal eulogies of Virgil (v.i.100–38) appear to draw on passages quoted in the introduction to this edition. Certainly, it was in his possession by the time he came to prepare for publication (in 1604) his contribution to the entertainments given for James on the occasion of the ceremonial entry to London. For notes Jonson provides are lifted directly from notes given by Pontanus. I shall begin, after introductory comments, by looking at these notes, partly for this reason, but principally because they provide a useful point of entry into the work done by the voice of Virgil, especially the more esoteric voice of the learned man's Virgil, throughout the corpus. Furnishing a 'ground' – defining and legitimising origin – for a master self/voice, and the order of things it names, especially the new order under the new sovereign James, the learned poet's voice at the same time furnishes, with other learned discourse, a form of control – necessarily socio-political as well as authorial – working to produce, in the social places where it is deployed, a hierarchy between a privileged elite of insiders, who understand such discourse, and an unprivileged majority of outsiders, who do not, and who are therefore excluded at once from the authorial meaning of the text and from what it names, both rendered opaque mysterious objects – *arcana*.

In *Poetaster*, this work of inclusion/exclusion is done in the place of production by the passage from *Aeneid* 4 which Virgil reads in Act V and which constitutes an opaque object, requiring the mediation of canoni-

---

[1] On the life and work of Pontanus (1542–1626), see Walther Killy, *Literatur Lexicon. Autoren und Werke deutscher Spracher*, 15 vols. (Munich: Bertelsmann Lexikon Verlag, 1988–93), vol. 9, pp. 204–6. For the dependence of his edition on the work of early modern Italian humanists, see Zabughin, *Virgilio nel rinascimento*, vol. 2, pp. 92–3.

cal commentaries to be understood. Further, the Virgilian passage itself includes a representation, as the monster Fame, of those it simultaneously excludes – an exclusion which is also staged. For the scene of Virgil's reading is staged as a secret and sacred ceremony in a closed space occupied by an elite audience of 'learned heads' (v.i.52) at the centre of power, the imperial court. A community, or, as I shall prefer to describe it, a *circle* of 'the same', to modify Stanley Fish's insightful phrase,[2] the universe of Virgil and his elite audience is placed in contrast and opposition to the universe of those 'outside', which is a universe of multiple, particular and ephemeral heterogeneity, 'every man in his humour'. That these universes are mutually exclusive (if also mutually defining) is pointed up by the moment when the ceremony of Virgil's reading is interrupted, 'prophan'd' (v.iii.165) and ended by one of these outsiders. This moment anticipates, if in inverted form, the pivot of the binary anti-masque/main masque structure, which comes to define the generic shape of the Jonsonian court masque. For, as we shall see in this chapter, the universe of the anti-masque is a universe of multiple, particular and ephemeral heterogeneity, like the universe of the satirical comedies; indeed, as Stephen Orgel pointed out long ago (and others have since reiterated), the anti-masques come increasingly and specifically to resemble early satirical comedies.[3]

In *Every Man In His Humour* (performed 1598), this hierarchical binary opposition is articulated, even as it is worked for in the place of production, by a quotation from the Sibyl's description in *Aeneid* 6 of the few permitted to escape from the underworld into the upper air – 'pauci, quos aequus amavit / Juppiter' (lines 129–30, quoted in *Every Man In*, III.i.21–2). In *Cynthia's Revels* (performed 1600), the quotation recurs, translated, in a context which makes explicit what the spectator/reader of *Every Man In* must divine, that the description is to be understood in terms of the canonical Neoplatonic mediations of the Virgilian underworld as a description of the few permitted, on account of the 'merit' of their 'true nobility, called virtue', to escape from the Dis or Tartarus of contingent, material existence into an absolute, fixed and transcendent place 'above'.[4] As we shall see, those who understand are granted, by

[2] Stanley Fish, 'Authors-Readers: Jonson's Community of the Same', in Stephen Greenblatt, ed., *Representing the English Renaissance* (University of California Press, 1988). The recurring 'imagery of circularity' in the Jonsonian corpus is discussed in Thomas M. Greene, 'Ben Jonson and the Centered Self', in Bloom, ed., *Ben Jonson*, especially pp. 89–92.

[3] Stephen Orgel, *The Jonsonian Masque* (Harvard University Press, 1965), pp. 72–6; Russ McDonald, *Shakespeare and Jonson, Jonson and Shakespeare* (Brighton: The Harvester Press, 1988), p. 170.

[4] *Cynthia's Revels*, v.i.33 and 31; for the canonical mediations of the Virgilian underworld see chapter 3, pp. 83–7.

virtue of their understanding, a means of 'grace', a means, that is, to escape from the multiple, particular heterogeneities of every man in his humour, to join the privileged homogeneous circle which the Virgilian voice in *Every Man In* both addresses and describes.

In *Poetaster*, Virgil and his privileged homogeneous circle are precisely placed 'above', at the highest level of a Neoplatonic scale of being which underpins the play, Virgil, in particular, being identified at once as an embodiment of '(p)oore vertue' (v.ii.33), and, more specifically, as a 'rectified spirit' 'refin'd / From all the *tartarous* moodes of common men' (v.i.100 and 102–3; my emphasis), refined, that is, from the material, impure – and Tartarean – moods motivating the 'common men' (and all the women) of the play, who are placed at the lowest level of the play's scale of being, the level closest to matter. The place of Virgil and his circle is the same as that occupied, in a well-known passage in *Timber*, by an elite of '(g)ood men', identified as absolute '*Spectators*' over 'the Play of *Fortune*' 'on the Stage of the world'.[5] Indeed, Virgil is likened to a 'right heavenly body' (v.i.105), just as the good men are described as 'the Stars, the Planets of the Ages wherein they live' – images which underscore not only the absolute, transcendent place of these spectator figures, but their normative and regulatory function, their function, that is, as over-seers.[6]

It is as just such an absolute, normative and regulatory figure, over-seeing the universe of material and temporal contingency – represented at once as a 'Play of Fortune' and as an 'underworld' – that Virgil is used throughout the corpus. Whether as the schoolboy's embodiment of a normative economy of Language/Life regulating 'proper' usage and conduct, or as the learned man's ground of knowledge, the figure of Virgil serves at once to circumscribe language and meaning, and to produce by inclusion/exclusion a hierarchy of privilege. Potentially too it could serve what might be described as a bourgeois ideology and ethos, inasmuch as the criteria of privilege could be acquired independently of rank or wealth, although such independence was rare in practice, as we have seen. In this chapter, we shall see how this potential is implied in Jonson's use of the learned voice of Virgil as a means of self-creation and, promotion, and, in the next chapter, how this potential is exploited in the Virgilian scenes in *Poetaster*, which explicitly promote 'vertuous merit' (v.i.93) as the criterion of privilege, like the passage in *Cynthia's Revels* cited above. This potential is, however, contained within

---

[5] *H&S*, vol. 7, p. 597; for a discussion of the relation of the passage to its source see Clayton, 'Ben Jonson "in travaile with expression of another"', pp. 399, 405–7.
[6] The same figure is used of 'Shakespeare' – constructed as central, transcendent, national overseer – in Jonson's prefatory poem to the first folio (discussed above, p. 5).

a traditional political structure of an absolute monarchy. Moreover, the relationship between the monarch and learned heads in general as well as Virgil in particular is characterised as a relationship of absolute reciprocity. 'Virgil', that is, serves 'the king', as he does throughout the corpus. Indeed, we shall see in this chapter that it is in the service of such a reciprocal relationship, more precisely in the service of a relationship of reciprocal legitimation with 'the king' that the learned voice of Virgil is mobilised in *The King's Entertainment* and the masques. We shall see too how in using Virgil for this end Jonson often draws on the traditional structure of hermeneutic authority, the 'ground' of meaning supplied by the canonical commentaries. What might be described as a Catholic hermeneutic and hierarchical ideology thus cohabit, more or less uneasily, with a more egalitarian bourgeois ethos and ideology.

The last general point I want to make is that, although the character and function of the voice and figure of Virgil remain constant, their use becomes more restricted. We shall see this in chapter 5 when I shall look at modifications to the use of Virgil in the Folio version of *Every Man In*, and at the presence/absence of Virgil in later masques and in the epigrams. Showing how this voice/figure is withdrawn from the universe of multiple, particular heterogeneity – the 'underworlds' of the anti-masques and the satirical comedies – I shall argue that this withdrawal implies not the more inclusive, accommodating older Jonson that critics have liked to imagine, but quite the opposite.

THE VOICE OF VIRGIL IN *THE KING'S ENTERTAINMENT* AND MASQUES: (RE)WRITING HISTORY, UNDERWRITING 'THE KING'

To situate Jonson's precise use of Virgil in his published version of *The King's Entertainment* we need to look briefly again at the public argument he had with Dekker over their respective contributions. The argument turns essentially on the question of propriety, and the related question of audience. For Jonson, whose version was published first, the proper audience for the forms proper to such an occasion are the 'sharpe and learned', any concession to the 'grounded judgements' of 'the multitude' not 'becoming' (*H&S*, vol. 7, p. 90). For Dekker, on the contrary, '(t)he multitude is now to be our audience', and learned discourse is consequently out of place both in the published text and at the occasional spectacle.[7] With more insight than later critics, who simply decode for

---

[7] Thomas Dekker, *The Dramatic Works*, edited by F. Bowers, 4 vols. (Cambridge University Press, 1953–61), vol. 2, p. 255.

an academic audience the meanings of Jonson's contributions, commenting at most that, at the occasion, they 'needed an Interpreter',[8] Dekker points to the ideological, and political work such discourse does in the context of broad heterogeneous audiences.

> To make a false florish here with the borrowed weapons of all the old Maisters of the noble Science of Poesie, and to keepe a tyrannicall coyle, in Anatomizing *Genius*, from head to foote, (only to shew how nimbly we can carve up the whole messe of the Poets) were to play the Executioner, and to lay our Cities houshold God on the rack, to make him confesse, how many paires of Latin sheets, we have shaken and cut into shreds to make him a garment. Such feates of Activitie are stale, and common among Schollers, (before whom it is protested we come not now (in a Pageant) to Play a Maisters prize) ...
>
> The multitude is now to be our Audience, whose heads would miserably runne a wooll-gathering, if we doo but offer to breake them with hard words. (pp. 254–5)

More than merely a 'fling at Jonson's scholarship' (*H&S*, vol. 10, p. 386), this criticises the use of scholarship as a form of strategic mystification, which serves to control and oppress the multitude: 'weapons ... to keepe a tyrannicall coyle ... to break them with hard words'. Indeed, inasmuch as Jonson's 'hard words' take the place of the 'symbolic devices' traditionally used on such occasions to distinguish, as Steven Mullaney has shown, citizen from non-citizen, they deal a death blow, executioner-like, to such modes of defining the community's sense of identity.[9] For, as Dekker indicates, Jonson's 'hard words' aim rather at self-advertisement ('only to shew' etc.), in the style of the competitive games played by scholars ('to Play a Maisters prize'), another, more restricted community, which uses such games at once to define itself, and to distinguish individuals within it, thus organising itself into a hierarchical structure, potentially, if not in fact, alternative to the socio-political hierarchy.[10] To

---

[8] Graham Parry, *The Golden Age Restor'd: The Culture of the Stuart Court 1603–42* (Manchester University Press, 1981), p. 6.

[9] See Stephen Mullaney, *The Place of the Stage. License, Play, and Power in Renaissance England* (University of Chicago Press, 1988), pp. 13–14. The relevant gloss to the phrase 'hard words' – 'a quasi-technical term for words which defy understanding unless interpreted by authority' – is given in Stephen Greenblatt, 'Remnants of the Sacred in Early Modern England', in Margreta de Grazia, Maureen Quilligan and Peter Stallybrass, eds., *Subject and Object in Renaissance Culture* (Cambridge University Press, 1996), p. 339.

[10] Specifically, Dekker alludes to a precise social practice, which John Stow describes in a passage from his *Survey of London* (1598) quoted by Rosemary O'Day in her discussion of the emergent competitive ethos in educational theory and practice, which she links to the competitive character of the patronage system. O'Day, *Education and Society*, pp. 52–3. From Stow's description it is clear that the specific practice, if not the ethos, belonged already (in 1598) to the past – hence Dekker's contemptuous, and provocative 'stale'.

display the learned origins of one's text is to display one's 'self' as thus differentially identified – distinguished. Such displays are, in short, exercises in the '*selfe-creating*' Dekker earlier shrewdly attributes to Jonson in *Satiromastix*.[11] Indeed, Jonson's 'learning' is explicitly represented in the play as a 'growth', something added to an original 'baseness' which it serves to conceal (*Satiromastix*, IV.iii.219-22). Though Dekker's is the sceptical gloss, it points to the twofold aspirations of Jonson's use of learning: to define a community, and hierarchy of privilege, and to furnish a ground – a defining and legitimising origin – for his texts and for a self, which, 'distinguished' from an original 'baseness' (whether social or, as in Dekker's critique, moral), serves to promote Jonson's upward social mobility.

The published version of *The King's Entertainment* does indeed display its learned origins, both in citations given in the description, and in notes which surround the descriptions and the speeches. These notes furnish visual advertisements of a generic likeness to the more elaborate editions of classical texts in circulation. This likeness is at one point – and a particularly important point – specific. For two notes to one of the most densely annotated passages are lifted directly from Pontanus's edition of the Virgilian *Opera*. The passage is from the speech addressed by the figure of 'Genius' to 'London' (represented on the arch at Fen Church) and tells of the origins and end of the city.

> thou now art blist to see
> That sight, for which thou didst begin to be.
> When ᶜBRUTUS plough first gave thee infant bounds,
> And I, thy GENIUS walk't auspicious rounds
> In every ᵈfurrow; then did I forelooke,
> And saw this dayᵉ mark't white in ᶠCLOTHO's booke.
>
> (*H&S*, vol. 7, p. 92)

Duplicating for the text they gloss the work of supplying origins which the text does for 'London', notes c and d read:

c Rather than the Citie should want a Founder, we choose to follow the received storie of *Brute*, whether fabulous, or true, and not altogether unwarranted in Poetrie: since it is a favor of Antiquitie to few Cities, to let them know their first Authors. Besides, a learned Poet of our time, in a most elegant worke of his *Con. Tam.&Isis*, celebrating *London*, hath this verse of her: *Æmula maternae tollens sua lumina Troiae*. Here is also an ancient rite alluded to in the building of

¹¹ *Satiromastix*, v.ii.138, in Dekker, *The Dramatic Works*, vol. 1, pp. 299–386.

Cities, which was, to give them their bounds with a plough, according to *Virg. Æn. li.10. Interea Aeneas urbem designat Aratro.* And *Isidore, lib.15.cap.2. Urbs vocata ab orbe, quod antiquae civitates in orbem fiebant; vel ab urbo parte aratri, quo muri designabantur, unde est illud. Optavitque locum regno et concludere sulco.* d *Primigenius sulcus dicitur, qui in condenda nova urbe, tauro et vacca designationis causa imprimitur;* Hitherto respects that of *Camd.Brit.*368 speaking of this Citie, *Quicunque autem condiderit, vitali genio, constructam fuisse ipsius fortuna docuit.* (ibid.)

Beginning with an originary lack – the 'want' of a 'Founder' or 'first Author' – note c proceeds to supply legitimising grounds (note the juridical register of 'unwarranted') for the substitution of this lack with the 'received storie' of Brute.[12] The ground of 'Antiquitie', which here merely serves to confirm the originary lack, is immediately supplemented ('Besides') by a line – 'London bearing aloft her lights in emulation of mother Troy' – from a contemporary poet in Camden's *Brittania*, possibly Camden himself (*H&S*, vol. 10, p. 390), whose legitimising authority is signalled by the epithet 'learned'. In addition ('Here also'), the received story of Brute is supplemented by 'an ancient rite of foundation' grounded in a line from Virgil: 'Meanwhile Aeneas marks out the city with a plough'. The line comes from *Aeneid* 5 (line 755), but in Pontanus's edition the running title on the page where it appears is 'Symbolarum Lib. X'.[13] That Jonson took his reference ('Æn. li. 10') from here is confirmed by the quotation he gives as supplementary ground, from the seventh-century scholar Isidore of Seville, which comes from the middle of Pontanus's note to this line.[14] Itself largely a quotation from the canonical Servius (see note 14), the quotation supplies for Jonson's text the ground supplied by Pontanus for the Virgilian, a ground which is double, a (fictive) etymological ground (*urbs* from *orbs* or *urbum*) being joined to the ground of ancient cultural practice. A quotation from a third-century scholar Festus, with which

---

[12] The political and ideological uses to which the Troy legend was put, and not only in England, is widely documented. See James, *Shakespeare's Troy*, chapter 1, note 14, for a comprehensive bibliography.

[13] 'Ad Quintum Aeneidos' is the running title on the facing page. Pontanus divides the *Opera* into seventeen books of 'Symbolae', the first of which comprises all the *Eclogues*, the second, *Georgics* 1, the third, *Georgics* 2, and so on until the seventeenth which comprises *Aeneid* 12. This is the only place where Jonson reproduces Pontanus's idiosyncratic system. A small ink mark on the page, between the quotations he uses from Isidore and Festus, may be another, literal trace of Jonson's copying of the note.

[14] *Urbs* derives either from *orbs*, because ancient cities were built in the form of a circle; or else from *urbum*, the curved part of the plough with which the walls were marked out, hence: 'He chose a site for his kingdom and enclosed it with a furrow.' See Virgil, *Symbolarum libri XVII*, edited by J. Pontanus, col. 1343. Up to 'designabantur' this is taken from the Servian gloss to *Aeneid* 1, line 12; the quotation which follows is made up of two half lines from the *Aeneid* (book 3, line 109, and book 1, line 425).

Pontanus's note begins, is then given in note d (though Festus is not named), to ground the foundational significance of the figure of 'the furrow' trodden by Genius: 'That furrow is called primigenial (or originary) which is imprinted by means of the pattern marked out by cow and bull when a new city is founded'. To this is added another quotation from Camden's *Britannia*, which includes not only another mention of genius but also a reference to the originary lack with which note c began: 'But whoever the founder, its fortunes taught the world it had been built with a vital genius'. Returning to this point of departure note d performs a circular movement, enclosing the text's origins in the bounds of its grounds, doubling the figure of the circular rite of foundation to which it alludes.

This figure of the circle is repeated in the narrative itself, the present moment of London's history being joined to the moment of its foundation as its fulfilment. The history of the nation is then explicitly represented, in the lines which follow, as 'severall circles' 'figur'd' in the book of Clotho (lines 289–91), an image of history as a book inscribed with circles which mirrors the printed text in which it features, a text surrounded by notes enclosing in its grounds the story of the city's – and the text's – origins.

At the same time, of course, readers unable to penetrate the Latin quotations are excluded from these grounds. Similarly, unlearned spectators would have been excluded from the allusion to the ancient rite of foundation and so from the meaning of Genius's speech at the occasional spectacle. For such readers and spectators the text is rather thickened (a literal, visual effect for readers), rendered opaque and 'strange'. This epithet is actually used by Jonson in another note which draws on Virgil and on the grounds of Virgil's learning given by Pontanus. The note is to the phrase 'masculine gums', which comes in a later speech by Genius addressed to the figure of a Flamen at the second arch at Temple Bar (pp.101–4). The note reads:

> Somewhat a strange Epithite in our tongue, but proper to the thing: for they were only *Masculine* odors, which were offerd to the Altars. *Virg.Ecl.8.* (p.103, note e)

The line from Virgil's *Eclogue* 8 (line 65) is then quoted, followed by a long explanatory comment on the use of the epithet from Pliny's *Natural History*, a reference to another chapter in Pliny and a quotation from the *Adversus nationes* (*c.* AD 300) by Arnobius. Except for the second reference to Pliny, which Jonson must have gone somewhere else to check, all this material is given by Pontanus in his note to the line from Virgil.[15] The ground of Virgil's learning here serves to authorise Jonson's usage, to draw within the bounds of the 'proper' what seems 'strange' in the vernacular.[16] The learned man's Virgil is thus joined with the school-boy's Virgil, the normative, regulatory model of Language who, in *Poetaster*, as we shall see, uses the same epithet 'strange' to police the language of Crispinus, which is banished – placed out of bounds – just as, in *Timber*, exemplary Virgilian practice serves to banish the use of archaisms.[17] Drawing on the ground of Virgil's learning to bring his own usage within the bounds of the 'proper', Jonson at the same time makes its 'strangeness' a function not of his own original usage, but of a spectator's/reader's ignorance.

It is not, however, only the meaning of his text that Jonson thus makes 'proper' to the 'learned', 'strange' to the 'ignorant', but the occasion it celebrates. The origins and end – the history and identity – of the nation, especially, as Dekker's critique indicates, of 'London', are thus turned over to the 'sharp and learned', made their 'proper' property, and the 'ignorant' multitude are estranged, dispossessed of the very ground – of 'London' – on which they stand. They are estranged too from 'the king', who is the end of the history told in the speeches, notably in the speech of Genius quoted above, which draws on *archana maronis* to serve the *arcana imperii*, producing an effect of a secret and sacred place, which is at once the ground of the authority of the king and the ground of the authority of the text-performance.[18]

Of crucial importance in the construction of this 'ground' (for both king and text) are the quotations from Camden's *Brittania* (published in Latin in 1586 and in a translation by Philemon Holland in 1610). For Camden 'understood the ways learning could serve the state',[19] and Jonson's quotations show, specifically, how Camden's learning could serve to unfold the 'original . . . Roman destiny . . . fulfilled in James's

---

[15] Virgil, *Symbolarum libri XVII*, edited by J. Pontanus, cols. 178–9

[16] Jonson's practice here in using a word with a technical register when alluding to religious ritual follows exactly the practice of the Catholic translators of the Bible, who, as they point out in their preface, prefer 'to keep in the text' such words, even though they may seem 'strange' 'to common English eares', and 'to tel their signification in the Margent' (as quoted in Görlach, *Introduction to Early Modern English*, pp. 267–8).

[17] Jonson actually uses the verb 'banish' in the passage in *Timber*. See chapter 1, pp. 40–3, and chapter 5, pp. 179–83.

[18] See Jonathan Goldberg, *James I and the Politics of Literature* (Baltimore and London: Johns Hopkins University Press, 1983), especially p. 56. For the very different occasion of Elizabeth's ceremonial entry, and its placing of London's citizens, see Mullaney, *The Place of the Stage*, pp. 11–13.

[19] Riggs, *Ben Jonson*, p. 14.

entrance' and to establish 'the legitimacy of the Roman name' of Britain, a legitimacy to which James passionately aspired.[20] Placed alongside the Virgilian text, as supplementary ground linking the Roman past to the British present, the contemporary 'learned poet' is implied to do for the British nation and for James what Virgil did for the Romans and for Augustus.[21] Building on this ground, Jonson both continues and repeats its work implicitly claiming for himself the same status as 'learned poet', who, like Virgil, supplies 'the beginnings, and hidden nature' of the name of Britain and the name/style of the king. But access to these grounds is confined to the learned; for those who are excluded the authority supplied by the notes is rather a function of their opacity, their character as *arcana*.

Even the occasional artefacts were rendered opaque by Latin quotations, including 'hard words' from Virgil. The arch at Temple Bar carried, as framing quotations, the relatively well known line from *Eclogue* 4 (line 6) declaring a return of the golden age, and a less familiar but similarly self-contained line from *Aeneid* 11 (line 362) appealing for an age of peace (*H&S*, vol. 7, p. 100). More obscurely, two of the figures at the first arch at Fen Church – two of the daughters of Genius – carried Virgilian quotations, which required that the spectator-reader be equipped at least with the context of the quotation. The first, carried by the figure of Sebasis (Veneration), was 'MIHI SEMPER DEUS' ('ever a god to me') (p. 87), which is from *Eclogue* 1 (line 7). Its full meaning is supplied by the Servian gloss on 'deus' as an allusion to Augustus, which discloses the quotation as a twofold compliment to James as one to whom, as to Augustus and to God, reverence is due.[22] The second quotation, carried by the figure of Prothymia (Promptitude), is still more opaque: 'QUA DATA PORTA' is, as Jonson explains in the published text, 'taken from another place in VIRGIL, where ÆOLUS at the command of JUNO, lets forth the wind' and where the winds show their promptitude of response 'to his high command.' (p. 88). The Virgilian context is here necessary for the 'word' to 'deliver' its meaning as a twofold figure of obedience to authority (Aeolus to Juno, the winds to Aeolus). It is indeed not insignifi-

---

[20] Golberg, *James I*, p. 47; see also Riggs, *Ben Jonson*, p. 17. Jonson later explicitly celebrates Camden for the 'name' 'my countrey owes him' as well as for 'his sight in searching the most antique springs' (epigram 14, lines 3–4, 8) (*H&S*, vol. 8, p. 31).

[21] Pontanus, following Servius, comments that celebration of the Roman people and especially Augustus was one of Virgil's objectives, which he achieved by representing their noble and ancient origins, their customs and feats. Virgil, *Symbolarum libri XVII*, edited by J. Pontanus, p. 6 (misprint for p. 7).

[22] Virgil, *Opera*, vol. 1, fo. 2v. See also Virgil, *Symbolarum libri XVII*, edited by J. Pontanus, cols. 5–6.

cant that both of these Virgilian 'hard words' – words, we should recall, which 'defy understanding unless interpreted by authority' (see note 9) – have to do with authority. For their opaque character at the moment of performance served to underwrite that authority through mystification, the effect being again of a secret and sacred 'place' (the word Jonson uses) – a *locus*, which is at once the meaning of the 'hard words' and the authority of 'the king'.

In the published version, the artefacts themselves are mediated through learned textual grounds. In particular, the figure of 'TAMESIS, the river' on the arch at Fen-Church, is described as 'alluding to VIRGILS description of Tyber', a passage in *Aeneid* 8 (lines 31–4), which is quoted (p. 86). But the description of the figure of Thames, which precedes and follows the quotation, is itself informed by the Virgilian passage, as well as by Pontanus's gloss.[23] The figure is thus described not as it 'was' seen, but as it 'should' have been seen – an ideal 'proper' perception which is defined for learned readers by its Virgilian textual ground.

The same work is done by the voice/figure of Virgil in the published versions of the court masques. Likewise surrounded with more or less dense notes, advertising a generic likeness to more elaborate editions of the texts they cite, these published versions similarly describe the spectacles as they should have been seen, an ideal 'proper' perception which their learned textual grounds supply for learned readers, and, especially, for the royal reader, who is identified again as the origin and end of these spectacles, and who, as spectator at the occasion, was placed at the point about which they were structured, the point, that is, precisely of 'proper' perception.[24] From this place, which Jonson identifies as a fixed, absolute place of redemption from the contingencies of material and temporal existence, including the contingencies of the occasional performance, 'ignorance' is excluded, an effect which is both dramatically staged, in the turn from anti-masque to main masque, notably in *The Masque of Queens* (1609), and represented in relation to the learned poet's voice, which, in *Oberon, The Fairy Prince* (1611), is, specifically, the voice of 'the most learned of poets' Virgil in the text, *Eclogue* 6, which furnishes the masque's principal textual ground. It is this masque, with

---

[23] The most striking example is the description of the mantle as 'thin, and bolne out like a sayle', which echoes the comment by Pontanus on the Virgilian phrase 'tenuis ... /carbasus' (thin lawn), that 'carbasus' was a kind of linen from which very thin sails used to be made: 'Carbasus ... genus est lini ... E carbaso texebantur tenuissima vela' (Virgil, *Symbolarum libri XVII*, edited by J. Pontanus, col. 1702). For other possible echoes see Clayton, '"Tempests, and such like Drolleries"', pp. 301–2.

[24] See Peter Womack, *Ben Jonson*, p. 60.

The Masque of Queens, in which the paradigmatic function of the figure of Virgil as ground to royal authority is architecturally figured, that will be the focus of what follows, after initial discussion of *The Masque of Blackness* (performed 1605, published 1608). I shall look not only at how Virgil is used, but at how the use and representation of this figure/voice relate, on the one hand, to the development of the form of the masque and, on the other, to the use of Virgil in *Poetaster*. In my discussion of *The Masque of Queens*, I shall also introduce the intertextual relation of *The Tempest* both to this particular masque and, more generally, to the binary structure which comes to define the form. This in turn will lead to discussion of differences in intertextual relations to Virgil, which continues when I look at *The Haddington Masque* (1608), where intertextual differences are bound up with a different relation to history and to nature, and, above all, *Hymenaei* (1606), the masque to which it is generally agreed Prospero's marriage masque most explicitly alludes. The discussion of *Hymenaei* will lead back to, in order to introduce *Poetaster* (chapter 5). For the Virgilian passage which furnishes a textual ground to the masque is the passage from *Aeneid* 4 which Virgil reads in Act V of *Poetaster*. And it is with the scene of this reading as well as with *Hymenaei* that *The Tempest* engages.

Particularly prominent in these four masques, the authority of Virgil is evoked as defining ground from the very outset, in the published version of the first masque, *The Masque of Blackness* (*H&S*, vol. 7, pp. 167–80). In particular, the description of the Tritons is informed by a Virgilian textual ground, like the description of Thames in *The King's Entertainment*.

Infront of this sea were placed sixe ᶠ*Tritons*, in moving, and sprightly actions, their upper parts humane, save that their haires were blue, as partaking of the sea-colour: their desinent parts, fish, mounted above their heads, and all varied in disposition. (p. 170)

This description is informed by the two passages cited in note f, from *Metamorphoses* 1 (line 333) and *Aeneid* 10 (lines 209–12). While the inserted clause beginning 'save that' combines a Virgilian epithet, 'hispida' (hairy), with an Ovidian, 'caeruleus' (precisely, 'blue, as partaking of the sea-colour'), 'their upper parts humane … their desinent parts, fish' follows very closely 'frons hominem praefert, in pristim desinit alvus' (*Aeneid* 10, line 211). The adjective 'desinent' is, in particular, a prominent, though not necessarily intended, advertisement of the Virgilian description. The first of only three examples in the *OED* (the other two are from a single text dated 1677), Jonson's use of the word – very 'precise and religious in folowing (the) copie'[25] – can indeed barely qualify as translation. For it fails effectively, if not officially, to make 'proper' to the vernacular a ('strange') Latinate form introduced to trace, as *religiously* as possible, the Virgilian ground, and shape, of the Tritons. Such a 'religious' mode of translation, for the Catholics translating the Bible as much as for Jonson translating Virgil, aspires at once to preserve and to appropriate the sacred authority of the source text by restricting to a minimum the inevitable departure that translation entails.

Jonson's explicit display of the textual grounds of his masques has been followed up by twentieth-century scholars (notably, D. J. Gordon, and Starnes and Talbert), who have argued that these grounds are invariably 'second-hand', drawn from standard dictionaries and mythographies, including, in particular, Comes' *Mythologiae*, from which, for example, Gordon suggests Jonson took the material on the Tritons for his note f here.[26] It is not my purpose to reinstate Jonson's credibility as a scholar; indeed, it should be clear that I am interested not in repeating the cardinal move of traditional scholarship, which privileges textual origins, but in analysing the ideological work done by this move in Jonson's texts. It would, however, appear that, for at least one of the four notes in which Virgil is cited, Jonson went to his copy of the *Opera* for supplementary material. The note is on 'horned', one of the features of Oceanus, the central, father figure of the masque, which is articulated principally through a dialogue between this father of rivers and his son Niger.[27]

OCEANUS, presented in a humane form, the colour of his flesh, blue; and shaddowed with a robe of sea-greene; his head grey; and [h]horned; as he is described by the *Ancients*: his beard of the like mixt colour: hee was gyrlonded with *Alga*, or sea-grasse; and in his hand a *Trident*. (p. 170)

---

25 From the preface to the Catholic translation of the Bible as quoted in Görlach, *Introduction to Early Modern English*, p. 267. See above introduction, p. 12.

26 D. J. Gordon, *The Renaissance Imagination: Essays and Lectures*, edited by Stephen Orgel (University of California Press, 1975), p. 132. See also T. De Witt Starnes and E. W. Talbert, *Classical Myth and Legend in Renaissance Dictionaries*, reprint (Westport, Conn.: Greenwood Press, 1973), p. 166. These scholars tend to assume that Jonson's published versions describe the masques as they were seen by the courtly audience, and do not recognise the extent to which the descriptions are informed by their textual grounds.

27 Jonson refers to Oceanus as father of rivers, p. 172, note k. For a summary of this myth and its survival as science into the seventeenth century, see David Quint, *Origin and Originality in Renaissance Literature. Versions of the Source* (New Haven and London: Yale University Press, 1983), pp. 34–5, 228.

Unlike the other features of this description, 'horned' is a feature which is not self-evidently proper to Oceanus and which might have appeared 'strange', arbitrary, original even. It is precisely to establish its proper character that the authority of the ancients is invoked, first in the general qualification 'as he is described by the *Ancients*' and then in the specific references given in note h. The first part of the note, which gives the 'natural' reason supplied by the ancients for the feature, and a quotation from Euripides, is taken from Comes' chapter on Oceanus, as Gordon has shown (Gordon, *The Renaissance Imagination*, pp. 137, 227). But, having translated 'cuiusmodi finguntur esse etiam fluvii'[28] 'And rivers sometimes were so called', Jonson adds, 'Looke *Virg. de Tiberi, et Eridano, Geor.4. Aeneid 8. Hor. Car.l.4. Ode 14* and *Eurip. in Ione.*' Comes gives no references, but in Pontanus's note to the first Virgilian passage mentioned, in *Georgics* 4 (lines 363–73), both Horace and Euripides are cited to underwrite Virgil's description of Eridanus as 'horned'.[29] Thus grounded in the authorities in which Virgil's text is grounded by Pontanus, as well as in the authority of Virgil himself, the apparently 'strange', arbitrary and original character of the epithet is erased, its 'proper' character established. At the occasion, of course, it was only the spectators with access to these grounds – and thereby qualified as 'learned' – who could enjoy the 'proper' significance of the horns of Oceanus. Others may have understood something else (cuckoldry?), perceived a 'strange', 'original' feature, or even not have distinguished the horns at all (as in the account given below).

The importance of the passage from *Georgics* 4, which is cited again in Jonson's next note i (p. 171), goes beyond the particular feature 'horned'. A description of the cave of Ocean, which David Quint has identified as the model for 'Renaissance ... depictions of the source' (Quint, *Origin and Originality*, p. 32), it provides not only a source for the figure of Ocean, father of rivers, but also an image for what the notes and the references perform – the return to source/origin/ground/father. Its presence is an index of a will to ground both this particular text-performance, and the form it inaugurates – the Jonsonian court masque – which was as yet without firm generic boundaries.[30] This doubles the quest, which is the motive of the masque's narrative, for the 'new name' (p. 177) of 'BRITANIA':

---

[28] Natalis Comes, *Mythologiae* (Venice, 1567), reprinted in *The Renaissance and the Gods* (New York and London: Garland, 1976), fo. 238v.

[29] Virgil, *Symbolarum libri XVII*, edited by J. Pontanus, col. 593.

[30] See *H&S*, vol. 10, p. 450; Enid Welsford, *The Court Masque* (Cambridge University Press, 1927), pp. 183–6.

With that great name BRITANIA, this blest Isle
Hath wonne her ancient dignitie, and stile,
A world, divided from the world . . .

(ibid.)

The last line translates a line from Virgil's *Eclogue* 1 (line 66), which
Jonson had already used in *The King's Entertainment* and which was
destined to become a 'commonplace of English political discourse' by
1628.[31] Here it serves to ground in ancient origins the 'new name' of
Britain thereby erasing its 'new' character, just as the earlier citations
serve to ground the epithet 'horned' in ancient origins. With this ancient
'new name' is grounded too the authority of the new king represented as
the 'sunne' of this world of Britain, whose 'State' is placed as the point of
proper perception (p. 171) – a proper perception which is in turn
supplied by the textual grounds of the published version.

A measure of the gap between this proper perception and the percep-
tions of particular spectators is provided by a version of the masque in a
letter from Dudley Carleton to Sir Ralph Winwood.

> At night we had the Queen's Maske in the Banqueting-House, or rather her
> Pageant. There was a great Engine at the lower end of the Room, which had
> Motion, and in it were the images of Sea-Horses with other terrible Fishes,
> which were ridden by Moors: The Indecorum was, that there was all Fish and
> no water. (As quoted in *H&S*, vol. 10, pp. 448–9)

Here there is no trace either of the Tritons or of Oceanus and Niger, let
alone any of the specific differentiating features mentioned by Jonson,
such as the 'desinent parts' of the Tritons, or the horns of Oceanus,
which appear not to have been perceived at all. Though Carleton was
an educated man, who may have been at Westminster School at the
same time as Jonson and who went on to Oxford, his version is not
informed by the textual grounds through which the spectacle is mediated in Jonson's version. Without these grounds the spectacle loses the
shape they give it, disappears to become something other in the representation of a spectator. For Jonson such re-presentations amounted
to what he calls, in a brief introduction to the published version of this
first masque, the '*oblivion*' of 'Ignorance' (*H&S*, vol. 7, p. 169).

His declared object in publishing is 'to redeeme' 'the *spirit*' of the

---

[31] Patterson, *Pastoral and Ideology*, p. 149 (for other examples, see her note 22). The line runs, 'et
penitus toto divisos orbe Britannos' (Fairclough translates: 'and the Britains wholly sundered
from the world'). The earlier citation in *The King's Entertainment* is in *H&S*, vol. 7, p. 84. See also
the first line of the inscription in the 1613 portrait of James by Crispin van de Passe, reproduced
in Riggs, *Ben Jonson*, p. 166.

spectacle from such oblivion, which he describes as one of 'two common evills', the other being the *'censure'* of Envy. This redemptory gesture is done '(i)n dutie ... to that Maiestie, who gave (the spectacle) ... authoritie and grace; and, (who) ... deserves eminent celebration' (ibid.). Origin and end of the occasional spectacle, royal authority is in turn upheld – advertised as well as supported – by the published version, which supplies its textual grounds. The two forms of authority are implied to ground each other, as they are in the Virgilian scenes in *Poetaster.* The enemies are the same too: in the play, the 'common evils' of ignorance and envy, embodied in 'common men' (v.i.103), oppose both the authors within it, especially Horace and Virgil, and 'the author' of it. As here too, these evils are associated with the universe of material and temporal contingency, which is the universe of the ignorant multitude, the body and occasional performance. In the play, the opposition of this universe to the universe of truth and transcendence, the secret and sacred place where the authority of the learned poet meets with the authority of the absolute monarch, is dramatised by the interruption of the scene of Virgil's reading, a moment which prefigures, if in inverted form, the structural pivot of the masque – the turn from anti-masque to main masque. Though this turn is not made in the first masque, the introduction which frames and mediates the published version is informed by the structure of oppositional worlds the turn will articulate. This suggests how, as we shall now see, the masques come to stage the exclusion of those they identify as their own enemies as well as, more generally, the enemies of learned poetic discourse.

In *Oberon, The Fairy Prince* (H&S, vol. 7, pp. 337–56), this exclusion is represented expressly in relation to 'the most learned of poets, *Virgil'*, in a note on the figure of Silenus, a figure who is central to the masque as he is to *Eclogue* 6, the principal textual 'place' (Jonson's word) on which the masque is grounded (p. 341, note c, p. 342, note d). Following a note on the 'nature of the *Satyres'* (p. 343, note b), whose light sports make up the anti-masque, the note on Silenus glosses, specifically, the command '(c)haster language' (line 50) with which he curtails the satyrs' mild ribaldry before announcing the '(s)olemne' (line 51) nature of the occasion – an anticipation of the turn from anti-masque to main masque, when the satyrs will be silenced and excluded, which is signalled in the '(b)ut' with which the note begins.

c But in the *Silenes,* was nothing of this petulance, and lightnesse; but on the contrarie, all gravitie, and profound knowledge, of most secret mysteries.

Insomuch as the most learned of Poets, *Virgil*, when he would write a Poeme of the beginnings, and hidden nature of things, with other great Antiquities, attributed the parts of disputing them, to *Silenus*, rather then any other. Which whosoever thinkes to bee easily, or by chance, done by the most prudent writer, will easily betray his own ignorance, or folly. To this see the testimonies of *Plato*, *Synesius, Herodotus, Strabo, Philostratus, Tertullian, etc.*

As Robert Evans points out, this note 'praise(s) Virgil as the most learned of poets even as it demonstrates Jonson's own erudition'.[32] More specifically, it echoes J. C. Scaliger's praise of Virgil, which is quoted by Pontanus in his notes to *Eclogue* 6: citing Plato and Aelian, Scaliger asserts that the representation of Silenus as a godlike prophet of Nature demonstrates Virgil's supreme and divine understanding.[33] In both places the notes do the work of what Jonson calls 'testimonies', a word with a juridical as well as religious register, which underscores their function as guarantors at once of the authority of Virgilian – and Jonsonian – practice, and of the 'ignorance, or folly' of those who fail to recognise this authority and who are consequently excluded.[34]

More generally, the note reproduces the inner/outer hermeneutic and epistemological structure I discussed earlier, in particular in relation to representations of Virgil as natural philosopher, a structure in which the truth of the text and the truth of nature are located in a 'hidden' place within.[35] Here, more specifically, the 'hidden nature of things' is associated with their 'beginnings', just as the truth of the text is identified with its 'springs' (sources) in the published versions of Jonson's masques including this one. Indeed, in so far as it supplies the Virgilian ground of the Jonsonian text as well as 'testimonies' to this Virgilian ground, the note produces for the Jonsonian text the structure it represents in relation to the Virgilian.

---

[32] Robert C. Evans, *Ben Jonson and the Poetics of Patronage* (Lewisburg: Bucknell University Press; London and Toronto: Associated University Presses, 1989), p. 234.

[33] Virgil, *Symbolarum libri XVII*, edited by J. Pontanus, col. 130. The quotation closes with the affirmation '*Quo enim quis doctior est, eo maiorem in eius scriptis deprehendit eruditionem.*' ('Indeed, the more learning a man has himself, the more he appreciates the erudition of Virgil.' (F. M. Padelford, *Select Translations from Scaliger's Poetics*, Yale Studies in English 26 (New York: Henry Holt and Co., 1905), p. 30)). Jonson's comment on readers who betray their ignorance and folly is the logical obverse of this affirmation.

[34] It is not clear where Jonson found the five 'testimonies' after Plato, perhaps in a dictionary providing references only, since as Herford and Simpson indicate, two of them (Herodotus and Philostratus) are not appropriate (*H&S*, vol. 10, p. 526). Their inappropriateness underscores the primarily rhetorical and ideological function of these proper names.

[35] See chapter 3, pp. 78–9; compare in particular Jonson's use of 'by chance' with the comment by the figure of Praetextatus in the *Saturnalia* that Virgil's learning might appear mere accident (quoted at the head of chapter 3).

Within the masque, the intertextual relation to the Virgilian ground is also signalled, in a different mode, by the figure of Echo. For the first words of the masque are the names of Virgil's satyrs, Chromis and Mnasyllos, called by an unnamed Satyre, who then sounds his cornet, thinks he is *'answer'd, but (is) deceived by the Echo'* (p. 341), a figure he recognises when he tries again (p. 342). Dramatically redundant, the repeated figure of Echo acknowledges, in poetic mode, the intertextual relation to the Virgilian 'place'. And the figure may itself be an echo of this textual place, though not of its opening scene. For the songs sung by Silenus in *Eclogue* 6 are described as 'the songs that of old Phoebus rehearsed, while happy Eurotas listened and bade his laurels learn by heart ... The re-echoing valleys fling them again to the stars.'[36] Here poetic creation – the origins of poetic utterance, including its own – becomes an object, like and with the origins of the universe, in a poem which is self-conscious in its echoes, as are all the eclogues.[37] It is a closing turn within a complex series of frames which tends infinitely to defer origin. In Jonson's text, the self-reflexivity of the figure of Echo, with its blurring of the intertextual boundary, the relation between inside and outside, self and other, which Jonson underscores by recalling the figure's relation to narcissism or 'selfe-love' (p. 342), is contained by the frame 'outside' of the notes in the published version. For, as in the other texts we have looked at, these notes function as a 'place' where origin and meaning are grounded, and the intertextual relationship – the relation between inside and outside, self and other – defined and stabilised as a relationship of legitimisation. With the change of 'place', that is, the mode of the intertextual relation changes, from a fusional, poetic mode to a discriminatory, juridical mode – the mode of the commentator.

In the long note quoted above, it is specifically the use of the figure of Silenus that is grounded in, and legitimated by Virgilian practice. Many years ago Stephen Orgel suggested that, in relation to the form of the masque, Silenus was a 'new sort of figure' inasmuch as he 'compre-

---

[36] 'omnia quae Phoebo quondam meditante beatus / audiit Eurotas iussitque ediscere laurus, / ille canit (pulsae referunt ad sidera valles)' (*Eclogue* 6, lines 82–4; I quote Fairclough's translation).

[37] Pontanus quotes the Servian gloss that Virgil acknowledges his general debt to Theocritus in the first line, though, as Coleman points out, *Eclogue* 6 as a whole is 'un-Theocritean'. See Virgil, *Symbolarum libri XVII*, edited by J. Pontanus, col. 124, and *Vergil: Eclogues*, edited by Coleman, p. 175. The description of the echoing valleys itself recalls Lucretius, as Pontanus notes (ibid., col. 144). Annabel Patterson has shown that such literary imitation is only one of the aims of the *Eclogues*; the political and ideological aims she foregrounds are of course relevant to Jonson's masque, which like Virgil's *Eclogues*, negotiates relations of, and with, structures of political power, even as it echoes textual models. Patterson, *Pastoral and Ideology, passim*.

hends' both parts – anti-masque and main masque (Orgel, *The Jonsonian Masque*, p. 84). Jonson's own notes, however, assert rather the non-innovatory character of this double role. For, while the note on Silenus grounds the main masque in the longer, main part of *Eclogue* 6, which comprises the songs of Silenus (lines 26-86), the first three notes (pp. 341–2) ground the anti-masque of satyrs in the scene with which, after an introductory frame (lines 1–12), the eclogue begins – the playful teasing of Silenus by the satyrs Chromis and Mnasyllos with the nymph Aegle (lines 13–26). The Virgilian 'place' thus serves to ground at once the double role of Silenus and the bi-partite structure of the form which this figure comprehends.

Within this likeness, however, there are significant differences between the two figures of Silenus. For, although Jonson describes the satyrs as the 'Play-fellowes' of Silenus (p. 341, note ab), his Silenus does not participate in their sports, exercising rather only the role mentioned later of 'ovr-seer [*sic*], or governour' to the satyrs (p. 342, note a), controlling both their language (as in the command quoted above) and their actions (he interrupts and ends their '*antique dance*' (p. 351)). Virgil's Silenus, on the other hand, participates in the satyrs' sports and even uses mild ribaldry such as Jonson's satyrs use and Jonson's Silenus curtails.[38] In this curtailment there may indeed be a trace of a will, at the intertextual level, to curtail the Virgilian model – modest as Servius says (see note 38), but perhaps not sufficiently modest for Jonson's idea of Virgil, chaste in language as in life.[39]

These differences point up how the bi-partite structure of the Virgilian text becomes, in the masque, a structure of oppositional worlds with their respective proper forms. This is underscored when Jonson's Silenus describes the palace of Oberon (Prince Henry) as an ideal 'other' world – a description which may owe something to Aelian's claim, quoted by Pontanus, that the songs of Silenus told of such worlds:[40] 'Do's not his *Palace* show / Like another Skie of lights?' (p. 346, lines 143–4). The absolute difference of this world to the world of the satyrs is

---

[38] Promising the satyrs the songs they request Virgil's Silenus declares that Aegle will have another kind of reward ('huic aliud mercedis erit' (line 26)), which Servius glosses as a veiled threat of sexual violation ('stuprum'), expressed modestly by Virgil ('verecunde dixit Virgilius'). Virgil, *Opera*, vol. 1, fo. 33r. In the exchange curtailed by Jonson's Silenus the satyrs precisely fantasise about sexual promiscuity with nymphs (p. 343, lines 45–8).

[39] See chapter 5, where I shall point out other examples of this will to curtail Virgilian practice, to make it 'more chaste'.

[40] Virgil, *Symbolarum libri XVII*, edited by J. Pontanus, col. 130. This also allows Jonson to accommodate within the frame of the Virgilian eclogue the native traditions of 'faery' land, which were quite other to the world of the Virgilian eclogue, but which Henry preferred.

subsequently underscored by Silenus in a dismissal of the satyrs, which prefaces a speech in praise of James – a speech which reworks the songs of Virgil's Silenus on the creation of the world and 'Saturn's reign' (*Eclogue* 6, line 41), as a song of perpetual re-creation, a renewal which is also a return to an absolute moment 'of gold' (p. 353, line 351).

> He is above your reach; and neither doth,
> Nor can he thinke, within a *Satyres* tooth:
> Before his presence, you must fall, or flie.
> He is the matter of vertue, and plac'd high.
>
> (pp. 352–3, lines 338–41)

There is no such dismissal by Virgil's Silenus who, on the contrary, addresses his songs implicitly to the satyrs throughout. That the relation between the two parts of the Virgilian model has acquired an opposi-tional and mutually exclusive character in the masque is underscored by the spatial metaphors here, which turn the opposition into a hierarchy between 'high' and 'low'. That this is a hierarchy of formal modes as well as of worlds is pointed up by a Sylvane, who, immediately before the dismissal by Silenus, anticipates its silencing and exclusion of the satyrs.

> Give place, and silence; you were rude too late:
> This is a night of greatnesse, and of state;
> *Not to be mixt with light and skipping sport.*
>
> (p. 352, lines 319–20; my emphasis)

Echoing Silenus's earlier chastisement of the satyrs' language, these lines epitomise the antithetical and mutually exclusive relation of the two worlds of the masque and of the formal modes proper to each. 'Com-prehended' here in the double figure of Silenus – in the anti-masque the satyrs' overseer, and in the main masque celebrator of the 'most secret mysteries' of absolute Majesty – these two worlds are comprehended in *Poetaster* by the paired authorial figures, Horace and Virgil.[41] For, while Virgil inhabits a 'main masque' universe of truth, unity and harmony 'above', Horace addresses and engages with – in order to regulate – the anti-masque universe of ignorance, folly and malice 'below'. It is to this universe 'below' that, in the note on Silenus with which we began, those who fail to understand Virgil's – and Jonson's – learned poetic discourse

---

[41] For an explicit evocation of Virgil and Horace as figures for different authorial selves/voices see the quotation at the head of chapter 5. Wesley Trimpi suggests the figure of Silenus-Socrates is recalled in Jonson's self-representations in later love lyrics. Wesley Trimpi, *Ben Jonson's Poems. A Study of the Plain Style* (Stanford University Press, 1962), pp. 216–18.

are said to be cast by 'their own ignorance or folly'. The exclusion which is performed by the turn from anti-masque to main masque thus mirrors the exclusion which is at once the condition of its 'proper' reception and an effect of its learned character.

This repetition is more overt still in *Poetaster*, in which the text Virgil reads is turned to mirror the structure of oppositional worlds which informs both the play and representations of it and its author. There is a similarly overt repetition in the framing introduction to the published version of *The Masque of Queens* (1609), which here takes the form of prefatory letters addressed to Queen Anne and Prince Henry (*H&S*, vol. 7, pp. 279–81). Most straightforwardly, Jonson closes the second of these by styling himself 'the most hearty Celebrater' of the Prince's 'Vertues', and so aligns himself, as author of the masque, with the authors, including Virgil, who are represented within it as the lower columns of the House of Fame, 'supporters' of the upper columns, the '*Heroes*, which those Poets had celebrated' (p. 313). This alignment is then reiterated, within the description, by the representation of himself as 'maker' of the figure of Bel-Anna for Queen Anne (pp. 312–13), the twelfth and last of the queens celebrated through the ages, who include the figure of Camilla as 'celebrated by Virgil' (p. 306). Finally, in the letter to Henry, the relation of the Prince to men of letters in general and to Jonson in particular is projected as a return – 'as heretofore' – to an ideal relation of mutual support, a relation which is exemplified by the relation of Augustus to 'learned heads' in general and to Virgil in particular in *Poetaster*. As an instance of this relation, a double reward is anticipated for the 'worke' of supplying '*authorities*' which Jonson has done for the published text,

your excellent understanding will not only justefie mee to your owne knowl-edge, but decline the stiffnesse of others originall Ignorance, allready armed to censure. (p. 281)

Jonson here represents hostile reception of his masque in the same terms as he represents both the enemies of the first published masque (though 'censure' is now an attribute not of 'Envy' but of 'Ignorance'), and the enemies of Virgil/Horace and 'the author' in *Poetaster*. More immediate-ly, his representation recalls the enemies represented within the masque as the anti-masque of witches, classified together as 'the opposites to good *Fame*' (p. 282), and individually as personifications of '*Ignorance, Suspicion, Credulity*, &c.' (ibid.), the first to be summoned by their leader, the Dame, being 'stupide *Ignorance*' (p. 287), since, as a note explains, 'the opposition to all *vertue* begins out of *Ignorance*' (p. 287, note o). To anticipate hostile reception of the learned published text as a repetition of the opposition the masque stages is pre-emptively to invalidate such reception, in short, to censor 'censure'.[42] As we shall see, *Poetaster* deploys similar pre-emptive textual strategies, which aspire to censor censure by placing 'the author', like and with Virgil/Horace, beyond the hostile, and dangerous criticism of those it classes as 'ignorant' and 'malicious' 'common men'.

The banishment of Ignorance which the masque stages is, in addition, linked to its reception as occasional spectacle (pp. 286–7). For the Dame's summoning of her 'drowsy Servant, stupide *Ignorance*' (p. 287, line 117) follows a short digression in which Jonson criticises, as inappropriate, explanatory explicitness such as Daniel uses in his spectacles.[43] To be less explicit, comments Jonson, requires a writer 'to trust' 'to the capacity of the *Spectator*', who is, in turn, expected to bring to such spectacles 'quick eares, and not those sluggish ones of Porters and Mechanicks'. The proximity of the virtual synonyms 'drowsy' and 'sluggish' aligns the universe of the anti-masque with the universe of 'common men' without the capacity to understand what they are shown. The exclusion the masque stages is thus linked with the effect of its learned character at the occasional performance as well as with the anticipated opposition to the published version.

The description of the anti-masque, which is named as such for the first time here (p. 282), characterises the universe represented by the witches as 'of strangenesse' (ibid.). This characteristic property is underscored by the use of the epithet 'strange' to qualify the witches' gestures (p. 283), their music and their dance (p. 301). Used normatively elsewhere, as we have seen, to mark the boundary of 'proper'/'improper' forms, the use of the word 'strange' here identifies improper, 'contrary' forms as the forms proper to the anti-masque. Specifically, its strangeness is translated, first, into the gestural code, as 'multiplicity of Gesture' (p. 282), which, in the dance, becomes multiple, back-to-front ('praeposterous'), 'contrary' forms (p. 301); second, into the vestimentary code, as 'all differently attir'd' (p. 283); third, into the aural code, as both 'hollow

---

[42] My analyses of Jonson's textual strategies here and in the next chapter will bear out Richard Burt's finely made argument for the complexities of Jonson's case with regard to the issues of censorship. Richard Burt, *Licensed by Authority. Ben Jonson and the Discourses of Censorship* (Ithaca and London: Cornell University Press, 1993).

[43] See *H&S*, vol. 10, p. 501 and Golberg, *James I*, p. 58; Jonson makes virtually the same criticism of Dekker in *The King's Entertainment* (*H&S*, vol. 7, p. 91).

and infernall' (p. 283) 'strange and sodayne' (p. 301) music, and 'confused noyse', which the witches make as they 'come from Hell' (pp. 282–3). This aural figure in particular represents, as indifferentiation, the effect of the multiple, particular differentiations of this universe 'of strangenesse'. It is an effect that characterises too the universe of the satirical comedies, which the later anti-masques will overtly resemble. For the universe of the satirical comedies is similarly a universe of 'strange', multiple, particular differentiations, every man in his humour (and the anti-masque figures in *Hymenaei* are expressly identified with the humours, as we shall see). This is translated not only into multiple plots and particularised characters, but into a multitude of particular languages, from the 'babble' of 'idiolects' in *Every Man In*, to the 'multiple vernaculars' of the vertiginously crowded universe of *Bartholomew Fair*.[44] Not so much 'a masque for the people' (Womack, *Ben Jonson*, p. 159) as a large scale anti-masque for the learned reader, *Bartholomew Fair* describes its universe of multiple vernaculars – the universe of London urban life – as 'full of noise' ('The Induction', line 79) and associates it with the Virgilian underworld, as the masque associates the 'confused noise' of its anti-masque of witches with hell.[45] The same association – of the multiple differentiations of London urban life with the Virgilian underworld – is made in *Every Man In*, as we shall see later, and, still more explicitly, in the last of the epigrams, which, in addition, uses the same aural figure – of confused noise – to characterise the effect of indifferentiation produced by multiple particular differences, the effect, we might say, of the babble of Babel, 'qui ressemble (confusément) au mot hebreu qui veut dire "confusion"'.[46]

To represent these universes of multiple, particular differences as confused noise is to confirm their place in and as an 'underworld', below the normative, 'proper' order, which, indeed, as contrary or negation,

---

[44] Womack, *Ben Jonson*, p. 80; Patricia Parker, *Literary Fat Ladies: Rhetoric, Gender, Property* (London and New York: Methuen, 1987), p. 25.

[45] See Clayton, '"Tempests, and such like Drolleries"', pp. 272, 277, 292, and Tudeau-Clayton, The Topography and Politics of Self-Knowledge in *Bartholomew Fair*.

[46] Geoffrey Bennington and Jacques Derrida, *Jacques Derrida* (Tours: Seuil, 1991), p. 163. Compare Quint on Milton's Satan: 'Babel and its implications are already suggested in the description of Satan's heavenly dwelling ... This Babelic confusion, moreover, has a literary corollary, and Satan becomes the figure of the autonomous, original author' (Quint, *Origin and Originality*, pp. 210, 211). He goes on to point out how Milton's affirmation of 'his unique authority and his authorial uniqueness' (p. 214) tends to align him with his Satan. It is precisely the strange – and diabolic – character of a universe of individual 'uniqueness' and originality that the anti-masque of witches represents. This association of the diabolic with original difference will return in *The Tempest*, as we shall see.

they serve to uphold.[47] It is as such a normative proper order – a main
masque universe – that Virgil and his circle are placed in *Poetaster*.
Specifically, the interruption of Virgil's reading by 'noise' (v.iii.12) from
one of the 'common men' (v.i.103) outside anticipates, in inverted form,
the turn from anti-masque to main masque. Indeed, the character from
the satirical comedy who interrupts Virgil is identified by the passage
Virgil reads with an anti-masque figure, the monster Fame.

The opposition represented as the noise of Lupus/the monster Fame
is identified as a threat not only to the 'proper' order Virgil and his circle
represent, but also to the order of the state. Similarly, the opposition of
the anti-masque of witches is identified as a threat to the 'soft peace' (p.
288) of the new political order under James as well as to the order of the
masque. 'Let us disturbe it, then' the Dame urges, referring to the soft
peace,

> and blast the light;
> Mixe Hell, with Heaven; and make Nature fight
> Within her selfe; loose the whole henge of Things;
> And cause the Endes runne back into theyr Springs,
>
> (p. 289, lines 146–9)

Here the new political order is aligned with the natural and both with
the masque's hierarchical structure of oppositional worlds – hell and
heaven – which the Dame seeks to confuse by 'mixing'. To mix these
worlds is thus to undo a system of differentiation which is at once
'proper' and natural, and which implies the order of the state. It is a
system in contrast to, and opposed by the confused noise of multiple
particular differentiations which it nevertheless contains by naming it as
its 'contrary', or negation. The binary structure of the masque thus
works at once to include and exclude opposition, to itself as well as to the
state, by representing such opposition – such difference – as a negation
of the proper and natural order.[48] The implication of generic modes in

[47] The term 'underworld' has been used casually by critics, especially of the world of Smithfield in
Bartholomew Fair. See, for example, Thomas Cartelli, '*Bartholomew Fair* as Urban Arcadia: Jonson
Responds to Shakespeare', *Renaissance Drama* 14 (1983), p. 156; Jonathan Haynes, 'Festivity and
the Dramatic Economy of *Bartholomew Fair*', in Bloom, ed., *Ben Jonson*, pp. 145–6. The use of the
term to designate urban, especially urban criminal life, is, however, of relatively recent origin –
the beginning of the twentieth century according to the *OED*. That such a use has a normative
ideological function, like Jonson's reiterated mapping of the classical topography over contemporary urban life, which may indeed have contributed to its emergence, is indicated by the
OED's relevant definition: 'A sphere or region lying or considered to lie *below the ordinary one*.
Hence also (fig.), a lower, or the lowest stratum of society' (4a; my emphasis). See further,
Tudeau-Clayton, 'The Topography and Politics of Self-Knowledge in *Bartholomew Fair*'.
[48] Womack pertinently uses the term 'syntax' of the binary structure of the masque (Womack, *Ben
Jonson*, p. 97), without however considering the violence of the suppression it articulates, which is

this structure raises the stakes of the imperative to generic decorum – overt in *Oberon* as we have seen – and consequently the stakes of the Shakespearean play which is characterised and criticised by Jonson (in *Bartholomew Fair*) as a monstrous hybrid, and which explicitly interrogates the binary structure of the Jonsonian masque – *The Tempest*.

This interrogation is staged overtly at two parallel moments of disruption from '*confused noise*' (*The Tempest*, I.i.59; IV.i.138). The second of these is particularly important here as the confused noise is further qualified in terms which echo Jonson's description of the witches' music, as '*strange*' and '*hollow*' (IV.i.138(SD)). Moreover, the noise disturbs a formal celebration of noble persons, performs, that is, the disturbance threatened by the witches, although in so far as the disturbed masque celebrates, specifically, a betrothal, intertextually linked to the wedlock of Dido and Aeneas, the parallel is rather with *Hymenaei*. Finally, the disturbance is brought about by a recognisable anti-masque figure, described, if not as a witch, then as a 'deformed'[49] 'disproportioned' (V.i.290) son of a witch, while his 'confederates' (IV.i.140), a jester and butler, are 'low-life' figures belonging to the universe of satirical comedy, like the figure in the opening scene who is associated with the first disruption of confused noise and who is actually called a 'noise-maker' (I.i.43-4) – the Boatswain.

As we shall see, *The Tempest* aligns its own performance with its 'noise-makers' and the contestatory thrust of their 'noise'. Of particular interest here, because it specifically contrasts with *The Masque of Queens*, is the attribution to Prospero, after his masque's disruption, of a commonplace speech (derived principally from Ovid's Medea), which evokes 'powers of troubling *Nature*' (p. 289, note q) and which in *The Masque of Queens* is spoken by Jonson's Dame (pp. 295–6).[50] For in both speeches the analogy between socio-political disorder and disorder in the natural world (commonplace in the early modern world, though Virgilian rather than Ovidian) is reiterated: the Dame claims 'we have set the

a violence we have seen articulated by other 'proper' systems of representation in chapter 2. It is, we might add, the violence of any total, and totalising ideological system, which invalidates – silences and excludes – difference and opposition by representing it as contrary, or negation.

49 See the 'Names of the Actors', in *The Tempest*, edited by Kermode, p. 2.

50 The specific relation is not mentioned in editions of *The Tempest* I have looked at. The likeness is both in the examples of magical powers/acts and in the incantatory, anaphoric structure of the speeches. While Jonson acknowledges his debt to Ovid (p. 294), critics have made the acknowledgement for Shakespeare; see Kermode's Appendix D. In his discussion of Prospero's speech, Bate includes Jonson's Dame's speech in his list of English Renaissance imitations of the Ovidian model without examining more specific connections between the two. (Bate, *Shakespeare and Ovid*, pp. 249–54.)

Elements at warres' (p. 295, line 228), and Prospero, evoking specifically, as we shall see, the eponymous performed tempest, declares he has 'set roaring war' (v.i.44) between earth and sea.[51] But while Jonson mobilises the analogy to underwrite the order of the absolute state, and to endorse a policy of repression, which the turn to the main masque stages, Shakespeare aligns the performed tempest (and *The Tempest*) with this figure of dis-order. Staging an interrogation of the main masque universe by the anti-masque universe the play indeed goes beyond this interrogation to evoke a radical 'noise' or otherness – a radical *negativity* – within nature, history and the human subject, which resists containment as negation within the binary structures of symbolic forms – whether of the masque or, more generally, of language – and which, consequently, cannot be mastered.[52]

This resistance of 'original difference' manifests itself at the level of the intertextual relation to Virgil, which is an explicitly contestatory relation, emblematised in the signed figure of the 'roaring' (noise-making) of the 'performed tempest' which seemed to make Neptune's 'dread trident shake' (1.ii.194, 204, 206). In contrast, the intertextual relation of *The Masque of Queens* to Virgil is a relation of likeness, and of legitimation in likeness, as in the other masques we have looked at. This is advertised again in the dense notes surrounding the published version, which again draw on Virgil as 'testemonye' (p. 293, note 11) (see also p. 295, note c). The likeness to Virgil is, however, advertised more overtly here, on the one hand, by Jonson's alignment of himself as author with the poets depicted on the House of Fame, including Virgil, whose 'support' of Aeneas/Augustus is architecturally figured, and, on the other, by his absolute identification of one of his queens 'Camilla; Queene of the Volscians' with the Virgilian model (pp. 306-7). For his 'description' of this figure consists simply in a brief location of the Virgilian context, a quotation (*Aeneid* 7, lines 803-11), and a summary of the next six lines. The only additions are comments which characterise the Virgilian lines as absolute perfection, to which, precisely, no addition can be made:

nothing can bee imagin'd more exquisite, or more honoring the person they describe. (p. 306)

---

[51] See further chapter 6, pp. 224-5. Ovid's Medea does not use the analogy.

[52] Though conscious of a possible strain of anachrony I draw here on the (Hegelian) distinction, as elaborated in the work of Julia Kristeva, between the notion of negation – the logical ground of the symbolic order of language which it therefore upholds – and negativity, which is other to – and disruptive of – the symbolic.

All which if the *Poet* created out of himselfe, without *Nature*, he did but shew, how much so divine a Soule could exceede her. (p. 307)

A transcendent object of reverence and admiration, like the divine soul of the poet, the Virgilian lines are left untouched by the difference of the imitator, a sacred origin/ground untouched by originality, as both Virgil and his lines remain virtually untouched in *Poetaster*. Specifically, Virgil's lines are praised for 'honoring' the queen they describe, anticipating Jonson's later claim 'to honor' Queen Anne through the name and figure of Bel-Anna (p. 312). Virgil provides, that is, the absolute authorising ground and precedent for the advertised twofold aim of the masque – to uphold the prince and to celebrate the queen.

In *The Haddington Masque* (performed 1608), Virgil is again the absolute model for Jonson's naming and upholding of 'the prince' (here James). In a speech, which follows and closes the 'sports' of Cupid and his boys, Hymen addresses Venus,

> Looke on this state; and if you yet not know,
> What Crowne there shines, whose Scepter here doth grow;
> Thinke on thy lov'd ᵇÆNEAS, and what name,
> MARO, the golden trumpet of his fame,
> Gave him, read thou in this. A Prince,
>
> (*H&S*, vol. 7, p. 256, lines 212–16)

Note b makes explicit that the 'name' which the absolute – 'golden' – voice of Virgil bestows on Aeneas and which Jonson bestows on James is that of Prince in his ideal person:

b *Aeneas*, the sonne of *Venus*, *Virgil* makes through-out the most exquisit patterne of *Pietie*, *Justice*, *Prudence*, and all other Princely vertues, with whom (in way of that excellence) I conferre my Soveraigne, applying, in his description, his owne *word*, usurped of that *Poets*. *Parcere subiectis, et debellare superbos*.[53]

Reiterated in editions and translations of the early modern period, the interpretation of Aeneas as paradigm for the leader/prince tends to erase the differences of history, as does its specific application here to James, who is made 'the same' as Aeneas.[54] More significantly, recent

[53] The quotation, from Anchises' speech to Aeneas (*Aeneid* 6, line 853), which alludes to Augustus, is used by James himself to close *Basilikon Doron* (*H&S*, vol. 10, p. 489). As Jonson's note implicitly acknowledges, his use of Virgil collaborates with James's.

[54] Pontanus, citing Scaliger, comments: 'Virgilius ... prudentissimi, religiosissimi, fortissimi Principis ideam et simulacrum effingit.' (Virgil fashions the idea and image of a most prudent, pious and courageous prince). Virgil, *Symbolarum libri XVII*, edited by J. Pontanus, p. 6. The interpretation is rehearsed by both Douglas and Phaer; Sidney's version of it is cited in Gordon, *The Renaissance Imagination*, p. 311, note 6.

history is similarly turned as a repetition of the same, when Hymen goes on to relate how 'when ᶜTreason would have burst' the 'thred' of James's life, John Ramsay (the bridegroom),

> Oppos'd; and, by that act, to his name did bring
> The honor, to be ᵈ*Saver of his King.*
> This *King,* whose worth (if gods for vertue love)
> Should VENUS with the same affections move,
> As her ÆNEAS; and no lesse endeare
> Her love to his safetie, then when she did cheare,
> (After a tempest) long afflicted *Troy,*
> Upon the *Lybian* shore; and brought them joy.

Identified in note c as 'that monstrous conspiracie of *E. Gowrie*', the complexities of recent history are reduced to an anti-masque/main masque structure, with Gowrie as the monstrous anti-masque figure, whose conspiracy the Virgilian figure of the tempest serves to represent as a disturbance of the 'natural order' (like the disturbance of the witches).[55] Aligned with nature as an analogous binary structure, history becomes a repetition of the same, which, like and with nature, under-writes the political order under James.[56] In (perhaps self-conscious) contrast, *The Tempest* foregrounds rather the differences of history, in particular the difference history has made to the Virgilian topography of 'the *Lybian* shore': 'This Tunis, sir, *was* Carthage' (II.i.80; emphasis mine).[57] It foregrounds too the absolute (in)difference of nature, most overtly, of course, through the Boatswain's, 'What cares these roarers for the name of king?' (I.i.16–17), which dismantles the Virgilian analogy between natural and political orders and invalidates its use to ground political authority. More generally, the play points up the limits of the power of 'the name' to control and master, again perhaps with con-scious reference to Jonson. For, as Anne Barton has remarked, the word

---

[55] For the complex circumstances of the killing of the Earl of Gowrie and his brother by John Ramsay, see 'Ruthven, John, third Earl of Gowrie', *DNB*, vol. 17, pp. 504–9; and for a discussion of the exemplary status of representations of Gowrie as monstrous, unnatural traitor, see Mullaney, *The Place of the Stage*, pp. 116–17.

[56] Jonson elsewhere treats history as repetition, for example, in his lines on Drayton's *Baron's Warres* (1627): 'in those, dost thou instruct these times, / That Rebells actions, are but valiant Crimes!' (*H&S*, vol. 8, p. 397, lines 43–4). Stephen Greenblatt touches expertly on this view of history as morally instructive repetition, which he calls 'the culturally dominant notion', citing Ralegh's *History.* Stephen Greenblatt, *Renaissance Self-Fashioning: From More to Shakespeare* (University of Chicago Press, 1980), pp. 201, 292.

[57] As Michael Srigley points out, Gonzalo reproduces contemporary understanding of the 'exact location of Carthage', and is not, as Kermode suggests, making a mistake. Michael Srigley, *Images of Regeneration: A Study of Shakespeare's 'The Tempest' and its Cultural Background*, Studia Anglistica Upsaliensia 58 (University of Uppsala Press, 1985), p. 53.

'name' has something of a 'talismanic' value in Jonson's work,[58] and nowhere more so than in these masques – *The Masque of Queens* and *The Haddington Masque* – which advertise the power of the name and the namer as much as the power of those named – a naming power which is exemplified as it is figured by the absolute 'golden trumpet' of Virgil.

Analogy is still more important in the first of the marriage masques, *Hymenaei* (performed and published 1606), which, as D. J. Gordon has shown, is about the divine principle of Union realised in analogous 'bodies': the universe, the microcosm of man, the institution of marriage, in particular, the marriages of James to Anne, and the Earl of Essex to Lady Frances Howard, and the body politic, in particular, the union of England and Scotland.[59] The last analogical level is foregrounded in a note to what is called '*the first* Masque, *of eight men*' (*H&S*, vol. 7, p. 213), which belongs generically and functionally to what will be named as the anti-masque in *The Masque of Queens*. For the eight men articulate in gesture the threat – to '*disturbe the Ceremonies*' (ibid.) – which the witches will articulate verbally. That their opposition is likewise the opposition of contraries is, again, signalled in the aural code, the music with which they enter being described as '*contentious*' (ibid.), which defines a generic mode at once in opposition to, and the opposite of the 'true musique' of Union which Hymen has just celebrated (pp. 212–3 (line 102)). This function, as contrary, is underscored by the iteration of the negative morpheme 'dis' in the note alongside the description, which compares the '*dis*ease, or *dis*temperature' (my emphasis) 'caused … by some abounding *humor*, or perverse *affection*' in '*naturall bodies*' to what happens in '*politick bodies*' when 'by the difference, or prædominant will of what we (*metaphorically*) call *Humors*, and *Affections*, all things are troubled and confused' (p. 213, note a). Like the anti-masque of witches, the masque of eight men stages as confusion – indifferentiation – the effect of the will to particular difference, every man in his humour. The relation with the satirical comedies is indeed here particularly overt inasmuch as the eight men are identified with the humours and affections. Again too, their effect is represented as the opposite or negation of the proper, healthful and natural order in place, which, as negation, it serves to uphold. The containment of difference and opposition as

---

[58] Anne Barton, *Ben Jonson, Dramatist* (Cambridge University Press, 1984), p. 181.
[59] Gordon, *The Renaissance Imagination*, pp. 158–74. That the last level of analogy was perceived as the masque's principal object is indicated in a spectator's summary of Hymen's speech in celebration of Union as 'an apostrophe to the union of the kingdomes' (John Pory to Robert Coton, as quoted in *H&S*, vol. 10, p. 466).

negation is thus again staged – here specifically to include/exclude (and so to censure) not only opposition to the political order under James, but more particularly opposition to his politics of union for England and Scotland.

Anticipating the binary anti-masque/main masque structure, and especially the anti-masque of witches, this moment also recalls the moment in *Poetaster* when the scene of Virgil's reading is disturbed by the 'noise' of Asinius Lupus, a character who is associated by his name with the humours/affections of ignorance and malice and by the Virgilian passage with a monstrous anti-masque figure. For Virgil and his privileged circle are themselves represented in terms of ideal true love and unity, and the relation between Virgil and Augustus as an ideal 'marriage', and this ideal is figured in the Virgilian passage by the scene of Juno's presence at the union of Dido and Aeneas, a scene which Jonson draws on to ground his '*second* masque' (p. 217) of Juno in *Hymenaei*. The eight men are, moreover, condemned as 'prophane' in their attempt to disturb the ceremony of the masque (p. 214, line 137), just as the ceremony of Virgil's reading is said to have been 'prophan'd' (*Poetaster*, v.iii.165) by the disturbance brought about by Asinius Lupus.

More significant still are the intertextual relations to these two parallel moments in the Jonsonian corpus which are articulated by *The Tempest*, in particular by its own moments of disturbance from 'confused noise', especially the second (*The Tempest*, iv.i.138). For the confused noise here disrupts, specifically, a formal masque celebrating the union of a noble couple, which, as critics have noted, shares features with Jonson's second masque of Juno in *Hymenaei*, although the shared Virgilian ground in *Aeneid* 4 has not been recognised.[60] As in *Hymenaei* too, the moment of disruption in *The Tempest* is marked by the iteration of the negative morpheme 'dis', which, in the masque, is personified as 'dusky Dis' (iv.i.89): Prospero is 'distemper'd' (iv.i.145), he bids Ferdinand not to be 'disturb'd' (line 160), while the anti-masque figure, 'this thing of darkness' (v.i.275), associated, like Lupus in *Poetaster*, with materiality, mortality and malice, is later described as 'disproportion'd' (v.i.290). The dis-rupture and its effects are, in addition, qualified both in *Hymenaei* and *The Tempest* by the adjectives 'confused' and 'troubled', the second being used, specifically, of the effect of the disturbance on the

---

[60] The resemblance between the Jonsonian and Shakespearean masques has been considered sufficiently striking to be included by Bullough in his 'sources' for *The Tempest*. Geoffrey Bullough, *Narrative and Dramatic Sources of Shakespeare*, 8 vols. (London: Routledge and Kegan Paul; New York: Columbia University Press, 1975), vol. 8, pp. 263–5, 329–33. Bullough does not mention the parallel disruptions.

author(ity) figure: Hymen (who is identified with 'the poet' by the spectator quoted in note 59) *'troubled spake'* (p. 213), while Prospero remarks apologetically that his 'old brain is troubled' (*The Tempest*, IV.i.159).

In contrast with both Hymen and Prospero, Virgil in *Poetaster* is untroubled at the disturbance, though silent until the noise- and trouble-maker Lupus is gagged. The position Virgil then assumes is the position assumed by the figure of Reason in *Hymenaei*, who, summoned by Hymen to deal with the trouble and confusion of the disturbance, enters to judge and condemn the 'ignorance' (p. 214, line 136) of *'humorous earthlings'* (line 152) and to order control and containment, just as Virgil, placed by virtue of the exercise of his reason above the 'tartarous moods' of 'common men', judges those motivated by such moods. Prospero too has recourse to reason (v.i.26–8), but it is a recourse which issues not in judgement and control but in forgiveness and release: 'Go release them' (v.i.30). This issue is predicated on the recognition of a common human kind, defined as participation in 'passion': 'myself, / *One of their kind*, that relish all as sharply / Passion as they' (v.i.22–4; my emphasis). Jonson's Virgil, on the other hand, precisely does not 'relish ... passion' and is, therefore, not of a kind with 'common men', but, like the figure of 'Reason', placed 'above' the passions/moods which char-acterise them. He is thus in a position to judge, an absolute spectator and overseer, like and with the elite of 'learned heads' he addresses, who throughout the Jonsonian corpus but most emphatically in *Poetaster* are represented as a different and superior, yet normative, human kind on account of their knowledge and virtue as well as of their 'Language'. The different move made by *The Tempest* dis-allows the differentiating superiority of such a position – and the power it bestows – and calls for its renunciation in recognition of the 'dis' or 'confused noise within' as the defining human condition – its common ground. More specifically, in its interrogation of the form of the masque it dis-allows the contain-ment as negation of this confused noise – or radical negativity – within nature and history as well as within the human subject.

These differences are underscored by what follows the respective moments of disrupture. In *Poetaster*, Virgil, speaking with absolute monologic authority, brings the play to a close once his judgement has been given, while in *Hymenaei*, Reason, speaking with the same author-ity, proceeds, once the disturbers have been contained, to explain the 'mysticke sence' (p. 214) of the disturbed ceremony and to introduce and explain the 'second masque' (p. 217) of Juno, which is then closed by a

dance in the form of a round – a figure of totality and closure as well as
of perfection. In *The Tempest*, it is specifically a dance that is broken up by
the dis-rupture, which is not contained. Rather it tends to displace, as
the art of the past, the masque of Juno and the total and closed Virgilian
vision of nature it embodies. In short, the play exposes as 'baseless' (*The
Tempest*, IV.i.151) 'the authoritie of *Virg.*' (*H&S*, vol. 7, p. 211, note d),
which, in *Hymenaei*, as in the other masques we have looked at, is
invoked, in the dense notes surrounding the published version, as
testimony to the 'solide *learnings*' on which it is 'grounded' (p. 209).

Of the twelve citations which invoke this authority no less than eight
refer to lines from *Aeneid* 4. Mediated by the canonical Servian commentary in terms of ancient cultural practices, on the one hand, and in terms
of natural philosophy, on the other, these lines, especially those describing the scene of Juno's presence at the 'union' of Dido and Aeneas, are
cited in the two kinds of secondary texts that D. J. Gordon has shown
Jonson drew on for most of his learning: the mythographies of Giraldi
and Comes, especially their chapters on Juno, and antiquarian works on
ancient cultural practices, especially ancient marriage rituals, by Barnaby Brisson and Antoine Hotman.[61] Thus mediated, the Virgilian
scene carries a twofold 'mysticke sence' authorising Jonson's combination, which Gordon finds unhappy, of the secrets of ancient culture and
the secrets of nature.

The Virgilian scene is particularly prominent in the notes surrounding the description of Juno as figure of the air and as '[b]governesse of
marriage' (p. 217). Note b gives '*Dant signum prima et Tellus, et Pronuba
Juno*' (*Aeneid* 4, lines 166–7, as quoted by Jonson), which Gordon suggests is taken from Comes, who later explains 'Pronuba' in terms of Juno
as figure of the air.[62] It is in these terms too that one of the semantically
dense details of Juno's costume – her 'Fascia, *of severall-coloured silkes*' (p.
217) – is explained in another note taken from Comes, who draws on
Servius: 'After the manner of the antique *Bend*, the varied colours
implying the severall mutations of the *Ayre*, as showres, dewes ...
tempest ... the facultie of causing these being ascribed to her by *Virg.
Aeneid. lib. 4.*' (ibid., note r; *Aeneid* 4, lines 120, 122 are quoted). As the

[61] Gordon, *The Renaissance Imagination*, pp. 174–6, Appendix VI. For a more detailed discussion,
which includes minor disagreements with Gordon, see Clayton, '"Tempests, and such like
Drolleries"', pp. 187, 305.
[62] Gordon, *The Renaissance Imagination*, p. 286. Compare 'Hinc Pronuba ... quod aeris benignitas
omnia in lucem evocet' ('Hence the epithet 'Pronuba' ... because the benevolent influence of the
air 'enlightens all things') (Comes, *Mythologiae*, lib. 2, cap. IV, fo. 44r) with Jonson's description of
Juno's effect in descending, 'As she enlightened all the *ayre*!' (p. 217, line 235).

echo of Servius indicates, this is the Neoplatonic cosmology, or grammar of Nature, folded into the Virgilian texts through the canonical
commentaries, and, as we saw in chapter 3, at once reproduced and
'disputed' in the early modern world.[63] Indeed, one of the key texts that I
looked at in chapter three – the *Somnium Scipionis* by the canonical
authority Macrobius – is cited directly (not via secondary works)
throughout, from the first note on Juno as 'the *ayre*' (p. 216, note n).
Jonson's spectacle of Juno as the air with '*(a)bove her the region of fire . . . and*
JUPITER . . . (figuring the heaven) *brandishing his thunder*' (p. 217) in effect
translates into the form of a masque such mediations, as natural philosophy of the marital relation between Jupiter and Juno: 'Juno is called his
sister and wife, for she is air: . . . she is called wife because air is
subordinate to the sky.'[64]

This mediation, as natural philosophy, of the scene of Juno's presence
at the union of Dido and Aeneas is suggested again by the context in
which Virgil's lines are quoted for a second time. Towards the close,
Hymen, calling upon the dancers to retire, describes how 'thrice hath
JUNO [a]mixt her *ayre* / With *fire*, to summon your repayre' (p. 222), a
description '(a)lluding', as note a comments, to Virgil's lines (which are
quoted). Mediated as natural philosophy by the mythographers such as
Comes, who, following Servius, interprets 'pronuba' in terms of Juno as
air, these lines are mediated in terms of ancient cultural practices by
antiquarian scholars such as Barnaby Brisson, who, likewise following
Servius, reproduce his gloss to the effect that, according to Varro,
'fulsere ignes' alludes to the ancient custom of carrying water and fire at
the marriage ceremony.[65] In his opening simulation of an ancient
marriage ceremony, Jonson may have drawn on this mediation, as there
are two 'auspices' who carry water and fire (p. 211), a feature which
Jonson explains (*pace H&S*) precisely by a reference to Varro (p. 215,
note c). In Hymen's speech, however, the word '*ayre*' (instead of water)
suggests not this mediation, as Gordon proposes, but the mediation, as
natural philosophy, of the relation between Jove and Juno, which the
second masque stages. This is underscored by lines in the closing speech

---

[63] Jonson's phrase 'mutations of the *Ayre*' has a semi-technical register, and virtually translates the
phrases 'de tempestatibus aeris' and 'de aëris affectionibus' discussed in chapter 3 (pp. 90–4 and
note 39).

[64] Stahl's translation of: 'Juno soror eius et coniunx vocatur. est autem Juno aer, et dicitur . . .
coniunx quia aer subiectus est caelo.' (Macrobius, *Somnium*, p. 69; Macrobius, *Commentary*, trans.
Stahl, p. 158) Stahl points out in a note that the Greek for air is an anagram of the name Hera,
which may well have inspired Jonson's JUNO/UNIO anagram.

[65] See Gordon, *The Renaissance Imagination*, p. 288. Gordon thinks this is the interpretation Jonson
alludes to here.

of Reason, when, advising Hymen to encourage the trembling bride, she comments, 'Tell her, what JUNO is to JOVE, / The same shall shee be to her *love*' (p. 224, lines 213–15), and then turns to the attendants:

> Up *youths*, hold up your lights in ayre,
> And shake abroad ᵇtheir flaming hayre.
> Now move united, (lines 217–19)

Example of the marital relation, and figure of the cosmic relation of air and fire, Juno and Jove furnish an 'example of unitie', as Ovid and Julia, in the guise of those very deities, are reminded in *Poetaster* (IV.v.138). As we shall see, this ironic reminder of the 'mysticke sence' of the figures of Juno and Jove points up, for those who recognise it, the contrast between this Ovidian scene and the Virgilian scenes, which exemplify the true love and unity figured, within the passage Virgil reads, by the image of cosmic 'union' when *'fire, and aire did shine'* (v.ii.65).

In *Hymenaei*, the total and closed character of the order thus exemplified and figured is finally recapitulated by the dance – in the 'perfect'st *figure*' of 'the *round*' (p. 224, line 404) – with which the masque is brought to a close. It is as a closed circle that we might characterise at once the privileged community of learned heads which constitute Virgil's stage audience in *Poetaster* and the bounded, bourgeois model of authorial self and text which Virgil embodies. It is in the service of such a bounded – and grounded – authorial self/text and of a privileged circle of learned heads with an absolute sovereign at its centre that we have seen the learned voice of Virgil is used in *The King's Entertainment* and in the masques we have looked at in this chapter. In his introduction to the published text of *Hymenaei*, Jonson uses another figure – of a banquet – which he also uses in *Poetaster* to represent the privileged circle addressed by the voice of the learned poet. Comparing, as he does in the introduction to the first masque, occasional performance with the body and essential meaning, 'grounded upon *antiquitie*, and solide *learnings*' which 'lay hold on more remov'd *mysteries*', with the soul, Jonson proceeds to represent, only to dismiss, those who criticise his use of such learning: 'I am contented, these fastidious *stomachs* should leave my full tables, and enjoy at home, their cleane emptie trenchers, fittest for such ayrie tasts' (pp. 209-10). Inclusion in Jonson's banquet of learning depends on the capacity of the reader/spectator; those included will share the same capacity and the banquet will confirm their identity as a circle of the same from which those with a different capacity are excluded as ignorant. It is as just such a 'heavenly' intellectual/spiritual banquet, opposed to the Ovidian 'banquet of sense' in Act IV, that the scene of Virgil's reading in Act V is represented in *Poetaster*. Virgil's text, which Augustus, 'like another soule . . . long(s) t'enjoy' (v.i.74), is, moreover, like the 'soul' of Jonson's masques, grounded on solid learning, which requires that readers/spectators share not only a 'capacity', but, more specifically, a prior mediation in order to be included in the removed mysteries of the text's meaning. The Virgilian text thus works to create a 'circle' amongst spectators/readers like that represented in the play as Virgil's stage audience.

This circle is an example of the unity which the masque of *Hymenaei* celebrates, evoking only to dismiss/exclude as confused noise the opposition of difference. Grounded in the learning which they share, this 'circle of the same' enjoys privileged access to the meaning both of the text and of what the text names. In *Hymenaei*, the naming, as analogous examples of union, of a politically crucial dynastic marriage,[66] of a contested politics of the union of England and Scotland, and of the institutions of marriage and the monarchy, is grounded in the solid learning of antiquity, specifically the 'remov'd mysteries' of ancient cultural practice and of nature which constitute the canonical ground of the Virgilian scene of union in *Aeneid* 4. For those outside the privileged circle of the learned, these politics and institutions tend rather to be covered – concealed and underwritten – by such present/absent – removed – mysteries, the mysteries of the *archana maronis*.

[66] See Gordon, *The Renaissance Imagination*, p. 157.

CHAPTER 5

Of 'chaste ear' and 'soveraigne worth': Jonson's use of Virgil as author

> I judge him of a rectified spirit
> By many revolutions of discourse
> (In his bright reasons influence) refin'd
> From all the tartarous moodes of common men;
> Bearing the nature, and similitude
> Of a right heavenly bodie:
>
> Let me be what I am, as *Virgil* cold;
> As *Horace* fat . . .[1]

If the focus of the previous chapter was very much on literal margins, what follows, on the one hand, places at the centre a dramatic text – *Poetaster* – which is often treated as marginal to the Jonsonian corpus. On the other, it places at the centre of that text the Virgilian scenes as a group (v.i–iii), and, in particular, the scene of Virgil's reading from *Aeneid* 4 (v.ii). This scene has been treated as marginal ever since the judgement of Herford and Simpson that it 'does not directly further the purpose of the play' but is rather a 'personal application of . . . ardour for poetry' (*H&S*, vol. 1, p. 431). Though some later critics have seen in such ardour precisely the purpose of the play, which they treat as an apology for poetry, in reaction, as Tom Cain points out in his comprehensive recent edition, to previous critics' reductive focus on fields of local historical reference, especially the so-called war of the theatres, there has been no modification to the perception of the *dramatis persona* of Virgil and the scene of his reading.[2] It is, moreover, still the field of local reference that is usually privileged as the location of the 'purpose of the

---

[1] From Horace's opening formal eulogy in *Poetaster* (v.i.100-5); and 'An Elegie', in *The Underwood*, no. 42, lines 1-2 (*H&S*, vol. 8, p. 199). I am grateful to Anne Barton for drawing my attention to the second quotation.

[2] See the excellent survey of the criticism in Jonson, *Poetaster*, edited by Cain, pp. 2-4, pp. 50-1, and for further bibliographical references in relation to the war of the theatres, Evans, *Ben Jonson and the Poetics of Patronage*, pp. 295-6.

play', even by Cain, who, though arguing diplomatically that the play is an '*ars poetica* and political and social satire combined', nevertheless focuses on the local objects of the satire. Within such a critical orientation the *dramatis persona* of Virgil is something of an embarrassment – 'almost too perfect to be a model for contemporary poets'[3] – simply because there is no obvious referential candidate. While the case for Shakespeare was rightly dismissed as anachronistic by Herford and Simpson, their own case for Chapman, which is still occasionally wheeled out, was argued, as Jonathan Bate comments, only 'plausibly ... not conclusively', and they themselves finally preferred the conclusion that 'Virgil is simply Virgil' – a conclusion effectively endorsed by Tom Cain, for whom the key figure is (again) Horace, the 'exalted status' of Virgil being merely 'strategically necessary to enable him to vindicate Horace'.[4]

The passage from *Aeneid* 4, which Virgil reads at court, has likewise been regarded as peripheral, its relation to the rest of the play loose and general. For Cain indeed it merely falls within the play's overall strategies to imitate Horace, as an example, with the Ovidian love scene, of *recusatio*, an illustration of a style that is renounced (p. 12), although he suggests more specific connections later (p. 25). Far from a mere *recusatio*, I shall argue that the Virgilian passage is as specifically embedded in the play's semantic structure as the Ovidian elegy which opens the play proper (1.i.44-85) and the Horatian satires which are drawn on in later scenes (III.i. and III.v). Specifically, I shall suggest, it is placed so as to re-present two structural and semantic oppositions. The first is the repeated opposition between a poet's 'circle' and vicious interpreters whose malicious misinterpretations break up the circle and silence the poet. In what Cain describes as an 'elegant symmetry' (p. 5), both Ovid and his circle in Act IV, and Virgil and his in Act V are disturbed and silenced on account of false accusations of treason spread by Lupus Asinius, who is identified by his name as an embodiment of malice (the wolf) and ignorance (the ass) and who, as others have noted though in a very general way, is associated with the 'monster' Fame in the Virgilian passage.[5]

Within this opposition, there is a second, which is likewise represented, if more opaquely, in the Virgilian passage. This is the opposition

[3] Jonson, *Poetaster*, edited by Cain, pp. 7 and 15.
[4] *H&S*, vol. 1, p. 436; Bate, *Shakespeare and Ovid*, p. 169; Jonson, *Poetaster* edited by Cain, pp. 10–11.
[5] Robert C. Jones, 'The Satirist's Retirement in Jonson's "Apologetical Dialogue"', *English Literary History* 34 (1967), p. 462; Alexander Leggatt, *Ben Jonson: His Vision and His Art* (London and New York: Methuen, 1981), pp. 99–100; Jonson, *Poetaster*, edited by Cain, p. 25.

between the two poets' circles. While the first is identified, at least by the absolute voice of Augustus, as a false, adulterate circle of a 'licentious' (IV.vi.53) poet, indulging in a banquet of sense, the second is identified as a true circle of a 'chaste' (V.i.108) poet, enjoying a heavenly banquet of true love – a 'spirituall coupling of ... soules', 'circular, eternall'.[6] In the Virgilian passage, this opposition is represented in the contrast between the false, adulterate love of Dido and Aeneas and the true, heavenly love of Jove and Juno/fire and air, 'example', as the 'counterfeits' (IV.vi.38) Ovid and Julia are reminded, 'of unitie' (IV.v.138). Critics, who have readily compared the relationship between Julia and Ovid with the relationship between Dido and Aeneas have not seen the contrasting figure of the gods/elements.[7] This blindness is, in part, due to the strategy of minimal indication which Jonson uses to preserve as *arcana* the canonical ground of the passage – its mediation as natural philosophy – and the implied structure of authority between learned insiders and ignorant outsiders. But it is also due to the discontinuities of history, which have virtually erased this mediation of the Virgilian text. The learned voice of Virgil thus excludes, in effect, not only the 'ignorant' readers/spectators it works to exclude, but the learned readers of posterity, who are, ironically enough, explicitly included in a gesture made by Horace at the close of the formal eulogies of Virgil in Act V, as we shall see. Their exclusion bears ironic witness to the pressure of history to change and erasure in the very scene which asserts the immunity and transcendence of Virgil, his place above the 'underworld' of 'the Play of Fortune' and its ignorant and malicious false interpreters.

This opposition, between a transcendent, immune poet/voice above, and ignorant and malicious interpreters below, is reiterated in representations of *Poetaster* and its 'author' in frames both outside and inside the play. For the reader, the first of these is a retrospective dedicatory epistle to the lawyer Richard Martin, who is presented with '*this peece ... of mine*' '*for whose innocence, as for the Authors you were once a noble and timely undertaker*', preserving for posterity '*that ... which so much ignorance, and malice of the*

---

[6] Lovel's definition of true love in *The New Inn* (III.ii.105 and 107) (*H&S*, vol. 6, p. 454), explicitly opposed, as Frank Kermode points out, to the 'banquet o'sense, like that of *Ovid*' (line 126). See Kermode, 'The Banquet of Sense', in *Renaissance Essays* (London: Routledge and Kegan Paul, 1971), pp. 90–3.

[7] While Waith sees the relationships as examples of passion over judgement, Leggatt sees them as examples of 'solipsistic love, neglectful of the world'. Eugene Waith, 'The Poet's Morals in *Poetaster*', *Modern Language Quarterly* 12 (1951), pp. 13–19; Leggatt, *Ben Jonson: His Vision and His Art*, p. 99.

times, then conspir'd to have supprest' (*H&S*, vol. 4, p. 201). Here interpretations exposing Jonson to legal prosecution[8] are construed retrospectively
as repetitions of what is staged through the figure of Lupus Asinius, who
conspires against authors and their 'peeces' by spreading dangerous
misinterpretations. While Virgil clears Horace of such misinterpretations in Act V, Horace himself defends Ovid, claiming the banquet of
sense to have been 'innocent mirth' (iv.vii.41). Though this claim of
innocence for Ovid is not unproblematic, contradicting as it does the
judgement of Augustus, the important point here is that the claim of
innocence for the author of *Poetaster* as well as for the authorial figures
Horace and Ovid, asserts the character both of their texts and their
'selves' as at once non-transgressive and whole, untouching as untouched.

The claim is repeated in another frame, an appended 'apologeticall
Dialogue' (*H&S*, vol. 4, p. 317), which was performed only once, being
as Herford and Simpson exactly comment 'so much like a repetition . . .
that it rather irritated than soothed'.[9] Repeating the case made in the
play for Horace by Virgil (v.iii.135–44), a figure named 'author' claims
the 'peece' 'innocent' of particular imputations (p. 320), which he
identifies as 'meere slanders' and 'lyes' spread by those who, previously
motivated by 'malice' and 'ignorance', had 'provoke(d)' him,

> To shew that VIRGIL, HORACE, and the rest
> Of those great master-spirits did not want
> Detractors then, or practisers against them
>
> (ibid., lines 103–5)

Here, the position of 'the author' both before and after the writing of his
'innocent' piece is identified with the second, if not with the first,
opposition between innocent authors and conspiratorial malicious misinterpreters, the opposition, that is, between the circle of the 'master-
spirits' Virgil/Horace, and the 'malicious, ignorant, and base / Interpreter' (v.iii.141–2): Lupus Asinius.

These repetitions inscribe the 'author' and his 'peece' in the 'circle' of
their innocence – an inviolable position in a place beyond criticism.
More provocatively still, this is where they are placed by two prologues,
frames within the play which aspire to pre-empt criticism by representing it as a conspiracy of ignorance and malice. They thus aspire to 'gag'
those who interpret the play in a way different from, and opposed to the

---

[8] See Riggs, *Ben Jonson*, p. 80.
[9] *H&S*, vol. 1, p. 29; see also Barton, *Ben Jonson, Dramatist.* p. 90, Burt, *Licensed by Authority*, pp. 5, 6.

author's own 'innocent' meaning, just as Lupus will be gagged, literally, in Act V.[10]

The first prologue is spoken by a figure of Envy (pp. 203–5), who 'prevented' from making her own 'spie-like suggestions' by discovering the play is set in Rome – itself a strategy of 'prevention' – turns to look amongst the audience for 'players' and 'poet-apes' – agents of detraction and misinterpretation within the play – who, 'arm'd / With triple malice', will attack the author's 'worke, and him'. Unable to discover any – another strategy of 'prevention' disguised as flattery – she is sinking in despair when a second, armed prologue enters. Addressing Envy as '(m)onster', he places his foot upon her head and 'tread(s) / (Her) malice into earth' (p. 205, lines 2–3). Performing an exclusion that anticipates the turn from anti-masque to main masque, this prologue goes on to represent the opposition Envy figures more specifically in terms of possible interpretations of the play and judgements of its 'author'. Presenting the 'case' that the 'Authour should, once more, / Sweare that his play were good',

> he doth implore,
> You would not argue him of arrogance:
> How ere that common spawne of ignorance,
> Our frie of writers, may beslime his fame,
> And give his action that adulterate name.
> Such ful-blowne vanitie he more doth lothe,
> Then base dejection: There's a meane 'twixt both.
> Which with a constant firmenesse he pursues,
> As one, that knowes the strength of his own *muse*.
> And this he hopes all free soules will allow;
> Others, that take it with a rugged brow,
> Their moods he rather pitties, then envies:
> His mind it is above their injuries.
>
> (pp. 205–6, lines 16–28)

Within the play arrogance is a fault of which Horace is accused by Demetrius (v.iii.307–8) and from which he is cleared by Virgil, who, using the first person plural, speaks as sovereign moral authority in a speech which, echoing this one, serves to endorse its representation of

---

[10] The play was, of course, specifically, 'a preemptive strike' against Dekker's *Satiromastix* (Evans, *Ben Jonson and the Poetics of Patronage*, p. 146). But the pre-emptive effect is more general, as is the structure of oppositional worlds which informs the play. This is not to deny that it has more specific objects; these have been overhauled from different points of view in discussions of the war of the theatres (see note 2).

the 'author' (v.iii.355–64). The accusation of arrogance is simply dismissed here as a misnaming – an 'adulterate name' (Virgil calls it a
'foule, abusive name' (v.iii.363)) – produced by false writers, who are
identified with forms of life close to matter, the offspring of 'ignorance',
which, in a Neoplatonic universe, is, like 'malice', a function of matter.
These critics are placed, that is, as Asinius Lupus will be placed, on the
lowest level of a scale of being which underpins the play, Virgil being
placed, as we shall see, at the highest level.

This denunciation of false representations of 'the author' by malicious and ignorant critics at once recalls the figure of Envy, and, like
this monster, anticipates the Virgilian passage, specifically the *'monster'*
(v.ii.97) *'Fame, a fleet evill'* (line 75), like Envy, *'covetous ... of tales, and lies'*
(line 96), and, like her, *'child'* of *'our parent earth, stird up with spight / Of all
the gods'* (lines 80–1).[11] It is, in particular, the 'fame' of the 'author' that is
said by the armed prologue to be contaminated by the malicious,
multiple, particular lies of the ignorant offspring of earth/matter.

These textual strategies, which seek at once to 'prevent' hostile and
dangerous interpretations, and to place 'the author' and his 'peece'
beyond them, might be taken, within the terms of the moral discourse of
the contemporary writers, who are here specifically anticipated, as
further, offensive and infuriating proof 'of *Arrogance*, / Of *Selfe-love*'
(*Satiromastix*, v.ii.220–1). Or they might be taken, within the terms of a
post-Freudian psychoanalytic discourse, as another symptom of the
retentive and controlling personality Edmund Wilson famously attributes to Jonson.[12] Or again, following Stanley Fish, who might be said
in an important sense to take Jonson at his word, they might be taken as
rhetorical moves to achieve a measure of independence from the institutions – here the theatre – on which as author Jonson is nevertheless
economically dependent.[13]

Without discounting these views, I want rather to look at these
strategies in relation to what Michel Foucault has called the 'author
function', especially in its articulation with moves to control textual
production and interpretation, particularly complex in Jonson's case, as

[11] Note the details of the translation, which embed the passage in the semantic structure of the play:
'stird up with *spight* / Of all the gods' for 'ira inritata deorum' (*Aeneid* 4, line 178) (compare:
'provoked to anger against the gods' (Fairclough)); '*covetous* ... of tales, and lies' for 'ficti pravique
tenax' (line 188) (compare: 'clinging to the false and wrong' (Fairclough)) (my emphasis).

[12] Edmund Wilson, 'Morose Ben Jonson' (1948), in *The Triple Thinkers: Twelve Essays on Literary
Subjects*, reprint (Harmondsworth: Penguin, 1962), especially pp. 245–7.

[13] Fish, 'Authors-Readers: Jonson's Community of the Same', *passim*. Fish's focus is of course the
poems and the structures of patronage within which they were produced.

Richard Burt has shown.[14] Most straightforwardly, this function is predicated on, even as it produces the effect of, both a stable, transcendent, authorial self, such as these representations of *Poetaster* and its 'author' imply, and a stable, transcendent, privileged meaning, or 'master-text', as Michael Bristol calls it, which is the property of the author (Bristol, *Carnival and Theater*, p. 119). The two come indeed to be identified, as in the representations of *Poetaster* quoted above, which claim 'innocence' at once for 'the author' and his 'peece', the two constituting, in effect, as Foucault says of the name of the author and his work(s), a single category (Foucault, 'Qu'est-ce qu'un auteur?', p. 77). The claim of 'innocence' recalls too Foucault's point that texts began to 'have' authors 'dans la mesure où l'auteur pouvait être puni' (p. 84). To represent as particular, false interpretations produced by malice and ignorance interpretations which would render 'the author' of *Poetaster* liable to punishment (like the author figures in the play), and to represent the 'author'/'work' as innocent is to seek at once to 'prevent' legal action (unsuccessfully in the case of *Poetaster*, as I indicated above) and, more generally, to 'prevent' the proliferation and dispersal of meaning in the place of reception by privileging the author's as the true, authoritative, whole – 'innocent' – meaning.

Such 'prevention' is especially necessary in the theatre, as the author/owner-ship of utterance – 'who says this?' – is complicated by the mediation of the actor's voice and person.[15] *Poetaster* reflects on this complication not only by making the players primary agents of false interpretation and detraction, but also by staging miniature plays-

---

[14] Michel Foucault, 'Qu'est-ce qu'un auteur?', *Bulletin de la société française de philosophie* 44 (1969), pp. 73–104; Burt, *Licensed by Authority, passim*. Others who have looked at Jonson's work in relation to the idea of the 'author function', if not in the same way, include: Michael D. Bristol, *Carnival and Theater: Plebeian Culture and the Structure of Authority in Renaissance England* (New York and London: Routledge, 1985), especially pp. 118–20; Riggs, *Ben Jonson*, pp. 351–3; and most thoroughly, though in relation mainly to poems, Sara van den Berg, 'Ben Jonson and the Ideology of Authorship', in J. Brady and W. H. Herenden, eds., *Ben Jonson's 1616 Folio* (Newark: University of Delaware Press; London and Toronto: Associate University Presses, 1991).

[15] See Womack, *Ben Jonson*, pp. 108–12. It is, I think, this complication, and the loss of control it entails, together with the ontological status of 'playing', that made the theatre such a problematic medium for Jonson. In this connection Dekker's portrayal of 'Horace'/Jonson at the theatre, in *Satiromastix*, is telling: amongst the promises 'Horace' is required to make at the close is not to 'sit in a Gallery, when your Comedies and Enterludes have entred their Actions, and there make vile and bad faces at everie lyne, to make Sentlemen [*sic*] have an eye to you, and to make Players afraide to take your part' (v.ii.298–301). Jonson is portrayed here as a dominating and intimidating author who seeks to (re)assert control over actors – and 'his' play – through facial gesture/comment. It is, of course, the 'players' that *Poetaster* identifies as primary agents of misinterpretation. On Jonson's problems with the theatre as a medium, see further J. Barish, 'Jonson and the Loathed Stage', in W. Blissett, J. Patrick and R. W. Van Fossen, eds., *A Celebration of Ben Jonson* (University of Toronto Press, 1973), especially pp. 34–5.

within-the-play, notably in Act III scene iv. Here Tucca has his page–
players perform miniature scenes which either are, or sound like, quotations (*H&S*, vol. 9, pp. 557–8), and which include an exchange taken
from Chapman which quite literally evokes – calls out – the question of
author/owner-ship of utterance: '1. PUR. Murder, murder. 2. PUR. Who
calls out murder?' (III.iv.241–2). These miniature borrowed plays-with-
in, together with other quotations scattered throughout the play, are
treated by the characters as common properties, properties, that is,
which, like other kinds of semantic matter – clothes and objects – can be
appropriated by any 'fellow-sharer' (III.iv.239).[16] At one point, however,
this free circulation, as common properties amongst fellow-sharers, of
borrowed utterances is curtailed by the introduction of the word 'plagiary', used in the sense of 'plagiarist'. Crispinus, the poetaster, sings a
song which is then discovered to belong to Horace: 'the ditti's all
borrowed; 'tis HORACES: hang him *plagiary*' (IV.iii.95–6). According to
the *OED*, this use marks the entry into the English language of the word
'plagiary' in this sense; indeed, examples of the cognate forms – 'plagiar-
ism', 'plagiarist' and 'plagiarise' – are not recorded before 1621, 1674
and 1716 respectively. The use of italics in Jonson's text underscores the
imported, foreign character of the word, which, for educated readers/
spectators, would have carried associations with formal legislation.[17] It is
precisely as a term of formal indictment that the word is used later, in
the trial of Demetrius and Crispinus (v.iii.218–20). The play's use of the
word thus marks the entry into the English language of what we might
call the juridical, formal correlate of the author function, which works,
like and with it, as a regulatory principle, 'of thrift in the proliferation of
meaning' 'by which one impedes the free circulation' of utterances,[18]
specifically through the formalisation of literary theft as indictable

---

16 This description by Tucca of one of his page-players, which immediately precedes the exchange
from Chapman, alludes of course to the actors' proto-capitalist practice of owning shares in their
company. See Gurr, *The Shakespearean Stage*, pp. 46-59. The phrase is used twice again in *Poetaster*
in Act IV scene iv (lines 7 and 10).

17 In Cooper's *Thesaurus* the definition of 'Plagiarius', 'He that stealeth away a man's children. He
that stealeth bookes', is followed by 'Plagiaria lex', 'A law made against those that weare called
Plagiarii'. Thomas Cooper, *Thesaurus linguae, Romanae et Britannicae* (London, 1565).

18 Michel Foucault, 'What is an Author?', in Paul Rabinow, ed., *The Foucault Reader*, reprint
(Harmondsworth: Penguin, 1991) pp. 118, 119. This quotation comes from a second version of
Foucault's paper given in English in 1970 and published in J. V. Harari, ed., *Textual Strategies:
Perspectives in Post-Structuralist Criticism* (Ithaca: Cornell University Press, 1979), pp. 141-6. For a
lucid analysis of the differences between the two versions see Harari's introduction, pp. 43-4.
The changes are given in French in footnotes to the first version of the paper (1969) in Michel
Foucault, *Dits et écrits 1954–1988*, edited by Daniel Defert and François Ewald, 4 vols. (Paris:
Gallimard, 1994), vol. 1, pp. 789–821.

158   *Jonson, Shakespeare and figures of Virgil*

offence ('hang him'). Here the utterances are identified as belonging to Horace, the figure (with Virgil) most closely associated with 'the author' of *Poetaster*, an association underscored by the self-conscious joke that the plagiarised lines resemble nothing written either by the historical Horace or by Jonson (*H&S*, vol. 9, p. 565), that, in short, they belong to 'the author' of *Poetaster*.

It goes perhaps without saying that neither 'plagiary' nor any of the cognate forms appear in the plays of the Shakespearean canon, plays without such strategies of 'prevention' and notably without a marked authorial function, until the publication of the first folio, when, as Magreta de Grazia has put it, Shakespeare is constructed as 'the authorial part' 'standing for the collective whole of production' (de Grazia, *Shakespeare Verbatim*, p. 39). Interestingly enough, this collective mode of production and absent authorial centre find confirmation, if not affirmation, in the Ovidian scenes in *Poetaster*, which are generally agreed to allude to a Shakespearean as well as to a Marlovian model, especially in the scene of Ovid's banquet of sense, which is staged as another play-within (the participants 'hire ... properties' (IV.iv.11) from the actors, as Womack points out), and which, Bate suggests, offers a 'poetics of play' like Shakespearean comedy.[19] But it offers too a play without an authorial centre, the participants all being author–players, and author–players without stable, transcendent selves. Ovid, in particular, is explicitly warned by his friend Tibullus that he will 'lose' his 'selfe' (I.iii.46) if he continues in his 'passionate' vein (line 59), which, as Cain comments, he does (*Poetaster*, edited by Cain, p. 20). Ovid is, in short, without the stable, transcendent self necessary to the 'author function'.

In contrast to the centreless Ovid and his centreless circle of playing is the 'marble' (IV.vi.76) – immobile – transcendent selfhood of the 'sovereign' (V.i.116) author Virgil, who stands at the absolute centre (with Augustus) of a circle of being/truth. As the lines from the 'apologeticall Dialogue' quoted earlier indicate, Virgil forms with Horace a pair associated with 'the author', each representing a different authorial self/voice, as in the lines quoted at the head of this chapter.[20] While

---

[19] Womack, *Ben Jonson*, pp. 109–11; Bate, *Shakespeare and Ovid*, p. 170; see also Barton, *Ben Jonson, Dramatist*, p. 84, and Jonson, *Poetaster*, edited by Cain, p. 23.

[20] In this poem, an 'Ovidian' voice is subsequently assumed, although the self-consciousness of the first lines detaches 'the author' from his own production in this vein. With Jonson's representation of Virgil and Horace as a pair, compare the historical Horace's representation of Virgil as his 'other half' ('animae dimidium meae'), quoted in Virgil, *Symbolarum libri XVII*, edited by J. Pontanus, p. 2.

Virgil's is the absolute, sovereign, bounded and detached – 'cold' – self/voice, which depicts and judges but does not engage with the universe of 'common men' and their 'moods', Horace's is the more earth-bound, relative, satiric voice, which engages with this universe to draw common men towards the absolute place of truth/being occupied by the sovereign authorial self. This 'co-operation' is underscored by Virgil's defence of Horace in Act V, which echoes the defence of 'the author' by the armed prologue, and is, in turn, echoed by the self-defence of 'the author' in the 'apologeticall Dialogue'. In the prologue, it is worth recalling, the 'mind' of 'the author' is explicitly placed, as Virgil is, 'above' the 'injuries' inflicted by the 'moodes' of his opponents, with which, nevertheless, like and through Horace, he engages.

Virgil is, moreover, described in terms of a 'chaste' economy of self- and text-fashioning suggestive of the economy sketched by Foucault. And Virgil's circle, idealised as an example of true 'chaste' love and unity, is a circle unified, more materially, by a shared 'profession' (v.i.76) of letters, and by a commitment to merit – judged in terms of virtue and understanding – as the primordial criterion of privilege. Like and with the economy of self/text-fashioning that Virgil exemplifies, this ideal-ised circle tends to promote what may be described as a bourgeois, professional ethos, characterised by an 'ideology of merit'.[21] More specifically, it tends to promote, even as it portrays, a circle of profes-sional men of letters, such as Pontanus gathers around Virgil in the introduction to his edition as what he calls 'testimonia' – testimonies which the formal eulogies to the 'soveraigne worth' (v.i.116) of Virgil effectively, and sometimes literally, as we shall see, translate.

The absolute character of the central, sovereign author and his text, which are identified, like 'the author' of *Poetaster* and his 'peece', is expressed not only formally and explicitly, but also tacitly by the translation of the passage read by Virgil (v.ii.56–97). For, like the translations we looked at in the previous chapter, this translation 'relig-iously' 'follows the copy',[22] which it thus leaves virtually intact, the proper property of its sovereign sacred author, unviolated by the differ-ence of the translator.

The passage is, nevertheless, embedded in the play's semantic struc-

---

[21] Magali Sarfatti Larson, *The Rise of Professionalism: A Sociological Analysis* (University of California Press, 1977), p. 113.

[22] Cain's adverb 'laboriously' (Jonson, *Poetaster*, edited by Cain, p. 221) is now a virtual synonym for 'religiously', with the pejorative inflections it has acquired. See my introduction where I cite, as here, the first Catholic translators of the Bible (introduction, p. 12 and note 32).

ture by anticipations such as those I pointed out earlier – in the first prologue of Envy and in the second prologue's representations of the malicious enemies of the author, which both look forward to the Virgilian figure of the monster Fame. More immediately associated with this figure is the character of Lupus Asinius. For Virgil breaks off with the phrase '(t)his monster' (translating 'haec' (*Aeneid* 4, line 189)), presumably looking off-stage in the direction of the clamouring Lupus, who arrives with his tales of treason against Horace. The Virgilian passage is thus embedded so as to re-present the play's foundational opposition between authors and their malicious misinterpreters, and, more specifically, to re-present Virgil's own enemies as well as the (same) enemies of 'the author', an inclusion of the malicious and ignorant common men it simultaneously excludes which looks forward to the masques. The structural pivot – the turn from anti-masque to main masque – is indeed anticipated, if in inverted form, by this moment of interruption, as it is more straightforwardly anticipated by the triumph of the second armed prologue over the first prologue of the monster Envy.

The association of Lupus with the monster Fame and of both with the universe of the anti-masques is underscored by a speech by Horace earlier in the play and an echo of it in the one significant modification to the Virgilian passage. The speech follows Ovid's banquet of sense, interrupted, like Virgil's reading, by Lupus, who has denounced it as a cover for treason. Angrily dismissing this as a misrepresentation of 'innocent pleasures' (iv.vii.41), Horace turns the accusation against the accuser by arguing that such misrepresentations themselves constitute a cover and that it is such as Lupus who are the real threat to the state, its 'moths, and scarabes', 'the dregs of courts' who '(c)are not whose fame they blast', and who, under a disguise of love towards their sovereign, 'vomit forth / Their ... prodigious malice', claiming to work in the interests of state security, but in fact tending to '(d)isturbe it most' with their 'false' cries (lines 44, 47, 49–50, 53). The imagery here places Lupus alongside the critics of 'the author' in a class of maliciously motivated monstrous ('prodigious') false-namers at a sub-human level of being close to matter, a class which the monsters 'bred of earth' – Envy and Fame – figure.

That such 'monsters' are the enemies not only 'of poetry'[23] and 'innocent' poets, but also of the state is the point made by Horace that is

---

[23] Jonson, *Poetaster*, edited by Cain, p. 25.

echoed by the one modification made to the translation of the Virgilian passage. For where the Latin text describes Fame as 'bred of earth' 'sister to Coeus and Enceladus',[24] Jonson's translation substitutes the names of the giants (which he gives in the marginal note*) with an explanatory gloss,

> *Shee was last sister of that Giant* race,*
> *That sought to scale* JOVES *court;*
>
> (lines 82–3)

An insertion of gloss into translation, which is not usually practised by Jonson when translating Virgil, but which is practised by others, such as Gavin Douglas and John Brinsley, this serves specifically to insert the political threat that Horace claims Lupus represents.[25] The Virgilian monster is thus aligned with the Jonsonian, both figures of an opposition 'bred of earth', motivated by malice and ignorance, spreading multiple, particular false representations – opinions – which work to undermine at once the order of an absolute state and the poet's 'innocent' authorial meaning. This looks forward to anti-masque figures, especially the witches of *The Masque of Queens*, whose threat is represented as a threat at once to the order of the state under James and the order of the masque, mutually reinforcing structures in a system of representation which is identified as at once proper and natural.

The foundational importance of this opposition in *Poetaster* may help to account for the flat contradiction between the unqualified condemnation by Augustus of Ovid's banquet of sense as 'worship of that idoll vice' (IV.iv.67) and Horace's representation of it to Lupus as 'innocent mirth / And harmlesse pleasures, bred, of noble wit' (IV.vii.41–2), which has puzzled critics, who have been uncertain, more generally, how the play judges Ovid, whether positively (Talbert and Nash, for example), negatively (Waith and Cain), or ambivalently (Barton).[26] Ambivalence there may be, but it is important to recognise too that the difference between

---

[24] 'illam Terra parens . . . / . . . Coeo Enceladoque sororem' (*Aeneid* 4, lines 178–9).

[25] For Douglas's insertion of gloss into translation, see Bawcutt, *Gavin Douglas*, pp. 120–1, and for Brinsley's see chapter 2, pp. 51–3. Compare specifically Phaer's marginal gloss: 'Giants that attempted to skale heaven' (Phaer, *The Nyne Fyrst Bookes*, fo. Fiiijr), and Bacon's comment: 'By the Earth is signified the nature of the vulgar, alwaies swolne and malignant and still broaching new scandals against superiors', the Giants signifying 'rebellious actions' and their sister Fame 'seditious reports', akin in their common end of political subversion. Francis Bacon, *The Wisedome of the Ancients . . . Done into English by Sir Arthur Georges* (London, 1619), reprinted in *The Renaissance and the Gods* (New York and London: Garland, 1976), pp. 49–50.

[26] Ernest Talbert, 'The Purpose and Technique of Jonson's *Poetaster*', *Studies in Philology* 42 (1945), pp. 225–51; Ralph Nash, 'The Parting Scene in Jonson's *Poetaster* (IV.ix)', *Philological Quarterly* 31 (1952), pp. 54–62; Waith, 'The Poet's Morals in *Poetaster*'; Barton, *Ben Jonson, Dramatist*, p. 84.

Augustus and Horace is the difference between an absolute and a relative position. According to the absolute position of Augustus, the 'licentious' Ovid's banquet of sense is vicious; according to the relative position of Horace, it is, compared to the malicious, undermining distortions of such as Lupus, innocent. This allows reiteration of the play's foundational opposition – crucial to the preventive, and defensive strategies of 'the author' – between 'innocent' authors and their malicious misinterpreters.

This in-between position – of Ovid and Julia as well as of their banquet of sense – is exactly the position of Dido and Aeneas in the Virgilian passage – in-between the absolute order of the gods/nature and the multiple distortions of the monster Fame. In both scenes there is, moreover, a false-naming, covering and permitting sexual licence, which, again, is relatively harmless compared to the maliciously motivated subversive false-namings of Lupus/Fame.[27] Bid at the outset not '(t)o be any thing the more god or goddess, for their names' (iv.v.17), the participants in the banquet are authorised to indulge in 'free licence' (line 18), specifically, 'to breake loving oaths' in adultery, as Dido does. Breaking troth/truth they cross over – transgress – from being to playing – and the banquet is, as we have seen, explicitly staged as a play – a point that is underscored at the moment of 'unmasking' when Augustus draws the distinction – 'I aske not, what you play? but, what you are?' (iv.vi.26). Peter Womack has insightfully identified this moment of unmasking by a figure of 'legitimate authority' (monarch/magistrate/father) as paradigmatic of the structure of Jonsonian comedy, in which the absence of such a figure is the condition of 'the play' (Womack, *Ben Jonson*, pp. 112–13). But to take the scene of the banquet, as he does, as a *mise en abyme* of the whole (p. 110) is strenuously to ignore the contrast to this scene of 'playing' which the Virgilian scenes of 'being' in Act V furnish, scenes in which the inevitable false naming of the theatrical medium – the 'acting' – is suppressed.

It is, more specifically, to ignore the indication of this contrast which is given in the banquet scene itself. The foolish citizen Albius, playing Vulcan, exhorts the quarrelling Ovid and Julia, playing Jove and Juno,

Here father, here mother, for shame, drinke your selves drunke, and forget this dissention: you two should cling together, before our faces, and give us example of unitie. (iv.v.135–8)

---

[27] Cain links the Virgilian passage to the play's preoccupation with false-naming without however noticing the distinction between more and less harmful kinds of false-naming. Jonson, *Poetaster*, edited by Cain, p. 25.

Applauded – 'excellently spoken' (line 139) – and so foregrounded, but without further explanatory comment, this invokes, for learned readers/ spectators, the mediation of the pagan deities as (Neoplatonic) natural philosophical discourse, and of Jove and Juno in particular as figures of the elements which, united as 'father' and 'mother', engender all things. It is a mediation we have seen associated with the passage from *Aeneid* 4, notably in *Hymenaei* where it furnishes the spectacle of Juno/Union with a ground of solid learning. Here the contrast between the 'dissention' of counterfeit deities and the 'unitie' of the true anticipates the scene of Juno's presence in the Virgilian passage *'when fire, and aire did shine'* (v.ii.65), indicating, if minimally, its hidden significance, including its relation to the representation of Virgil and his circle as examples and figures themselves of a community of 'true Love', '(t)hat ... combines' '(i)n equall knots': 'in a calme, and *god-like unitie*'.[28]

The contrast between the Ovidian and Virgilian scenes, and more particularly between the characters of Ovid and Virgil, is explicitly drawn in the speech by Augustus absolutely condemning the banquet. For the dismissal of Ovid and his circle as vicious is followed by a description of those Augustus will 'prefer' (i.e. promote), which antici- pates the formal 'preferment' of Virgil in Act V scene ii (where the verb is used again (line 38)).

> I will preferre for knowledge, none but such
> As rule their lives by it, and can becalme
> All sea of humour, with the marble *trident*
> Of their strong spirits: Others fight below
> With gnats, and shaddowes, others nothing know.
>
> (IV.vi.74–8)

The type Virgil exemplifies is portrayed here in terms of the scene of Neptune's calming of the tempest in *Aeneid* 1 (lines 124–57), moralised as the exercise of reason over turbulent desires (translated into the Jon- sonian idiom 'humours'). The portrait justifies, even as it announces, both the formal preferment and, more particularly, the investment of Virgil with authority as judge in Act V, when he will exercise the monologic authority that Neptune exercises over the unruly winds. Those he judges are indeed placed, like and with 'the others' here, 'below', in the realm of the turbulent humours which Virgil has mas- tered and which, in Ovid's case, is, specifically, the humour of the

---

[28] 'Epode', *The Forest*, XI (*H&S*, vol. 8, pp. 109–13), lines 43, 49, 53 (my emphasis). The poem is contemporary with *Poetaster* (*H&S*, vol. 11, p. 40).

passion 'they ... call Love', '(i)nconstant, like the sea' '(r)ough, swelling, like a storme': '(i)n a continuall *tempest*.'[29]

The same scene from *Aeneid* 1 and the same emblem of Neptune's (and Virgil's) authority are invoked in *The Tempest* when Ariel describes retrospectively the '(p)erform'd ... tempest' which seemed to make the 'dread trident' of 'the most mighty Neptune shake' (1.ii.194, 204, 206).[30] Further, the opening scene of the performed tempest itself invokes the Virgilian scene through the speech of the Boatswain, whose mocking imperative 'use your authority' (1.i.23) at the same time echoes the 'use your authoritie' (v.iii.398) with which Augustus invests Virgil as judge over 'the others', especially over their language, in *Poetaster*. *The Tempest* thus engages with and contests ('shakes') not only the authority of Virgil, but the way this authority is used, by Jonson in particular, to exclude – 'put down' and silence – the multiple, particular voices of common men. For Virgil and his circle are placed throughout the corpus, but most explicitly in *Poetaster*, 'above' common men and women, as a different and superior human kind, a difference and superiority that is marked precisely by the difference between the normative Language of this circle and the multiple, plural languages used by 'the others', judged, as we shall see, and contained by the normative Language as its own contrary, a 'strange' deformation or noise, like the confused noise of the anti-masque.[31]

This absolute opposition between the (main masque) universe of Virgil and his circle and the (anti-masque) universe of 'the others below' is re-marked in another speech which anticipates the Virgilian scenes, and which, with the rest of the scene and the next two scenes (III.i–

---

[29] Ibid., lines 37, 39, 40, 43 (my emphasis). For early modern moralisations of the Virgilian tempest see further, chapter 6, pp. 209–11 and note 32.

[30] The imported, Latinate character of the word 'trident' is signalled by the use of italics in the Quarto of *Poetaster* (1601) and in the Quarto of the *Masque of Blackness* (1608) (see chapter 4, p. 127). The word is not, however, distinguished by special typeface in the Quarto of *Neptune's Triumph* (1623–24) (*H&S*, vol. 7, p. 694), which furnishes a fairly precise indication of its entry into the English lexicon. (See further chapter 6, note 85.) Jonson's use of the epithet 'marble' to qualify Neptune's trident may have been influenced by Giraldi's descriptions of statues of Neptune, 'cum buccino [i.e. trumpet] et fuscina [i.e. trident], qualem marmoreum'. Lilius Gregorius Giraldus, *De deis gentium* (1548), reprinted in *The Renaissance and the Gods* (New York and London: Garland, 1976), p. 216.

[31] Arguing that the play is 'about language' A. H. King has provided a valuable socio-linguistic analysis of the languages of the satirised characters (and their historical counterparts). A. H. King, *The Language of Satirized Characters in Poetaster: A Socio-Linguistic Analysis, 1597–1602*, Lund Studies in English, 10 (Lund: G. W. K Gleerup, 1941), p. xiii. Unfortunately, though he promises a sequel, which will analyse the 'norm, the speech and writing of Horace and Virgil, the talk of Mecoenas and Caesar' (ibid., p. xiii), this does not seem to have been published.

III.iii.10), is taken from the ninth of the first book of satires by the historical Horace.[32] Suggesting, like the parasitic bore of the original, that Horace might engineer promotion with Mecœnas for the two of them, and adding, specifically, that they might oust 'VIRGIL, VARIUS and the best of them' (III.i.244–5), the poetaster Crispinus is roundly rebuked, like the bore, for failing to understand the ethos of the patron's house. But while the Horace of the original condemns such self-interested manoeuvrings as evils utterly foreign to the pure house of Mecœnas,[33] Jonson's Horace qualifies these 'evils' as 'low' and 'common' (III.i.255), 'poore affections / Of under-mining envie, and detraction, / Moodes, onely proper to base groveling minds' (III.i.251–3). These additions embed the satire in the play's structure of oppositional worlds, with Crispinus placed alongside Lupus, and the hostile critics of 'the author' of *Poetaster*, in a world 'below' of those 'common' men motivated by the 'under-mining' moods of envy and detraction. Similarly, additions to the description of the community at the house of Mecœnas align it with the world of the Virgilian scenes. 'Each man hath his place' (III.i.257), which exactly translates the closing words of the original description,[34] is supplemented by: 'And to his merit, his reward of grace: / Which with a mutuall love they all embrace' (lines 258–9). In its specification of individual 'merit' as the community's criterion of differentiation and its description of the commitment to this criterion as a shared and unifying 'love' this looks forward to the Virgilian scenes, their ideology of merit and their idealisation of this ideology as an illustration of a true love which '(p)reserves communitie' 'in a calme, and god-like unitie', a unity figured by the gods/elements in the Virgilian passage. Such unity, such love, are objects of incredulous wonder to Crispinus (as to the bore of the original) – 'You report a wonder! 'tis scarce credible, this' (line 260) – a response which only serves to confirm his exclusion from this universe and its absolute difference from the universe of common men like him.

This characterisation of Virgil's circle – as a loving community whose members are differentiated by, and unified in their commitment to merit – is summed up by Augustus in the lines with which he closes the formal eulogies of Virgil.

---

[32] All references will be to Horace, *Satires, Epistles and Ars Poetica*, translated by H. R. Fairclough, reprint (Cambridge, Mass.: Harvard University Press; London: Heinemann, 1978), pp. 104–11.

[33] 'domus hac nec purior ulla est / nec magis his aliena malis', ibid., p. 108, lines 49–50.

[34] 'est locus uni / cuique suus', ibid., lines 51–2.

> This one consent, in all your doomes of him,
> And mutuall loves of all your severall merits,
> Argues a trueth of merit in you all.
>
> (v.i.139–41)

'... one ... all ... / ... all ... / a trueth ... all': lexical repetitions with the repetition of a regular iambic pattern together foreground the whole which transcends the particular – 'severall' – differences. The effect is of totality and stasis, closure and exclusion, the closure and exclusion of the circle – the figure to which, we might say, this speech aspires. The effect repeats and epitomises the effect of the formal eulogies themselves. Literally circular inasmuch as they open and close with a speech from the same speaker – Horace – these speeches are all eight lines long, a generalising, 'embracing' conclusion of two lines being added to the last. More importantly, they sound the same, exemplifying in their measured, restrained mode the normative 'chaste' economy of Language which Virgil represents and which is in absolute contrast to the verbal as well as sexual licence exemplified by those outside, notably in the quick-fire exchanges of the circle of Ovid's banquet of sense. The formal eulogies are indeed not exchanges so much as monologic affirmations, which are finally interchangeable, the different speakers speaking with one 'voyce'[35] and with 'one consent'.[36]

This formalised consent is, however, preceded by a moment of dissent, the only such moment in these scenes – another contrast to what goes on outside, especially in the scene of Ovid's banquet, which, as we have seen, is characterised by 'dissention'. Inviting, first, an estimation of Virgil from those he addresses as 'gentlemen, / (That are of his profession, though rankt higher)' (v.i.75–6), Augustus then turns to Horace instead: 'Or HORACE, what saist thou that art the poorest, / And likeliest to envy, or to detract?' (v.i.77–8). This suggestion, that Horace might belong with the maliciously motivated outsiders and enemies to the learned poet's circle on account of his poverty, is criticised by Horace as itself how such 'common men' (line 79) think. He goes on to

---

[35] From epigram 128 (*H&S*, vol. 8, pp. 80–1), line 11, discussed below.
[36] In *Satiromastix* this idealised circle is neatly turned into a circle of two: Horace and the stupid, sycophantic Asinius Bubo, who is a Horace/Jonson sound-alike reproducing his master's voice (II.ii.11–20) and 'judgement' (I.ii.151–2). This is to expose the 'dictatorial underside' (as Boehrer rightly calls it) to Jonson's aspirations to a 'community of the same' as well as to his use of the term 'judgement'. Bruce Thomas Boehrer, 'Renaissance Overeating: The Sad Case of Ben Jonson', *PMLA* 105:5 (1990), p. 1079. As Riggs points out, *Satiromastix* also paints a very different picture of Horace/Jonson as professional author, 'immersed in the grubby round of commissions that bring in his meager livelihood' (Riggs, *Ben Jonson*, p. 81). The picture is, in short, of the venal and sordid profession that *Poetaster* makes the profession of the law.

argue against making 'a difference ... for ... poornesse' (line 80), and for making the crucial criterion rather possession of knowledge and virtue (lines 81–93), an argument Augustus accepts as 'holsome sharpnesse' (line 94), agreeing to 'put no difference more / Betweene the great, and good, for being poore' (lines 97–8). This exchange allows for the articulation of a distinction between legitimate opposition (Horace) and illegitimate (Lupus), a distinction which will be reiterated explicitly in Virgil's condemnation of Lupus, and which carries obviously crucial implications for 'the author' of *Poetaster*. It allows too, precisely as an instance of such legitimate opposition, the case for 'vertuous merit' (v.i.92) and against wealth as the primordial criterion of privilege. This case is then further advanced through the formal preferment of Virgil, which Virgil himself moralises as '(p)oore vertue rais'd, high birth and wealth set under' (v.ii.33), he being, like Horace, a '*poet* (void / Of birth, or wealth, or temporall dignity)' (lines 30–1). Such a preferment, it is agreed, goes against both 'custom' (line 36) and 'fortune' (line 38), but is in accordance with the 'harmonie' (line 41) of a 'humane order' (v.i.66) governed by 'reason' (v.ii.42). It is such an order that Augustus takes upon himself to institute both in the particular preferment of Virgil and in his more general advancement of 'learned heads' (v.i.51).

In advocating as properly human a rationally constructed order based on virtuous merit, these scenes undoubtedly suggest the 'egalitarian' potential Don Wayne sees in Jonson's 'neoclassicism' in general, even the 'revolutionary tendencies' Boehrer claims for 'Jonsonian virtue' – a virtue here embodied in a Virgil explicitly preferred above, and against the traditional criteria of wealth and rank.[37] Indeed, these scenes suggest, more specifically, not just in the ideology of merit promoted by Virgil's preferment, but in the formal testimonies to his worth and in the economy of self- and text-fashioning they describe, a professional, bourgeois ideology and ethos of selfhood and authorship within a community/republic of letters. This is signalled, crucially, when Augustus privileges identity bestowed by a shared 'profession' as men of letters over difference of rank, in his address to the 'gentlemen' that are of Virgil's 'profession, though rankt higher' (v.i.75–6). Nevertheless, this ideology and ethos are contained within a structure of absolute political authority, just as Jonson's use of learning in general and of Virgil in particular always serves 'the king'. It is, after all, Augustus, once 'corrected' by Horace, who controls access to the privileged circle of letters.

---

[37] Don E. Wayne, *Penshurst: The Semiotics of Place and the Poetics of History* (London: Methuen, 1984), p. 151; Boehrer, 'Renaissance Overeating', p. 1081.

There are 'testimonies', as we shall shortly consider, but there is no formal system of testing administered by the members of the circle, which is how a professional bourgeois community works. Recognition of merit, that is, is ultimately a function of the authority of an absolute monarch. There is, moreover, nothing egalitarian, much less revolutionary, about the hierarchical and oppositional relation which the play articulates between the universe of this privileged elite and the universe of common men and women which it includes/excludes.

The egalitarianism of these scenes, as of the representation and use of Virgil throughout the corpus, is, finally, no more egalitarian than an education system which allowed access to learning in general and to Virgil in particular only exceptionally to those of unprivileged social origins such as Jonson, who could then use what they had acquired in the service of their own 'self-creating' upward mobility, as Jonson's critics claimed he did.[38] The truly egalitarian tendencies lay rather with the anti-humanist as well as anti-hierarchical thrust of more radical Protestant discourses, which, as we saw in earlier chapters, promote godliness and plainness over the humanists' virtue and eloquence, exemplified and figured by Virgil. Whatever is 'new' – bourgeois and egalitarian – about these scenes and whatever the implied personal stakes, they are, moreover, 'covered', on the one hand, by the representation of Virgil's circle as an example of an absolute, ideal (Neoplatonic) 'love' and unity, and, on the other, by the location of this circle in history, as an ideal 'prior order' (Wayne, *Penshurst*, p. 150). The modest social origins of both Horace and Virgil were indeed grounded in received history, though Horace was reputedly poorer than Virgil, whose father was a small landowner. There were likewise historical grounds for the enthusiasm of Augustus for Virgil's poetry and for the scene of Virgil's public reading from *Aeneid* 4 at the imperial court.[39]

But of greater interest for our purposes are the more immediate historical, and textual grounds for the formal eulogies of Virgil (v.i.100–38). For both as a mode of legitimation and in their descriptions, these eulogies serve to promote a professional, bourgeois ethos and ideology of letters. The textual grounds to these eulogies are furnished by the last of three chapters of 'testimonia' given by Pontanus at the end of the

[38] See chapter 5, pp. 119–20. Still more explicit than this phrase of Dekker's is his comment that Horace/Jonson is 'ambition, and does conspire to be more hye and tall, as God a mightie made him' (*Satiromastix*, IV.iii.254–5).
[39] The enthusiasm of Augustus is mentioned in Virgil, *Symbolarum libri XVII*, edited by J. Pontanus, pp. 2, 15. According to Donatus, Virgil read books 2, 4 and 6 of the *Aeneid* at the imperial court. Donatus, 'Vita', in Colin Hardie, ed., *Vitae Vergilianae antiquae*, 2nd edn (Oxford: Clarendon Press, 1966) p. 13. This is not recorded by Pontanus.

introduction to his edition – itself a monumental testimony to the emergent enterprise of a professionalised humanism. Entitled '(t)estimonia quorundam eruditorum' – 'testimonies', we might accurately translate, 'of certain "learned heads"' – this chapter gathers comments in praise of Virgil from a group of early modern (principally Italian), humanist authors, scholars and critics.[40] Turning these testimonies as formal eulogy Jonson furnishes grounds for the authority – and consequently the promotion – of Virgil, just as he furnishes grounds to the authority of his own, and Virgilian texts, by the citation of what he calls 'testimonies' in notes to his masques and *The King's Entertainment*, as we saw in the previous chapter. Both modes of legitimation do indeed belong to the formal apparatus of a professionalised academy: the legitimation of text by 'testimonies' given in notes and the legitimation of an authorial 'self' by 'testimonies' from members of the 'profession' 'rankt higher'. What is more the grounds given for the promotion of Virgil include arguments which apologists for the humanities have continued to make, notably in relation to Shakespeare – a continuity which helps to account for the (anachronistic) identification of Jonson's Virgil with Shakespeare. They bear traces too of recurring contradictions of the humanist project, such as the contradiction of the single, yet plural character of the central sovereign author, and the contradiction between the affirmation of his absolute, universal value and the exclusion of common men, and women.

The defining term of the eulogies is *castitas*, the term J. C. Scaliger uses (with *frugalitas*) to characterise the greatness of the Virgilian style, in one of the passages from the *Poetics* selected by Pontanus as this scholar's testimony.[41] Explicitly evoked in the second speech, by Gallus, in the phrase 'chaste ... ear' (v.i.108), it is implicitly introduced in the first speech by Horace, to define an economy not only of text-fashioning, but also (and first) of self-fashioning. Echoing the verb Scaliger uses of Virgil's 'collected' style ('collegit'), in contrast to Homer's profusion ('fudit'), and his claim that Jupiter could not write better verses (see note 41), Horace asserts that Virgil is 'most severe / In fashion, and collection

---

[40] Virgil, *Symbolarum libri XVII*, edited by J. Pontanus, pp. 22–5. There are slight marks in the margins of this chapter in Jonson's copy, and a few words are underlined. As far as I can tell, these marks indicate either disagreement on usage, or endorsement of the point being made about Virgil.

[41] 'Virgilius semper sublimi spiritu ... Nec Jupiter meliores versus faciat ... Neque enim in mole frequentiave orationis, sed *in castitate atque frugalitate magnitudo constituta est*. ... Fudit Homerus, hic collegit: ille sparsit, hic composuit.' Virgil, *Symbolarum libri XVII*, edited by J. Pontanus, pp. 23–4 (my emphasis). The association of Virgil and his texts with *castitas* is widespread; see, for example, the description of the *Aeneid* as 'castius nihil' and of Virgil as 'castus' in Willes, *De re poetica*, pp. 110, 115.

of himselfe, / And then as cleare, and confident, as JOVE' (lines 105–7).

This assertion is the climax of a speech in which Scaliger's attribution to Virgil of a 'sublime spirit' is elaborated in terms of a Neoplatonic ascent, a passage and process of refinement from the underworld (or Tartarus) of 'tartarous moodes of common men' (line 103), through 'revolutions of discourse' (line 101), under the influence of 'reason' (line 102), to 'the nature and similitude / Of a right heavenly bodie' (lines 104–5).[42] This explicitly places Virgil at the highest level of a Neoplatonic scale of being, the lowest level of which is occupied by Lupus, the poetaster and the critics of 'the author', the 'common men' of the play who are figured, in the passage Virgil reads, by the monster Fame 'bred of earth'. The economy of 'collected' self/text-fashioning Virgil exemplifies is thus a measure and function of an achieved transcendent, immutable and immune selfhood – to which 'common men' have no access – a selfhood emblematised, in the earlier portrait by Augustus, in the Virgilian figure of Neptune's 'marble *trident*'.[43]

This single economy of text/self-fashioning is further elaborated in the next speech by Gallus.

> And yet so chaste, and tender is his eare,
> In suffering any syllable to passe,
> That, he thinkes may become the honour'd name
> Of issue to his so examin'd selfe;
> That all the lasting fruits of his full merit
> In his owne *poemes*, he doth still distaste:
> As if his mindes peece, which he strove to paint,
> Could not with fleshly pencils have her right.
>
> (lines 108–15)

Father–author, Virgil subjects his 'issue' to the same rigorous scrutiny that he subjects his 'examin'd selfe'. Called 'Exercise' in *Timber*, such scrutiny is identified as the second requisite of the true poet (after 'naturall wit') and illustrated by an anecdote about Virgil which may lie behind the image of poems as 'issue' here.

It is said of the incomparable *Virgil*, that he brought forth his verses like a Beare, and after form'd them with licking. *Scaliger*, the Father, writes it of him, that he

---

[42] This description echoes the 'Doctrine … of the *Scala a Tartaro ad primum ignem*', which Henry Reynolds attributes to Zoroaster in his summary of the natural philosophical discourse inherited from the ancients. Reynolds, *Mythomystes*, pp. 53–4; see also chapter 3, pp. 108–12.

[43] For an expert summary of the (Platonic) derivation of this idea of the self, and its subsequent history, see Charles Taylor, *Sources of the Self: The Making of The Modern Identity* (Cambridge University Press, 1989), especially pp. 115–20; in relation to Jonson, see Greene, 'Ben Jonson and the Centered Self', in Bloom, ed., *Ben Jonson*, especially, pp. 94–5.

made a quantitie of verses in the morning, which afore night he reduced to a lesse number. (*H&S*, vol. 8, p. 638)[44]

Like the fashioning of the poet's self by 'severe ... collection', the verses here are fashioned by 'reduction', a gathering in and curtailment, rather than a Homeric and, we might add, Shakespearean expansiveness (see note 45). This is the economy of text/self-fashioning Virgilian *castitas* represents: like the economy of the 'author function', it is an economy of curtailment, limitation, exclusion and, finally, closure. It is, moreover, an economy at once of a transcendent, bounded and immune self – always like itself – and of bounded, homogeneous 'issue', like each other and like their 'father–author' with whom they can consequently be identified (and, as Foucault points out, formal homogeneity is crucial to the author function). It is an economy which the eulogies themselves illustrate, as I have indicated, palpably restrained in their diction, syntax and rhythm, sounding like each other and like the sovereign, master – and dictatorial – voice at their centre. It is an economy, finally, that is in absolute contrast and opposition to the heterogeneous, plurivocal economy of the unbounded selves and freely circulating 'issue' outside. It is, in particular, in contrast to the economy represented by Ovid and his circle, which is an economy of linguistic as well as sexual 'licence', as the purge and prescriptive diet administered by Virgil to one of this circle – the poetaster Crispinus – will confirm.[45]

'But', Tibullus begins, not so much to contradict what has been said as to develop the 'soveraigne worth' (line 116) Virgil's 'issue' have for 'our lives',

> That, which he hath writ,
> Is with such judgement, labour'd and distill'd,
> Through all the needfull uses of our lives,
> That could a man remember but his lines,
> He should not touch at any serious point,
> But he might breathe his spirit out of him.
>
> (lines 118–23)

---

[44] Though the anecdote is recorded by Pontanus, Jonson is closer to the version by Donatus (quoted in *H&S*, vol. 11, p. 284). No explanation has been given for the reference to J. C. Scaliger, who does not record the anecdote in the *Poetics*.

[45] The variety of 'languages' in the various circles outside the circle at court is shown by King, who, interestingly, suggests Ovid is a 'borderline' case between those who speak well and those who speak badly (King, *The Language of Satirized Characters in Poetaster*, pp. xvi, 64). It is worth recalling that it is for his incapacity to exercise restraint that 'Shakespeare' is criticised in the well-known lines in *Timber*: 'sometimes it was necessary he should be stop'd' (*H&S*, vol. 7, p. 584). Shakespeare is portrayed here as something of a verbal prodigal, like the Ovid of *Poetaster* (with whom, as we have seen, there are other likenesses), and like Scaliger's Homer. It will, of course, be to Homer that Dryden will liken Shakespeare, while he will liken Jonson to Virgil. (I am grateful to Ian Donaldson for this reminder.)

Here the economy of *castitas* is turned towards ethical praxis, which is subject to the same rigorous scrutiny to which language has been subject. What this 'labour' has produced is a pure moral essence ('distill'd'), which will serve to inform the moral life of the man who remembers the poet's lines 'at any serious point'. Pure and absolute, like the normative Language Virgil illustrates, and likewise produced by 'Exercise', this moral information is nevertheless supplementary to, and separate from the formal order (a separation betrayed by the opening 'but'), as it is in the pedagogical and exegetical discourses and practices I discussed in earlier chapters, and as it is in the 'testimonies' of the early modern humanists given by Pontanus. Specifically relevant here is again the testimony of J. C. Scaliger, who praises Virgil's supreme knowledge of human life – 'Humanam vitam nemo melius, ac prudentius Virgilio novit' – while another testimony, by M. A. Maioragio, opens with an assertion of the self-evident usefulness to the moral life of the Virgilian text – 'Quid autem utilitatis haec in se habeant, quis est adeo stupidus, quin intelligat?'[46] This moral usefulness is invested with absolute, universal value by these scholars, as it is by Tibullus through the universalising figures of 'our lives' and 'a man', and through the suggestion of essence in 'distill'd'. It is of course a universality that is contradicted by the exclusive character of the circle Virgil addresses. Or rather the universality of this exclusive circle serves to confirm the identity of the 'common men' outside as 'others below' the normative humankind it represents.[47]

This exclusion is not only represented, and staged, but, as we have seen, worked for in the place of production by the learned character of the passage Virgil reads. It is indeed Virgil's 'learning' (line 129) that Horace treats in the last of the speeches of formal eulogy. This underscores its importance in Jonson's representation and use of Virgil as well as its separation from the schoolboy's *norma loquendi* and *norma vivendi* – a separation which we have seen throughout produced by exegetical and pedagogical discourses, including, foundationally, the discourses of the canonical commentaries of Servius and Macrobius, who both represent Virgil as supremely learned. This is echoed in the early modern 'testimonies' given by Pontanus, and notably in a passage from Fabio

---

[46] 'There is no one who understands human life so well and so wisely as Virgil.' 'Who can be so stupid as not to realise their intrinsic usefulness?' Virgil, *Symbolarum libri XVII*, edited by J. Pontanus, pp. 23, 24–5.

[47] Universal moral value has also been attributed to Shakespeare; as Cain points out, it was this speech that led Gifford to identify Jonson's Virgil with Shakespeare (Jonson, *Poetaster*, edited by Cain, p. 217).

Paolini's *Hebdomades* (1589) (marked in Jonson's copy), which first asserts what Virgil's learning is *not* – 'verborum volubilitas inanis . . . materia digna philosopho'[48] – like Jonson's Horace.

> His learning labours not the schoole-like glosse,
> That most consists in *ecchoing* wordes, and termes,
> And soonest wins a man an empty name:
> Nor any long, or far-fetcht circumstance,
> Wrapt in the curious generalties of artes:
>
> (lines 129–33)

While Paolini goes on to use a figure (from Cicero) to represent the poems as 'blossoming' and 'flowing' from an infinite knowledge of the arts,[49] Horace renders this relation of knowledge to poems in more strictly philosophical terms.

> But a direct, and *analyticke* summe
> Of all the worth and first effects of artes.
>
> (lines 134–5)

Then, with a generalising summarising move, Horace subsumes the particular figures of 'Virgil' in a single figure of an abstract principle – 'life':

> And for his *poesie* 'tis so ramm'd with life,
> That it shall gather strength of life, with being,
> And live hereafter, more admir'd, then now.
>
> (lines 136–8)[50]

This transcendent principle of 'life' is what guarantees a continuity of the 'admiration' to which the eulogies themselves bear witness. Readers of posterity are thus included in the circle of the same that the learned poet addresses, a circle, which, like the poet and his texts, is immune from the discontinuities and difference of history. As I have indicated, this immunity tends to be belied by the failure of modern readers to recognise in the canonical mediation of the Virgilian passage as natural philosophical discourse the ground of its intertextual relation to the play. This is not, however, to deny continuity. Indeed, not only is the universal human value of the central, sovereign author (whether Virgil

---

[48] 'An empty torrent of words . . . matter worthy of a philosopher'. Virgil, *Symbolarum libri XVII*, edited by J. Pontanus, p. 24.
[49] 'ex infinita . . . artium cognitione efflorescunt, atque redundant . . . illa . . . carmina', ibid.
[50] Compare Paolini: 'Sed *admirabile est* . . . quam unus inter omnes Latinos emineat . . . noster Maro: in quo tot *sunt congesta* bona atque virtutes . . .' (ibid.; my emphasis.) 'Ramm'd' is an effective translation of 'congesta sunt'.

or Shakespeare) reiterated, but continuity is itself a recurring object of attention: how to represent that which is immanent – as 'life', essence, nature, or 'real presence' – and which guarantees not merely survival, but continued 'admiration'.

The admiration towards Virgil is underscored in the play by the ceremonial reception he receives from Augustus, who declares they will exchange names – 'to CAESAR, VIRGIL / ... shall be made / A second sur-name, and to VIRGIL, CAESAR' (v.ii.3–5) – a declaration which, like an earlier use of the verb 'cherish' (v.i.67), evokes the marriage ceremony. More equal indeed than a marriage, their union – a union of Learning/ Virtue and Power – exemplifies the general relation between Augustus and 'learned heads' which Horace has earlier characterised as an integrating and holy relationship of absolute reciprocity.

> PHOEBUS himselfe shall kneel at CAESARs shrine,
> And deck it with bay-garlands dew'd with wine,
> To quite the worship CAESAR does to him
>
> (v.i.44–6)

The relationship here is exactly the 'perfect if closed reciprocity' which Stanley Fish identifies as 'the essence ... of the transaction between Jonson's poetry and the community of its readers', a 'community of the same', like the community of learned heads with Virgil and Augustus at their centre.[51] It is such a relation of reciprocity, and more precisely, of reciprocal legitimation that *The King's Entertainment* and masques work to achieve, the voice of the learned poet grounding the authority of 'the king' in an order which is identified as at once true, proper and natural, and from which oppositional voices are included/excluded as the con-fused noise of multiple, particular opinions – the voices of malice, ignorance and envy, the tartarous moods of common men. The com-munity of the same is, thus, finally, a monovocal community, the exclusion of other voices – the exclusion staged in the turn from anti-masque to main masque – being a condition of the reciprocity that its members enjoy.

That such exclusion is necessary for the learned poet to address his homogeneous audience, and, especially, the absolute 'eare' (v.iii.165) of the sovereign is underscored by Augustus's command that the doors be guarded 'and let none enter' (v.ii.55) and by the silence of Virgil at the interruption of Lupus. The interruption is, moreover, represented by

---

[51] Fish, 'Authors-Readers: Jonson's Community of the Same', pp. 252–3. See above, pp. 116, 166.

Augustus as a profanation of a sacred ceremony when he apologises to Virgil,

> Our eare is now too much prophan'd (grave MARO)
> With these distastes, to take thy sacred lines:
> Put up thy booke, till both the time and wee
> Be fitted with more hallow'd circumstance
> For the receiving so divine a worke.
>
> (v.iii.165–9)

That it is not only the book that is sacred, but the poet himself is indicated by what follows the interruption. For Virgil maintains his silence until the bringer and embodiment of 'distastes' – the tastes, we might say, of Dis – is gagged. The sovereign poet is thus kept apart, like and with his sacred book, from the tartarous moods of common men and their profaning noise, which he depicts, but with which he never directly engages.

When he does finally speak it is to approve as '(f)aire and just' (v.iii.135) Caesar's treatment of Lupus, whom Virgil condemns, without addressing, as a 'malicious, ignorant, and base / Interpreter' (lines 141–2), who will disturb the order of the state, as a '*satyrick* spirit' (line 138) will not – an explicit reiteration of the distinction made earlier between illegitimate and legitimate opposition, crucial to the defence both of Horace and 'the author' of *Poetaster*. Virgil speaks, that is, as absolute judge, a role which is immediately formalised by his appointment as Praetor (juridical magistrate) in the trial of Demetrius and the poetaster Crispinus. Structuring the trial through his short questions and commands Virgil then assumes the sovereign second person plural 'to tender our opinion' (line 344), an 'opinion' which is actually a judgement, exonerating Horace and condemning Crispinus and Demetrius, in terms which echo and endorse the second prologue's defence of 'the author' of *Poetaster*. The absolute, definitive and monologic character of the sovereign voice is confirmed when the speech receives no answer. It is, indeed, unanswerable.[52]

Likewise unanswered and unanswerable is Virgil's second formal speech, which at once judges and corrects the language of the poetaster Crispinus (v.iii.531–65). Virgil here exercises fully and specifically the

---

[52] The example of Virgil is an important exception to Peter Womack's point that the aspirations of Jonson's father figures to monologic discourse are ineffective, although his related point about the gap between the categories of such discourse and the 'heteroglot city' obviously bears on the relation between Virgil's master voice, and the multiple voices of 'others below'. See Womack, *Ben Jonson*, pp. 81, 85.

normative, regulatory function which he exercises punctually and briefly in what precedes through critical comments on examples of the
poetaster's language: 'strangely worded' (line 297), 'it stickes strangely'
(line 517). In chapter 4 we saw how Jonson uses 'strange', on the one
hand, of his own usage, which the ground of Virgil's learning serves to
draw within the bounds of the 'proper'; on the other, of the universe of
the anti-masque, which is thus at once included and excluded as contrary to the 'proper' normative universe of the main masque it therefore
serves to uphold. Virgil's critical comments similarly include and exclude the language of Crispinus as contrary to the normative system of
proper Language. This exclusion is then spectacularly staged by the
purge administered to Crispinus, which Virgil follows up by prescribing
a 'holsome dyet' (line 536). With distinctly schoolmasterly intonations,
as I indicated in chapter 1, this monologic speech reproduces, even as it
mobilises, the *norma loquendi* of the schoolboy's Virgil. More specifically, I
compared it with an overtly pedagogic passage in *Timber*, which likewise
mobilises Virgil as *norma loquendi*, exemplifying the 'abstinence' (line 558)
that Crispinus is prescribed here. Virgil is mobilised, that is, in both texts
to produce the economy of 'proper' Language he exemplifies and
figures, a 'chaste' economy of curtailment and abstinence, of 'collection'
and 'thrift', in contrast and in opposition to the economy of formal and
sexual licence Ovid and his circle (including the poetaster Crispinus)
exemplify and represent.

The Virgilian economy of *castitas* tends, finally, to the close of 'play' –
a tendency which the poet's last words dramatise: 'So: now dissolve the
court' (line 611). For this brings to a close both the trial and the play
which is *Poetaster*. All that follows is a short speech by Augustus, which
confirms the closure by reiterating the structure of oppositional worlds
which has informed the play, and which informs representations of it:
on the one hand, 'low, ... despised objects' (lines 619–20), 'flat, grovel-
ling soules' (line 621) and their 'discords' (line 615) motivated by 'Envy'
(line 624); on the other, the 'high' (line 619) community of self-present
'selves' (line 621) united in 'mutual loves' (line 623) and distinguished by
'merit' (line 624). This is the community of 'all true arts, and learning'
(line 618), an exclusive, proto-professional community of men of letters,
guardians of learning, and of the normative economy of proper, chaste
Language and Life exemplified and figured by the sovereign, chaste and
learned author at their centre.

THE BEST MASTER: VIRGIL IN *TIMBER*

As we saw at the close of chapter 1, Virgil is placed as example and figure of an absolute economy of proper Language and Life, preserved by a community of the learned and virtuous, in a passage in *Timber*, which is translated from Quintilian, and which deals with the proper Language to be acquired and practised by the educated schoolboy, and, especially, with the use of archaisms. This is the 'place' occupied by the figure of Virgil throughout the pages of these posthumously published notes which treat reading and writing practices. This is indicated by modifications – both minor and more major – which Jonson makes to texts he translates. While minor modifications insist at a general level on the absolute character of the Virgilian model, more major modifications insist on the specifically 'chaste' character of the absolute model Virgil represents for the implied audience of these pages, which is just such an (ideal) privileged community as the passage from Quintilian describes and as *Poetaster* represents as Virgil's stage audience.

The minor modifications which underscore the absolute character of the Virgilian model usually consist in added phrases, as in the following quotations (added phrases in bold type): '**incomparable** *Virgil*'; '**the best writers** ... *Virgil* ... *Horace*'; 'the **best Masters** of the *Epick*, *Homer* and *Virgil*'.[53] It is, moreover, Virgil that is cited as authorising example for the definition of a poem, in one of the few passages that appear to be Jonson's own.

> even one alone verse sometimes makes a perfect *Poeme*. As, when *Aeneas* hangs up, and consecrates the Armes of *Abas*, with this Inscription;
> *Aeneas haec de Danais victoribus arma.*
> And calls it a *Poeme*, or *Carmen*. (p. 635)

Virgil's naming of the inscription as 'carmen' – 'rem carmine signo' (*Aeneid* 3, line 287) – authorises the definition of a poem by Virgilian example, and the Virgilian example is, in turn, invested with an absolute character by Jonson's phrase 'Perfect *Poeme*'.

More interesting, however, than minor modifications and additions are more specific, and more substantial modifications Jonson makes to passages which he translates from Vives and Quintilian (critical authorities he draws on extensively in *Timber*), on the use of particular forms – hyperbole and archaisms. For, in each case, Virgilian practice is turned

---

[53] *H&S*, vol. 8, pp. 638, 639, 647. Compare the phrase 'master-spirits', used of Virgil and Horace in the 'apologeticall Dialogue' to *Poetaster* (quoted above, p. 153). Details of these modifications are given in Clayton, '"Tempests, and such like Drolleries"', pp. 172–4.

so as to illustrate a *restrained, limited,* 'chaste' use of these forms – a turn which, in both cases, is a turn against the critical authority being translated and, in the first case, a turn against the consensus of critical opinion.

On hyperbole Jonson begins by following Vives, allowing the use of the figure merit according to the Erasmian criterion of 'amplification': 'Superlation, and overmuchnesse amplifies' (*H&S*, vol. 8, p. 624).[54] But restrictions are immediately introduced: 'It may be above faith, but never above a meane.' Vives' statement of what is required – that hyperbole be above faith but not above a mean[55] – has here been turned into a concession – 'may' – and an absolute negative – 'never' – a modification which registers a pressure to curtailment. More indicative still of this pressure is Jonson's procedure in supplying examples. For, omitting three examples from Virgil, which Vives gives between the two statements Jonson has translated (see note 56), Jonson goes instead to another authority, the elder Seneca, who, in his collection of rhetorical pieces entitled *Suasoriae*, quotes Virgil, but as an example, specifically, of a *restrained* use of hyperbole. Jonson gives this example and the contrasting example Seneca gives of unrestrained use (Vives gives no such examples), a contrast which underscores the restraint of Virgilian practice.

It was ridiculous in *Cestius,* when hee said of *Alexander: Fremit Oceanus, quasi indignetur, quod terras relinquas*; But propitiously from *Virgil:*–
> *Credas innare revulsas*
> *Cycladas.*

He doth not say it was so, but seem'd to be so. Although it be somewhat incredible, that is excus'd before it be spoken.[56]

Framed by a figure of excuse, the figure of hyperbole, as practised by Virgil, is contained within 'proper' boundaries. That these boundaries

---

[54] 'Superlatio, seu nimietas ... ad amplificationem pertinet'. J. L. Vives, *De ratione dicendi,* as quoted in *H&S*, vol. 11, p. 269.

[55] 'supra fidem iubent esse, sed non supra modum', ibid.

[56] Cestius descripsit: sic fremit Oceanus quasi indignetur quod terras relinquas ... Vergilius quid ait? qui de navibus:
> credas innare revulsas
> Cycladas. (*Æn.* viii. 691–2.)
Non dicit hoc fieri sed videri. Propitiis auribus accipitur, quamvis incredibile est, quod excusatur antequam dicitur. (Seneca, *Suasoriae,* as quoted in *H&S*, vol. 11, p. 270)
Jonson's minor modifications – the addition of 'ridiculous' and the translation of 'propitiis auribus' as an adverb 'propitiously' – sharpen the contrast between the two examples. The Virgilian examples given by Vives are: *Eclogue* 5, line 62; *Aeneid* 4, line 177 (from the description of Fame, translated in *Poetaster*); *Aeneid* 7, line 808 (from the description of Camilla, quoted by Jonson in *The Masque of Queens*). Not quoted by Herford and Simpson, who only supply the passages Jonson translates, they may be found in Juan Luis Vives, *Opera omnia,* edited by G. Majansio, reprint, 8 vols. (London: Gregg Press, 1964), vol. 2, p. 125.

are more Jonsonian than Virgilian is indicated not only by the departure from Vives, who qualifies neither the use of hyperbole nor the practice of Virgil in this way, but also, more generally, by the departure from the consensus of critics, who have always agreed on, if not always approved of, Virgil's 'sustained use' of hyperbole, especially in the *Aeneid*.[57] Indeed, the use of such 'qualifying' words as Jonson makes typical of Virgilian practice – a use which 'strictly, eliminates the hyperbole', as Hardie says – is, as he shows, only an occasional Virgilian strategy (Hardie, *Virgil's 'Aeneid'*, p. 244). Making what is occasional typical, Jonson limits Virgilian practice to exemplify an economy of restraint, necessarily in contradictory tension with a figure which is by definition an excess, associated with strong, even 'excessive emotion' (p. 243).[58]

Similar limiting moves are made by Jonson when translating Quintilian on the use of archaisms in general, and on Virgilian practice in particular, in the two passages I quoted at the close of chapter 1. In the first passage, which is translated from the second book of the *Institutio*, a difference from Quintilian is initially signalled by the omission of his affirmative statement that exposure to, and use of ancient authors may improve a schoolboy's style.[59] Then, although recommending, like Quintilian, that 'both, the old and the new' should be read when the boys' 'judgements are firme, and out of danger', Jonson inserts next Quintilian's earlier warning about the possible negative effects of excessive and premature exposure to 'modern' authors: 'take heed, that their new flowers, and sweetnesse doe not as much corrupt, as the others drinesse, and squallor' (*H&S*, vol. 8, p. 618)[60] – a limiting move register-

---

[57] Philip R. Hardie, *Virgil's 'Aeneid': 'Cosmos' and 'Imperium'* (Oxford: Clarendon Press, 1986), p. 289.

[58] Interestingly, the declared 'ultimate aim' of Hardie's long discussion of Virgil's use of hyperbole in the *Aeneid* is 'to show how Vergilian hyperbole may be, in Quintilian's phrase, a "*decens veri superiectio*"'. (p. 244). Hardie shares, that is, Jonson's aspiration to bring the Virgilian use of this figure within the boundaries of the 'decent' or 'proper', though he defines these boundaries less strictly.

[59] 'suaserim … antiquos legere, ex quibus si assumatur solita [*sic*], ac virilis ingenii vis … tum noster hic cultus clarius enitescet'. *M. Fabii Quintiliani institutionum oratoriarum libri XII. Et declamationes XIX* (Paris, 1528), lib. II, ca. vi. fo. xvr. This is Jonson's copy, now in the library of Emmanuel College, Cambridge, from which I shall usually quote. Butler translates: 'I should strongly recommend the reading of ancient authors, since if we succeed in absorbing the robust vigour and virility of their native genius, our more finished style will shine with an added grace.' M. Fabius Quintilianus, *The Institutio Oratoria*, edited and translated by H. E. Butler, 4 vols., reprint (Cambridge, Mass.; Harvard University Press; London: William Heinemann, 1963), vol. I, II.v.23.

[60] The Latin runs: 'Alterum, quod huic diversum est, ne recentis huius lasciviae flosculis capti, voluptate quadam prava deleniantur, et praedulce illud genus … adament.' Quintilian, *Institutionum oratoriarum*, lib. II, ca. vi, fo. xvr. For the aversion to the coinage of new words in *Poetaster*, see King, *The Language of Satirized Characters in Poetaster*, pp. xviii–xix, 60–2.

ing a pressure towards restraint in relation to the new as well as to the old. The ideal standard of 'Language' that such doubly bounded use represents is then immediately linked, as it is not by Quintilian, to Virgilian practice and, contrastively, to Spenserian: '*Spencer*, in affecting the Ancients, writ no Language: Yet I would have him read for his matter; but as *Virgil* read *Ennius.*' Here, though the ostensible compari-son is between the schoolboy-reader of Spenser and Virgil as reader of Ennius, there is an implicit contrast between Spenserian display in 'affecting the Ancients' and Virgil's relation to Ennius, which is placed (as it is by Pontanus) on the side of temperance.[61]

Such temperance with respect to both archaisms and neologisms is advocated again in the second passage, some two hundred lines later, which is translated from the first book of *The Institutio* (chapter 10) (*H&S*, vol. 8, p. 622). For, to the opening definition of Custom as the 'Mistresse of Language' – exactly translated from Quintilian – Jonson adds his own exhortation against the frequent coinage of new words – 'But we must not be too frequent with the mint, every day coyning' – and Quintilian's against persistent recourse to archaisms – 'Nor fetch words from the extreme and utmost ages', giving as the reason for such twofold regula-tion of the authority of custom Quintilian's criterion of clarity: 'since the chiefe vertue of a style is perspicuitie, and nothing so vitious in it, as to need an Interpreter'. The pressure to curtailment registered in these negative prescriptions is signalled too by a change in the order of sentences. For, while Quintilian's caution about the use of archaisms follows an affirmation of their felicitous effects, Jonson reverses the order so that the affirmation is framed by the caution, a qualifying move underscored by the addition of 'sometimes' to the translation of the affirmation, which is then further qualified by the use of a contrastive conjunction – 'But' – for Quintilian's 'Ergo' – to introduce the ideal normative 'Language' – 'the eldest of the present, and newest of the past'.

Words borrow'd of Antiquity, doe lend a kind of Majesty to style, and are not without their delight *sometimes*. For they have the Authority of yeares, and out of their intermission doe win to themselves a kind of grace like newnesse. *But* the

---

[61] Virgil, *Symbolarum libri XVII*, edited by J. Pontanus, p. 14. The extent of Virgil's use of Ennius has continued to be debated. Cordier, for example, argues for extensive use. A. Cordier, *Etudes sur le vocabulaire epique dans l'Enéide* (Paris: Les Belles Lettres, 1939). Jonson's position on Virgil's use of archaisms is not such a marked departure from critical consensus as it is in the case of Virgil's use of hyperbole.

eldest of the present, and newest of the past Language is the best. (ibid.; emphasis mine)[62]

In what follows, the pressure to curtailment emerges as a pressure, specifically, to the curtailment of contemporary practices. For, in his translation of Quintilian's rhetorical question – 'quid est aliud vetus sermo, quam vetus loquendi consuetudo?' – 'For what was the ancient Language ... but the ancient Custome?' – Jonson inserts a qualifying clause to 'Language' – 'which some men so doate upon' – and so introduces what will shortly be quite overt – a critique of those amongst his contemporaries 'affecting the Ancients'. Their practice will be (again) explicitly set against the practice of Virgil, the contrast being here anticipated in the verb 'doate' – signalling an excessive, uncontrolled affective relation – to which Virgil's 'chaste' relation to 'Antiquity' will furnish a corrective.

The examples of Virgilian practice are taken from Quintilian, but from the next chapter (11) on spelling. Jonson places the examples immediately after his (exact) translation of Quintilian's description of the community of the learned and virtuous as the guardians of the normative standards of 'Language' and 'Life'. Virgil is thus placed, as he is in *Poetaster*, at the centre of this community, as the example and figure of the Language/Life it preserves, from which those who 'doate' upon other forms and practices, like Ovid and his circle and, especially, Crispinus, are to be excluded, 'banish'd'.

For what was the ancient Language, which some men so doate upon, but the ancient Custome? Yet when I name Custome, I understand not the vulgar Custome: For that were a precept no lesse dangerous to Language, then life, if we should speake or live after the manners of the vulgar: But that I call Custome of speech, which is the consent of the learned; as Custome of life, which is the

---

[62] The Latin runs: 'Verba a vestutate repetita non solum magnos assertores habent, sed etiam afferunt orationi maiestatem aliquam, non sine delectatione, nam et auctoritatem antiquitatis habent, et quia intermisssa sunt, gratiam novitati similem parant. Sed opus est modo, ut neque crebra sint haec neque manifesta ... nec utique ab ultimis et iam obliteratis repetita temporibus ... oratio vero, cuius summa virtus est perspicuitas, quam sit vitiosa, si egeat interprete? Ergo ut novorum optima erunt maxime vetera, ita veterum maxime nova.' Quintilian, *Institutionum oratoriarum*, Lib. I, ca. x. Butler translates: 'Archaic words not only enjoy the patronage of distinguished authors, but also give style a certain majesty and charm. For they have the authority of age behind them, and for the very reason that they have fallen into desuetude, produce an attractive effect not unlike that of novelty. But such words must be used sparingly ... nor above all must they be drawn from remote and forgotten ages ... But what a faulty thing is speech, whose prime virtue is clearness, if it requires an interpreter to make its meaning plain! Consequently in the case of old words the best will be those that are newest, just as in the case of new words the best will be the oldest.' Quintilian, *The Institutio*, trans. Butler, vol. I, I.vi.39–41.

consent of the good. *Virgill* was most loving of Antiquity; yet how rarely doth
hee insert *aquai*, and *pictai*! *Lucretius* is scabrous and rough in these; hee seekes
'hem: As some doe *Chaucerismes* with us, which were better expung'd and
banish'd. (ibid.)

In his representation of Virgilian practice here Jonson departs significantly from Quintilian, a departure which moves in the same direction
as his departure from Vives. For, while Quintilian simply states that
'Vergil, always a passionate lover of antiquity, inserted *pictai vestis* and
aquai in his poems',[63] Jonson restricts Virgil's relation to one that is
'loving' 'yet' restrained ('how rarely doth hee insert') – an illustration,
once again, of *castitas*.

The departure from Quintilian is then signalled in a peculiarly literal
way. For, having given the Virgilian examples, Jonson sets aside the Latin
critic – indeed he does not return to him again in *Timber* – and turns to his
copy of Virgil. For in what follows the Virgilian examples he echoes the
gloss given to one of them – 'pictai vestis' – by Pontanus, who comments
that poets of old, especially Lucretius, would frequently use *aï* (for *æ*)
because this was ancient usage, and Martial condemned this licence, as
well as the use of obsolete words, amongst the poets of his day.[64] Two lines
from the relevant epigram are quoted.[65] Jonson quotes the second line of
this epigram – 'quae per salebras altaque saxa cadunt' – in the next but
one sentence after his condemnation of Lucretius and those who practise
Chaucerisms. But its imagery is already present in the terms with which
he condemns Lucretius: 'scabrous and rough'.[66] Using Martial's imagery
to condemn the example of Lucretius given by Pontanus, Jonson then
follows Martial by turning to what he takes to be an equivalent contemporary licence: Chaucerisms. Those who dotingly indulge in Chaucerisms are placed, with Lucretius, as examples of unrestrained use, in
contrast to Virgil, whose ideal restraint they serve to underscore, like the
contrasting example given in the passage on hyperbole.

---

[63] Butler's translation of: 'unde *pictai vestis*, et *aquai* Virgilius amantissimus vetustatis carminibus
inseruit'. Quintilian, *The Institutio*, trans. Butler, vol. 1, 1.vii.18. I quote from the Latin in Butler's
edition, as in Jonson's copy of Quintilian the second example is not *aquai* but *aulai*. This indicates
that he was probably not using his copy here.

[64] Virgil, *Symbolarum libri XVII*, edited by J. Pontanus, col. 1831. The phrase 'pictaï vestis', from
Aeneid 9 (line 26), is translated by Fairclough: 'broidered robes'.

[65] I quote from M. V. Martialis, *Epigrams*, edited and translated by W. C. Ker, 2 vols. (Cambridge,
Mass.: Harvard University Press, 1950), vol. 2, pp. 300–1 (book 11, epigram 90). Pontanus quotes
lines 5–6.

[66] The first two lines describe poems 'affecting the ancients' as a rough ride. Ker translates 'No
poems win your favour that speed on a gentle path, only those that fall over rough places and
high cliffs.'

Traces of the pressure towards Virgilian restraint may be detected even in Jonson's own writing here. For between the condemnation of Lucretius/contemporary doaters and the quotation from Martial there are two sentences, the first spreading over several lines in an expansive amplification of the trope of figurative discourse as 'flowers'.[67] The second sentence opens with the interjection 'Marry', which carries a spontaneous, dialogic thrust, making immediate curtailment of Jonson's own writing/self here the first object of the negative prescription which follows.

Marry, we must not play, or riot too much with them, as in *Paranomasies* [*sic*]: Nor use too swelling, or ill-sounding words; *Quae per salebras, altaque saxa cadunt.*

Recalling, with the quotation from Martial, the examples of unrestrained usage he has condemned, Jonson curtails his own practice, drawing it within the bounds of the 'proper' normative economy Virgil represents for the community of 'proper' speakers/writers ('we'). As the negative prescriptions signal, this is an economy of abstinence – *castitas* – tending to curtail the expansive, and expensive, indulgence of pleasure – moral and social as well as verbal: 'play, or riot'. It is an economy 'objectively' where Peter Womack finally places Jonson, 'on the side of "Lent"' (Womack, *Ben Jonson*, p. 135), incompatible by definition with 'play on the word',[68] as it is incompatible with hyperbole, and, we might add, the world of (the) play.

THE BEST MASTER WITHDRAWN: THE TWO VERSIONS OF *EVERY MAN IN* AND LATER MASQUES

The tendency of this economy to the curtailment and closure of play assumes, as we have seen, literal form both in *Poetaster*, which is effectively closed by Virgil's last words, and in the Quarto version of *Every Man In* (published 1601), which closes with Judge Clement's quotation of the last line of *Eclogue* 3: '*Claudite iam rivos pueri, sat prata biberunt*' (v.iii.448–9).[69] In chapter 2 I pointed out that this quotation works not only as a form of closure, but also as a form of control, which mobilises the structure of

---

[67] 'Some words are to be cull'd out for ornamant and colour, as wee gather flowers to straw houses, or make Garlands; but they are better when they grow to our style; as in a Meadow, where though the meere grasse and greennesse delights, yet the variety of flowers doth heighten and beautifie.'

[68] W. Shakespeare, *The Merchant of Venice*, iii.vi.43.

[69] Fairclough translates: 'Shut off the rill now, my lads; the meadows have drunk enough.' For Puttenham's translation see above, chapter 2, p. 59.

authority folded into the Virgilian text to produce a hierarchy of privilege between learned insiders with access to the ground of the quotation's canonical mediation, and ignorant outsiders. The same work is done by another Virgilian quotation earlier in the play – the description by the Sibyl of the privileged few who escape the under-world – which, as I indicated at the outset of chapter 4, likewise requires access to the ground of canonical mediations and so aspires to produce the elite it describes.

In the Folio version, the play is no longer closed by the Virgilian quotation but by a vernacular echo of Pontanus's version of the Servian gloss, from which the specifically Virgilian intonations have disap-peared.[70] This might seem a demystifying move of accommodation, all the more so as the form the closure now takes expressly includes the public theatre audience (see note 70). There is, moreover, another Virgilian quotation in the Quarto version – the opening words of the *Aeneid* quoted by Clement in Act V (v.iii.263) – which is removed from the Folio version, together with the most explicitly authorial speeches, with which the Virgilian voice is associated. But the earlier quotation from *Aeneid* 6 is retained, and the ironic thrust of its significance is even underscored, as we shall see. What I want to suggest is that, given this remaining quotation and its emphasised ironic thrust, the other re-movals may by symptomatic not so much of accommodation as of withdrawal, not so much of a closing as of a widening of the gap between the absolute 'upper air' of those whom Jove loves and the 'underworld' of the place of the play.

The association of the Virgilian voice with an absolute authorial perspective is indicated by the names of the characters to whom the quotations are attributed – Judge Clement and Prospero – who are thereby identified as agents of a benevolent, controlling authorial over-

---

[70] Closing, as in the Quarto version, with an apparently inclusive, reconciliatory gesture (belied in the former by the exclusive effect of the Virgilian quotation), Clement declares that Brayne-worme (the type of ingenious servant, formerly Musco) will be his 'mistris' for the evening: 'BRAYNE-WORME! to whom all my addresses of courtship shall have their reference. Whose adventures, this day, when our grand-children shall heare to be made a *fable*, I doubt not, but it shall find both spectators, and *applause*' (v.v.87–91; my emphasis). In his note to the closing line of *Eclogue* 3 Pontanus repeats the Servian allegorical interpretation, then gives two other examples of formal modes of closure, the first being the use of 'dixi' in forensic discourse, the second being the use of 'plaudite' in the theatre: 'Potest etiam allegoria esse, pro, satis cantatum est, discedite: sicut peractae caussae (sic) symbolum est, Dixi: *fabulae peractae, Plaudite*.' (This may be under-stood, allegorically, for enough has been sung, have done. Similarly, a case is closed with the symbolic device 'I have spoken', a fable with an appeal for applause.) Virgil, *Symbolarum libri XVII*, edited by J. Pontanus, col. 85 (my emphasis).

seer.[71] It is, moreover, on hearing that Matheo claims to be 'an Author' (v.iii.262) that Clement quotes the first words of the *Aeneid*, introducing, as an authorial, absolute measure of the would-be author, the figure who will shortly perform this function as a *dramatis persona* in *Poetaster*. Further, the most explicitly authorial speeches which follow – the impassioned speech of Lorenzo (v.iii.312–43) and Clement's reply (lines 344–8) – which set the nature of true poetry against the false poetry of poetasters anticipate the Neoplatonic system of oppositions which will inform the Virgilian scenes in their relation to the rest of the play: true poetry is spiritual, absolute, uncontaminated by 'earthly' (line 330) thoughts, 'fit to be seene / Of none but grave and consecrated eyes' (lines 332–3), exactly as 'grave MARO' (*Poetaster*, v.iii.165) will be 'seen' in *Poetaster*. False poetry is, however, preferred in the contemporary world of '(o)pinion' (line 312) 'governd altogether by the influence of humour' (lines 344–5). In the Folio version, Lorenzo's speech has disappeared, together with the Virgilian quotation, while Clement merely gestures towards the absolute position of his earlier speech, defining the nature of the true poet in terms relative to the urban perspective of his addressee.

There goes more to the making of a good *Poet*, then a Sheriffe, Mr KITELY . . . I will do more reverence to him . . . then I will to the Major, (i.e. Mayor) out of his yeere. (v. v. 39–43)

Clement here is more the benevolent city magistrate immersed in the relative perspectives of contemporary, urban life than the detached, learned scholar overseeing and regulating from an absolute authorial position 'above', like, and by means of, the Virgilian model he quotes.

Yet this model has not disappeared from the play. The retained Virgilian quotation occurs in an exchange between the young man Prospero (called Well-Bred in the Folio version) and two comic butts, Bobadilla and the would-be poet Matheo, who are obsessed with the criterion 'fashion gentlemen use' (i.iii.154). The ironic thrust of the quotation against those to whom it is addressed is underscored in the Folio version, which adds 'of fashion' to Matheo's criticism of Prospero's brother: 'he doth not carrie himselfe like a gentleman' (ii.iii.15) ('he doth not carry himselfe like a gentleman of fashion' (Folio version, iii.i.19–20)). 'Oh Signior Matheo', replies Prospero, 'that's a grace peculiar but to a few; *quos aequus amavit Jupiter*' (ii.iii.16–17; unchanged in the Folio

---

[71] The character of Prospero with its Virgilian associations may have influenced the naming of the Virgilian figure in *The Tempest*, particularly as Shakespeare is identified as one of the 'principall Comoedians' of the first performance of *Every Man In* in 1598. See *H&S*, vol. 3, p. 403.

version, except for Matheo's name, which is Mr Matthew). That this
description by the Sibyl of the few who escape from the underworld into
the upper air is to be understood in terms of the canonical Neoplatonic
mediations as a description of the few allowed to escape from the prison-
house of the body and the underworld of material and temporal contingency – precisely, the world of 'fashion' – is confirmed by a translation
in *Cynthia's Revels*, 'some few, / Whom equall JOVE hath lov'd' (v.i.37–8),
which is used, without irony, of those who stand out as true courtiers,
'The better race in court / That have the true nobilitie, call'd vertue'
(lines 30–1). In *Every Man In* – both versions – there is irony, but only for
those with access to the quotation's canonical ground. This is signalled
by Matheo's response to the quotation – 'I understand you sir' (I.iii.18) –
and Prospero's retort – 'No question you do sir', to which 'or you doe
not' has been added in the Folio version (III.i.24), which again serves to
underscore the irony. For those who do understand, the irony works as a
form of 'grace', which allows them to escape the underworld of every
man in his humour, its multiple, particular opinions, into the upper air
of an absolute authorial master position. But, in the Folio version, this is
the only remaining trace of such a position, now all but withdrawn, a
touchstone still for those few readers/spectators – now very few – whose
own responses will determine their place, whether in the underworld or
with the privileged authorial circle of those the Virgilian voice both
addresses and describes.

The wider gap between the two worlds, which these changes to the
Virgilian presence in *Every Man In* suggest, is confirmed by a more
restricted use of Virgil in later court masques. As we saw in chapter 4,
Virgil is used from the outset to ground local features of the form,
whether of the anti-masque or (more often) the main masque, until
Oberon when a single Virgilian text – *Eclogue* 6 – is used to ground not
only particular features but the binary structure of the form. Subsequently, as the anti-masque comes increasingly to resemble the early
satirical comedies, without their authorial master figures, Virgil is used
to ground local features of the main masque only. This is strikingly
illustrated by *The Masque of Augurs* (performed 1621, published 1622)
(*H&S*, vol. 7, pp. 624–47). The main masque, in verse, draws on a wealth
of learning displayed in dense notes, including Servian mediations of
Virgilian knowledge of ancient ritual practice, which, as in *The King's
Entertainment*, cover – conceal and underwrite – the authority of James,
who is associated with Aeneas/Augustus (p. 642, note p; p. 643, note r).
The anti-masque, in prose, is a miniature satirical comedy with a cast of
noisy, incompetent London commoners, including a 'rare Artist . . . a

Projector of Masques', who 'speakes all languages in ill *English*' (p. 633) and who produces, as a second anti-masque, '*a perplex'd Dance of straying, and deform'd Pilgrims, taking severall pathes*' (p. 638). With baroque self-reflexivity this anti-masque within the anti-masque represents, in the mode of the earlier anti-masques, especially in the symbolic form of dance, the 'confused' strangeness of multiple, particular differences, which the framing anti-masque represents in the mode of the satirical comedies, especially in its plural, particular idiolects, and above all in the babelic English of the Projector of Masques, 'deformed' by contamination with multiple vernaculars ('all languages'), which is virtually incomprehensible, virtually, indeed, noise. Simply '*frighted away*' (p. 638), this universe has no point of contact with the universe of the main masque. There is no figure like Silenus to comprehend them both. And the voice of Virgil is to be heard only in the main masque, the anti-masque being now a place where such a voice is out of place.

'IMBARQU'D FOR HELL': VIRGIL'S 'VOYCE' IN THE EPIGRAMS[72]

The absolute separation between the universe of the main masque and the universe of the anti-masque/satirical comedy, and the confinement of the figure/voice of Virgil to the first, are echoed in the *Epigrams* (*H&S*. vol. 8, pp. 21–89). Reproducing this separation in their division between poems in praise of the virtuous/learned and poems in condemnation of the vicious/ignorant, they confine the voice of Virgil, with one ambivalent exception, to the first group. As others have shown, these poems represent individuals as ideal, moral paradigms,[73] so that, as a group, they represent, as Stanley Fish has argued, a community of 'the same', like the community of 'learned heads' in *Poetaster*, whose speeches are interchangeable, as Fish suggests the poems of praise are.[74] Once again Virgil is, both more and less explicitly, a central, shared, guiding and unifying master voice to this community. This is underscored, if somewhat paradoxically, by the ambivalent exception mentioned above, the last poem of the collection in which, for the first time, the universes of the vicious/ignorant and virtuous/learned are brought together, in a parodic descent into the 'underworld' of Fleet Ditch, sewer and rubbish tip of London city. For, as with the quotation from *Aeneid* 6 in *Every Man*

---

[72] The phrases quoted are from epigram 128, discussed below.
[73] For example, G. A. E. Parfitt, 'The Poetry of Ben Jonson', *Essays in Criticism* 18 (1968), pp. 18–31; David Wykes, 'Ben Jonson's "Chast Booke" – *The Epigrammes*', *Renaissance and Modern Studies* 13 (1969), pp. 76–87.
[74] Fish, 'Authors-Readers: Jonson's Community of the Same', p. 250; see above, pp. 116, 166.

In, the Virgilian intertext is mobilised both to point up the absolute separation between the two universes, even as they are brought together, and to produce an analogous division amongst readers.

In 'Inviting a Friend to Supper' (epigram 101), a poem exceptionally in praise of a community rather than an individual, a reading from Virgil's poetry is offered as entertainment for the guests.[75] As in *Poetaster*, the community is unified around their shared texts, 'Of which we'll speake our minds, amidst our meate' (line 23). A line Jonson has added to his sources, this aligns intellectual exchange with the sharing of food, both rituals serving to unify the community. Again too, malicious informers are explicitly excluded (line 36), another addition, which marks the 'absolutist position' occupied by Jonson in the poem 'seeing all, controlling all, and defining all' (Boehrer, 'Renaissance Overeating', p. 1075), the position occupied in *Poetaster* by Virgil and 'the author', who simultaneously include and exclude their enemies as malicious and ignorant false interpreters. The poem also puts more emphasis than its sources on moderation (line 35), which has led critics to see in the poem 'a utopian vision of *restrained* conviviality' (p. 1072; my emphasis), a restraint which Joseph Loewenstein suggests the 'plain style' of the poem itself illustrates.[76] Both banquet and poem illustrate, that is, the economy – of *castitas* – figured and exemplified in *Poetaster* by Virgil, and by the privileged circle of those invited to, and unified by, the intellectual banquet of his poetry reading.

This economy is associated, however, not only with this particular poem and its occasion, but with the collection as a whole, which is described, in one of the poems of condemnation, as 'my chast booke' (epigram 49, line 6). Significantly enough the addressee here is a figure called Play-wright, who inhabits a universe of 'language' (line 4), 'manners' (line 5) and meanings (line 3) which are dismissed as inappropriate to such a book – an inclusion/exclusion of the forms it defines as its own contraries which recalls both the masques and the Virgilian scenes in *Poetaster*. More specifically, it is the licence, both verbal and sexual – the 'bawdrie' (line 3) – of the world of Play-wright that is condemned as contrary to the book's 'chaste' character – an incompatibility between

---

[75] In this much analysed poem, Jonson draws on Martial and Juvenal (*H&S*, vol. 11, pp. 20–1; compare Greene, *The Light in Troy*, pp. 278-86); in his version of the ideal banquet, Juvenal specifically recommends Homer and Virgil as appropriate entertainment. This entertainment is described by Boehrer as an 'immoderate, even hypersophisticated pleasure' (Boehrer, 'Renaissance Overeating', p. 1074); the comment is a measure of the strain of anachrony in his analysis.

[76] Joseph Loewenstein, 'The Jonsonian Corpulence: Or, The Poet as Mouthpiece', *English Literary History* 53 (1986), p. 491.

the universe of (the) play and the Virgilian economy of *castitas* which again recalls *Poetaster*. That the poems exemplify this economy, like the speeches in the Virgilian scenes in *Poetaster*, is borne out by what Peter Womack calls their 'laconic monumentality' (Womack, *Ben Jonson*, p. 85). Comparing them to the 'didactic pronouncements' of father figures in the satirical comedies, he points out how both are 'forms which lift their language out of the play of dialogue and seek to constitute it as authoritative' (ibid.) to constitute it, that is, as a stable, transcendent Language such as the Virgilian economy of *castitas* exemplifies and represents.

It is similarly to lift above dialogic play the moral position attributed to, and urged on individuals that Virgil is mobilised, as moral authority, in specific allusions in poems of praise. Epigram 74, addressed to Lord Egerton, for instance, closes with an echo of Virgil's *Eclogue* 4 (*H&S*, vol. II, p. 14). The particular conditions given in the three dependent clauses introduced by 'Whil'st' (a temporal as well as conditional conjunction), which make up the rest of the poem, are thus turned into the absolute conditions which will make a man fit to judge at any moment in history, irrespective of the particular institutional structures within which he works.

> Whil'st thy weigh'd judgements, EGERTON, I heare,
> . . .
> Whil'st I behold thee live with purest hands;
> . . .
> Whil'st thou art certaine to thy words, once gone,
> . . .
> The *Virgin*, long-since fled from earth, I see,
> T(o)'our times return'd, hath made her heaven in thee.

In epigram 70, addressed to Sir William Roe, a similar effect is produced by a Virgilian *sententia* taken from a Senecan essay on the shortness of life on which Jonson's poem is based.[77] Translating 'Optima quaeque dies miseris mortalibus aevi / prima fugit' (*Georgics* 3, line 66-7) – 'Each best day of our life escapes us first' (line 6) – Jonson urges engagement to 'true causes' (line 4) as the proper response to the human condition of temporal confinement, which the Virgilian voice at once describes and, in its timelessness, transcends. That this voice addresses a common human condition is signalled by an inclusive use of the first

---

[77] I examine the relation of the poem to its Senecan base, and the different philosophical positions implied in their respective treatments of the Virgilian *sententia* in Clayton, '"Tempests and such like Drolleries"', pp. 165–7.

person plural, 'our life' (for 'miseris mortalibus'), which is countered in
the next line by an explicitly exclusive use: 'we (more than many) these
truths know' (line 7). As in *Poetaster*, that is, the assertion of the absolute,
universal value of Virgil as moral guide for 'our lives' (*Poetaster*, v.i.120) is
belied by the confinement of that moral understanding to a privileged
few, who are consequently placed 'above' common men and women
whom they oversee and judge.

It is expressly as the shared 'voyce' of an exclusive 'we' that Virgil is
invoked in another epigram addressed to William Roe on the occasion
of his departure for the continent (epigram 128). This voice at once
unifies the exclusive community and lifts it out of the contingencies of
time and space, like, and with the subject of the poem, whose journey is
projected as a circle, figure of an inviolable, bounded self-same self such
as we have seen attributed to Virgil in *Poetaster* as well as to the privileged
community he addresses.

>   may all thy ends,
> As the beginnings here, prove purely sweet,
> And perfect in a circle alwayes meet.
> So, when we, blest with thy returne, shall see
> Thy selfe, with thy first thoughts, brought home by thee,
> We each to other may this voyce enspire;
> This is that good ÆNEAS, past through fire,
> Through seas, stormes, tempests: and imbarqu'd for hell,
> Came backe untouch'd. This man hath travail'd well.
>
>   (lines 6–14)

The 'we' here share not only the Virgilian epic narrative, but an
understanding of it as moral/spiritual discourse, specifically as a 'prog-
ress' of the soul/self confronted by trials and conflicts.[78] Roe will return
'untouch'd', the same as him-self, and the same as 'good Aeneas', both
above differences, whether of the self, of time ('(t)his is that' erases
historical distance and difference), or of place – the particular 'manners
and men' (line 2) encountered on particular journeys. Their place
'above' is shared by the community of 'we', again a community of the
same, including those readers who understand the Virgilian 'voyce' and
escape, like and with Roe/Aeneas, from the 'hell' of multiple, particular
and ephemeral difference.

---

[78] On the early tradition of interpretations of the *Aeneid* as a moral/spiritual pilgrimage, see Jones,
'The Allegorical Traditions', especially, pp. 126–7, and Baswell, *Virgil in Medieval England*, pp.
110–30. For early modern versions in England, see Tudeau-Clayton, 'Supplementing the *Aeneid*'
(forthcoming).

There is no such escape for the heroes 'imbarqu'd for hell' four poems later, in the last of the collection, 'The Famous Voyage' (epigram 133). For they merely return whence they came once their journey is over (line 292), whereas Aeneas passes from the realm of Tartarus to Elysium, the place of the virtuous. This is one of the differences between Aeneas and these heroes, who, unlike Roe, are *not* the same as the Virgilian hero. Signalled more and less explicitly, these differences furnish a level of ironic comment, for the reader who recognises them, together with the canonical mediation of the Virgilian descent into Hades as a Neo-platonic allegory of the descent of the soul into the 'prison-house' of the body and material and temporal existence. For it is the body, especially its 'lower' organs and functions, that is the focus of this poem – the voyage is full of farts and smells – which is one of the reasons critics have tended either to ignore it or to dismiss it as a 'bad joke' (*H&S*, vol. 2, p. 341).[79] Another reason for a modern critic's difficulty with this poem is the wealth of local allusion in which it is immersed. Precisely, for this is the universe of the particular and ephemeral – a universe epitomised in the fart. The fitness of the poem as a conclusion to the collection has consequently been missed. For the intertextual relation to the Virgilian descent and its canonical ground allows the poem to bring together the universes of the learned/virtuous and ignorant/vicious and to perform as it were a 'last judgement', which finally divides them, and casts readers into analogous categories.

There are two moments when the ironic level of commentary furnished by the canonical ground of the Virgilian intertext breaks through the comic surface. In the prologue, when classical versions of the descent, especially Virgil's, are apparently dismissed in favour of the contemporary voyage, comparisons are made which boast the latter's 'filth, stench, noyse ... / ... confused' (lines 9–10) for what the classical versions 'boast of STYX, of ACHERON, / COCYTUS, PHLEGETON' (lines 7–8). That this contemporary universe of stench and confused noise is, rather, precisely what these features of the Virgilian underworld represent, emerges in the lines which follow and which describe how, for the Virgilian 'cryes of *Ghosts*' (line 16),

---

[79] See also G. B. Johnston, *Ben Jonson: Poet* (New York: Columbia University Press, 1945) p. 29. For an unembarrassed reading which endorses mine, though without detailed consideration of the Virgilian intertext, see Leggatt, *Ben Jonson*, pp. 263–5. The canonical mediations of the Virgilian underworld are discussed above, chapter 3, pp. 83–7.

> women, and men,
> Laden with plague-sores, and their sinnes, were heard,
> Lash'd by their consciences, to die, affeard.
>
> (lines 16–18)

The place of the Virgilian ghosts is taken here by a scene which furnishes emblem and instance of the corruption and pain – physical and moral – suffered in, and on account of the body, according to the canonical Neoplatonic mediations of the rivers of the underworld – Phlegethon, Acheron, Styx and Cocytus – which have just been evoked and apparently dismissed.[80] The relation between physical and moral/spiritual pain and corruption is, in addition, formally articulated, 'sinnes' being aligned by syntax with 'plague-sores' and 'Lash'd by their consciences' being aligned by sound as well as by syntax with 'Laden with plague-sores'.

This relation is articulated again, through a metaphor of kinship, in the second passage where the serious level of ironic comment breaks through the comic surface. On one of the walls at the entrance to Fleet Ditch there are 'monsters', as at the entrance to the Virgilian Hades,

> stench, diseases, and old filth, their mother,
> With famine, wants, and sorrowes many a dosen,
> The least of which was to the plague a cosen.
>
> (lines 70–2)

Diseases, famine, want and sorrows/cares are all Virgilian (*Aeneid* 6, lines 273–6). But the Virgilian Grief, Age and Fear have been replaced, first, by 'stench', a property as well as symptom of material corruption, second, by 'the plague', a modern instance of disease which is linked to the Virgilian monsters by the kinship metaphor. Most important is the addition of 'old filth, their mother', which invokes the putative etymological connection made by the Neoplatonists between *materia* and *mater*, and the consequent identification of matter as the origin not only of material corruption – stench and diseases – but also of moral turbulence and pain – sorrows.[81] It is an identification that has already been evoked, less explicitly, a few lines earlier, when the heroes encounter the first monster, 'Mud' (line 62), and '(t)horough her wombe ... make their famous road' (line 66), the descent into hell being figured as birth

---

[80] Acheron is associated by Macrobius, specifically, with pangs of regret at past deeds and words, Cocytus with whatever drives men to grief and tears, Phlegethon with the passions of anger and desire. Macrobius, *Somnium*, p. 43.

[81] See, for example, Landino, in Stahel, 'Cristoforo Landino's Allegorization', fo. H6r. Compare Janet Adelman, *Suffocating Mothers* (New York and London: Routledge, 1992), pp. 6, 242–3, 255.

through the womb of mother-matter, as in the Neoplatonic interpretations.

These glimpses of the canonical ground of the Virgilian intertext are supplemented by the recognition of irony in the differences between the two 'descents', especially between their respective heroes. Not only do the contemporary heroes remain confined within the realms of Tartarus, but they are said to pass the monsters at the entrance to the underworld 'unfrighted' (line 73). This might sound like praise, but read in relation to Aeneas's reaction of terror at the same moment ('trepidus' (*Aeneid* 6, line 290)), becomes rather the opposite.[82] Similarly, the most overtly advertised differences from the Virgilian model are apparently couched as commendation – the contemporary heroes 'Sans helpe of SYBIL, or a golden bough, / Or magick sacrifice … past along!' (lines 48-9) – but will be recognised as condemnation, if the significance of these differences is understood. While the absence of sacrifices such as Aeneas performs (*Aeneid* 6, lines 236–54), and the absence of the Sibyl signal an absence of the piety which characterises the Virgilian hero ('pius Aeneas'), the absence of the golden bough signals, if more opaquely, the absence of his moral/spiritual discernment. For the golden bough was invariably given a moral gloss, from Servius, who likens it to the Pythagorean letter Y and its moral significance (the choice of virtue/ vice), to Pontanus, who suggests it signifies 'prudentia', and Phaer, whose marginal gloss 'wisdome that overcommeth all things' may echo Erasmus's, 'wisdom set apart in a hidden place and found only by a few'.[83] These moral meanings are of course themselves 'hidden', the figure of the golden bough exemplifying the hidden wisdom it signifies. In Jonson's poem, those who understand its significance recognise the absence, in the contemporary heroes, of the wisdom that by virtue of this recognition they understand themselves to possess, with Aeneas, Virgil and 'the author'. In such recognitions lies the 'grace' – of irony – which allows 'those few whom just Jove loves' to escape from the underworld of multiple, particular heterogeneity, the 'confused noise' of contemporary urban life, into the absolute 'upper air'.

---

[82] Compare Gavin Douglas on the fear of Aeneas in the tempest: 'he that dredis na thyng, nor kan haf na dred, is not hardy, but fuyll hardy and beistly'. Douglas, *Virgil's 'Aeneid'*, vol. 2, p. 25, note 1. This gloss is also relevant to characters' reactions in the opening scene of *The Tempest.*

[83] See Virgil, *Opera*, vol. 2, fo. 328v; Jones, 'Allegorical Interpretation in Servius', p. 221; Virgil, *Symbolarum libri XVII*, edited by J. Pontanus, col. 1389; Phaer, *The Nyne Fyrst Bookes*, n. pag.; for the Erasmian gloss see chapter 2, note 59 and for a range of interpretations in medieval England, Baswell, *Virgil in Medieval England*, pp. 95, 110–12.

CHAPTER 6

Shaking Neptune's 'dread trident': The Tempest and figures of Virgil

The relation of *The Tempest* to Virgil's *Aeneid* has remained an object of critical attention, despite the 'shifting' of 'emphasis' by 'revisionist' versions of the play, which place 'New World material at the centre', and especially 'power relations in the New World',[1] and which effectively ignore the 'Old World' Virgilian material. The intertextual relation to this material has thus usually been (re)considered by critics who practise more traditional forms of historical or formal criticism,[2] although there is now a full length study, by Donna B. Hamilton, which has been insightfully described as 'New Historicism in a gentle mode'.[3] For Hamilton attempts to bring together what she calls the 'master poetic discourse' of Virgil's *Aeneid* and 'the master discourses of high politics' to suggest that 'in the rehandling of these discourses, Shakespeare constructed an argument for constitutionalism' (Hamilton, *Virgil and The Tempest*, p. xi). The play continues, that is, to be treated, in the revisionist mode, as about 'power relations' but power relations within England as well as in the colonies of the New World and Ireland: 'the language of colonization also imaged the impact and implications of absolutism within England itself' (p. 64).[4]

---

[1] Meredith Anne Skura, 'Discourse and The Individual: The Case of Colonialism in The Tempest', *Shakespeare Quarterly* 40 (1989), p. 44.

[2] Bono, *Literary Transvaluation*, pp. 220–4; Gary Schmidgall, *Shakespeare and the Courtly Aesthetic* (University of California Press, 1981), especially pp. 165–73; John Pitcher, 'A Theatre of the Future: The *Aeneid* and *The Tempest*', *Essays in Criticism* 34:3 (1984), pp. 193–215; Miola, 'Vergil in Shakespeare', pp. 254–6; Wiltenburg, 'The *Aeneid* and *The Tempest*'. See introduction, p. 3 and note 8.

[3] Lachlan Mackinnon, 'Shakespeares for our Age', *The Times Literary Supplement*, 6 March 1992, p. 12. Hamilton's book expands on, without substantially modifying the arguments of an earlier (misleadingly titled) article, Donna B. Hamilton, 'Defiguring Vergil in *The Tempest*', *Style* 23 (1989), pp. 352–73.

[4] While Hamilton and Skura argue that revisionist accounts have been too narrow in their scope, Felperin criticises the 'claims', made by Schmidgall as well as by Hamilton, 'for a specifically Jacobean political commentary' in the play, as too 'partial and local', like the revisionist accounts in terms of New World discourses. Felperin, 'Political Criticism', pp. 51, 54.

Yet this revisionist version of the play's intertextual relation to Virgil's *Aeneid* fails, like more traditional versions, to address more than cursorily the historically specific mediations of Virgil (poet and texts), and the ideological stakes of their (re)production and circulation. The result, at the simplest level, is that traces of these mediations in certain features of the play are not recognised, notably, the traces of Virgil as natural philosopher/magician, and as bearer of 'Language' in the character and story of Prospero, and the traces of the Virgilian grammar of nature in the opening storm scene and the betrothal masque. Not to recognise these traces is not to recognise, at a second level, how the play dramatises the 'power relations' at stake in the imitation of Virgil. It is, in short, not to recognise the full scope of the 'politics of imitation' (Hamilton's misleading sub-title), which is what I have tried to outline, in relation to Virgil, in preceding chapters.[5] Specifically, here, we might recall how pedagogic and exegetic practices mediating Virgil to school-boys were used to serve the colonialist project: the normative, regulatory discourses by which the native (Irish or New World) savage was to be 'reduced' to 'civilitie' were the discourses by which the English school-boy was to be 'informed' as a 'man' and these normative discourses were represented, as they were exemplified by Virgil.[6]

To fail to recognise the ideological stakes of the imitation of Virgil in general is necessarily to fail to recognise the ideological stakes of a particular imitation which, as we shall see, engages in an interrogatory and finally ironic relation to this figure of master discourses. Indeed, the other feature which Hamilton's revisionist account shares with more traditional accounts is the assumption that the relation is neither con-testatory nor conflictual. While earlier accounts tend simply to fore-

---

[5] Heather James has argued that the intertextual relation with Virgil is interrogatory and subversive, but, like Hamilton, she does not address the historically specific mediations of Virgil and so misses the scope of the political and ideological implications of the relation. Heather James, *Shakespeare's Troy*, chapter 6.

[6] See chapter 2, pp. 48–9. Comparisons with Shakespeare come to mind again. For Shakespeare has likewise been used, notoriously, as the central author of a liberal humanism both to serve the colonialist project and to reproduce structures of authority – and class – within English culture. That there is always already a politics to the reproduction of Shakespeare in British society is implied in the on-going debates about the teaching of Shakespeare in secondary schools. See, for example, Judith Judd, 'Bard only for the bright', *The Independent*, 21 March 1993, p. 3. Like Virgil too, Shakespeare is associated, for adolescents, with normative forms of 'proper' language. In the test on Shakespeare for fourteen year olds instituted by the national curriculum, the formal scheme for marking provides a list of 'Assessment Objectives', which include 'use punctuation and grammar correctly'. The test paper for 1994 tells the student: 'Your work will be assessed for your knowledge and understanding of the play and the way you express your ideas. Your spelling and handwriting will also be assessed.' (My thanks to Barbara March for providing me with the material quoted here.)

ground likenesses, construing the relation in terms of source, echo or allusion,[7] later accounts admit or even foreground differences but without displacing, or disfiguring either 'master' – Virgil or Shakespeare.[8] This may be due in part to the persistent hold of the traditional structure of literary history – the structure of canonised master figures. But it may also be due to the hold of the will to the place of the master as the will motivating imitation/commentary. This is borne out by the following: 'Shakespeare, then, is involved both in demonstrating his mastery of the master poetic discourse and in responding to the master discourses of high politics' (Hamilton, *Virgil and The Tempest*, p. xi). A performative disguised as a constative, epitomising the performative project of the whole book, such discourse, intent as it is on entitlement as master, tends to repeat, without recognising that it repeats the (repeated) will to the place of the master which is dramatised by the play, in particular through Antonio, who is not only the brother, but also the supplanting imitator of the 'Virgilian' Prospero. Antonio's question 'How came that widow in?' (II.i.74) is indeed a commentator's question, at once advertising and seeking the origins of, the Virgilian presence. Ironically, if perhaps inevitably, it has done more than any other feature of the play to provoke repetitions in versions of the intertextual relation to Virgil's *Aeneid*. Commentary thus runs to commentary, as imitation runs to imitation, in the pursuit of the place of the master/meaning.

The place to which such an advertisement points is the *locus* of the authorised and authorising textual origin or source – such sources as schoolboys' imitations were required to resemble in order to be recognised as legitimate productions, and such sources as Jonson's notes to

---

[7] R. S. Conway, *New Studies of a Great Inheritance: Being Lectures on the Modern Worth of some Ancient Writers* (London: John Murray, 1921), pp. 165–89; J. M. Nosworthy, 'The Narrative Sources of *The Tempest*', *Review of English Studies* 24 (1948), pp. 281–94; Colin Still, *Shakespeare's Mystery Play: A Study of The Tempest* (London: Cecil Palmer, 1921); Colin Still, *The Timeless Theme. A Critical Theory Formulated and Applied* (London: Ivor Nicholson and Watson, 1936); Srigley, *Images of Regeneration*.

[8] See introduction, p. 3. It is the need to include difference in an account of the intertextual relation that motivates Hamilton's work which, however, does not go beyond a traditional formalism, and which does not 'defigure' either master. See Hamilton, 'Defiguring Vergil'. In one of two versions of this relation, Jan Kott runs through likenesses he sees only to come to the completely unexpected conclusion that the 'Virgilian myths are invoked, challenged and finally rejected'. Jan Kott, 'The *Aeneid* and *The Tempest*', *Arion* NS, 3/4 (1976), p. 444. This is mere assertion; no attempt is made to show how the challenge is articulated or in what it consists. Kott's other version focuses on repetitions, as the title indicates. Jan Kott, 'The Tempest, or Repetition', *Mosaic* 10:3 (1977), pp. 10–36. The most obvious repetitions today are perhaps the repetitions of Kott's own readings of Shakespeare in Jan Kott, *Shakespeare our Contemporary*, translated by B. Taborski (London: Methuen, 1964). Like Kott (whom he does not cite), Felperin reads the play's relation to the *Aeneid* as illustrative of a cyclical vision of history as repetition. Felperin, 'Political Criticism', pp. 52–6.

The King's Entertainment and to his masques display as 'testimonies' – legitimising ground – to their authority. That textual origin/source furnishes privileged access to the place of the master is no doubt the most persistent assumption, and motive, of traditional editorial and interpretative practices, although this has of course been challenged, at least theoretically, by '(i)ntertextuality, or con-textualization'.[9] In practice, however, 'intertextuality' has often turned out to be source studies under another name, while contextual studies, although they do replace the source with 'a shared code' or with 'congruent texts, irrespective of Shakespeare's knowledge of them',[10] nevertheless turn these codes or congruent texts – mediated through what are today institutionally recognised master discourses – into a master text which serves to ground or, we might say, to 'reduce'/'colonise' the play and the reader. And the will to the place of the master – and, we might add, to master Will – remains the same.

Entitlement as master within the institutionalised forms and practices of the humanities continues, that is, to call for supplementary productions which display at once a measure of likeness to institutionally recognised master discourses, or sources (a likeness marked as 'authority'), and a measure of difference from them (marked as 'originality'). The relative weight of these measures has of course varied: the shift from the Renaissance to the Romantics, or, more specifically, from Jonson to Johnson, might indeed be epitomised in the shift in the value of the term 'original' (in this sense): demonised (and feminised) in Jonson's *The Masque of Queens*, it is idealised, by the beginning of the eighteenth century, as *The Ground of Criticism in Poetry*.[11] It is in the Renaissance that, as Quint has argued so well, 'original' in this sense begins to acquire a positive value, although (except in his discussion of Milton) he does not associate this with what I have called the 'Protestant turn', when the radical and irreducible difference of originality emerges as potentially dis-ruptive of likeness to 'authoritative' (and legitimising) origin and indeed of likeness to any symbolic form, and so to the very possibility of mastery.

---

9 Francis Barker and Peter Hulme, 'Nymphs and Reapers heavily vanish: The Discursive Contexts of *The Tempest*', in John Drakakis, ed., *Alternative Shakespeares*, p. 196.

10 Stephen Greenblatt, *Shakespearean Negotiations: The Circulation of Social Energy in Renaissance England* (Oxford: Clarendon Press, 1988), p. 86; Barker and Hulme, 'Nymphs and Reapers', p. 196.

11 The title of a book by John Dennis published in 1704, cited in Quint, *Origin and Originality*, pp. 216–17, 256. See chapter 4, pp. 136–7. Sherman discusses the anachronism of 'originality' as a criterion in the analysis of early modern reading and writing practices in Sherman, *John Dee*, pp. 122–7.

This dis-rupture is dramatised in *The Tempest*, notably at two moments of '*confused noise*' in Act I, scene i and Act IV, scene i, when the production of symbolic forms is challenged by that which is other to the symbolic, the negativity of 'noise' from 'below'. This negativity is not only of an 'original' irreducible self, but of nature and history too. The play thus stages, at the most general level, the dis-rupture by a 'new world' of an old world paradigm. It is a disrupture that Marjorie Nicolson's old-fashioned but still interesting book on the effects of the new science on poetry epitomised in the figure of the breaking of the circle – a figure which is of particular relevance to the second moment in *The Tempest*, when the dis-rupture is marked by the breaking up of a 'graceful dance'.[12] It is, moreover, in the very passage in Bacon's work which inspired Nicolson's title – a passage from *The Advancement of Learning*, elaborated in the *Novum organum* as the doctrine of the Idols of the Tribe – that Michel Foucault detected the emergence of a critique of likeness as epistemological ground. Indeed, in its articulation of this critique, Bacon's argument, like the play, foregrounds the '*negative, or privative*', which man's mind prefers to ignore, just as it '*doth usually suppose and feign in nature a greater equality and uniformity than is in truth*' imagining '*relatives, parallels*, and *conjugates*, whereas no such thing is'.[13] Foregrounding the otherness of nature (and of God) to 'human disposition' (ibid.), the passage exposes as fiction the model of nature as a total, closed system of relations of likeness, just as the mediation of the Virgilian order of nature came to be recategorised as fiction with what I have called the 'Protestant turn'. It is a turn, or shift that, as Quint puts it, entailed a turn in 'all realms of human thought and discourse, formerly closed, now irreversibly open-ended' (Quint, *Origin and Originality*, p. 220). More specifically, it is a turn that tended inevitably to the displacement of a degenerative model of knowledge of nature by a progressive model: no longer a fixed system of relations of likeness received from the ancients, knowledge of nature consists rather in (potentially infinite) relations to be construed on the (bottomless) ground – or 'abysm' (1.ii.50) – of difference.

---

[12] Marjorie Hope Nicolson, *The Breaking of the Circle: Studies in the Effect of the 'New Science' on Seventeenth-Century-Poetry*, rev. edn, (New York and London: Columbia University Press, 1962). As Hardie points out, Nicolson's book illustrates the 'division between poetic and scientific discourses that has lasted to the present day'. Hardie, *Virgil's 'Aeneid'*, p. 6. Hardie's work is, in turn, of particular relevance in so far as it proceeds to illustrate the imbrication of these discourses in the poetry of the ancients, especially Virgil.

[13] Francis Bacon, *The Advancement of Learning*, edited by G. W. Kitchin, reprint (London: Dent, 1965), pp. 132–3. See Foucault, *Les mots*, pp. 65–6.

There is to such a turn a politics – a politics of knowledge. This is implied in the moments of '*confused noise*' in *The Tempest*, although more obviously perhaps in the first. For here the 'authority' (I.i.23) of the Virgilian grammar of Nature, inflected in relations of likeness, is challenged by an emergent, technical and specialised discourse from 'below' – from, that is, the very class of unprivileged seamen to whom Virgil's knowledge of nature was, as we saw in chapter 3, particularly exposed. Their representative, the Boatswain, is actually called a 'noise-maker' (lines 43–4), and so associated with the 'roarers' (line 16) he describes of a nature different from, and indifferent to the forms of 'human disposition'. At the second moment, a 'vision' (IV.i.118) of nature, marked as Virgilian, is dis-rupted (and ended) by the return of another figure 'from below'. Identified as '(t)hou earth' (I.ii.316), 'on whose nature / Nurture can never stick' (IV.i.188–9), Caliban embodies a nature not to be reduced to civility or indeed to 'nature' by the normative, regulatory discourses which Prospero – Virgilian natural philosopher, master, father and schoolteacher – represents. It is a resistance to formation marked both in his language and in his body, 'disproportioned in his manners / As in his shape' (V.i.290–1).

This description of Caliban as '*dis*proportioned' recalls the figure, within Prospero's masque, of 'dusky Dis' (IV.i.89), likewise a 'thing of darkness' (V.i.275) and likewise a figure 'from below', specifically, from the Virgilian underworld – 'dusky Dis' being a precise translation of Virgil's 'atri ... Ditis' (*Aeneid* 6, line 127).[14] A personification of the privative morpheme, 'Dis' recalls the 'disdain and discord' (IV.i.20), which are evoked by Prospero before the masque, in his speech of warning to Ferdinand, and which Stephen Orgel has insightfully described as anti-masque figures.[15] The figure is then recalled again, after

[14] Neil Forsyth points out, if rather cautiously, how the 'poetic and intellectual tradition ... tended to find ... significant' not only etymological relations, but accidental phonetic relations between words and goes on to show Milton's self-conscious play with the name 'Dis' and 'dis'-words, a play which he suggests is present in the Virgilian epic too. Neil Forsyth, 'Of Man's First Dis', in Mario A. di Cesare, ed., *Milton in Italy: Contexts, Images, Contradictions* (Binghampton, N.Y.: MRTS Press, 1991), especially pp. 352–4, 357–9.

[15] Shakespeare, *The Tempest*, edited by Orgel, p. 47. Elsewhere Orgel comments suggestively that 'the play seems a story of privatives: withdrawal, usurpation, banishment, the loss of one's way, shipwreck', but he does not develop the idea, which, moreover, he considers only thematically. Stephen Orgel, 'Prospero's Wife', reprinted in Stephen Greenblatt, ed., *Representing the English Renaissance* (University of California Press, 1988), p. 231. For another example of the association of the privative morpheme with the god of the underworld, see the description of the entertainment given for Queen Elizabeth and Mary in 1562, which includes the figure of Disdain who 'declares that his master Pluto ... has sent Malice to require ... the freeing of Discord' (as quoted in Welsford, *The Court Masque*, p. 153). Disdain and discord, the personifications evoked by Prospero, are here overtly associated with their 'master' Pluto, otherwise known as Dis.

the masque, in the 'distempered' (IV.i.145) condition of Prospero as well as in the 'disproportioned' body of Caliban. In particular, the return of 'Dis' at the dis-rupture of the masque by another thing of darkness marks the failure both of Prospero's particular masque, and, more generally, of the binary structure of the generic form of the Jonsonian masque, which works, like language, to contain negativity as negation.[16]

In so far, of course, as this revision of the structure of the masque is marked in language, as the return of 'dis', and in the return of a recognisable, 'dis-proportioned', anti-masque figure, it would appear to make again the move of containment. Indeed, the 'dis'-words which come after the disrupture – dis-tempered and dis-proportioned – epitomise, like dis-cord before it, the binary structure of the masque, and of language, which contain negativity as negation. This containment is, however, countered, on the one hand, by what follows the moment of disruption – Prospero's recognition of the 'dis' or 'confused noise within' as the common ground of the human condition, and his renunciation of control. On the other hand, what is done in language and action is supplemented – and sometimes supplanted – by the 'noise' with which the play, like the 'isle', is 'full' (III.ii.133).

There is, specifically, the *'confused noise'* called for by the stage directions at both moments of dis-rupture. As we have seen, Jonson uses this aural figure, notably of the anti-masque of witches in *The Masque of Queens*, to represent, as indifferentiation, the effect of the multiple, particular differences which define the universe of the anti-masque/satirical comedy, and which are contained as the contrary/negation of the proper and natural order. In contrast, the confused noise in *The Tempest* is not thus contained. Indeed, in any particular performance the noise called for may actually erase the words of the dramatic text, as they are erased, inadvertently perhaps, in the BBC's film version of the first scene, which might exactly be described as 'confused noise'.

More importantly still, noise is evoked throughout the play. Not only do characters describe noises which, in any performance, may more or less erase the words of the dramatic text, but the language of the whole play tends to insist on its own character as sound, and especially as *imitative* sound, sound, that is, which aspires to reproduce the noises of nature and so to erase or to dis-rupt from within the condition of the symbolic order, which is not-noise. This is done, first, through iteration

---

[16] As we saw in chapter 4, the moment most specifically recalls the interruption of the marriage masque in *Hymenaei* by the anti-masque of humours, an interruption which is similarly marked by a proliferation of 'dis'-words. See chapter 4, pp. 144–5.

of onomatopoeic words: '*Bow-wow*', '*Cock a diddle dow*', '*Ding-dong*' in the first of Ariel's songs (i.ii.384, 389, 406); 'claps' and 'cracks' in Ariel's description of the tempest (i.ii.202, 203); 'twangling' and 'hum' in Caliban's description of the noises of the isle (iii.ii.135, 136); 'roaring, shrieking, howling, jingling' (v.i.233) in the Boatswain's description of the 'strange and several noises' (line 232) heard by the ship's crew, to cite just a few examples. It is Caliban, in particular, whose discourse is marked by such words (eg. 'sucks', 'mow', 'chatter', 'hiss' (ii.ii.1, 9, 14)) – traces of what Miranda describes, in another example, as the 'gabble' he uttered prior to his education into 'words' (i.ii.358, 360), a gabble that tends, moreover, to return under the influence of alcohol: ''Ban, 'Ban, Cacaliban' (ii.ii.184). Caliban here returns to an infantile playing with his name as if it were a piece of the excrement he makes it 'sound like' (caca) – a playing that itself mirrors the 'original' naming of Caliban, which is generally agreed to play on the noun 'cannibal'. Together with Miranda's description of such savage/infantile discourse as 'gabble' this tends to associate the noise to which the onomatopoeic character of the play's language aspires with the 'noise' which precedes education into language and which is excluded/repressed by it. Caliban may thus be seen to represent not only a radically (in)different new world 'savage'/ nature, but also a radically indifferent nature/savage 'within', to be informed by education into language, and, more specifically, into 'Language', the normative, 'proper' and 'natural' 'civilising' Father tongue Virgil represents. The resistance in his discourse may thus be understood as an 'original' resistance to such in-formation, a resistance which is shared by other 'noise-makers' in the play, whose language aspires to reproduce the 'noise' of nature and so to erase from within the distinctions of the symbolic order.[17]

Even Caliban's schoolteacher Miranda expresses resistance at this level, joining her pupil and the other noise-makers, under the influence

[17] Skura interprets Caliban as the figure of a childish 'will' whose vengefulness 'is associated with an infantile need to dominate and with the scatological imagery of filth' (Skura, 'Discourse and the Individual', pp. 63–4), but she does not relate this to the character of his discourse, only commenting in passing that 'any child might complain that he was taught to speak and now his "profit on't" is to be trapped in the prison-house of language' (p. 64, note 101). The Wordsworthian figure here betrays Skura's universalisation of a historically specific construction of the human subject, especially the child, in its relation to language, which obscures the way that *The Tempest* marks a historical shift. Within the tradition of thought still exemplified in Jonson's writing, for example, education into language, especially, the 'proper' language of the educated elite, is not a prison-house but a means to escape from the prison-house of the body. This difference between Jonson and Wordsworth entails a rewriting of the Neoplatonic vision which informs much of Wordsworth's writing as it does Jonson's.

not of alcohol but of sexual desire. As I indicated in chapter 2, the only initial resistance shown by Miranda to in-formation by her father/ schoolteacher is the withdrawal of attention to which Prospero alludes with paternal/schoolmasterly irritation (I.ii.78, 87, 106). But under pressure from what we might call the noise of sexual desire she breaks the bounds/bonds of the paternal prescriptions, to tell Ferdinand first her name (III.i.36–7), then her desire (lines 53–7). Still more significant is the move of self-curtailment and chastisement that she makes after expressing her desire. For in making this move she recollects not only the paternal prescriptions, but also her 'self', which is to say the 'self' in-formed by, and sounding like her father, the schoolteacher-self who has chastised Caliban.[18]

> But I prattle
> Something too wildly, and my father's precepts
> I therein do forget.
>
> (lines 57–9)

Reining in her libidinal self, Miranda names its utterances as excess – unbounded, infantile 'noise', wild, like the noises of nature, especially the sea,[19] and like Caliban's infantile/savage 'gabble' (with which 'prattle' nearly rhymes). Yet, even as she represses it, the 'noise' of her libidinal self (as well as of her pre-verbal self with which the libidinal self is associated) returns in the material, bodily sound of the word 'prattle'. Like, and with, the other onomatopoeic words of the play, including 'gabble', 'prattle' aspires to reproduce the 'noise' it describes and so to disrupt from within the symbolic order which represses such noise.

But there are not only onomatopoeic words. The whole play, and especially the descriptions of nature, are full of rhythmic patterns and sound repetitions – assonances, consonances and alliterations – which work to produce onomatopoeic effects, to produce, that is, 'noise' which is other to the symbolic, whether, as the verbal content of the descriptions suggest, the noise of nature, or a more indeterminate noise from 'within', 'below', or 'before'.[20] The most striking examples are, of

---

[18] See above, chapter 2, pp. 49–50 and note 11.

[19] Miranda uses 'wild' of the waters in the tempest (I.ii.2), as does Ariel (I.ii.380).

[20] In Kristeva's terms, the disruption of the symbolic by the semiotic – a recollection or echo of the pre-verbal phase, a recollection, specifically, of the 'mother'/wife to whose absence Stephen Orgel's seminal essay drew attention. See Orgel, 'Prospero's Wife', *passim*. The indeterminacy produced by formal repetitions is analysed as a stylistic effect in Russ McDonald, 'Reading *The Tempest*', *Shakespeare Survey* 43 (1991), especially p. 25.

course, Miranda's and Ariel's descriptions of the tempest, which, more specifically, attempt to translate into language that which has been represented by other modes of representation in the opening scene.[21] With regard to Miranda's description, I have already mentioned its use of spondees, which Eritreo recommends, in his edition of Virgil for schoolboys, as appropriate to express what he describes, in another example of onomatopoeia, as the 'colluctatio' of a tempest (see chapter 3, p. 107). In addition, there are alliterations: of *w* ('wild waters . . . would . . . welkin's'), *p* ('(p)ut . . . pour . . . pitch'), *s* ('sky . . . seems . . . stinking . . . sea'), which works as consonance too; and assonances: of *ee* ('seems . . . sea . . . cheek'), and *or* (the internal rhyme 'roar/pour'). All work to imitate the 'noise' of the tempest which the speech describes.

At the same time, the 'noise' to which her lines aspire may be heard in relation to her intense compassion: 'O, I have suffered / With those that I saw suffer!' (I.ii.5–6), 'O, the cry did knock / Against my very heart!' (lines 8–9). Indeed, in lines which echo these, both 'meanings' of such 'noise' are conflated, compassion such as Miranda here expresses being attributed to the sea in Prospero's story of how they were abandoned,

> To cry to th'sea that roar'd to us; to sigh
> To th'winds, whose pity, sighing back again,
> Did us but loving wrong.
>
> (I.ii.149–51)

A consolatory as well as compassionate echo to the human cry of abandonment, the noise of nature, especially the noise of the sea (*la mer*), is invested here with connotations of a pre-verbal relation with the maternal body (*la mère*), a 'noise' which the rhythms and repetitions of Prospero's lines aspire to re-member or echo, like and with Miranda's lines.

To this effect, both Prospero and Miranda use 'roar', a word that recurs in various forms no less than ten times throughout the play, an epitome as well as an example of the aspiration of the play's language to erase the distinctions of the symbolic order by making '*confused noise*

---

[21] See the opening stage directions: '*a tempestuous noise of thunder and lightning heard*'. The limited technical means to represent such 'noise' is of course mocked by Jonson (see Gurr, *The Shakespearean Stage*, p. 186). Typically, the play explores the relationship between the various modes of representation that make up a performance text. One of these relations – *between* language and music – has been elided by the tendency of critics casually to describe the effects of sound repetition as the 'music' of the play (for example, McDonald, 'Reading *The Tempest*', p. 24).

within'. While the word aspires to erase distinctions at the level of sound, the repetitions aspire to erase distinctions at the level of semantic categories, notably the distinction between the categories of the human and the natural. For 'roar' is used not only of the noise made by nature, especially by the sea, and by animals, but also of the noise made by human 'noise-makers' – the 'roarers' (I.i.16) from below, especially Caliban and his 'confederates' (IV.i.140), Trinculo and Stephano.[22]

Nevertheless, despite this aspiration to 'confused noise', the word 'roar' remains a word/not-noise, which marks, even as it aspires to cross, the limit between language and the confused noise within nature/ the self. Indeed, the difference which marks this limit – the difference a vowel makes – at the same time marks the word as an internally echoing *form*, a formal echoing that is doubled at the level of words by the internal rhyme 'roar'/'pour'. This 'hollow' self-echoing of imitative forms is at once illustrated and underscored by the hastily improvised fictions of Antonio and Sebastian, who make 'noise' out of 'nothing' in order to cover their intent to murder. 'While we stood here securing your rep*o*se', Sebastian begins, 'Even now, we heard a hol*low* burst of bel*low*ing/ *L*ike bu*ll*s, or rather *l*ions' (II.ii.305–7; my emphasis). His words are immediately supplemented and echoed by Antonio's:

> *O* 'twas a din to fright a monster's ear,
> To make an earthquake! *sure* it was the *roar*
> Of a wh*o*le herd of lions.
>
> (lines 309–11; my emphasis)

The repetition of the onomatopoeic 'low', with the repeated labials in 'like' 'bulls' and 'lions', the assonance of *o*, the alliteration of *b* with the onomatopoeic 'burst' in particular, and the internal rhyme 'sure'/'roar' (which echoes Miranda's 'roar'/'pour') all work to create – or make believe in – the illusion of 'noises' of nature, an illusion which is underscored by Alonso's 'I heard nothing' (II.i.309), especially by the homonymic echo of 'herd' (line 311). The herd that is heard is, indeed,

---

[22] 'Roar' is used four times: I.ii.2 (of the sea); I.ii.372 (of Caliban under torture); II.i.310 (of the 'lions' conjured up by Sebastian and Antonio); IV.i.261 (of Caliban, Stephano and Trinculo pursued by Prospero's hunters). 'Roaring' is used four times: I.ii.204 (of the noise of the performed tempest); IV.i.193 (of Caliban, Trinculo and Stephano under Prospero's torture); v.i.44 (of the tempest); v.i.233 (of the noises heard by the crew). 'Roar'd' is used once: I.ii.149 (of the sea). 'Roarers' is used once: I.i.16 (of the wind and waves, 'with an overtone of rioters' (Shakespeare, *The Tempest*, edited by Orgel, p. 98)).

heard only: the only 'noises' here are those of language hollowly echoing itself. The duplicitous imitator of the Virgilian Prospero, and *his* imitator produce here not only an example, but an image of language itself, especially the imitative language of the play, as a hollow – treacherous and false – imitator of nature, whose aspirations to produce noises of nature turn out to be echoes only of itself.[23]

The play thus, on the one hand, aspires to go beyond the containment of negativity as negation, to dis-rupt and to erase the symbolic order by making '*confused noise within*'. On the other, it ironises its own aspirations and exposes the limits of representation, its necessary incapacity to capture the radical alterity of the noise within nature, history and the self. In marking the radical alterity and (in)difference of nature, history and an 'original' self to symbolic forms, the play stages what I have called the Protestant turn, the turn, that is, away from a universe in which magic is inherent to knowledge and symbolic forms are related 'sympathetically' (in Dee's sense) at once to nature and to human minds/bodies, and therefore efficient as forms of *control*. This universe is dis-placed as the past, an 'old world' from which the 'new' 'dis-enchant-ed' world has definitively turned. By this turn, 'magic' and 'charming' can be used of the forms used by a poet – the patterns, for example, of sound and of metre – only in the transferred and attenuated senses such terms carry when used by critics of the language of *The Tempest*, to describe an aesthetic or rhetorical effect of *expression* rather than a form or mode of *knowledge*.[24]

The ironic thrust of the play's own 'original' difference thus goes beyond the authority of a particular master figure 'Virgil' (discussed more closely in what follows). More radically, in its marking of the (in)difference of nature and of an 'original' self to symbolic forms it ironises the very will to the place of the master. Most obviously exempli-fied by the imitator and usurper Antonio, and his imitator Sebastian,

---

[23] Ferdinand uses the adverb 'hollowly' (III.i.70) of false, ungrounded utterances, opposed to 'true', when he swears his love to Miranda: 'O heaven, O earth, bear witness . . . / And crown . . . / If I speak true! if *hollowly*, invert / What best is boded me to mischief!' (III.i.69-71; my emphasis) What this points up is the recourse to a natural/supernatural order as the absent/present ground – guarantor – of false or true utterances, a ground, which, arguably, 'disappears' with the onset of the modern era. Indeed, the 'hollow', ungrounded character of language haunts the Shake-spearean canon, though it is variously regarded: in the comedies as enabling – a reason for liberation and joy; in the tragedies as disabling – a reason for terror and despair.

[24] McDonald cites critics who read Caliban's speech on the noises of the isle 'as evidence . . . of the magical atmosphere of the setting', 'magical' here being used loosely, in the sense I describe. McDonald, 'Reading *The Tempest*', p. 24.

this will to the place of the master is exemplified too by their parodic doubles Caliban and Stephano – an internal rhyme at the level of plot which underscores the irony.

The logic of this irony, which is both psycho- and ideo-logical, is the dis-investment from the will to mastery, which the play's mode of closure dramatises. It is a mode of closure which I have suggested may be in self-conscious contrast to what takes place in *Poetaster* and Jonson's masques, especially *Hymenaei*. For, while in the Jonsonian texts recourse to 'Virgil'/'Reason' issues in judgement and containment, Prospero's recourse to reason issues in forgiveness, a renunciation of mastery over his enemies (v.i.20–32) which is immediately followed by a renunciation of mastery over nature (lines 34–57). This is predicated, as I pointed out, on Prospero's recognition of a common 'human' (line 20) 'kind' (line 23), defined precisely as participation in '(p)assion' (line 24) or 'fury' (line 26), the darkness of Dis in the self as in nature,[25] a darkness which cannot be mastered, controlled or contained by symbolic forms including, especially, language.[26] This has 'levelling' implications which Jonson's texts never allow and indeed work to 'prevent', and which extend to spectators'/readers' reception of the performed play/published text. For we have seen how Jonson's texts tend to mobilise forms of control over reception, including the voice of the 'best master' Virgil, a figure which, in *Poetaster* in particular, is used in the service of the 'author function' to control, limit, and, finally, to close proliferation of meaning. The end of *The Tempest* moves in the opposite direction. For Prospero steps forward as actor as well as *dramatis persona* to yield up control into the 'good hands' (Epilogue, line 10) of the immediate spectators – a control which is figured in images of the control over nature which he has exercised through magic and which he has renounced within the play (lines 5-13). The spectators are then invited explicitly, as the whole play invites them implicitly, to make the same move of renunciation, and on the same ground – the ground of a shared human condition of darkness – and to set actor-author(ity) figure, and the play, 'free' (the last word of the play). It is an invitation which critics, within the institutionalised forms of the hu-

---

[25] 'fury' is also used of the sea (I.ii.395) and is the name of one of Prospero's dogs (IV.i.257). For the contrast with Jonson see chapter 4, pp. 145–6.

[26] Compare Gilman on 'the lesson prepared for Prospero, and for the audience at the disruption of the masque – a lesson learned not by mastering a body of knowledge, but by suffering the loss of mastery and undergoing a therapeutic process of dislocation and recovery'. Ernest B. Gilman, '"All eyes": Prospero's Inverted Masque', *Renaissance Quarterly* 33 (1980), p. 230.

manities, with the place of the master/author at stake, cannot perhaps afford to hear.[27]

THE TEMPEST, THE 'NEW WORLD' AND VIRGIL

If, as I have been arguing, the play stages at this general level the 'Protestant turn' from an old to a new 'dis-enchanted' world, the question remains of its relations more specifically with (so-called) New World discourses as well as with Virgilian figures. The relation between these two contexts in turn needs to be revised in the light of previous chapters. For there is more to this relation than the likeness with the *Aeneid* which, as others have shown, was asserted not only to lend heroic 'colour' to the colonialist project, but to legitimate and, as Richard Waswo has argued, to naturalise it.[28] As we have seen, the figure of the schoolboy's Virgils was also, less obviously, but perhaps more significantly, implicated in the colonialist project in so far as it was central to the practices of an education mobilised to 'reduce' the native 'savage' to 'civility', just as it 'informed' the English schoolboy, made a 'man' of him. Virgil was, in short, the embodiment and bringer of 'civilising' 'proper' 'Language', like the coloniser, schoolteacher and father Prospero. At the same time, we have seen how, with the New World discoveries, a difference, or gap, opens up between the Virgilian geography/cosmography and new maps of the world/the universe – a difference or gap which was part of, even as it contributed to a more general emergent critique of the ancients as the 'fathers of knowledge'. The intertextual relation of New World discourses – understood in a broad

---

[27] It is worth noting that gestures of dis-interested dis-respect towards, and dis-investment from the formal apparatus of an education in the humanities recur in the Shakespearean canon. More importantly, the relation of this apparatus to the socio-political structure is explicitly fore-grounded. Take the example of Launcelot Gobbo in *The Merchant of Venice*: in his playful strategies to get his blind father (!) to call him 'Master' he (mis)-uses Latin forms ('ergo')(ii.ii.57 and 60) and classical figures, 'Fates and Destinies, and such odd sayings, the Sisters Three, and such branches of learning' (ii.ii.62–4). Launcelot's flounderings point up the 'odd' character of the discourse acquired through an education in the humanities and the relation between the acquisition and practice of this 'master' discourse and entitlement to the style of 'Master', the title of a gentleman. The irony – that Shakespeare serves in effect a function of social differentiation in English culture like that performed by the classical learning Gobbo mocks – might be pointed out to students and spectators (Gobbo might, for instance, be heard to quote 'To be, or not to be' as an example of 'odd sayings . . . branches of learning').

[28] Richard Waswo, 'The History that Literature Makes', *New Literary History* 19 (1988), pp. 541–64. The argument has been developed and extended to the present in Richard Waswo, *The Founding Legend of Western Civilization: From Virgil to Vietnam* (Hanover, N.H. and London: New England/ Wesleyan University Press, 1997). Hamilton points out that allusions to the *Aeneid* are also used in accounts of the colonialist project in Ireland. Hamilton, *Virgil and The Tempest*, pp. 65–6.

sense – to Virgil (poet and texts) thus consisted in differences as well as in likenesses. And it is as a relation of difference(s) and likeness(es), indeed of differences *in* likenesses – a dialectical or dialogical imitation – that I have suggested we might consider the intertextual relation of *The Tempest* to Virgil.

Likeness to Virgil is, of course, most obviously asserted by the location of the play, set as it is in the Old World rather than the New, and, more specifically, on the stretch of sea between the Italian and North African coasts, which is the site of the tempest in *Aeneid* 1. New World discourses are thus alluded to, or played over, the *locus* – geographical as well as textual site – of the opening scene of the Virgilian epic, a mode of allusion I suggested in chapter 1 we might compare to Brant's allusion to Columbus's voyage of discovery in his illustration to the tempest in *Aeneid* 1.[29] However, while Brant's allusion merely asserts likeness between New World voyages and Old World epic, the play inserts difference into likeness, the difference that history makes to geography: 'This Tunis, sir, was Carthage' (II.i.80). Reproducing what was contemporary knowledge, Gonzalo's assertion marks the historical distance and topographical difference between the world of *Aeneid* 1 (and 4) and the world of the play, which is, more generally, to mark history as difference rather than as analogy or likeness.[30] It is, moreover, a difference which is linked to theatrical performance when Antonio says to Sebastian that in their return from Tunis they have all been 'sea-swallow'd', 'though some cast again, ... to perform an act ... ' (II.i.246–7). The performance of the play is thus advertised as a supplementary/supplanting theatrical recasting of the Virgilian master *locus*, which is dis-placed as the past.

It is as a supplementary/supplanting actor that Prospero 'casts' Antonio in his narrative of the betrayal and usurpation following his 'cast(ing)' of the 'government' on his brother (I.ii.75). In this narrative

[29] See chapter 1, pp. 23–4 and figure 1. Nosworthy, amongst others, notes the likeness between the setting of the play and the site of Virgil's opening tempest. Nosworthy, 'The Narrative Sources', p. 290. I do not rehearse all the likenesses to Virgil's *Aeneid* that have been suggested to date, which range from the generally recognised, such as the harpy episode (which underscores Prospero's 'Virgilian' features), and the first exchange between Ferdinand and Miranda, to the more or less contested, such as the likeness of Ariel to Virgil's Mercury (Kott, 'The *Aeneid* and *The Tempest*', pp. 427–8), and the likeness of the basic 'purgatorial' structure of the play to the pattern of *Aeneid* 6 (Still, *The Timeless Theme*; Srigley, *Images of Regeneration*). For reasons of economy I point out only likenesses which have not been noticed and repeat only those of relevance to my focus on the play's articulation of contestatory difference from the Virgilian model.

[30] For the possibly self-conscious difference from Jonson, see chapter 4, pp. 142–3. For the contemporary accuracy of Gonzalo's comment, see ibid., note 57 and Cooper's entry under 'Carthago': 'The countrey where it stoode, is nowe called Tunyse.' Cooper, *Thesaurus*.

there are again likenesses to Virgil, but these emerge only in the context of early modern mediations, on the one hand, of the *Aeneid* and, on the other, of the life and character of the poet. Prospero's description of his retirement when he was 'transported / And rapt in secret studies' (lines 76–7), 'neglecting worldy ends, all dedicated / To closeness and the bettering of my mind' (lines 89–90), follows the pattern (even the vocabulary) of descriptions of the type of contemplative Neoplatonic natural philosopher/mage/true poet exemplified by the 'learned scholler' Virgil, who, in the narrative of the *Lyf*, is similarly a learned and retiring scholar. In the *Lyf*, in addition, the scholar Virgil loses lands, if not a dukedom, to greedy kinsmen because of this retirement (see chapter 3, pp. 98–9).

Other details of Prospero's narrative recall, rather, early modern mediations of the *Aeneid* as moral/spiritual discourse, in Landino's commentary and Vegio's imitation.[31] Informed by the binary, hierarchical opposition of the contemplative life over the active, these mediations turn both the tempest sent by Juno and the wars against Turnus into figures of the turbulence brought about by the desire for what Prospero calls 'worldly ends', which disrupts the virtuous hero's (higher) pursuit of 'closeness and the bettering of (his) mind'.[32] Turnus, in particular, mediated as the embodiment of a diabolic, this-worldly ambition which disrupts the virtuous man's pursuit of the contemplative life occupies a place, or function, very like the place occupied by Antonio in Prospero's narrative. Virtually identified as a personification of ambition through explicit references (i.ii.105; ii.i.237 and v.i.75) and through a comparison with the commonplace emblem of ambition, ivy

[31] See above chapter 1, pp. 25–6 and notes 11 and 12, and for the relations between the two and their circulation in early modern England, Tudeau-Clayton, 'Supplementing the *Aeneid*' (forthcoming).

[32] Gavin Douglas summarises Landino's commentary in a note to his translation of the tempest in *Aeneid* 1: 'Cristoferus Landynus, that writis moraly apon Virgill, says thus: Eneas purposis to Italy, his land of promyssion; that is to say, a just perfyte man entendis to mast soveran bonte and gudnes, quhilk as witnessyth Plato, is situate in contemplation of godly thyngis or dyvyn warkis. His onmeysabil ennymy Juno, that is fenʒeit queyn of realmys, entendis to dryve him from Italle to Cartage; that is, Avesion, or concupissence to ryng or haf warldly honouris, wald draw him fra contemplation to the actyve lyve; quhilk, quhen scho falis by hir self, tretis scho with Eolus, the neddyr part of raison, quhilk sendis the storm of mony warldly consalis in the just manis mynd. Bot ... fynaly by the fre wyll and raison predomynent, that is, ondirstand, by Neptun, the storm is cessit.' Douglas, *Virgil's Aeneid*, vol. 2, p. 29, note to line 100. In Vegio's *Supplementum* Turnus is turned into an *exemplum* of ambition, especially in the speech by Latinus made over his body, which begins (in Douglas's translation), 'O dampnabill pryde and ambitioun' (ibid., vol. 4, p. 155). See further, Tudeau-Clayton, 'Supplementing the *Aeneid*' (forthcoming).

(I.ii.85–7), Antonio is associated, like Turnus, with the archetypal 'deceiver' (Epilogue, line 7) – the devil.[33]

However, just as difference is inserted into the topographical likeness with the site of the Virgilian tempest, difference is inserted into the likeness with the moral 'map' grafted on to the Virgilian tempest by early modern commentary/imitation. This is done, crucially, through the syntax and figures (of waking and procreation) in Prospero's narrative: 'I, thus neglecting worldly ends' 'in my false brother / Awak'd an evil nature' (I.ii.89, 92–3); 'my trust / Like a good parent, did beget ... A falsehood' (lines 93–5). The relation of the contemplative to the active life is here turned from an atemporal, binary, hierarchical opposition into a linear relation of temporal process, at once historical and natural cause and effect. The structures of allegory, which turn history in general as well as the Virgilian epic in particular into repetitions of the same (as in Jonson's *Haddington Masque*, discussed in chapter 4), are thus 'confused' by the form of a linear narrative which turns history (as well as nature) into temporally embedded process marked by change, difference, dis-rupture. More specifically, the hierarchical relation of the contemplative life over the active, which the early modern – Catholic – mediations of the Virgilian tempest promote, is put into question by this narrative, which makes one man's pursuit of the good of the contemplative life the cause of another's 'evil' desire for the active. This effect is underscored by Prospero's role as head of state as well as natural philosopher. For the pursuit of the contemplative life, in this case, appears rather as a dereliction of duty and so the opposite of good.[34]

As this suggests, it is not only the hierarchical relation of the contemplative life over the active that is put into question, but, more generally, the relation of the moral order to the political. Of particular importance here is the alignment of moral and political orders in Landino's mediation of the Virgilian tempest: the virtuous man's superior reason

---

[33] On ivy as the emblem of ambition, see the speech of Silvanus to Elizabeth at Kenelworth in J. Nichols, *The Progresses and Public Processions of Queen Elizabeth*, 2 vols. (London: The Society of Antiquaries, 1788), vol. 1, p. 84. On Vegio's association of Turnus with the devil, see Brinton, *Maphaeus Vegius*, p. 28, Hijmans, '*Aeneia Virtus*', pp. 152–3, 154. The 'narrative function' of Vegio's Turnus, and of Antonio in Prospero's narrative, is like that of the devil, 'something in the way' 'the Adversary', as Neil Forsyth puts it, a 'function', which he points out is signalled in the etymology of *diabolos*. Neil Forsyth, *The Old Enemy: Satan and the Combat Myth* (Princeton University Press, 1987), p. 4.

[34] This problem is raised already in an earlier play – *Henry 6, part 2* – in which the aspiration of the king to the contemplative life provokes the ambition of subordinates and political turmoil. Early modern mediations of the Virgilian tempest are explicitly mobilised here too. See Clayton, '"Tempests, and such like Drolleries"', pp. 216–20.

(Neptune), which suppresses the turbulent effects of ambition (the tempest), is likened to a supreme magistrate and a prince.[35] This is, of course, to extend into the moral allegory the likeness drawn in the first epic simile between Neptune and a statesman who brings a popular rising under control (*Aeneid* 1, lines 148–57). This Virgilian scene is explicitly invoked in the opening scene of *The Tempest*, which puts into question its alignment of political and natural orders, just as the form of Prospero's narrative puts into question the alignment of moral and political orders in early modern moral mediations of the Virgilian tempest. In each case, the alignment is dis-rupted by the difference within analogy, the difference on which it is grounded. The same is done to another traditional and commonplace (if not specifically Virgilian) analogy – between ship and state – which is likewise invoked in the opening scene and likewise undone by the foregrounding of the difference within analogy.

In marking the difference within these received relations of likeness the play at the same time asserts its own 'original' difference in the relation of likeness to the Virgilian model. The intertextual relation thus 'mirrors' the dis-ruptures performed by the play – a mirroring that is underscored by the use of theatrical metaphors to represent both the past and present 'acts' of the usurping imitator Antonio. Foregrounding its own performance as present pass-time, the play underscores both its original difference and the difference of the present from the 'maps' – moral and political as well as topographical – of the Virgilian *locus*, which are dis-located as the other place of the past.

This dis-location of the Virgilian *locus* by the original, contestatory and usurping difference of the imitation is overtly represented in Ariel's retrospective description of the '(p)erform'd ... tempest' (1.ii.194), especially in the signed image of its shaking of Neptune's 'dread trident' (discussed further below). Alluding to the Virgilian scene of Neptune's suppression of the tempest to which the opening scene – precisely the 'perform'd tempest' – alludes too, Ariel's description recalls not only the allusion, but the ironic mockery to which the Virgilian scene is exposed through the figure of the Boatswain, one of the play's 'noise-makers', whose resistance is both more generally and radically to the symbolic order of language, and, more specifically, to the authority of the Virgilian model.[36] Both forms, or levels, of resistance will in turn be

---

[35] Landino in Stahel, 'Cristoforo Landino's Allegorization', fo. H3v and fo. H4r.
[36] Heather James anticipates my point that the Boatswain's speech interrogates the Virgilian scene, but she does not see the more radical aspects of his interrogations nor Ariel's echo of them. James, *Shakespeare's Troy*, chapter 6.

re-presented at the second moment of 'confused noise', when another noise-maker 'from below' dis-rupts a universe specifically marked as Virgilian.

But before looking in detail at these particularly explicit articulations of dis-rupture in relation to the Virgilian model I want to look at what might appear a less explicit articulation, in the ironic commentary of Antonio and Sebastian on the discourses of Gonzalo in Act II, scene i. It is, of course, here that Gonzalo introduces the name of 'widow Dido' (ii.i.73) triggering the question from Antonio which I described earlier as a commentator's question and which has itself triggered subsequent commentary on the relation of the play to Virgil's *Aeneid*. It is, however, important to recognise that the question belongs to an on-going commentary made by Antonio and Sebastian from the very outset of the scene on both the form and content of Gonzalo's discourse. It is, moreover, from the outset that this discourse is associated with the Virgilian model, for Gonzalo's opening speech declares itself as a self-conscious imitation of the speech 'of consolation' given by Aeneas to his companions after the tempest, on the 'theme of woe' (ii.i.6). As we saw in chapter 2, its self-consciousness is signalled by its inclusion of the 'outside' – the framing formal classification of the Virgilian speech – 'inside', an inclusion which points up the learned, 'set' character of this particular imitation and the inevitable tendency of the practice of imitation to turn 'matter' into mere 'words' (see chapter 2, pp. 76–7).

This is underscored by Antonio and Sebastian, the ironic shadows of imitation/commentary (in both senses of the genitive), who deride both the laboured, 'set' character of Gonzalo's Virgilian discourse and its failure to achieve its consolatory purpose, its failure, in short, to 'work'. Their derision echoes and underscores the derision of the Boatswain in the opening scene, which is likewise directed at the discourse of both Virgil and Gonzalo, and which again points up the failure of such discourse to 'work'. I suggested in chapter 1 that this ineffectiveness registers the failure of the Old World and Renaissance humanist ideal of the virtuous and eloquent statesman – an ideal which Gonzalo embodies, like the Virgilian model and the specific Virgilian figures (of Neptune and Aeneas), with which he is associated. Both ideal and model are dis-placed in the other place of the past by the irony of the play's noise-makers. This function of the intertextual relation – its marking of historical time – is indeed given a literal turn by Sebastian, who begins the mocking commentary on the laboured, learned form of Gonzalo's words: 'Look, he's winding up the watch of his wit; by and by it will strike ... One: tell' (II.i.13–15) The ironic shadows of imitation/commentary tell time, mark the negativity – dis-location – of history.

This irony extends to the other, more familiar 'set piece' of Gonzalo's – on his ideal commonwealth (II.i.139–64). As others have pointed out, Gonzalo's ideal includes a paradisiacal vision of nature like that embodied in Prospero's masque.[37] What has not been noticed, however, is that the two ideal worlds share Virgilian associations (specifically, associations with *Georgics* 1) and, more importantly, that they are both disrupted, and dis-located as the past, by the negativity – 'noise' – of a 'new world' figure, which they fail to contain.

We can see this more clearly if we take a closer look at the relation of Gonzalo's speech to its recognised source in Montaigne's essay on the cannibals.[38] For Montaigne's account of the New World tribal communities is not simply reproduced, but placed within a framing conditional: 'Had I plantation of this isle ... / ... / And were the King on't' (II.i.139, 141). This frame turns Montaigne's 'what ... we see by experience' into an imagined ideal, a fiction like and not, as Montaigne claims, 'dissonant' from the 'imaginarie commonwealth' of Plato, and the 'pictures' of a 'golden age' produced by the ancient poets, including Virgil in his *Georgics*.[39] The mediated character of this 'picture' of the New World is, moreover, advertised through the explicit naming of its formal mode (not in Montaigne): Gonzalo 'would by contraries / Execute' (lines 143–4) his ideal commonwealth, that is, by means of the formal mode of negation, which is, at least in part, how the Virgilian vision in *Georgics* 1 is articulated.[40] Like the formal self-consciousness of his opening speech of consolation, this underscores the formal, set or given character of Gonzalo's discourse. More importantly, it points up the likeness to Old World, and, specifically, Virgilian visions of the golden age, points up, that is, how the vision of Gonzalo (indeed of Montaigne) remains within

---

[37] For example, Maus, 'Arcadia Lost', pp. 193–4; François Laroque, *Shakespeare's Festive World*, translated by Janet Lloyd (Cambridge University Press, 1993), pp. 221–2.

[38] Michel de Montaigne, *Essais*, 3 vols. (Paris: Flammarion, 1969), vol. 1, pp. 251–63.

[39] Florio's translation in John Florio, *The Essayes, or Morall, Politike, and Millitarie Discourses of Lo: Michaell de Montaigne ... now done into English* (London, 1603), p. 102. Montaigne quotes *Georgics* 2, line 208, but the language of his 'picture' of the New World suggests rather the *locus classicus* in *Georgics* 1 (lines 125–8), quoted in note 40.

[40]   ante Jovem *nulli* subigebant arva coloni;
                   ne signare *quidem* aut partire limite campum
                   fas erat: in medium quaerebant, ipsaque tellus
                   omnia liberius, nullo poscente, ferebat.

                                              (*Georgics* 1, lines 125–8; my emphasis)
    'Before Jove's day no tillers subdued the land. Even to mark the field or divide it with bounds was unlawful. Men made gain for the common store, and Earth yielded all, of herself, more freely, when none begged for her gifts' (Fairclough).

the binary terms/limits – 'bounds' – of the Old World models. Like Prospero's Virgilian vision, it fails to contain, as negation or 'contrary', the radical negativity of the new world/New World – a failure that the dis-rupture of the masque will dramatise. Here this failure is signalled, on the one hand, by the ineffectiveness of the speech in its consolatory purpose: like the opening speech, it has no purchase on the 'noise' of Alonso's subjectivity, specifically the 'noise' of his grief, as Alonso's laconic comment – 'Thou dost talk nothing to me' (line 170) – points up.[41] On the other hand, the failure is signalled by the disruptive ironic commentary of Antonio and Sebastian, telling time. The ironic shadows of imitation/commentary 'translate' the radical negativity of a new world, which cannot be contained by Old World forms, and which indeed call for new forms, new visions.

PROSPERO'S VIRGILIAN MASQUE AND THE FALL INTO DIS-STORY

This dis-location of Old World forms and visions is dramatised by the dis-rupture of Prospero's masque, which is marked by '*confused noise*' and which points up the radical negativity at once of history, individual subjectivity and a nature (in)different to the forms received from the ancients, the 'fathers of knowledge', and, specifically, Virgil. For the vision of nature embodied in the masque clearly evokes Virgilian *loci*: first, *Aeneid* 1 and 4, especially the scene of Juno's presence at the 'wedlock' of Dido and Aeneas, a scene mediated as natural philosophy, notably in Jonson's *Hymenaei*, the marriage masque to which it is agreed Prospero's masque alludes;[42] second, the universe of *Georgics* 1, likewise mediated, if also interrogated, as natural philosophy, as we have seen. More generally, the masque evokes the 'proportioned' 'charming' form of Virgil's verse, mediated as knowledge of nature.

That the masque, and the exchanges between Ferdinand and Prospero which immediately precede it, include precise verbal echoes of *Aeneid* 1 and 4 has, of course, been pointed out by others: Baldwin notes that Ceres' description of Iris (iv.i.78–9) echoes *Aeneid* 4 (lines 700–1),

---

[41] This will be echoed by 'I heard nothing' (line 312), which points up the 'hollowness' of verbal imitations of nature as this comment points up the 'hollowness' of formal imitations of textual *loci*.

[42] See chapter 4, pp. 144, 146–8. The word 'wedlock' is Stanyhurst's and comes in his strategically opaque discussion of the scene, revealing/concealing its significance as 'secretes of Nature', specifically as alchemical knowledge. Stanyhurst, *Translation of the First Four Books of the Aeneis*, p. 7. See above, chapter 3, note 59.

while Bernhard Smith suggests that Ferdinand's allusion to the 'mur-kiest den' (IV.i.25) which 'shall never melt / Mine honour into lust' (lines 27–8) recalls the 'speluncam' (*Aeneid* 4, line 124) in which Dido and Aeneas consummate their passion.[43] To these we might add what seems to me a particularly pleasing echo of 'ipsa Paphum sublimis abit' (*Aeneid* 1, line 415) in Iris's description of Venus '*(c)utting the clouds towards Paphos*' (IV.i.93).[44] With these verbal details Ceres' question whether '*Venus or her son*' '*(d)o now attend the queen*' (lines 88–9), with its emphasis on the singular alliance between the habitual enemies Juno and Venus, and Iris's reply, with its allusion to the '*wanton charm*' (line 95) attempted on Miranda and Ferdinand, evoke the Virgilian narrative of Dido and Aeneas as a contrasting *exemplum*, or contrary to the '*contract of true love*' (line 84). The ideal of true love is indeed 'executed', like Gonzalo's commonwealth, by contraries, which are here intertextual, Miranda and Ferdinand being identified as not Dido and Aeneas. To this Ceres adds a parallel Ovidian 'contrary', in her allusion to the '*plot*' of Venus and Cupid through which '*dusky Dis (her) daughter got*' (line 89), a contrary which introduces, specifically, the underworld figure of the negative or contrary – Dis.[45]

It is precisely as an *exemplum* of 'false' love or lust, in contrast to an ideal of 'lufe ... rewlyt by messure', that Gavin Douglas treats the story of Dido and Aeneas in his long prologue, or '(p)reambill' to *Aeneid* 4.[46] His preamble appears to be recalled in what might be described as the preamble to Prospero's masque – the exchanges between Prospero and Ferdinand (IV.i.13–32 and lines 51–6). For the respective discourses share key metaphors: love/lust as seed and the outcome as good/bad fruit;

[43] Baldwin, *William Shakespere's Small Latine*, vol. 2, pp. 479–81; Kermode, note to IV.i.25. Kermode points out that Stanyhurst translates 'speluncam' 'den'. He uses 'den' again to translate 'speluncam' in line 165 (identical to line 124), as does Henry Howard. Henry Howard, Earl of Surrey, *The Aeneid*, edited by Florence H. Ridley (University of California Press, 1963), p. 119. The epithet 'murkiest' may owe something to 'nocte tegentur opaca' (*Aeneid* 4, line 123), translated by Stanyhurst 'they shal be in darknes al hooveld'. Stanyhurst, *Translation of the First Four Books of the Aeneis*, p. 98

[44] Compare, for example, the rather more pedestrian rendering by Day Lewis, 'she herself was gone through the air to Paphos'. Lewis, *The Eclogues, Georgics and Aeneid of Virgil*, p. 146.

[45] The figure of Dis is discussed above, pp. 199–200. In a very interesting analysis of the masque as at once Virginian and Ovidian John Gillies focuses on the Ovidian narrative of the rape of Proserpina to argue that Prospero's masque is informed by Ovidian oppositions, and, especially, an Ovidian association of temperance and fertility, which he suggests informs too colonialist accounts of Virginia. John Gillies, 'Shakespeare's Virginian Masque', *English Literary History* 53 (1986), pp. 673–707. In making his case he ignores the overt specific Virgilian echoes I have cited. The masque is surely Virgilian as much as it is Virginian and Ovidian; indeed, we might see the Virgilian and Ovidian *exempla* as blended in another Erasmian exercise of 'copy'. Both *exempla* illustrate a universe that is at once moral and cosmographical, the key term being, as Gillies rightly points out, temperance.

[46] Douglas, *Virgil's 'Aeneid'*, vol. 2, pp. 147–54 (quotation from p. 150 (line 125)).

uncontrolled desire as 'ane unbridillyt hors'.[47] And they are informed by
the same 'natural philosophy' (we might say physiology) of love/lust:
love is engendered by what Prospero calls 'fire in th'blood' (IV.i.53), heat
which, when 'excessyve' (Douglas), and uncontrolled, turns into lust,
expelling honour, producing hate, and, specifically in the case of Dido,
'disdeyn' (which Douglas gives as the reason for her suicide).[48] In
contrast, 'lufe ... rewlyt by messure' is a love marked by moderation,
'(i)n temperat warmnes, nowthir to cald nor hait' (line 127), that is to say,
precisely Ferdinand's 'white cold virgin snow' (IV.i.55), which '(a)bates
the ardour of (his) liver' (IV.i.56).[49]

Temperance is indeed the common and key term to the moral and
natural philosophical discourses informing the masque.[50] At the most
obvious level, it is articulated in the repetition of the commitment by
the true lovers *'that no bed-right shall be paid / Till Hymen's torch be lighted'*
(IV.i.96–7). It is, however, also articulated at the level of the formal
structure of the masque, specifically through the organisation of the
figures of the four elements. As in the mediations as natural philosophy
of the scene of Juno's presence at the 'wedlock' of Dido and Aeneas, all
four elements are included. They are, however, introduced in an order
which formally realises the delay intrinsic to the idea of temperance. In
terms of Brant's woodcut illustration to the Virgilian universe in *Georgics*
I (figure 4), the masque moves from the centre – the *'earth'* (line 82)
figured by Ceres – via the *'wat'ry arch'* (line 71) figured by Iris – to *'th' sky'*
(line 70), or air, figured by Juno, and, finally, after a delay of twenty-five
lines, to fire, evoked in the phrase 'Hymen's torch ... lighted' (line 97).[51]
This phrase recalls, immediately, Prospero's speech of warning to Fer-

---
47 Ibid., p. 150 (line 117). Compare Prospero's 'do not give dalliance / Too much the rein' (IV.i.51–2). Chaucer too uses 'imagery of fruition' in relation to the Dido and Aeneas story; see Baswell, *Virgil in Medieval England*, pp. 264–5.
48 Ibid., p. 150 (line 121), and p. 154 (line 256). Recall the 'disdain and discord' (IV.i.20) evoked by Prospero as the outcome of lust.
49 Douglas twice uses a verb – 'refrain' – which has a semantic field overlapping that of 'abate', once in an admonition – 'Refreyn ȝour curage' (line 204) – once in a condemnation of young men who 'lyst not thar heyt refreyn' (line 154).
50 See Gillies, 'Shakespeare's Virginian Masque', *passim*; and James, *Shakespeare's Troy*, chapter 6. Temperance/chastity is of course the defining term of the Virgilian economy/character in the Jonsonian corpus, as we have seen.
51 The element of water, which is absent from the Virgilian scene, is similarly introduced through the adjective 'watrye' by Richard Stanyhurst, to make up the set of four, as he explains. Stanyhurst, *Translation of the First Four Books of the Aeneis*, p. 7. Jonson too adds 'watrie *Meteors*' in the fuller description of his masque of Juno in *Hymenaei* (*H&S*, vol. 7, p. 231). In Prospero's masque Iris's 'watry' character is emphasised in lines which echo Virgil's description of Iris at the end of *Aeneid* 4 (see above, note 43), the adjective 'roscida' (*Aeneid* 4, line 700) being expanded in the description of Iris as one who diffuses *'honey-drops, refreshing showers'* (IV.i.78–9).

dinand – 'take heed / As Hymen's lamps shall light you' (lines 22–3) – and more distantly, perhaps, the close of *Hymenaei* when Hymen's torches are raised (and described in terms of the Virgilian scene). A synecdoche of the ceremony, and metonymy of the institution of marriage, Hymen's torch figures the containment of sexual desire within symbolic forms – whether the ceremonial forms of marriage or the masque, or simply forms of language – a containment that will be dis-rupted when the lustful violator of Proserpine – Dis – returns in the lustful, and 'dis-proportioned', would-be violator of Miranda – Caliban.

This delay in the completion of the circle of the four elements realises, in the masque's 'Virgilian' natural philosophical discourse, the temporal dimension which is explicitly foregrounded in the moral discourse ('Till *Hymen's torch be lighted*'). Moral, and specifically sexual temperance are thus turned in terms of cosmic order, or, more precisely, cosmic *proportion* projected along the time axis. It is 'proportion' – a term with numerical, musical and architectural senses as well as cosmographical – that John Orrell suggests informs the structure of Prospero's masque, as, he shows, it informs the structure of Jonson's *Hymenaei*.[52] Looking at line numbers only, he identifies the recurrence of 'the ratio of the diapason, 1:2', but does not see that this ratio is figured too in patterns of rhyme and rhythm – patterns, incidentally, which formally distinguish, and separate, the masque from the rest of the play. For, while the rhyme pattern organises lines into couplets, an emphatic tetrameter rhythm marks these units of two as twice four. This is particularly prominent in the song sung by Ceres and Juno (lines 106–17), which is not merely four lines followed by eight, as Orrell points out, but two couplets, followed by four, of four beat lines. The recurrence of the number four is, of course, specifically significant in so far as it echoes the number of the elements figured in the masque. As in the organisation of these figures, the temporal dimension is formally realised, the language of the masque being, we might say, language 'rewlyt by messure', language, that is, tempered, and tempered not only as an aural figure of cosmic proportion and the lovers' temperance, but in order to produce such proportion/temperance, to work, that is, 'sympathetically', which is to work in the manner of magic charms, as Ferdinand's description of the masque – '(h)armonious charmingly' (line 119) – precisely (or, as Orrell suggests,

---

[52] John Orrell, 'The Musical Canon of Proportion in Jonson's *Hymenaei*', *English Language Notes* 15 (1978), p. 178, note 14. Only Orrell has pointed out this dimension of the (generally recognised) relation of Prospero's masque to Jonson's.

'correctly') puts it. For Ferdinand's phrase implies the 'sympathetic' model of nature and the human mind/body, discussed in chapter 3, especially in relation to the quantitative form of Virgilian metre, mediated, like and with music, as a form of knowledge.[53]

The mode of the masque, especially the song sung by the figures of air and earth, is thus incantatory, a mode which aspires, that is, to produce the effect – of a tempered/proportioned order – which it figures. As such it is not simply, as Louis Montrose suggests of the generic form of the masque, and of Jonson's masques in particular, 'art functioning very close to ritual' but art *as* ritual, art, that is, which aspires to a symmetry (precisely, a likeness of measure in proportion), not primarily between initially disjunct social groups (Montrose's focus), but between the human and natural.[54] It is, finally, art that aspires to a magical control of nature, a control predicated on a belief in a 'sympathetically' related system or order.[55] It is a control that, as Ferdinand again precisely puts it, '(m)akes this place Paradise' (line 124) – the figure which Gabriel Naudé uses of the knowledge achieved by his type of natural philosopher/mage, exemplified by Virgil, and which Thomas Elyot uses, specifically, of the knowledge of nature disclosed in *Georgics* 1.[56]

The numerical structure of the masque may allude to this Virgilian paradise (as well as to *Hymenaei*), since, as Duckworth (following Le Grelle) has shown, *Georgics* 1 is constructed according to 'mathematical proportion', in particular the Golden Mean ratio (of which the diapason is an instance).[57] More specifically, and verbally, the universe of the Virgilian poem is evoked at the outset by the words with which Iris

---

[53] See chapter 3, pp. 101–8, and recall the linking of the origin of metre to God's creation of the universe according to a certain logic, or *ratio* of number. Recall too the title of Puttenham's chapter on the quantitative form of the ancients: 'Of *Proportion* Poeticall' (my emphasis; see chapter 3, pp. 104–5).

[54] Louis A. Montrose, 'Sport by Sport O'erthrown: *Love's Labours Lost* and the Politics of Play', reprinted in Gary Waller, ed., *Shakespeare's Comedies* (London and New York: Longman, 1991), p. 65.

[55] Interestingly, Claude Levi Strauss, from whom Montrose takes his definition of ritual, likens native systems of thought/knowledge precisely to the 'système de correspondances' elaborated by the ancients and by late medieval/early Renaissance thinkers (such as Albert the Great). Claude Levi-Strauss, *La pensée sauvage* (Paris: Plon, 1962), pp. 54–60. The dis-ruption of Prospero's masque marks this universe as the past and so implies a critique of such contemporary forms as Jonson's which aspire to the condition of ritual in a universe where such correspondences no longer 'work'.

[56] 'In his Georgikes / lorde what pleasaunt varietie there is: the divers graynes / herbes / and flowres / that be there described / that reding therin hit semeth to a man to be in a delectable gardeine or paradise.' Elyot, *The Book named The Governor*, fo. 32v. See chapter 3, note 37 and for Naudé's representation of Virgil, ibid., pp. 96–7.

[57] George E. Duckworth, *Structural Patterns and Proportions in Vergil's 'Aeneid': A Study in Mathematical Composition* (Ann Arbor: University of Michigan Press, 1962), pp. 36–44.

summons Ceres: '*Ceres, most bounteous lady*' (line 60), which renders
exactly 'alma Ceres', the phrase with which the goddess of the earth is
summoned at the opening of the Virgilian poem.[58] Ceres' earth, which
Iris goes on to describe, is, moreover, characterised by what Elyot calls,
in relation to the Virgilian poem, 'pleasaunt varietie' of 'divers graynes':
'*wheat, rye, barley, vetches, oats and pease*' (line 61).[59] It is too an earth
laboured – its '*banks with pioned and twilled brims, / Which spongy April ...
betrims*' (lines 64–5), its vineyards '*poll-clipt*' (line 68). The Virgilian poem
too foregrounds such labour, which 'Ceres was the first to teach men',[60]
and which consists primarily of specific techniques to master nature:
'labor omnia vicit' (labour conquered the world' (Fairclough) (line 145)).
In both Prospero's masque and in Virgil's poem, that is, Ceres' earth is
nature 'tempered' by labour – and, as we saw in chapter 2, school-
teachers readily moralised the Virgilian descriptions of labour in such
terms. Indeed, such moral discourse is introduced into the masque
through allusions to '*cold nymphs chaste crowns*' (line 66) and to '*the dismissed
bachelor*' (line 67) '*lass-lorn*' (line 68) – chastened – as the vineyard
(described in the same line) is '*poll-clipt*'.

But nature is 'tempered' in the Virgilian poem not only by labour but
by other forms of human control, in particular, ritual dance. At the
outset, fauns and dryads, who are described as 'nymphs' in Fleming's
explanatory expansion, are summoned to accompany the poet's song in
dance.[61] Then, those who have 'cut' 'Ceres golden grain' 'in noonday
heat' (Fairclough) (line 297), are called upon to practise piety towards the
gods, especially Ceres, by performing sacrifices, songs and dances in the
spring (lines 335–50). These forms of piety are to be practised specifically
in order to prevent bad weather – tempests. Dis-temper in nature is thus
to be prevented through forms which aspire to draw nature into a

---

[58] *Georgics* 1, line 7. The figure of earth in the scene of Juno's presence at the 'wedlock' of Dido and Aeneas in *Aeneid* 4 is Tellus not Ceres.

[59] See note 56. Five of the six crops listed by Iris appear in a passage on strategies for planting (*Georgics* 1, lines 71–83), as translated by Abraham Fleming: 'wheat and rie'; 'vitches' 'otes' 'pease'. Fleming, *The Bucoliks ... with his Georgiks. All newly translated into English verse*, p. 4. The term 'farra' (line 73) in this passage, which Fleming translates 'corn', is glossed by Cooper, 'Al maner of corn: properly meale of wheate or *barley* where the corne is beaten in a mortar' (my emphasis). Cooper, *Thesaurus*, s.v. 'farra'.

[60] Fairclough's translation of 'prima Ceres ... mortalis ... instituit' (*Georgics* 1, line 147).

[61] 'et vos, agrestum praesentia numina, Fauni, / (ferte simul Faunique pedem Dryadesque puellae!) / munera vestra cano' (*Georgics* 1, lines 10–12), translated by Fleming: 'And O you Fawnes (of Woods, the Gods, and Cattel-keepers too) / You present Gods of Husband-men, you fawns, and Driads, you / (The Nymphs of Trees, and chiefly Okes) set hither ward your foote.' Servius links the phrase 'ferte pedem' to the poet's use of metre, which may be relevant to the phrase 'country footing' (IV.i.138) in Prospero's masque, especially given its emphatic tetrameter rhythm, a rhythm characteristic, of course, of popular forms. See Virgil, *Opera*, vol. 1, fo. 54r.

symmetrical relation of correspondence with human bodies 'rewlyt by messure'.

That the *'graceful dance'* (SD) performed by the *'temperate nymphs'* (IV.i.132) and *'sunburn'd sicklemen'* (line 134) at the close of Prospero's masque carries the significance of such forms of ritual dance is indicated by the epithets *'graceful'*, *'temperate'*, and *'properly'* (in *'Reapers, properly habited'* (SD)) – 'properly' being, of course, cognate with 'proportion'. The partners are, moreover, associated with the elements, respectively, of air and water – *'nymphs ... of the ... brooks'* (line 128) – and fire and earth – *'sunburn'd sicklemen ... / ... from the furrow'* (lines 134–5), and, perhaps, with gender inflected formal patterns. For Iris summons the nymphs in three rhyming couplets, and the sicklemen in two (plus a half line), a numerical figure of 3:2, which, as Jonson's *Hymenaei* recalls, is a proportion of the female and male numbers, the number five being the figure of perfect union (*H&S*, vol. 7, p. 216).

As a genre of course the court masque, especially the Jonsonian court masque, makes self-conscious use of the symbolic form of dance, which it tends to invest explicitly with such significances as these indications to Prospero's masque supply.[62] In *The Masque of Queens*, for instance, the third dance of the queens is expressly described as a *'numerous* composition', a figure of mathematical *'proportion'*, in contrast to the witches' 'contrary' dance (*H&S*, vol. 7, pp. 315, 316, 301). In *Hymenaei* too it is specifically in their dance with the 'powers' of Marriage that the 'untemp'red *Humors'* and affections are said to be 'sweetly temper'd' (pp. 213, 221).[63]

Of importance here too are the 'ritual dances' of popular cultural traditions, which, as Brissenden points out, continued to mark 'the seasonal round of the year' in sixteenth-century English rural life, despite being 'long ... under attack by the church', and which belonged to the forms of festivity François Laroque has described so fully, arguing that cultural productions at all levels were influenced by them, especially by their mode of structuring time.[64] In particular, Laroque suggests that Prospero's masque brings together 'popular and scholarly' references,

[62] McDonald asserts simply that the dances performed in Shakespeare's play 'fulfill precisely the same functions they do in Jonson's masques: the representation of harmony between the upper and lower worlds'. McDonald, 'Reading *The Tempest*', p. 162. This is the meaning seen too by Brissenden in his interesting if straightforward book on dance in the Shakespearean corpus. Alan Brissenden, *Shakespeare and the Dance* (London and Basingstoke: Macmillan, 1981), pp. 96–102.

[63] See chapter 4, pp. 136–7, 148. For the (Platonic) idea of dance as a figure of proportion and the (Pythagorean) idea of it as a means to temper humours, see Paul Bourcier, *Histoire de la danse en Occident* (Paris: Seuil, 1978), p. 30.

[64] Brissenden, *Shakespeare and the Dance*, p. 2; Laroque, *Shakespeare's Festive World, passim*.

evoking at once the rural tradition of 'harvest-home' and ancient pagan rites associated with Ceres, although he does not mention the Virgilian examples of such rites (pp. 221–3). As he points out, the two forms of ritual were actually compared by contemporary observers, such as Paul Hentzer in 1598, and such comparisons served to fuel Protestant attacks on festive traditions (pp. 158, 356). However, he does not consider the significance of the graceful dance (only its 'rustic style'), or the abrupt breaking up of both the dance and the masque, commenting merely that Prospero's speech on the revels expresses 'a farewell to festivity' in the sense that, with the masque, it 'rounds off the festive calendar' (p. 223). Rather, I would argue, the speech should be taken precisely in relation to the dis-rupture of the masque and the dance, as a farewell to a universe in which festive forms, including ritual dance, 'worked' in linking human beings to each other and to nature through 'sympathy', within what Laroque describes as 'the magic, primitive view' (p. 201) of time – as a cycle of recurring binary oppositions. With the dis-rupture of the masque and the return of 'Dis' in the dis-tempered condition of Prospero, this universe is dis-located as the past, dis-rupted by a radical negativity of a 'new world', which the binary structures, whether of the court masque or popular festive forms, or indeed, as we have seen, of language, fail to contain as negation, or 'contrary'.[65]

Most immediately, it is the symbolic form of dance that fails to contain the 'confused noise within'. Indeed, an argument like that David Lindley makes about music in the play (and John Hollander makes more generally about music in the early modern world) could be made about this form too.[66] That is, the metaphysical meaning of dance, as a form which tempers and orders even as it figures a tempered and proportioned cosmic order – a meaning celebrated most elaborately in John Davies's poem *Orchestra* (1596) (and the only meaning of dance hitherto seen in *The Tempest*) – is dis-placed by the 'dancing' (iv.i.183) of the 'disproportion'd' (v.i.290) Caliban and his 'confederates' (iv.i.140). Though only described by Ariel, this 'dancing' – an ironic counterpoint to the 'graceful dance' of Prospero's masque – may be compared with

---

[65] Compare these suggestive interpretations of Prospero's speech on his masque: 'inspired ... by his failure to assimilate the nature of Caliban into his European idea of a moralised nature'. (Gillies, 'Shakespeare's Virginian Masque', p. 702); 'Prospero's invocation of last things, of an ultimate collective destiny, effectively brackets human history within a containing structure of radical indeterminacy and a containing discourse of radical unknowing'. (Felperin, 'Political Criticism', p. 57).

[66] Lindley, 'Music, masque and meaning in *The Tempest*' (see above, chapter 3, pp. 84–5); Hollander, *The Untuning of the Sky*.

the witches' dance in *The Masque of Queens*, especially since, as I pointed out in chapter 4, the language used of the sounds which accompany the disrupture of Prospero's masque – '*a strange, hollow, and confused noise*' – echoes the description of the witches' gestures and the accompanying noise and music. This is all the more important since, as we saw, the description of the witches, foregrounding as it does the 'strangeness' of particular differences, may be extended to the generic universes of the anti-masque and the Jonsonian satirical comedy. It is this generic universe that disrupts and displaces the total, closed Virgilian universe of Prospero's masque – a universe in which magic is inherent to knowledge and the symbolic forms of dance, music and language control by 'sympathy'. It is, finally, the likeness of these forms to nature/the self/history that is dis-rupted by what I have called the Protestant turn – a turn which is a turn from a form or mode of relation as well as a form of religion, the root sense of 'religion' being of course 'relation'. It is indeed arguably here rather than in any explicit verbal attacks that the vital, or deadly, impact of the Protestant turn lay, for its turn to particular difference tends, as we have seen, to render repetition hollow.

The hollow character of this universe and its place as the past are pointed up by the stage directions: '*they heavily vanish*'. For 'vanish' is the verb Jonson uses of the anti-masque of witches at the onset of the main masque in *The Masque of Queens*: 'the *Hagges* . . . quite vanishd' (*H&S*, vol. 7, p. 301) (and again of the first anti-masque in *Pleasure reconcil'd to Vertue* (p. 483)). Linked by sound as well as, distantly, by etymology with 'vain' and 'vanity', the verb attributes to the universe of the 'main masque' the insubstantial, ephemeral and illusory character attributed, in Jonson's texts, to the universes of the anti-masques and the satirical comedies. This is underscored by Prospero's farewell speech on the end of the 'revels' (iv.i.148): the 'vision' described by Ferdinand as 'harmonious charmingly' is now dismissed as 'melted' (line 150), an 'insubstantial pageant faded' (line 155), a 'vision' of 'baseless fabric' (line 151).[67] The 'paradise' of a total, fixed and proportioned order of nature – the Virgilian 'vision' – is thus dis-placed as 'baseless', not-knowledge and as

---

[67] Kermode, following Welsford, suggests this speech 'significantly resembles Jonson's lament for the ephemeral beauty of his masque' ('Introduction', in *The Tempest*, p. lxxiii). But it is important to set against this 'lament' the affirmation – which often follows it – of the solidity of the printed text and the truths it celebrates, compared, we should recall, with the 'spirit' or 'soul', in contrast and in opposition to the (insubstantial and ephemeral) 'body' of the performance. The hierarchy of printed text over particular performance is another of the (mutually reinforcing) hierarchies that Jonson's texts assert and *The Tempest* undermines.

the past, by the turn, or fall, into the radical negativity – the confused noise – of nature/history.

Like and with his Virgilian 'vision', Prospero falls subject to this negativity, as Miranda's description of him underscores: 'Never *till this day* / Saw I him . . . so *distemper'd*' (lines 144–5; my emphasis). The formal alignment of the phrases 'this day' and 'distemper'd' – and the near homonyms 'this' and 'dis' – link Prospero's subjection to the 'dis'-within to a subjection to difference in time, a difference which is at once of the self and of history. The Protestant turn is thus marked not only as a turn to selfhood as particular subjectivity, but to particular subjectivity as constructed by differentially related moments in time/history, history and time being no longer collectively experienced repetitions of the same, but particularised, linear narratives marked by dis-rupture and difference.[68] The moment thus dis-allows the immunity and transcendence of the self-same self Jonson's Virgil represents, especially in *Poetaster*, and his consequent position as overseer and judge over common men, which is also the position of the figure of Reason in *Hymenaei*, called upon by Hymen to control the humours and affections by which, like Prospero, he is 'troubled'. The difference makes the move of reason not judgement and containment, but forgiveness and renunciation of control. Prospero's fall into dis-temper, and into history as *this* story – particularity rather than repetition – is indeed followed by recognition of a common human kind precisely in this 'dis', which is a recognition of sameness in irreducible difference (v.i.21–8). This is underscored by his acknowledgement of the 'disproportion'd' Caliban as 'his' (v.i.275–6), the words 'distempered' and 'disproportioned' being virtual synonyms and, literally, of course, sharing the 'dis' within.[69] Prospero's recognition of, and identification with this universe of 'dis' is then confirmed in his renunciation of control over nature (v.i.33–57), which echoes not only Ovid's Medea but, more immediately, the principle witch in Jonson's anti-masque, whose immediate subordinate is called, not insignificantly, 'Ignorance'.[70]

---

[68] Heather James has coined the fine phrase 'negative epiphany' for what happens to Prospero here, though she uses it only to characterise his psychological experience. James, *Shakespeare's Troy*, chapter 6.

[69] Interestingly, 'disproportion'd' occurs in only one other place in the Shakespearean corpus (*Othello*, I.iii.2), where it is effectively glossed by what follows as 'difference' (line 7), a difference which is, specifically, a textual difference – *this*, as distinct from *that*, story.

[70] See chapter 4, pp. 139–40. Both ignorance and fury are of course opposites to Reason and in Jonson's Neoplatonic system the one implies the other, for, as he comments in a note on the witches, 'the opposition to all *vertue* begins out of *Ignorance*' and amongst her offspring is '*fury*' (*H&S*, vol. 7, p. 287, note o), the passion which Prospero recognises specifically as his (v.i.26).

More importantly, the speech aligns not only the author(ity) figure
with the universe of 'dis', but the '(p)erform'd ... tempest' (I.ii.194) –
both the opening scene and the play. For, in a modification to the
Ovidian speech, and the Jonsonian imitation, the itemised acts of
magical control over nature are put into a temporal sequence, which
turns them into a narrative of the production in time of a particular
tempest.[71] In another modification to the Ovidian speech (again not in
the Jonsonian imitation), the winds raised in order to produce this
tempest are described as 'mutinous' (line 42). The epithet recalls at once
the Virgilian *locus*, where the winds are thus characterised, in particular
in Neptune's speech of rebuke, as we shall see, and the opening scene of
the play, where the Virgilian analogy (immediately after Neptune's
speech) between human and natural orders is invoked only to be
mocked by the Boatswain. Himself arguably mutinous in his derision,
the Boatswain is associated with the 'mutinous' 'roarers' he describes by
the phrase 'noise-maker' (I.i.43–4), used of him by 'noble' passengers to
whom the epithet might equally well be applied within the hierarchy of
authority on board ship. There is indeed here a levelling 'confusion'
which is an effect of the dis-mantling of another received, though not
Virgilian, analogy – between ship and state. Both analogies are dis-
mantled by the foregrounding of the difference within, which produces
a paradoxical 'levelling' effect of 'the same', the sameness in difference
that Prospero will recognise and that will lead to his renunciation of
control.

What is at stake in such levelling confusions is indicated in another
modification to Prospero's 'Ovidian' speech: his description of the
tempest he has raised as 'roaring war' (v.i.44). Virgilian rather than
Ovidian, and so, like 'mutinous', another signal of the Virgilian *locus*
'behind' the opening scene, the figure of tempest as war is used in
Jonson's imitation, as we have seen, to represent the dis-order of nature
produced by the witches, which is qualified as 'unnatural', like the

---

[71] As translated by Golding Medea's speech runs:

> By charmes I make the calme Seas rough, and make the rough seas plain
> And cover all the Skie with Cloudes, and chase them thence again.
> By charmes I rayse and lay the windes ...

(As quoted in Kermode's edition, p. 148)

In Prospero's lines the tense is not, as here, the generalising simple present, but the present
perfect (signifying a particular, if perhaps repeated act), while the raising of the winds is placed
before (rather than after) the production of the tempest in what is therefore a temporal (and
implicitly causal) sequence:

> I have bedimm'd
> The noontide sun, call'd forth the mutinous winds,
> And 'twixt the green sea and the azur'd vault
> Set roaring war ...

(lines 41–4)

witches themselves, and which is contained by the 'proper' and 'natural' order of the main masque as its 'contrary'.[72] Prospero's use of the figure aligns it rather with what is performed by, and in, the play. While the epithet 'roaring' reiterates the play's most insistent onomatopoeia and so links the performed tempest and its effects to the aspiration of the play's language to erase the distinctions of the symbolic order and to (re)produce 'confused noise within', the noun 'war' points to the history – dis-story – that such more and less radical confusions tend to produce. At the most general and radical level, nature, history and the human subject are made 'the same' in (in)difference to symbolic forms (and 'war' the 'natural' condition of (in)different selves, as for Hobbes).[73] At a more specific level, received analogical structures are dis-mantled, producing an effect of sameness in difference, as in the opening scene of the play, when the 'noble' passengers are brought 'down' to the same level as the common man, the Boatswain. For, as the Boatswain's insistence that they 'keep below' (I.i.11) indicates, those who occupy the highest place in the structure of authority in the state belong, as passengers, to the lowest place in the structure of authority on board ship. The traditional analogy between ship and state is thus dis-rupted by the difference within and an effect of levelling 'confusion' is produced, which invalidates the use of the analogy to underwrite a hierarchical socio-political system and an absolute form of government.

Among the many examples of such use both before and after *The Tempest* I should like briefly to consider one in particular here. For, coming after the play, it appears to revisit and revise the opening scene in a way which betrays recognition of what is at stake in its dismantling of analogies even as they are reinstated in order to make the case for absolutism.

This revisionary scene is in John Barclay's *Argenis* (Paris, 1621), a Latin prose romance, which receives scant attention today but which was '(o)ne of the most popular books written and published during the

---

[72] See chapter 4, pp. 136–40. In a note praising the comparison made after Neptune's speech, Douglas adds that Virgil consistently compares 'battell tyll spayt or dyluge of watyr, or than to suddan fyr, and to nocht ellis'. Douglas, *Virgil's 'Aeneid'*, vol. 2, p. 29, note to line 92.

[73] As we shall see, the Restoration version recognises the play's anticipation of the civil war and its implicit levelling democratic ideology, both of which it, rightly, associates with the treatment of the sailors and of nature's roarers. Hobbes's philosophical system – notably its postulate of 'roaring war' as the 'natural' condition of human kind (in contrast to Hooker's postulate of social hierarchy as 'natural') – comes out of even as it reacts to the civil war. The turn we are dealing with – which I have called the Protestant turn – thus entails a re-vision of the 'natural' and of 'nature', which I take to be always ideologically inflected, as the inverted commas are intended to indicate.

seventeenth century',[74] and which was translated into English no less than three times during the decade following its first publication.[75] Set within the same location as *The Tempest* (and *Aeneid* 1) *Argenis* uses the figure of the tempest throughout, both to unify the loose episodic form and to promote its advertised 'purpose': 'to make an institution or ordering both of a King and his Kingdome'.[76] At two moments, in particular, a tempest drives the hero Poliarchus, Aeneas-like, from his intended course on to the shore of North Africa, where he is entertained by Queen Hyanisbe (identified in the key as Elizabeth I). Both tempests (though in particular the second) have Virgilian features,[77] and, more importantly, both are invested by subsequent commentary (in the form of dialogues) with political significance. This serves to reinstate, even as it mobilises, both the Virgilian analogy between natural and political orders, and the traditional analogy between ship and state – both of which are used to argue the case for absolutism.

In the first instance, the king of Sicily, Meleander, is advised '*Aeolus*-like' to 'bridle' the 'ambitious winds' of the noblemen (chiefly Lycogenes) whose aspirations have caused the unrest and disorder which is figured throughout as a tempest.[78] In the second instance, the argument made here through the Virgilian analogy between natural and political orders is reinforced through the analogy between ship and state. The ground for the comparison is prepared in the description of the behaviour of the sailors during the tempest.

The Mariners began to hinder one the other by their sudden haste, and making an outcry among themselves, with the roaring of the Sea, they seemed to second the winds terrour ... And now one began to advise, and every one to

---

[74] Fletcher, *The Intellectual Development of John Milton*, vol. 2, p. 564. References will be to John Barclay, *Argenis* (Leyden, 1627).

[75] The first of these translations, interestingly enough by Jonson, was lost in the fire of 1623 (see 'An Execration upon Vulcan', *The Underwood* 43, lines 95-7 (*H&S*, vol. 8, p. 207)). I shall refer to the second translation, done by Kingsmill Long and published in 1625, specifically the second edition as this includes a translation of the 'key.' Kingsmill Long, *Barclay, his Argenis, or, the Loves of Poliarchus and Argenis* (London, 1636). Though the last years of his life (1616–21) were spent in Rome where he wrote *Argenis*, John Barclay spent the previous years (1606–15) in London seeking favour (unsuccessfully) from James (and *Argenis* may be read at one level as a continuation of this project). He may, therefore, have seen an early performance of *The Tempest*. See David Dalrymple, *Sketch of the Life of John Barclay* (Edinburgh, 1783), pp. 2–5.

[76] 'The Key' in Long, *Barclay, his Argenis*, n. pag.; compare 'Clavis', in Barclay, *Argenis*, pp. 764–5.

[77] See Clayton, '"Tempests, and such like Drolleries"', p. 257, notes 24 and 26.

[78] Long, *Barclay, his Argenis*, p. 285. Long's 'bridle' translates 'utre' (Barclay, *Argenis*, p. 305), which suggests rather a Homeric context (the 'bag' of winds given by Aeolus to Odysseus); 'bridle' suggests rather the Virgilian context (*Aeneid* 1, line 63). Moreover, 'ambitious' is an addition of Long's which evokes the early modern politico-moral mediations of the Virgilian tempest by Landino and Vegio (see above note 32).

command; that the hurly-burly of such as were unskilfull in Sea-busines, was
like to bring no lesse danger than the storms violence.

(Long, *Barclay, his Argenis*, p. 508)

The intertextual relation to the opening scene of *The Tempest* is here
pointed up by Long's translation, notably his use of 'roaring' and his
addition of the phrase 'they seemed to second the winds terrour'.[79]
Crucially, of course, it is not, as in *The Tempest*, noble passengers that get
in the mariners' way – making the noise which seconds that of the winds
– but the mariners who get in each other's way. And the struggle for
authority is a struggle within the structure of authority on board ship
and not between putatively analogous structures.

This suppression of the 'confusion' produced in the opening scene of
the play allows for the analogy between ship and state to be mobilised in
a dialogue which follows the tempest, and which takes place between the
shipwrecked noble Poliarchus (who is, conveniently, not involved in the
'hurly-burly' on board ship) and Hyanisbe. Hyanisbe relates how,
confronted with an unstable political situation – later described as a
storm – provoked by the ambitions of a foreign power (identified in the
key as Philip of Spain), she does not possess sufficient authority to raise
the funds she needs but must go to the people's representatives in
Parliament. Horrified at this limitation of her authority, Poliarchus
argues that to raise funds by imposing taxes is a prerogative of the
sovereign which serves as a valuable reminder to the people 'that they
are borne to subject themselves, and not to rule: who, where those
Tributes are not ordinary, or under the power and authority of their
King ... grow refractory, or foolishly or dangerously insolent' (Long,
Barclay, his Argenis, p. 534). Limitation of the sovereign's authority, he
implies, will tend to provoke insubordination from those 'unskilful in
state business' – a parallel which is made quite explicit by the use of the
same word – 'tumultus' – translated by Long as 'hurly-burly' – to
describe both the political situation in Hyanisbe's kingdom and the
situation on board ship during the tempest.[80] Another 'tumultus', the
tempest serves to figure the disorder that will be provoked where
aspirations 'to advise, and ... to command' in the state as on board ship
are not controlled by an absolute sovereign authority.

---

[79] Compare the Boatswain's 'you do assist the storm' (*The Tempest*, i.i.14) and 'A plague upon this
howling! they are louder than the weather or our office' (lines 35–7).

[80] Barclay, *Argenis*, pp. 545, 586; Long, *Barclay, his Argenis*, pp. 508, 546. Barclay's description of the
political situation in Hyanisbe's kingdom as 'tanto ... motu' (p. 578) is translated by Long 'so gret
a storme' (p. 538). The case for absolutism constitutes at the same time a critique of the regime
under Elizabeth (associated with Dido in her own reign).

Barclay's revision thus reinstates, as a legitimising 'ground' for absolutism, both the traditional analogy between ship and state and the
Virgilian analogy between natural and political realms, which are both
dis-mantled by the opening scene of *The Tempest*, the second through
explicit assertion of the (in)difference of nature to socio-political structures (discussed further below), and the first through the dramatisation
of the difference (and conflict) between those who are skilful in sea
business and those who are skilful in state business – the effect of which is
to 'confuse' them, make them 'the same'.[81]

Authorial recognition that the play undermines such received
legitimising 'grounds' may even be signalled by another detail of Prospero's Ovidian speech. For where Ovid's Medea (as translated by
Golding) claims 'I make the Mountains shake', Prospero declares 'the
strong-bas'd promontory / Have I made shake' (v.i.46–7).[82] The turning
of mountains into a strong-based promontory introduces a contrastive
echo of an image in the other, earlier speech of farewell, which dismisses
the Virgilian 'vision' of nature, set forth in the masque, as 'baseless'. The
verb in turn recalls the earlier, explicitly Virgilian, and more overtly
signed image, used by Ariel to describe the effect of the performed
tempest as shaking Neptune's 'dread trident' (discussed below). These
echoes invest the image with value as an emblem of the play's performed
interrogations of the forms and figures used to ground/base human
structures of authority. Shake-speare's tempest shakes not only the
received authority of the legitimising ground/base of the Virgilian
master *locus*, in particular the Virgilian analogical vision of nature, but,
more generally, the ground of analogy, and, more generally still, the
ground of language. For, as we have seen, the play recognises that
language, like and with analogy, may be 'hollow', without an inherent
relation of likeness to a nature (in)different to human symbolic forms
and to the socio-political structures of authority they are used to ground.

'WHERE'S THE MASTER?' (*THE TEMPEST*, I.i.9)

This (in)difference of nature, in particular to language, and to the
structure of political authority it is used to ground, is, of course, the

---

[81] A conscious will to outdo the Shakespearean play may be signalled in a speech by an
author-figure Nicopompous, who, summarising the narrative of *Argenis* in a projection of the
book he proposes to write, claims 'our Countrie-men ... will love my booke above any
Stage-Play, or Spectacle on [*sic*] the Theater' (Long, *Barclay, his Argenis*, p. 193).

[82] See Kermode's edition, p. 148. There is no equivalent act in the Jonsonian imitation. Note again
the use of the present perfect instead of the present, which turns the act/event into a particular, if
perhaps repeated act/event in a period of time linked to the present.

explicit thrust of the Boatswain's comment, which specifies precisely 'the *name* of King' (1.i.17; my emphasis) as the object of the (in)difference of nature's 'roarers'.[83] As I pointed out earlier, in relation to the play's aspiration throughout to (re)produce the confused noise within nature, these very words might in any particular performance become mere 'noise', because of the 'confusion' produced by the supplementary modes of representation used to make the '*tempestuous noise*' which the stage directions call for, and which the Boatswain's words describe. Ironically too, the noise-maker's words include 'roarers' – the first instance of the onomatopoeia that will recur in various forms through-out the play epitomising as well as exemplifying both its aspiration to reproduce the confused within nature, and the hollow, self-echoing character of language.

As we have seen, 'roar' and 'roaring' are used by Miranda and Prospero respectively in their retrospective descriptions of the per-formed tempest. More importantly still, 'roaring' is used in Ariel's retrospective description, in what I have suggested is the first, and more prominent, of the play's signed figures. For here the 'roaring' (1.ii.204) of the '(p)erform'd . . . tempest' (1.ii.194) is overtly linked to the contestatory difference of Shake-speare's performed tempest from the Virgilian mas-ter *locus*.

> the fire and cracks
> Of sulphurous roaring the most mighty Neptune
> Seem to besiege, and make his bold waves tremble,
> Yea, his dread trident shake.
>
> (lines 203–6)[84]

Though the semantic value of '(y)ea' here cannot be determined (so much depends on voice and gesture), it may have served to advertise, and inflect ironically, the quotation marks around the phrase 'dread trident'. For the Latinate, even Virgilian intonations of the phrase must have been prominent to contemporaries, at least to those who had a minimum of grammar school education, as they are not to modern spectators and scholars. For it translates more exactly than any of the extant translations, which were all published before the first recorded

83 For the Jonsonian intonations to 'name' see chapter 4, pp. 142–3. While Jonson asserts the power of the poet to bestow 'names', especially in his masques, Shakespeare's play exposes at the same time its ends – in the sense of limits as well as of purposes.

84 Shakespeare is written 'SHAKE-SPEARE' in, for example, the list of actors to *Sejanus* (*H&S*, vol. 4, p. 471), and was regularly juggled with, notoriously by Robert Greene, but also, visually, on the Shakespearean coat of arms, and by Thomas Fuller ('*Hasti-vibrans*, or *Shake-speare*'). See E. K. Chambers, *William Shakespeare: A Study of Facts and Problems*, 2 vols. (Oxford: Clarendon Press, 1930), vol. 2, pp. 18–22, 182, 245. I discuss Jonson's punning allusion to the name below.

use of the noun 'trident' (1599), 'saevem tridentem' (*Aeneid* 1, line 138), a phrase from the speech in and by means of which Neptune asserts authority over the winds and so calms the tempest (*Aeneid* 1, lines 132–41).[85] Specifically, the 'dread trident' is claimed as an ensign of his sovereignty over the sea – 'imperium pelagi' (line 138) – a territorial sovereignty that, in their mutinous raising of 'confusion' (Fairclough's translation of 'tantas ... moles' (line 134)), the winds have attempted to usurp.

The political analogue, implicit in the whole speech, is subsequently elaborated in the first extended simile of the epic, which Douglas particularly recommends to the reader's attention, as, no doubt, did countless grammar school teachers ('yea').[86] Neptune is likened to 'sum man of gret autorite' (Douglas's translation of 'gravem ... virum quem' (line 151)), who brings a popular uprising under control, initially through the authority of his presence and then through the authority of his discourse – 'ille regit dictis animos' (line 153): 'he with speche their wood (i.e. insensed) myndes doth aswage' (Phaer, *The Nyne Fyrst Bookes*, fo. Aii^v). This makes explicit what the effect of the speech implies, that the power Neptune's dread trident stands for is effectually immanent in the discourse claiming it, a master(ing) discourse as well as a discourse of the master, a point economically signalled by the use of 'regit' – the verb denoting regal power – to describe the effect of his words. The power Neptune's dread trident stands for thus mirrors the ideological and cultural value of the figure of Virgil for the early modern English schoolboy faced with, and obliged to take in, the paradigmatic example of extended analogy, synecdoche of the normative master Language, and Language of the masters, that Virgil represents – a Language no doubt shot through with 'dread', given the punitive pedagogical practi-

---

[85] While Douglas gives 'thre granyt ceptour wand', and Phaer 'mace threforked large', Stanyhurst omits the phrase altogether. Douglas's difficulty with 'tridens' is pointed out by Bawcutt, who suggests it is a general difficulty until the end of the sixteenth century (Bawcutt, *Gavin Douglas*, pp. 131-2). Still more precisely significant are the entries under 'tridente' in the 1598 and 1611 editions of Florio's Italian–English dictionary: the 1598 definition 'a threforked mace,' becomes in 1611, 'a trident, or threforked mace'. John Florio, *A Worlde of Wordes, Or Most Copious, and exact Dictionarie in Italian and English* (London, 1598); John Florio, *Queen Anna's New World of Words, or Dictionarie of the Italian and English tongues* (London, 1611). In the following year (1612), Thomas Dekker, with his eye as always on a relatively heterogeneous audience, still feels obliged to gloss his description of Neptune carrying 'a Silver Trident, *or Three-forked Mace*' (Dekker, *The Dramatic Works*, vol. 3, p. 232; my emphasis). This signals the bookish and specifically Latinate register of the word at the moment of the first productions of *The Tempest*. The foreign character of the word in the first decade of the seventeenth century and its entry into the English lexicon are signalled too by the use of special typeface in the published versions of Jonson's texts, including *Poetaster*. See chapter 5, note 30.   [86] Douglas, *Virgil's 'Aeneid'*, vol. 2, p. 29, note to line 92.

ces which, as Ong has shown, accompanied the acquisition of, and in-formation by, this master discourse.[87]

Indeed, 'dread' is already associated with Virgilian images of paternal and regal authority in the immediately preceding lines.

> Jove's lightnings, the precursors
> O'th'*dreadful* thunder-claps, more momentary
> And sight-outrunning were not:
>
> (lines 201–3; my emphasis)

These lines recall the admonitory tale, told by the Sibyl to Aeneas, of Salmoneus, who suffers eternal torment in Hades precisely for having dared to imitate Jove's lightning and the thunder of Olympus: 'flammas Jovis et sonitus imitatur Olympi' (he mimicked the thunder and lightning of Jove almighty (Day Lewis); *Aeneid* 6, line 585), which is, the Sibyl declares, to imitate that which cannot be imitated: 'non imitabile fulmen' (line 590). Ariel's words deny the Sibyl's and align the performed tempest with the challenge of Salmoneus to Jove, which, like the challenge to Neptune in the next lines, is at the same time a challenge to the 'dreadful'/'dread' figure of paternal and cultural authority, Virgil.

The same twofold challenge – to Jove/Virgil – is made in a passage in *The Advancement of Learning*, in which, asserting the 'precedence' of 'these times' in their 'virtuous emulation with antiquity', specifically in the field of '*cosmography*', Bacon quotes Virgil's description of the universe in *Georgics* 1 – the canonical mediation of which as knowledge of nature we looked at in chapter 3 – only to claim that 'these times' would be justified in asserting not only '*imitabile fulmen*, in precedence of the ancient *non imitabile fulmen*' 'but likewise *imitabile coelum*' (Bacon, *The Advancement of Learning*, p. 79). Here the Sibyl's (and Virgil's) words are directly negated, as they are, if less directly, by Ariel's description. What is more this negation is likewise associated with the overturning of the forms of knowledge received from the ancients, and, in particular, with the rewriting of the order of the universe received from Virgil. In both texts too the assertion of the 'precedence of these times' dis-places the ancients, and specifically Virgil, in the past, and replaces a degenerative, closed model of knowledge of nature with an open, progressive model. In Ariel's description, this dis-placement is done not only by the direct challenge to the Sibyl's words, but also, less directly, by the ironic inflections of 'yea', which in addition point up the bookish learned

---

[87] Ong, 'Latin Language Study as a Renaissance Puberty Rite', *passim*. See above, chapter 2, pp. 47–8.

character of the 'dread-ful' Virgilian model, rather as, we saw earlier, the ironic commentary of Antonio and Sebastian points up the bookish learned character of Gonzalo's Virgilian eloquence.

The repeated question 'Where's the master?' (I.i.10 and 12), and the master's disappearance after line 4 in scene one, thus acquire a signifi- cance beyond the anticipation of Prospero's story, which is what critics have usually suggested.[88] The question is, moreover, addressed to the Boatswain, a character whose discourse, in this scene at least, interro- gates forms and figures of (the) master(y), both at more general and more specific levels, and so tends to provoke the question. Expanding on his previous terse assertion of the (in)difference of nature's roarers to the symbolic order and to the structure of political authority grounded on it, the Boatswain evokes, only to mock ('yea'), the first extended simile of the Virgilian epic, in a speech which is addressed to Gonzalo, a charac- ter who fits Virgil's description of the man of authority.[89]

> You are a counsellor; if you can command these elements to silence, and work the peace of the present, we will not hand a rope more; use your authority: if you cannot, give thanks you have lived so long, and make yourself ready in your cabin for the mischance of the hour, if it so hap. (I.i.20–6)[90]

The stakes of this challenge are not merely, as Orgel suggests, the 'sympathies' of an audience[91] but the effect of (alternative) authority it tends to provoke. Using the imperative form which he invites Gonzalo to use in order, like Virgil's Neptune/man of authority, to bring the 'roarers' under control, the Boatswain mockingly promises that, if

[88] There are telling modifications in the Restoration version here: the 'master', doubled as Stephano, reappears (I.i.47) after leaving the stage temporarily (line 11). The spectacle of a master who disappears for good must have been particularly disturbing at this post-revolutionary (and post-1649) moment of reaction. In another, more recent attempt to revise the scene, Falconer asserts that the master's presence is signalled by the sound of his whistle which 'indicates that all is under control' (Falconer, *Shakespeare and the Sea*, pp. 13 and 58). But there is no further indication of the master's presence in the scene. Altogether Falconer works very hard to turn the scene into an image of order: the Boatswain, specifically, is firmly declared to be 'doing no more than his duty' in his treatment of the court party and he is 'neither a revolutionary nor one who prides himself on taking liberties' (p. 59). This interpretation is determined by the ideological project of the whole book (see note 93).

[89] Compare Virgil's 'pietate gravem ac meritis' (line 151), 'a man honoured for noble character and service' (Fairclough), with the description of Gonzalo in the 'Names of the Actors' as 'an honest old Councellor' (*The Tempest*, p. 2). This description approaches the classic, humanist definition of a good orator 'Vir bonus, dicendi peritus', which Servius adds in his gloss to Virgil's description. Virgil, *Opera*, vol. 1, fo. 163r.

[90] I here agree with Orgel that Kermode's emendation of 'present' to 'presence' is unnecessary, although it would underscore the political dimension.

[91] 'Even a Sunday sailor will feel the justice of the Mariners' [*sic*] expostulations'. Shakespeare, *The Tempest*, edited by Orgel, p. 14.

Gonzalo succeeds, the 'hands' he represents – a representative function indicated in the absence of a proper name as well as in the use of 'we' – will stop work in collective recognition of, and deferral to the authority of Gonzalo, which is also the authority of the Virgilian grammar of nature inflected in relations of likeness to structures of political authority. His irony, of course, tends to produce the opposite effect, undermining the authority of both Gonzalo and Virgil by pointing up that their language does not 'work' (in both senses of the verb), and is therefore 'use'-less to the work of the 'hands' he represents ('we will not hand a rope more'), whose (alternative) authority is thus asserted.

This is to subvert not only the authority of Virgil as 'best master' (Jonson), but the hierarchy of forms of discourse as discourses of knowledge. It overturns, that is, the 'precedence' (to use Bacon's apposite word) of the discourses of the ancients over the emergent, technical and specialised discourses of non-privileged artisans, especially the discourse of seamen (to whom, as we saw in chapter 3, Virgil's *Georgics* were particularly recommended as a source of knowledge). Indeed, the Boatswain's words anticipate, even as they *work* to produce the conditions for 'preferring', as the discourse of knowledge, 'the language of Artizans, Countrymen and Merchants, before that of Wits and Scholars' – a preference, or privileging, expressed by Thomas Sprat in 1667 which, as Stone points out, entailed profound socio-political changes.[92] Specifically, here, we might contrast the expressed intention of Augustus in *Poetaster* to 'prefer' for knowledge men such as Virgil – figure of a normative Language used by a socio-political, as well as intellectual and moral elite of 'learned heads' at the centre of power, the court.

The preferring, or privileging of the seaman's discourse as a discourse of knowledge, and the socio-political changes it calls for, are dramatically signalled by the Boatswain's insistence that his noble passengers 'keep below' (line 11). His orders meet with some resistance, in particular from Sebastian and Antonio, whose insults – 'dog' (line 41) 'cur' (line 42) as well as 'noise-maker' (lines 42–3) – seek to humiliate the Boatswain, 'put him down', by classifying him as belonging to the realm 'below' the human and his language as belonging to the realm 'below' language. Their use of hierarchically organised categories to underwrite the social order is of course a recurring ideological strategy of the dominant class, which we have seen exemplified in previous chapters, notably in the

---

[92] Stone, 'The Educational Revolution', p. 80 (including the quotation from Thomas Sprat).

Jonsonian corpus, where, specifically, we have seen how the universe of 'common men' is represented as an 'underworld' of confused noise. *The Tempest*, though in particular this scene, dis-mantles such hierarchies. For it is undoubtedly the Boatswain, and the seaman's discourse, that prevail in the struggle for the place – 'above' – of authority (the 'upper hand'): his retort to the insults, '(w)ork you then' (line 42), neatly puts the insulters down by pointing out the redundancy of their discourse, as he has pointed out the redundancy of Gonzalo's and Virgil's discourse, to those that 'work'. He thus places them where they belong physically as passengers – 'below'.[93]

At the same time, the description of the Boatswain as a noise-maker associates this representative of the 'lower orders' with the more radical contestation/resistance of an indeterminate 'confused noise within' which will shortly dis-rupt the production of the symbolic order in this scene as it will later dis-rupt the masque.[94] Indeed, we have seen how the play aspires throughout to produce 'confused noise' and so to dis-rupt from within the condition of the symbolic order, which is not-noise. It is at this level that we find traces of the resistance of the Boatswain at his return in the fifth act, when he appears to have a different relation to

---

[93] With typical, if typically limited, insight, Johnson glossed the Boatswain's discourse as 'perhaps the first example of sailor's language exhibited on the stage' (as quoted in W. Shakespeare, *The Tempest*, edited by H. H. Furness (New York: Dover Publications Inc., 1964), p. 11). His doubts about the accuracy of this language were subsequently refuted by Malone whose expressed admiration for Shakespeare's nautical competence has been echoed by later critics. Typically, this admiration is directed not towards the sailors in the play (and the social group they represent), but towards 'Shakespeare' whose agreed authority on sea-business is now the subject of an entire book, which concludes with the hypothesis that Shakespeare must have spent time at sea (as a Lieutenant no less!). Falconer, *Shakespeare and the Sea*. The ideological 'point' of this project(ion) as of the whole book (which determines its interpretation of the Boatswain mentioned in note 88) is disclosed in the opening – the 'greatest of dramatists remained profoundly impressed ... by the greatest naval tradition the world has seen' (p. xii) – and the concluding raptures on the 'sea tradition that has ... enriched much that is greatest in English life. Shakespeare knew and felt its power and has paid his tribute.' (p. 150) I cite this not for its insight into the play but as an example of the way Shakespeare was still used in 1964, and no doubt, in certain institutions, today, to serve jingoistic ends.

[94] Golding uses 'confused was the noyse' in his translation of the Ovidian tempest in *Metamorphoses* 11, which Erasmus recommends with the Virgilian tempest in *Aeneid* 1 as parallel *loci* for imitation, in *De copia* (see chapter 2, p. 74). Arthur Golding, *Ovid's Metamorphoses: The Arthur Golding Translation* (1567), edited by J. F. Nims (New York: MacMillan, 1965), book 11, line 572. This is especially interesting because the cries given adjacent to the stage directions, 'A *confused noise within*' appear to be taken from Golding's translation of cries described in the Ovidian *locus* (see Clayton, '"Tempests, and such like Drolleries"', p. 227). Ironically, the relation of the stage directions to the cries has been perceived as confused and confusing by editors and commentators, who have usually (and sometimes, like Barton and Orgel, silently) followed Cappell's emendations to the first folio, which identify the cries *as* the confused noise, that is, 'confused' with it, rather than as audible, separate and distinct, verbal utterances. It is impossible to decide between the two interpretations from the folio.

figures of authority.[95] For his discourse is marked here by a deference for the king ('sir' (v.i.229)), which contrasts with his earlier subversive indifference. Yet the contrast at the same time serves to underscore the *difference* between structures of authority on land and at sea, which the opening scene foregrounds through the Boatswain, who, on land, acknowledges his place 'below', as, on ship, he asserts the place 'below' of the noble and royal passengers. More interestingly perhaps, his discourse here is marked not only by deference but by traces of the noise-making of the opening scene (and of the play). For his description of the 'strange and several noises' (line 232) heard by the ship's crew – 'Of roaring, shrieking, howling, jingling chains' (line 233) – is one of the most sustained examples of the aspiration of the play's language to (re)produce 'noise'. Like Caliban, indeed like Miranda, the Boatswain subjects his 'self' to forms and figures of authority, suppressing overt resistance, which nevertheless remains as a trace in the aspiration of his language to 'roar'.

It is, moreover, to the model of knowledge implied in the Boatswain's discourse in the opening scene that the play will turn. With a technically precise, specialised vocabulary, which registers the splitting of knowledge into increasingly particularised 'fields' and 'languages', his discourse is at the same time marked by what we might describe as a spontaneous informality as well as by a sense of present and particular contingency – 'the mischance of the hour, if it so hap' (i.i.25–6). The implied model of knowledge is a relative, open, provisional, particular (this/'dis'), use-orientated model, which recognises its own ends (in the sense of limits as well as purposes). The Boatswain's knowledge and control are confined to his ship; he cannot control the elements of nature and knows he cannot. He knows, that is, the irreducible otherness of nature, which Prospero will discover in and for him-'self' and which will lead to his renunciation of mastery. In the turn from mastery the play will also, more specifically, turn from the 'best master' Virgil whose 'vision' of nature will be dis-located as 'baseless' art/not-knowledge, and as the past. In the Boatswain's speech, as in Ariel's, such dis-location is achieved through irony, specifically the ironic evocation of the scene of Neptune's 'dread trident' speech to the winds and the extended analogy which follows it.

It is not, however, only the authority of the Virgilian model that is critically glanced at by the Boatswain, but the uses to which it is put. In

---

[95] I am grateful to Ian Donaldson for drawing my attention to this point.

Figure 5   *Neptune calming the Tempest*, oil sketch on wood panel by P. P. Rubens, 1635

particular, early modern European artists regularly used – *drew on* – the scene of Neptune's speech in ways which served to 'link Neptune with the contemporary ruler',[96] suggesting a legitimising affinity between control of the natural world and political power. This is done not only in representations of Neptune (Freedman's focus), but also in occasional paintings of the Virgilian scene done for men of power, like that done by Rubens for the voyage, in 1633, of the cardinal infante Ferdinand, brother of Philip IV of Spain, from Barcelona to Genoa, on his way to assume the governorship of the Spanish Netherlands (figure 5).[97] It is the affinity implied in such representations that the Boatswain's speech derides, dis-figuring at once Virgil and nature, and dis-allowing the uses made of both to legitimate absolute political power and (as in the Ruben's sketch) a politics of suppression.

Still more specifically, though not unconnected to such visual representations, the Boatswain's mocking imperative 'use your authority' recalls the phrase with which Augustus invests Virgil with authority as judge in *Poetaster* – an investment which is anticipated and justified by a portrait of Virgil in terms of this scene of Neptune's 'dread trident' speech. The portrait makes Virgil a 'man of gret autorite', like Neptune, authorised to judge 'common men', who are placed 'below' and associated with the (sea-like) instability and 'confused noise' of the humours, which Virgil has mastered with the 'marble *trident*' of his spirit. This authority is then confirmed in the scene of his judgement in Act V when he delivers two monologic speeches, which, like Neptune's speech to the winds, and 'Reason''s to the 'untemper'd' 'humours' and 'affections' in *Hymenaei*, are absolute in their achievement of mastery, an achievement which bears witness to the authority of the discourse, as does the closure which follows.

As a final illustration of *The Tempest*'s critical engagement with such

---

[96] Luba Freedman, 'Neptune in Classical and Renaissance Visual Art', *International Journal of the Classical Tradition* 2:2 (1995), p. 231. Ascensius uses the vocabulary of visual representation when he comments that in the figure of Neptune Virgil exactly ('ad unguem') 'paints' ('depingit') the role of a prudent prince. Virgil, *Opera*, vol. 1, fo. 162v. As Hardie points out, Augustus had been portrayed 'in the role of Neptune driving his chariot over the waves' (Hardie, *Virgil's 'Aeneid'*, p. 204).

[97] See *Neptune Calming the Tempest* in James Cuno, Marjorie B. Cohn et al., *Harvard's Art Museums. 100 Years of Collecting* (New York: Harry N. Abrams, 1996), pp. 170–1. The painting conveys not only nature's endorsement of Ferdinand's power but an appeal for him to exercise his power in putting down the 'rebellious northern Dutch provinces' (ibid., p. 170). Such applications of the Virgilian scene to contemporary politics are not uncommon, and can be traced back until the fourteenth century at least, when an English commentator links it to the Peasants' revolt of 1381 (Baswell, *Virgil in Medieval England*, pp. 144–6).

uses of Virgil we may take the exchange which immediately follows Ariel's mocking allusion to Neptune's/Virgil's 'dread trident', and which invokes early modern mediations of Neptune as Reason.

> *Pros.* Who was so firm, so constant, that this coil
> Would not infect his reason?
> *Ari.*   Not a soul
> But felt a fever of the mad,
>
>   (I.ii.207–9)[98]

Prospero's two lines articulate a dis-turbance of one universe – the fixed ('firm' and 'constant') universe of 'reason' (Neptune's 'dread'/Virgil's 'marble', 'trident') – by another universe – of confused noise, 'this coil'.[99] The performed tempest is thus turned in terms of a masque-like binary structure, specifically anticipating the later moment when Prospero himself fails to be 'firm', falling into 'infirmity' ('Be not disturbed with my infirmity' (IV.i.160)) and distemper. Marking the failure of the binary structures of symbolic forms to contain negativity as negation, the return of Dis in this distemper and in the disproportioned figure of Caliban, together with the noise with which the play is full, specifically dis-allow Virgil/Neptune/Reason immunity to such negativity, and their 'Language' the privileged position or place 'above' as an absolute, transcendent master(ing) discourse overseeing and silencing the voices of common men 'below'.

RESTORATIONS OF THE MASTER

Particularly telling traces of the subversive effects of the 'perform'd tempest' are furnished by corrective moves made in texts which follow in its wake, and which betray recognition of these effects even as they seek to 'correct' them. I have already looked at one example – John Barclay's *Argenis* – and the way it restores analogical structures dis-mantled by the play, in order to promote the case for absolutism. To close I want to consider briefly perhaps the most telling case of all – the Restoration version of the play, especially its more popular operatic

---

[98] For the mediation of Neptune as reason see, for example, the summary of Landino's commentary above, note 32.

[99] Also 'Dis' coil according to Ferdinand (as quoted by Ariel): 'Hell is empty / And all the devils are here' (lines 213-14).

form by Thomas Shadwell (1674).[100] For this revises, specifically, both the treatment of the sailors, and the intertextual relation with the Virgilian master *locus*. This relation is 'restored' as a relation of likeness, and used to underwrite a 'restored' structure of political authority, and an authoritarian politics of suppression.

If we take, first, the treatment of the sailors, and in particular the Boatswain's discourse in the opening scene, there are changes which betray recognition of disturbing elements even as these are neutralised. The 'name of king', for instance, has been replaced by the 'name of duke' (I.i.22), 'command' (in the next speech) by 'advise (I.i.25) and (perhaps most significantly) 'authority' by 'wisdom' (I.i.26). Further, this version drops entirely the crucial juxtaposition – 'work the peace of the present, we will not hand a rope more' (*The Tempest*, I.i.22–3) – which points up the opposition and struggle between (the discourse of) those who 'work' with words and (the discourse of) those who work with hands. At the same time these changes effectively erase the Virgilian intertext and the challenge to it. More importantly still, the effect of alternative authority to the Virgilian model provoked by the Boatswain's speech and by the competence of the sailors is erased by the transformation of their specialised, technically precise – use-full – discourse into patently use-less, nonsensical *jargon*.[101] This strategy of invalidation through satiric deformation puts the sailors' discourse, and the sailors, 'down', restores, that is, the hierarchy subverted by the treatment of the sailors' discourse, and the sailors, in the Shakespearean play. This effect is reinforced by the identification of the sailors with the earlier play's 'low' comic figures, the master being doubled as Stephano, the Boatswain as Trinculo.

[100] For the popularity of this version of the play at the time of its production and through the eighteenth century, see Maus, 'Arcadia Lost', pp. 189–90; Shakespeare, *The Tempest*, edited by Orgel, pp. 64–9. Maus attributes this popularity to the politics of the play, which, she argues, 'redefines the limits and uses of sovereignty' (p. 190). Her argument is chiefly made through analysis of the figure of Prospero. She does not consider the politics either of the treatment of the sailors or of the intertextual relation to Virgil, which indeed she does not mention. In my discussion of the play I shall refer to Dryden, *The Works*, vol. 10, pp. 1–103, while, in my discussion of the masque added by Shadwell, I shall use Thomas Shadwell, *The Complete Works*, edited by Montague Summers, 3 vols. (London: The Fortune Press, 1927), vol. 2, pp. 265–7.

[101] An authority on nautical matters comments: 'The Scud never goes against the wind'; 'A perfectly absurd order. There is no such thing as a "Seere-Capstorm", and there never has been such a thing'; 'In fact it may be generally remarked of this whole Scene, that the words and phrases put into the mouth of the Boatswain are manifestly used by a person who did not understand them.' Shakespeare, *The Tempest*, edited by Furness, pp. 393–4. Similar strategies are, of course, used by Jonson in his satirical comedies and later anti-masques. For the language and competence of Shakespeare's sailors see above, pp. 233–5 and note 93.

This strategy of invalidation continues to be deployed in the scenes on land, where its more specific object is Puritan, egalitarian ideology and attempts in the New World to construct forms of government on this ideological ground. For the sailors' talk on shore is almost at once of government. '(L)et us have a Government' (ii.iii.51) declares Ventoso (an additional, significantly named, sailor) to which Stephano responds: 'I was Master at Sea, and will be Duke on Land' (lines 56–7) – a response which acknowledges the political significance of the figure of the master in the opening scene of the earlier play. Stephano's claim to the place of the master meets with opposition from Ventoso, or, rather, from the ideology for which he is evidently a parodic mouthpiece: 'I am a free Subject in a new Plantation, and will have no Duke without my voice' (lines 60–1). To Stephano's whispered offer of advancement in exchange for his 'voice' Ventoso publicly denounces such corruption: 'I'le have no whisperings to corrupt the Election; and to show that I have no private ends, I declare aloud that I will be Vice-Roy, or I'le keep my voice for my self' (lines 64–6).[102] The patent absurdity of his self-contradiction confirms the judgement carried in his name – that the 'new world' discourse and ideology are so much 'wind' or cant (like the sailors' discourse in the opening scene) – use-less, because unworkable, unworkable because inherently contradictory, 'private ends' necessarily working against each other and so against collective ends, the particular will to dominance – 'Each wou'd to rule alone the rest devour' (iv.iii.269), as Ariel puts it – tending necessarily to 'Civil War' (ii.iii. 79 and 141) – an issue to the 'Protestant turn' which the earlier play points to without, however, calling for the reaction which the later play calls for. Like the Hobbesian universe it implies, in which the 'natural' condition of man is 'roaring war', this calls for an absolute form of government to which individual wills are entirely subject, and which will 'put down' voices of difference/dissent.

Achieved as an effect through the strategy of invalidation by derision, such 'putting down' is more directly re-presented in the masque written by Thomas Shadwell to close the operatic version of the play. Its staged scene of suppression recapitulates, in the mode of the masque, the treatment of the sailors within the play, which it endorses. More importantly, the treatment of the sailors is linked to the intertextual relation to

---

[102] Ventoso's discourse is a parody of discourses in circulation in England during the Civil War and Interregnum period as well as in the contemporary 'new plantations' where attempts at more democratic systems of government were being made, notably in Massachusetts, a colony of 20,000 inhabitants virtually independent from the British Crown.

the Virgilian master *locus* in *Aeneid* 1, which is overtly revised in a way which betrays recognition of, even as it suppresses, the contestatory character of this relation and the implied authorial alignment with dissenting voices 'from below'.

Within the 'play proper' (i.e. what precedes the masque), this contestatory intertextual relation is dealt with rather by the elimination of all traces of it. In addition to the changes to the Boatswain's discourse mentioned above, there are no allusions to 'widow Dido' and 'widower Aeneas' (*The Tempest*, II.i.75 and 76), no ironic comments from Sebastian and Antonio (repentant rather than ironic), no spectacle of the harpy, and no (dis-rupted) Virgilian betrothal masque of Ceres and Juno. Still more significant than these erasures is the truncated version of Ariel's retrospective description of the performed tempest: otherwise virtually reproducing the speech in the earlier play, this stops short at 'I did flame distinctly' (I.ii.118), stops short, that is, of the images of opposition to Virgilian figures of paternal and regal authority (discussed above, pp. 229–31). That this excision betrays recognition, at some level, of the subversive thrust of these images, especially the second, is borne out by the masque, which draws precisely on the textual ground of the scene of Neptune's 'dread trident' speech to which Ariel's second, and signed image alludes. What is more this image, cut from the play proper, is re-introduced in the masque, grafted on to the master *locus* by an act of textual coercion that mirrors the advertised end of the masque: 'to teach' the 'sawcy Element to obey'.[103]

The epithet 'sawcy' recalls the sailors as they are treated within the play.[104] Judged (with their discourse) as windy – Ventoso – the sailors do indeed return in the masque as the '*roaring Winds*' (p. 266) of Aeolus, whose threat to '*disturb*' (p. 265) is the threat represented by the Jonsonian anti-masque. A measure perhaps of post Civil War fears, this anti-masque of 'winds' is not even performed on stage but merely evoked verbally as the threat that is to be (and so in effect is already) contained. First, Amphitrite requests her spouse Neptune to order Aeolus to '*keep*' '*his boystrous Prisoners*' '*(i)n their dark Caverns*' (ibid.). This is followed by a similar request from Oceanus, who asks Neptune to '*(c)onfine the roaring winds*' (p. 266). In response to these requests, Neptune summons Aeolus and bids him '*make no noise / Muzzle your roaring boys*', to

---

[103] Shadwell, *The Complete Works*, vol. 2, p. 265 (without line references).

[104] Associated specifically with ships and, by metonymy, with sailors from the end of the sixteenth century, the epithet suggests (often verbally expressed) insubordination from those placed 'below' in institutional structures of authority.

which Amphitrite adds, '*Let 'em not bluster to disturb our ears*,' describing the effect of such 'blustering' as war. These '*(b)lusterers*' (as Aeolus will address them), 'boys*terous*' '*roaring* boys' (ibid.; my emphasis) recall not only the 'boys' within the play[105] and their 'windy' ('blustering') discourse (Ventoso), but both the Virgilian and Shakespearean textual *loci*, which are blended together as one.[106] More precisely, the Shakespearean *locus* is contained within the Virgilian, both at the formal level (it is the Virgilian *locus* that provides the ground of the masque) and at the level of its treatment of figures and forms of authority. The contestatory difference – 'noise' – staged by Shakespeare's performed tempest is, in short, censored – 'muzzled' – exactly as the roaring boys/winds are muzzled.[107] This is done most overtly in the lines at the thematic and formal centre of the masque when Aeolus submits to Neptune's authority.

> *You I'll obey, who, at one stroke can make,*
> *With your dread Trident, the whole Earth to quake.*

(ibid.)

'At one stroke' of the revisionary pen the signed figure of the roaring of the performed tempest which seemed to 'shake' Neptune's 'dread trident' is turned into an affirmation of the absolute power to suppress such roaring – and to instil 'dread' – that Neptune's 'dread trident' stands for. Shake-speare's performed tempest does not shake but joins with, or is subsumed under the authority of Virgil's/Neptune's dread trident to make quake/shake.[108] This specific textual coercion epitomises the way the earlier play is turned so as to suppress its contestation of figures and forms of authority. Especially, as we have seen, the Shakespearean treatment of the sailors, which validates their discourse (their 'voice'), is turned so as to invalidate them, and the democratic ideology implied in their validation. The play is thus made to 'call for' the

---

[105] The sailors use 'boy' or 'boys' to address each other in Act II scene iii (lines 101, 103, 104, etc.).

[106] While the characters of the masque and the language of Amphitrite's speech – which represents the winds as '*prisoners*' in their '*dark Caverns*' – evoke primarily the Virgilian *locus* – the language used by Oceanus and Neptune – '*noise*', '*roaring Winds*'/'*roaring Boys*' – evokes the Shakespearean. The repetition of 'roaring' suggests Shadwell has picked up the earlier play's key, recurring onomatopoeia. It goes without saying perhaps that the earlier play's insistence on language as (imitative) sound – its aspiration to 'roar' – exemplified by the use of this word – is otherwise not to be found either in the masque or in the play which precedes it. This is another level at which the play's 'noise-making' may be said to be suppressed by the later version.

[107] 'Muzzle' has the specific sense of 'censor' from the end of the sixteenth century according to the *OED*. Compare the staged 'gagging' of Lupus in *Poetaster*, discussed above, chapter 5, pp. 153–4.

[108] Maus actually gives 'shake' for 'quake' in her quotation of these lines, which suggests she has registered, if subconsciously, the revisionary move. Maus, 'Arcadia Lost', p. 200.

suppression – muzzling – of the contestation that Shake-speare's performed tempest stages, and for the restoration of the figures and forms of
authority it interrogates ('shakes'). Such restoration is promoted both by
the masque and the play which precedes it, as the necessary condition
for the prevention of civil war and the preservation of the country's
restored '*soft peace*' (p. 267).[109]

It is not, however, just the play that is thus coerced to underwrite the
restoration of the master, but the author Shakespeare, 'the ultimate
patriarchalist authority figure' (Maus, 'Arcadia Lost', p. 205). Placed at
the centre and apex of a structure of English authors, 'Shakespeare' is
twice explicitly compared to a monarch whose authority (in the second
instance) is declared inviolable: 'Shakespear's pow'r is sacred as a
King's'.[110] This construction of Shakespeare as sovereign author works
to the same ideological end as the textual coercions and censorings
which follow – the endorsement of the (restored) structure of political
authority in place.

As I indicated in my introduction, this construction and use of
Shakespeare may be compared to the construction and use of Virgil in
early modern English culture, especially by Jonson in *Poetaster*, where the
sacred authority of Virgil is similarly likened to, even as it is aligned with
the equally sacred authority of an absolute monarch. Between this figure
of Virgil and the Restoration figure of Shakespeare is the Shakespeare
that Jonson constructed for his prefatory poem to the first folio (*H&S*,
vol. 8, pp. 390–2). Not only does this poem revise other Jonsonian
figures of Shakespeare, but it also constructs Shakespeare as equivalent
to the ancients, and so universal, and as the unifying centre of 'Great
Britain', authorising British nationalism and British imperialism, as I
pointed out. By way of conclusion, I would like to draw attention to the

---

[109] The same phrase is used by Jonson, in *The Masque of Queens*, of the recently established order
under James I, which the witches seek to disturb, like the winds of Aeolus (see chapter 4, p. 138).
Whether conscious or not, the echo underscores how this masque is doing much the same
ideological work as Jonson's – underwriting the structure of political authority in place and
advocating authoritarian repression of dissent. That there are nevertheless differences is
signalled by modifications to the Virgilian scene of Neptune's speech. For Neptune's authority
is asserted at the request of Amphitrite and it is expressly *her* '*will*' that Neptune orders Aeolus
and his winds to obey. This suggests Neptune's absolute authority is the expression of the 'will'
of his 'people' (Amphitrite), who collectively submit to this representative of their common will.
Further, Neptune does not directly address the winds (as in the Virgilian scene) but issues his
orders to Aeolus, who in turn addresses his 'boys'. This suggests an articulation of the
sovereign's authority through intermediary institutions. At any rate these differences do tend to
endorse Maus's argument that the play redefines forms of sovereignty (see above, note 100).

[110] Dryden, *The Works*, vol. 10, p. 6, line 24. In relation to other English authors Shakespeare is
described as 'Monarch-like' (line 7).

way that this fashioning of Shakespeare as 'The AUTHOR' (title) punningly alludes to his name. First, when the equivalent authority of 'Shakespeare' to the ancients is claimed, particular authors are named and 'called upon' to hear the British author 'shake a Stage' (line 37), that is, to acknowledge his power/authority. Then, as the poem reaches its climax, the paternal analogy is mobilised – 'Looke how the fathers face / Lives in his issue' (lines 65–6) – in order to assert the immanence of '*Shakespeare's* minde, and manners' (line 67) in his 'lines' (line 68), an assertion which seals 'Shakespeare' as 'The AUTHOR' (or, we might say, in the 'author function'). This immanence is then inscribed by a literal writing of the author's name in his 'lines', 'In each of which, he seemes to shake a Lance, / As brandish't at the eyes of Ignorance' (lines 69–70). Whether or not a conscious revision of Ariel's signed image (even perhaps of *Launce*lot Gobbo's subversive ignorance[111]), these lines turn Shakespeare as Father/Author into a 'main masque' figure of reason, knowledge and authority, wielding the dread-inspiring authority of his name, overseeing and mastering the underworld of ignorance, fury and noise, like, and not in opposition to, Virgil's/Neptune's/Reason's 'dread trident', the figures/names of authority which *The Tempest*'s noise, and noise-makers, shake.

[111] See above, note 27. The semantic proximity of 'launce', 'spear' and 'trident' is signalled in a thematically arranged word list dating from 1668: under the category of weapons, group 3 has 'spear' listed alongside 'launce' and 'pike', while 'Trident' is listed on the next line alongside 'Halbert' and 'Partizan' (as quoted in Görlach, *Introduction to Early Modern English*, p. 141).

Bibliography

PRIMARY SOURCES

EDITIONS OF VIRGIL

Opera ... P. Melancthonis illustrata scholiis, Lyon, 1537.

Opera ... cum XI commentariis (Venice, 1544), reprinted in *The Renaissance and the Gods*, 2 vols., New York and London: Garland 1976.

Bucolica, Georgica et Aeneis ... Nicolai Erythraei ... opera ... restituta, Venice, 1555.

Georgica, P. Rami ... praelectionibus illustrata, Paris, 1564.

Bucolica P. Rami exposita, Paris, 1572.

Bucolica, Georgica, Aeneis ... notationibus illustrata ... opera et industria Jo. A. Meyen, Venice, 1576.

Poemata novis scholiis illustrata, quæ Henr. Steph ... dedit, Paris, 1583.

Symbolarum libri XVII, quibus ... Bucolica, Georgica, Aeneis ... declarantur ... per J. Pontanum, Augsburg, 1599.

Opera omnia, argumentis, explicationibus, notis illustrata, auctore Jo. Ludovico de la Cerda, 3 vols. (separately titled), Leyden, 1612–19.

Opera omnia ... cum commentario Frid. Taubmanni, Wittenberg, 1618.

Virgil, edited and translated by H. Rushton Fairclough, 2 vols., reprint, Cambridge, Mass.: Harvard University Press; London: William Heinemann, 1974.

Vergil: Eclogues, edited by R. Coleman, Cambridge University Press, 1977.

Vergil: Georgics, edited by Richard F. Thomas, 2 vols., Cambridge University Press, 1988.

OTHER PRIMARY SOURCES

Anon., *This boke treateth of the lyfe of Virgil, and of his death, and many other marvayles that he did in his lyfe tyme by witchecrafte and nygromancy, through the develles of hell*, London?, 1550?.

Ascham, Roger, *The Scholemaster* (1570), in G. Gregory Smith (ed.), *Elizabethan Critical Essays*, 2 vols., reprint, Oxford University Press, 1964, vol. 1, pp. 1–45.

Bacon, Francis, *The Wisedome of the Ancients . . . Done into English by Sir Arthur Georges* (London, 1619), reprinted in *The Renaissance and the Gods*, New York and London: Garland, 1976.

The Advancement of Learning, edited by G. W. Kitchin, reprint, London: Dent, 1965.

Barclay, John, *Argenis*, Leyden, 1627.

Brinsley, John, *Virgils Eclogues, with his booke De Apibus*, London, 1633.

A Consolation for Our Grammar Schooles, reprinted with an introduction by T. C. Pollock, New York: Scholars Facsimiles and Reprints, 1943.

Ludus literarius (1612), reprinted in *English Linguistics 1500–1800*, no. 62, Menston: The Scholar Press, 1968.

A Consolation for Our Grammar Schooles (1622), reprinted in *The English Experience*, no. 203, Amsterdam and New York: Da Capo Press, 1969.

Brisson, Barnaby, *De ritu nuptiarum . . . De iure connubiorum*, Paris, 1564.

De formulis et sollemnibus populi Romani verbis, Libri VIII, Frankfurt, 1592.

Comes, Natalis, *Mythologiae* (1567), reprinted in *The Renaissance and the Gods*, New York and London: Garland, 1976.

Cooper, Thomas, *Thesaurus linguae, Romanae et Britannicae*, London, 1565.

Dee, John, *The Elements of Geometrie . . . translated by H. Billingsley with a very fruitfull Preface made by M. I. Dee*, London, 1570.

Dekker, Thomas, *The Dramatic Works*, edited by F. Bowers, 4 vols., Cambridge University Press, 1953–61.

de Phares, Simon, *Recueil des plus célèbres astrologues et quelque hommes doctes*, edited by Dr Ernest Wickersheimer, Paris: Champion, 1929.

Donatus, Aelius, 'Vita', in *Vitae Vergilianae antiquae*, edited by Colin Hardie, 2nd edn, Oxford: Clarendon Press, 1966.

Douglas, Gavin, *Virgil's 'Aeneid' translated into Scottish Verse*, edited by D. F. C. Coldwell, Scottish Text Society, 4 vols., Edinburgh and London: Blackwood, 1957–64.

Drayton, Michael, *The Works*, edited by W. J. Hebel, reprint, 5 vols., Oxford University Press, 1961.

Dryden, John, *The Works*, edited by H. T. Swedenberg, Jr, 19 vols., University of California Press, 1956–79.

Elyot, Thomas, *The Book named The Governor* (1531), reprinted in, *English Linguistics 1500–1800*, Menston: The Scholar Press, 1970.

Erasmus, Desiderius, *De ratione studii*, edited by J.-C. Margolin, *Opera omnia*, vol. 1-2. Amsterdam: North Holland, 1971.

Adagiorum chilias tertia, edited by F. Heinemann and E. Kienzle, *Opera omnia*, vols. II-5, II-6. Amsterdam and Oxford: North Holland, 1981.

De duplici copia verborum ac rerum commentarii duo, edited by Betty I. Knott, *Opera omnia*, vol. 1-6. Amsterdam, New York, etc.: North-Holland, 1988.

Literary and Educational Writings 2, edited by Craig R. Thomson, *Collected Works of Erasmus*, vol. 24. Toronto University Press, 1978.

Fenner, Dudley, *The Artes of Logike and Rhetorike set foorth in the English tounge*, London, 1584.

Fleming, Abraham, *The Bucoliks of Publius Vergilius Maro, Together with his Georgiks. All newly translated into English verse*, London, 1589.

Florio, John, *A Worlde of Wordes, Or Most Copious, and exact Dictionarie in Italian and English*, London, 1598.

   The Essayes, or Morall, Politike, and Millitarie Discourses of Lo: Michaell de Montaigne . . . now done into English, London, 1603.

   Queen Anna's New World of Words, or Dictionarie of the Italian and English tongues, London, 1611.

Fraunce, Abraham, *The Lawiers Logike, exemplifying the praecepts of Logike by the practise of the Common Lawe* (1588), reprinted in *English Linguistics 1500–1800*, no. 174, Menston: The Scholar Press, 1969.

   The Arcadian Rhetorike (1588), edited by Ethel Seaton, Oxford: Basil Blackwell, 1950.

Fulgentius, Fabius Planciades V.C., *Opera*, edited by R. Helm, rev. edn. by J. Préaux, reprint, Stuttgart: Teubner, 1970.

   Fulgentius the Mythographer, translated by Leslie G. Whitbread, University of Ohio Press, 1971.

Giraldus, Lilius Gregorius, *De deis gentium* (1548), reprinted in *The Renaissance and the Gods*, New York and London: Garland, 1976.

Golding, Arthur, *Ovid's Metamorphoses: The Arthur Golding Translation* (1567), edited by J. F. Nims, New York: MacMillan, 1965.

Harvey, Gabriel, *Ciceronianus*, introduced by H. S. Wilson and translated by C. L. Forbes, Lincoln: University of Nebraska Press, 1945.

Horace (Quintus Horatius Flaccus), *Satires, Epistles, Ars Poetica*, edited and translated by H. R. Fairclough, reprint, London: William Heinemann; Cambridge, Mass.: Harvard University Press, 1978.

Howard, Henry, Earl of Surrey, *The Aeneid*, edited by Florence H. Ridley, University of California Press, 1963.

Humphrey, Lawrence, *The Nobles, or of Nobility* (1563), reprinted in *The English Experience*, no. 534, Amsterdam: Da Capo Press, 1973.

Jonson, Ben, *Ben Jonson*, edited by C. H. Herford, Percy and Evelyn Simpson, 11 vols., Oxford: Clarendon Press, 1925–52.

   The Alchemist, edited by F. H. Mares, reprint, Manchester University Press, 1979.

   Poetaster, edited by Tom Cain, Manchester University Press, 1995.

Kempe, William, *The Education of Children in Learning* (1588), in *Four Tudor Books on Education*, edited by Robert D. Pepper, Gainesville, Fla.: Scholars Facsimiles and Reprints, 1966.

Long, Kingsmill, *Barclay, his Argenis, or, the Loves of Poliarchus and Argenis*, London, 1636.

MacIlmaine, Roland, *The Logike of the Most Excellent Philosopher P. Ramus Martyr*, translated by Roland MacIlmaine (London, 1574), edited by C. M. Dunn, Northridge, Calif.; San Fernando Valley State College, 1969.

Macrobius, Ambrosius Theodosius, *Commentary on the Dream of Scipio*, translated by W. H. Stahl, New York: Columbia University Press, 1952.

I Saturnali di Macrobio Teodosio, edited by N. Marinone, Turin: Unione Tipografico-Editrice Torinese, 1967.

Macrobius. *The Saturnalia*, translated by P. V. Davies, New York and London: Columbia University Press, 1969.

Saturnalia, edited by J. Willis, Leipzig: Teubner, 1970.

Commentarii in somnium scipionis, edited by J. Willis, Leipzig: Teubner, 1970.

Marlowe, C., *Dr Faustus*, edited by David Bevington and Eric Ramussen, Manchester University Press, 1993.

Martial (Martialis, Marcus Valerius), *Epigrams*, edited and translated by W. C. Ker, 2 vols., Cambridge, Mass.: Harvard University Press, 1950.

Mirandula, Octavianus, *Illustrium poetarum flores*, Leyden, 1555.

Montaigne, Michel de, *Essais*, 3 vols., Paris: Flammarion, 1969.

Nashe, Thomas, *The Works*, edited by R .B. McKerrow, revised by F. P. Wilson, 5 vols., Oxford University Press, 1966.

Naudé, Gabriel, *Apologie pour tous les grands personnages qui ont esté faussement soupçonnez de magie*, Paris, 1625.

Nichols, J. *The Progresses and Public Processions of Queen Elizabeth*, 2 vols., London: The Society of Antiquaries, 1788.

Phaer, Thomas, *The Nyne Fyrst Bookes of the Eneidos of Virgil converted into Englishe vearse*, London, 1562.

Phaer, Thomas and Thomas Twyne *The xiii bookes of Æneidos. The thirtenth [sic] the supplement of Maphæus Vegius*, London, 1584.

Puttenham, George, *The Arte of English Poesie* (London 1589), reprinted in *English Linguistics 1500–1800*, Menston: The Scholar Press, 1968.

The Arte of English Poesie, edited by G. D. Willcock and A. Walker, reprint, Cambridge University Press, 1970.

Quintilian (Marcus Fabius Quintilianus), *M. Fabii Quintiliani institutionum oratoriarum libri XII. Et declamationes XIX*, Paris, 1528.

The Institutio Oratoria, edited and translated by H. E. Butler, 4 vols., reprint, Cambridge, Mass.: Harvard University Press; London: William Heinemann, 1963.

Ramus, Petrus, *Dialecticae libri duo, Audomari Talei praelectionibus illustrati*, Paris, 1556.

Dialectique (1555), edited by Michel Dassonville, Geneva: Droz, 1964.

see also Talon

Reynolds, Henry, *Mythomystes* (1632), reprint, Menston: The Scholar Press, 1972.

Selden, John, *De dis syris, syntagmata II*, 2nd edn, Leyden, 1629.

Shadwell, Thomas, *The Complete Works*, edited by Montague Summers, 3 vols., London: The Fortune Press, 1927.

Shakespeare, William, *The Tempest*, edited by Horace Howard Furness, New York: Dover Publications Inc., 1964.

The Riverside Shakespeare, edited by G. Blakemore Evans et al., Boston: Houghton Mifflin Co., 1974.

The Tempest, edited by Anne Righter (Barton), reprint, Harmondsworth:

Penguin, 1982.

The Tempest, edited by Stephen Orgel, Oxford University Press, 1987.

The Tempest, edited by Frank Kermode, 6th edn, reprint, London and New York: Routledge, 1994.

Sidney, Philip, *The Complete Works*, edited by A. Feuillerat, 4 vols., Cambridge University Press, 1912–26.

The Poems of Sir Philip Sidney, edited by William A. Ringler, Jr, Oxford: Clarendon Press, 1962.

Spenser, Edmund, *Poetical Works*, edited by J. C. Smith and E. de Selincourt, Oxford University Press, 1970.

Stanyhurst, Richard, *Translation of the First Four Books of the Aeneis* (Leyden 1582), edited by E. Arber, London: The English Scholars' Library, 1880.

Talon, Omer (Talaeus, A.), *Rhetorica, e Petri Rami . . . praelectionibus observata*, Paris, 1577.

Vives, Juan Luis, *Opera omnia*, edited by G. Majansio, 8 vols., reprint, London: Gregg Press, 1964.

Webbe, William, *A Discourse of English Poetrie*, edited by E. Arber, London: The English Scholars' Library, 1870.

A Discourse of English Poetrie, in G. Gregory Smith (ed.), *Elizabethan Critical Essays*, 2 vols., reprint, Oxford University Press, 1964, vol. 1, pp. 226–302.

Willes, Richard, *De re poetica* (1573), translated by A. D. S Fowler, Oxford: Basil Blackwell, 1958.

Willich, Jodochus, *Dialysis quatuor librorum in Georgicis Virgilii. Signorum prognosticorum de tempestatibus aeris physica explicatio*, Frankfurt, 1551.

SECONDARY SOURCES

Adams, H. M., *Catalogue of Books Printed on the Continent of Europe 1501–1600 in Cambridge Libraries*, 2 vols., Cambridge University Press, 1967.

Adelman, Janet, *Suffocating Mothers*, New York and London: Routledge, 1992.

Allen, Don Cameron, *Mysteriously Meant: The Rediscovery of Pagan Symbolism and Allegorical Interpretation in the Renaissance*, Baltimore and London: Johns Hopkins University Press, 1970.

Appelt, T. C., *Studies in the Contents and Sources of Erasmus' Adagia, with particular reference to the First Edition, 1500 and the Edition of 1526*, University of Chicago Press, 1942.

Attridge, Derek, *Well-Weighed Syllables: Elizabethan Verse in Classical Metres*, Cambridge University Press, 1974.

'Puttenham's Perplexity: Nature, Art, and the Supplement in Renaissance Poetic Theory', in Patricia Parker and David Quint (eds.), *Literary Theory/Renaissance Texts*, Baltimore and London: Johns Hopkins University Press, 1986.

Baldwin, T. W., *William Shakespere's Small Latine and Lesse Greeke*, 2 vols., Urbana: University of Illinois Press, 1944.

Barber, Charles *Early Modern English*, London: André Deutsch, 1976.

Barish, Jonas, 'Jonson and the Loathed Stage', in W. Blissett, Julian Patrick and R. W. Van Fossen (eds.), *A Celebration of Ben Jonson*, University of Toronto Press, 1973.

Barker, Francis and Hulme, Peter, 'Nymphs and Reapers heavily vanish: The Discursive Con-texts of *The Tempest*', in John Drakakis (ed.), *Alternative Shakespeares*.

Barton, Anne, *Ben Jonson, Dramatist*, Cambridge University Press, 1984.

Bassnett-McGuire, Susan, *Translation Studies*, reprint, London and New York: Routledge, 1988.

Baswell, Christopher C., *Virgil in Medieval England: Figuring the 'Aeneid' from the Twelfth Century to Chaucer*, Cambridge University Press, 1995.

Bate, Jonathan, *Shakespeare and Ovid*, 2nd edn, Oxford: Clarendon Press, 1994.

Bawcutt, Priscilla, *Gavin Douglas: A Critical Study*, Edinburgh University Press, 1976.

Belyea, Barbara, 'The Notion of "Equivalence": The Relevance of Current Translation Theory to the Edition of Literary Texts', in Jacques Flamand and Arlette Thomas (eds.), *La traduction: l'universitaire et le practicien*, University of Ottawa Press, 1984.

Bennington, Geoffrey and Derrida, Jacques, *Jacques Derrida*, Tours: Seuil, 1991.

Berg, Sara van den, 'Ben Jonson and the Ideology of Authorship', in Jennifer Brady and W. H. Herenden (eds.), *Ben Jonson's 1616 Folio*, Newark: University of Delaware Press; London and Toronto: Associate University Presses, 1991.

Bernard, John D. (ed.), *Vergil at 2000: Commemorative Essays on the Poet and his Influence*, New York: AMS Press, 1986.

Birch, David, *Language, Literature and Critical Practice*, London and New York: Routledge, 1989.

Bloom, Harold (ed.), *Ben Jonson. Modern Critical Views*, New York, New Haven and Philadelphia: Chelsea House Publishers, 1987.

Boehrer, Bruce Thomas, 'Renaissance Overeating: The Sad Case of Ben Jonson', *Publications of the Modern Language Association* 105:5 (1990), 1071–82.

Bolgar, R., *The Classical Heritage and its Beneficiaries*, Cambridge University Press, 1954.

Bono, Barbara J., *Literary Transvaluation: From Vergilian Epic to Shakespearean Tragicomedy*, University of California Press, 1984.

Bourcier, Paul, *Histoire de la danse en Occident*, Paris: Seuil, 1978.

Brinton, Anna Cox, 'The Ships of Columbus in Brant's Virgil', *Art and Archaeology* (September 1928), 83–6 and 94.

   Maphaeus Vegius and his Thirteenth Book of the Aeneid: A Chapter on Virgil in the Renaissance, Stanford University Press, 1930.

   Descensus Averno: Fourteen Woodcut Reprints reproduced from Sebastian Brant's Virgil, Stanford University Press, 1930.

Brissenden, Alan, *Shakespeare and the Dance*, London and Basingstoke: MacMillan, 1981.

Bristol, Michael D., *Carnival and Theater: Plebeian Culture and the Structure of Authority in Renaissance England*, New York and London: Routledge, 1985.

Bullough, Geoffrey, *Narrative and Dramatic Sources of Shakespeare*, 8 vols., London: Routledge and Kegan Paul; New York: Columbia University Press, 1975.

Bulman, James C., 'Shakespeare's Georgic Histories', *Shakespeare Survey* 38 (1985), 37–47.

Burt, Richard, *Licensed by Authority. Ben Jonson and the Discourses of Censorship*, Ithaca and London: Cornell University Press, 1993.

Calder, I. R. F., 'John Dee studied as an English Neoplatonist', PhD thesis, The Warburg Institute, University of London, 1952.

Cameron, A., 'The Date and Identity of Macrobius', *Journal of Roman Studies* 56 (1966), 25–38.

Campbell, Oscar James, 'The Dramatic Construction of *Poetaster*', *The Huntington Library Bulletin* 9 (1936), 37–63.

Cartelli, Thomas, '*Bartholomew Fair* as Urban Arcadia: Jonson Responds to Shakespeare', *Renaissance Drama* 14 (1983), 151–72.

Cascardi, Anthony J., *The Subject of Modernity*, reprint, Cambridge University Press, 1994.

Caspari, F., *Humanism and the Social Order in Tudor England*, University of Chicago Press, 1954.

Cave, Terence, *The Cornucopian Text: Problems of Writing in the French Renaissance*, Oxford University Press, 1979.

Céard, J., 'Virgile, un grand homme soupçonné de magie', in Chevallier (ed.), *Présence de Virgile*.

Chambers, E. K., *William Shakespeare: A Study of Facts and Problems*, 2 vols., Oxford: Clarendon Press, 1930.

Charlton, K., *Education in Renaissance England*, London: Routledge and Kegan Paul, 1965.

Chevallier, R. (ed.), *Présence de Virgile*, Paris: Les Belles Lettres, 1978.

Christie, R. C., *The Old Church and School Libraries of Lancashire*, Chetham Society, 2nd series, no. 7, Manchester: Charles Simms, 1885.

Clarke, M. L., 'Virgil in English Education since the Sixteenth Century', *Virgil Society Lecture Summaries* 39 (1957).

Classical Education in Britain 1500–1900, Cambridge University Press, 1959.

Clayton, Margaret, 'Ben Jonson "in travaile with expression of another": His Use of John of Salisbury's *Policraticus* in *Timber*', *The Review of English Studies* NS 30:120 (1979), 397–408.

'"Tempests, and such like Drolleries": Jonson, Shakespeare and the Figure of Vergil', PhD thesis, University of Cambridge, 1986.

see also Tudeau-Clayton

Comparetti, D., *Virgilio nel medio evo*, 2 vols., Livorno: Francesco Vigo, 1872.

Vergil in the Middle Ages, translated by E. F. M. Benecke, London: Swan Sonnenschein; New York: MacMillan, 1895.

Virgilio nel medio evo, 2 vols., edited by Giorgio Pasquali, Florence: La Nouva Italia, 1937–41.

Vergil in the Middle Ages, translated by E. F. M. Benecke, introduced and edited by Jan Ziolkowski, Princeton University Press, 1997.

Conley, C. H., *The First English Translators of The Classics*, New Haven: Yale University Press; Oxford University Press, 1927.

Conway, R. S., *New Studies of a Great Inheritance: Being Lectures on the Modern Worth of some Ancient Writers*, London: John Murray, 1921.

Cordier, A., *Etudes sur le vocabulaire épique dans l'Enéide*, Paris: Les Belles Lettres, 1939.

Courcelle, Pierre, 'Les Pères de l'Eglise devant les enfers virgiliens', *Archives d'histoire doctrinale et littéraire du Moyen Age* 22 (1955), 5–74.

Cranz, F. Edwards and Kristeller, P. O. (eds.), *Catalogus translationum et commentariorum: Medieval and Renaissance Latin Translations and commentaries*, Washington: The Catholic University of America Press, 1960– .

Culler, Jonathan, 'English in the Age of Cultural Studies', *Bulletin de la société des anglicistes de l'enseignement supérieur* 40 (1996), 8–24.

Cuno, James, Cohn, Marjorie B. et al., *Harvard's Art Museums. 100 Years of Collecting*, New York: Harry N. Abrams, 1996.

Dalrymple, David, *Sketch of the Life of John Barclay*, Edinburgh, 1783.

de Grazia, Margreta, *Shakespeare Verbatim: The Reproduction of Authenticity and the 1790 Apparatus*, Oxford: Clarendon Press, 1991.

de Man, Paul, *The Resistance to Theory*, Theory and History of Literature, 33, Minneapolis: University of Minnesota Press, 1986.

de Nolhac, Pierre, *Pétrarque et l'humanisme*, Paris: Champion, 1907.

Derrida, Jacques, *Acts of Literature*, edited by Derek Attridge, New York and London: Routledge, 1992.

see also Bennington

di Cesare, Mario A., 'Seeking the Renaissance Vergil', in Lotte Hellinga and John Goldfinch (eds.), *Bibliography and the Study of Fifteenth-Century Civilisation*, London: British Library, 1987.

Dobbs, Betty Jo Teeter, *The Foundation of Newton's Alchemy or 'The Hunting of the Greene Lyon'*, Cambridge University Press, 1975.

Dollimore, Jonathan and Sinfield, Alan (eds.), *Political Shakespeare*, Manchester University Press, 1985.

Drakakis, John (ed.), *Alternative Shakespeares*, London and New York: Methuen, 1985.

Dryoff, J. M., 'Approaches to the Study of Richard Stanyhurst's translation of Virgil's *Aeneid*', PhD dissertation, University of Boston, 1971.

Duckworth, George E., *Structural Patterns and Proportions in Vergil's 'Aeneid': A Study in Mathematical Composition*, Ann Arbor: University of Michigan Press, 1962.

Duncan, Douglas, *Ben Jonson and the Lucianic Tradition*, Cambridge University Press, 1979.

Dutton, Richard, *Ben Jonson: To the First Folio*, Cambridge University Press, 1983.

Evans, Malcolm, 'Deconstructing Shakespeare's Comedies', in Drakakis (ed.), *Alternative Shakespeares*.

Signifying Nothing: Truth's True Contents in Shakespeare's Text, Brighton: The Harvester Press, 1986.

Evans, Robert C., *Ben Jonson and the Poetics of Patronage*, Lewisburg: Bucknell University Press; London and Toronto: Associated University Presses, 1989.

Falconer, A. F., *Shakespeare and The Sea*, London: Constable, 1964.

Felperin, Howard, 'Political Criticism at the Crossroads: The Utopian Historicism of *The Tempest*', in Nigel Wood (ed.), *The Tempest, Theory in Practice*, Milton Keynes and Philadelphia: Open University Press, 1995.

Ferguson, William, *Scotland's Relations with England: A Survey to 1707*, Edinburgh: John Donald, 1977.

Fish, Stanley, 'Authors-Readers: Jonson's Community of the Same', in Stephen Greenblatt (ed.), *Representing the English Renaissance*, University of California Press, 1988.

Fletcher, Harris F., *The Intellectual Development of John Milton*, 2 vols., Urbana: University of Illinois Press, 1956 and 1964.

Forsyth, Neil, *The Old Enemy: Satan and the Combat Myth*, Princeton University Press, 1987.

'Of Man's First Dis', in Mario A. di Cesare (ed.), *Milton in Italy: Contexts, Images, Contradictions*, Binghampton, N.Y.; MRTS Press, 1991.

Foucault, Michel, *Les mots et les choses*, Paris: Gallimard, 1966.

'Qu'est-ce qu'un auteur?', *Bulletin de la société française de philosophie* 44 (1969), 73–104.

'What is an Author?' in Paul Rabinow (ed.), *The Foucault Reader*, reprint, Harmondsworth: Penguin, 1991.

Dits et écrits 1954–1988, edited by Daniel Defert and François Ewald, 4 vols., Paris: Gallimard, 1994.

Fowler, Alastair, 'The Beginnings of English Georgic', in Barbara K. Lewalski (ed.), *Renaissance Genres: Essays on Theory, History and Interpretation*, Harvard University Press, 1986.

Freedman, Luba, 'Neptune in Classical and Renaissance Visual Art', *International Journal of the Classical Tradition* 2:2 (1995), 219–37.

French, Peter, *John Dee: The World of an Elizabethan Magus*, London: Routledge and Kegan Paul, 1972.

Frost, William, 'Translating Virgil, Douglas to Dryden: Some General Considerations', in George de Forest Lord and Maynard Mack (eds.), *Poetic Traditions of the English Renaissance*, New Haven and London: Yale University Press, 1982.

Gillies, John, 'Shakespeare's Virginian Masque', *English Literary History* 53 (1986), 673–707.

Gilman, Ernest B., '"All eyes": Prospero's Inverted Masque', *Renaissance Quarterly* 33 (1980), 214–30.

Girard, René, *Shakespeare: les feux de l'envie*, Paris: Bernard Grasset, 1990.

Goldberg, Jonathan, *James I and The Politics of Literature*, Baltimore and London: Johns Hopkins University Press, 1983.

Goold, G. P., 'Servius and the Helen Episode', *Harvard Studies in Classical Philology* 74 (1970), 101–68.

Gordon, D. J. *The Renaissance Imagination. Essays and Lectures*, edited by Stephen Orgel, University of California Press, 1975.

Görlach, Manfred, *Introduction to Early Modern English*, reprint, Cambridge University Press, 1993.

Grafton, Anthony, 'Renaissance Readers and Ancient Texts: Comments on Some Commentaries', *Renaissance Quarterly* 38 (1985), 615–49.

Grafton, Anthony and Jardine, Lisa, *From Humanism to the Humanities*, Cambridge, Mass.: Harvard University Press, 1986.

Greenblatt, Stephen, *Renaissance Self-Fashioning: From More to Shakespeare*, University of Chicago Press, 1980.

    Shakespearean Negotiations: The Circulation of Social Energy in Renaissance England, Oxford: Clarendon Press, 1988.

    'Remnants of the Sacred in Early Modern England', in Magreta de Grazia, Maureen Quilligan and Peter Stallybrass (eds.), *Subject and Object in Renaissance Culture*, Cambridge University Press, 1996.

Greene, Thomas M., *The Light in Troy: Imitation and Discovery in Renaissance Poetry*, New Haven and London: Yale University Press, 1982.

    'Ben Jonson and the Centered Self', reprinted in Harold Bloom (ed.), *Ben Jonson*.

Gurr, Andrew, *The Shakespearean Stage 1574–1642*, 3rd edn, Cambridge University Press, 1992.

Gusdorf, Georges, *La révolution galiléene*, 2 vols., Paris: Payot, 1969.

Halliday, F. E., *A Shakespeare Companion 1550–1950*, reprint, London: Gerald Duckworth, 1955.

Hamilton, Donna B., 'Defiguring Vergil in *The Tempest*', *Style* 23 (1989), 352–73.

    Virgil and The Tempest: The Politics of Imitation, Columbus: Ohio State University Press, 1990.

Harari, J. V. (ed.), *Textual Strategies: Perspectives in Post-Structuralist Criticism*, Ithaca: Cornell University Press, 1979.

Hardie, Philip R., *Virgil's 'Aeneid': 'Cosmos' and 'Imperium'*, Oxford: Clarendon Press, 1986.

Hawkes, Terence, *That Shakespeherian Rag*, London and New York: Methuen, 1986.

Haynes, Jonathan, 'Festivity and the Dramatic Economy of Jonson's *Bartholomew Fair*', in Harold Bloom (ed.), *Ben Jonson*.

Helgerson, Richard, *Self-Crowned Laureates: Spenser, Jonson and the Literary System*, University of California Press, 1983.

Hijmans, B. L., Jr, '*Aeneia Virtus*: Vegio's *Supplementum* to the *Aeneid*', *The Classical Journal* 67 (1971–2), 144–55.

Hill, Christopher, *Intellectual Origins of the English Revolution*, Oxford University Press, 1965.

Holderness, Graham (ed.), *The Shakespeare Myth*, Manchester University Press, 1988.

    'Preface: "All This"', in Holderness (ed.), *The Shakespeare Myth*.

'Bardolotry: Or, The Cultural Materialist's Guide to Stratford-upon-Avon', in Holderness (ed.), *The Shakespeare Myth*.

Hollander, John, *The Untuning of the Sky: Ideas of Music in English Poetry 1500–1700*, Princeton University Press, 1961.

Howell, W. S., *Logic and Rhetoric in England, 1500–1700*, Princeton University Press, 1956.

Hubaux, Jean, *Le réalisme dans les Bucoliques de Virgile*, Paris: Champion, 1927.

Hughes, Merrit Y., *Virgil and Spenser*, University of California Press, 1929.

Hulubei, A., 'Virgile en France au seizième siècle', *Revue du seizième siècle* 18 (1931), 1–77.

Hutton, James, 'Some English Poems in Praise of Music', *English Miscellany* 2 (1951), 1–63.

Jackson, W. A., Ferguson, F. S. and Pantzer, K. F., *A Short Title Catalogue of Books Printed in England and Scotland 1475–1640*, 2nd edn, revised and enlarged, 3 vols., London: The Bibliographical Society, 1976–1991.

James, Heather, 'Cultural Disintegration in *Titus Andronicus*: Mutilating Titus, Vergil, and Rome', *Themes in Drama* 13 (1991), 123–40.

Shakespeare's Troy: Drama, Politics and the Translation of Empire, Cambridge University Press, 1997.

Jardine, Lisa, *Francis Bacon: Discovery and the Art of Discourse*, Cambridge University Press, 1974.

'Humanism and the Sixteenth-Century Arts Course', *History of Education* 4 (1975), 16–31.

see also Grafton

Javitch, Daniel, *Poetry and Courtliness in Renaissance England*, Princeton University Press, 1978.

Jayne, Sears, *Library Catalogues of the English Renaissance*, University of California Press, 1956.

Johnston, G. B., *Ben Jonson: Poet*, New York: Columbia University Press, 1945.

Jones, J. W., Jr, 'Allegorical Interpretation in Servius', *Classical Journal* 56 (1960–61), 217–26.

'The Allegorical Traditions of the *Aeneid*', in Bernard (ed.), *Vergil at 2000*.

Jones, Robert C., 'The Satirist's Retirement in Jonson's "Apologetical Dialogue"', *English Literary History* 34 (1967), 447–67.

Joseph, B. L., *Elizabeth Acting*, rev. edn, Oxford University Press, 1964.

Judd, Judith, 'Bard only for the Bright', *The Independent*, 21 March 1993.

Kallendorf, Craig, 'Cristoforo Landino's *Aeneid* and the Humanist Critical Tradition', *Renaissance Quarterly* 36 (1983), 519–46.

'Maffeo Vegio's Book XIII and the *Aeneid* of Early Italian Humanism', in Anne Reynolds (ed.), *Altro Polo: The Classical Continuum in Italian Thought and Letters, A volume of Italian Studies*, University of Sydney, 1984.

In Praise of Aeneas, Virgil and Epideictic Rhetoric in the Early Italian Renaissance, Hanover, N. H. and London: University of New England Press, 1989.

'Introduction: Recent Trends in the Study of Vergilian Influences', in Craig

Kallendorf (ed.), *Vergil. The Classical Heritage*, New York and London: Garland, 1993.

Kantorowicz, E. H., *The King's Two Bodies: A Study in Medieval Political Theology*, Princeton University Press, 1957.

Kaster, Robert A., *Guardians of Language: The Grammarian and Society in Late Antiquity*, University of California Press, 1988.

Kavanagh, James H., 'Shakespeare in Ideology', in Drakakis (ed.), *Alternative Shakespeares*.

'Ideology', in Frank Lentricchia and Thomas McLaughlin (eds.), *Critical Terms for Literary Study*, University of Chicago Press, 1990.

Kearney, Hugh, *Scholars and Gentlemen: Universities and Society in Pre-Industrial Britain 1500–1700*, London: Faber and Faber, 1979.

Kermode, Frank, 'The Banquet of Sense', in *Renaissance Essays*, London: Routledge and Kegan Paul, 1971.

The Classic, London: Faber and Faber; New York: Viking, 1975.

'Institutional Control of Interpretation', in *Essays on Fiction 1971–82*, London, Melbourne and Henley: Routledge and Kegan Paul, 1979.

Killy, Walther, *Literatur Lexicon, Autoren und Werke deutscher Spracher*, 15 vols., Munich: Bertelsmann Lexikon Verlag, 1988–93.

King, A. H., *The Language of Satirized Characters in Poetaster: A Socio-Stylistic Analysis, 1597–1602*, Lund Studies in English 10, Lund: G. W. K. Gleerup, 1941.

Knight, W. F. Jackson, *Virgil The Aeneid*, reprint, Harmondsworth: Penguin, 1973.

Kott, Jan, *Shakespeare our Contemporary*, translated by B. Taborski, London: Methuen, 1964.

'The *Aeneid* and *The Tempest*', *Arion* NS 3/4 (1976), 424–51.

'*The Tempest*, or Repetition', *Mosaic* 10:3 (1977), 10–36.

Laroque, François, *Shakespeare's Festive World*, translated by Janet Lloyd, Cambridge University Press, 1993.

Larson, Magali Sarfatti, *The Rise of Professionalism: A Sociological Analysis*, University of California Press, 1977.

Laslett, Peter, *The World we have lost: England before the Industrial Age*, 2nd edn, New York: Charles Scribner's Sons, 1971.

Lathrop, H. B., *Translations from the Classics into English. From Caxton to Chapman 1477–1620*, Madison: University of Wisconsin Press, 1933.

Leedham-Green, Elisabeth, *Books in Cambridge Inventories: Book-lists from Vice-Chancellor's Court Probate Inventories in the Tudor and Stuart Periods*, 2 vols., Cambridge University Press, 1986.

Leggatt, Alexander, *Ben Jonson: His Vision and his Art*, London and New York: Methuen, 1981.

Lestringant, Frank, *L'atelier du cosmographe ou l'image du monde à la Renaissance*, Paris: Albin Michel, 1991.

Lévi-Strauss, Claude, *La pensée sauvage*, Paris: Plon, 1962.

Levin, Richard, 'The Poetics and Politics of Bardicide', *Publications of the Modern Language Association* 105:3 (1990), 491–504.

Lewis, C. Day, *The Eclogues, Georgics and Aeneid of Virgil*, Oxford University Press, 1966.

Lindley, David, 'Music, Masque and Meaning in *The Tempest*', in David Lindley, (ed.), *The Court Masque*, Manchester University Press, 1984.

Llewellyn, Nigel, 'Virgil and The Visual Arts', in Charles Martindale (ed.), *Virgil and his Influence*, Bristol Classical Press, 1984.

Loane, Helen A., 'The *Sortes Vergilianae*', *The Classical Weekly* 21:24 (1928), 185–9.

Lockyer, Roger, *The Early Stuarts: A Political History of England 1603–1642*, London and New York: Longman, 1989.

Loewenstein, Joseph, 'The Jonsonian Corpulence: Or, The Poet as Mouthpiece', *English Literary History* 53 (1986), 491–518.

Lord, M. L. 'The Use of Macrobius and Boethius in some Fourteenth Century Commentaries on Virgil', *International Journal of the Classical Tradition* 3:1 (1996), 3–22.

Low, Anthony, *The Georgic Revolution*, Princeton University Press, 1985.

MacKinnon, Lachlan, 'Shakespeares for our Age', *The Times Literary Supplement*, 6 March 1992.

Maguiness, W. S., 'Maffeo Vegio continuatore dell'Eneide', *Aevum* 42 (1968), 478–85.

Mambelli, G., *Gli annali delle edizioni virgiliane*, Florence: Leo S. Olschki, 1954.

Marder, L., *His Exits and Entrances: The Story of Shakespeare's Reputation*, London: J. Murray, 1964.

Margolies, David, 'Teaching the Handsaw to fly: Shakespeare as a Hegemonic Instrument', in Holderness (ed.), *The Shakespeare Myth*.

Margolin, Jean-Claude, 'Erasme, lecteur et exégète de Virgile', in Chevallier (ed.), *Présence de Virgile*.

Massena, Victor, Prince D'Essling, and Muentz, Eugène, *Petrarque ses études d'art, son influence sur les artistes, ses portraits et ceux de laure. L'Illustration de ses écrits*, Paris: Gazette des Beaux Arts, 1902.

Maus, Katherine Eisaman, 'Arcadia Lost: Politics and Revision in the Restoration *Tempest*', *Renaissance Drama* NS 18 (1982), 189–209.

Ben Jonson and the Roman Frame of Mind, Princeton University Press, 1984.

McDonald, Russ, *Shakespeare and Jonson, Jonson and Shakespeare*, Brighton: The Harvester Press, 1988.

'Reading *The Tempest*', *Shakespeare Survey* 43 (1991), 15–28.

McPherson, David, 'Ben Jonson's Library and Marginalia. An Annotated Catalogue', *Studies in Philology* 71:5 (1974), v–106.

Miola, Robert S., 'Vergil in Shakespeare: From Allusion to Imitation', in Bernard (ed.), *Vergil at 2000*.

Montrose, Louis, 'Of Gentlemen and Shepherds: The Politics of Elizabethan Pastoral Form', *English Literary History* 50 (1983), 415–59.

'Sport by Sport O'erthrown: *Love's Labour's Lost* and the Politics of Play', reprinted in Gary Waller (ed.), *Shakespeare's Comedies*, London and New York: Longman 1991.

Mortimer, Ruth, 'Vergil in the Light of the Sixteenth Century: Selected Illustrations', in Bernard (ed.), *Vergil at 2000*.

Mullaney, Steven, *The Place of the Stage. License, Play and Power in Renaissance England*, University of Chicago Press, 1988.

Nash, Ralph, 'The Parting Scene in Jonson's *Poetaster* (IV.ix)', *Philological Quarterly* 31 (1952), 54–62.

Nicolson, Marjorie Hope, *The Breaking of the Circle: Studies in the Effect of the 'New Science' on Seventeenth Century Poetry*, rev. edn, New York and London: Columbia University Press, 1962.

Norbrook, David, *Poetry and Politics in the English Renaissance*, London, Boston, Melbourne and Henley: Routledge and Kegan Paul, 1984.

Norris, Christopher, 'Post-Structuralist Shakespeare: Text and Society', in Drakakis (ed.), *Alternative Shakespeares*.

Nosworthy, J. M., 'The Narrative Sources of *The Tempest*', *The Review of English Studies* 24 (1948), 281–94.

O'Day, Rosemary, *Education and Society 1500–1800*, New York and London: Longman, 1982.

Ong, W., 'Latin Language Study as a Renaissance Puberty Rite', in *Rhetoric, Romance and Technology*, Ithaca and London: Cornell University Press, 1971.

Orgel, Stephen, *The Jonsonian Masque*, Harvard University Press, 1965.

'Prospero's Wife', reprinted in Stephen Greenblatt (ed.), *Representing the English Renaissance*, University of California Press, 1988.

Orrell, John, 'The Musical Canon of Proportion in Jonson's *Hymenaei*', *English Language Notes* 15 (1978), 171–8.

Padelford, F. M., *Select Translations from Scaliger's Poetics*, Yale Studies in English 26, New York: Henry Holt and Co., 1905.

Parfitt, G. A. E., 'The Poetry of Ben Jonson', *Essays in Criticism* 18 (1968), 18–31.

Parker, Patricia, *Literary Fat Ladies: Rhetoric, Gender, Property*, London and New York: Methuen, 1987.

Parry, Graham, *The Golden Age Restor'd: The Culture of the Stuart Court, 1603–42*, Manchester University Press, 1981.

Patterson, Annabel, *Pastoral and Ideology: Virgil to Valéry*, Oxford: Clarendon Press, 1988.

Shakespeare and the Popular Voice, Oxford and Cambridge, Mass.: Basil Blackwell, 1989.

Phillips, M. M., *The Adages of Erasmus: A Study with Translations*, Cambridge University Press, 1964.

Pitcher, John, 'A Theatre of the Future: The *Aeneid* and *The Tempest*', *Essays in Criticism* 34:3 (1984), 193–215.

Proudfoot, L., *Dryden's 'Aeneid' and its Seventeenth-Century Predecessors*, Manchester University Press, 1960.

Quint, David, *Origin and Originality in Renaissance Literature. Versions of the Source*, New Haven and London: Yale University Press, 1983.

Rabb, Theodore, 'Sebastian Brant and The First Illustrated Edition of Vergil', *Princeton University Library Chronicle* 21:4 (1960), 187–99.

Rabinow, Paul (ed.), *The Foucault Reader*, reprint, Harmondsworth: Penguin Books, 1991.

Riggs, David, *Ben Jonson. A Life*, Cambridge, Mass. and London: Harvard University Press, 1989.

Roberts, R. J. and Watson, A. N., *John Dee's Library Catalogue*, London: The Bibliographical Society, 1990.

Robinson, F. G. *The Shape of Things known: Sidney's 'Apology' in its Philosophical Tradition*, Cambridge, Mass.: Harvard University Press, 1972.

Rosenmayer, Thomas G., *The Green Cabinet: Theocriticus and the European Pastoral Lyric*, University of California Press, 1969.

Ross, Charles S., 'Maffeo Vegio's "schort Cristyn wark"', with a Note on the Thirteenth Book in Early Editions of Virgil', *Modern Philology: A Journal Devoted to Research in Medieval and Renaissance Literature* 78:3 (1981), 215–26.

Ross, David O., Jr, *Virgil's Elements: Physics and Poetry in the Georgics*, Princeton University Press, 1987.

Sayle, R. T. D., 'Annals of Merchant Taylors' School Library', *The Library*, 4th series, no. 15 (1934–5), 457–80.

Schmidgall, Gary, *Shakespeare and the Courtly Aesthetic*, University of California Press, 1981.

Schneider, Bernd (ed.), *Das Aeneissupplement des Maffeo Vegio*, Acta Humaniora der VCH Verlagsgesellschaft, 1985.

Shell, Alison, 'Picking the Critical First Eleven', *The Times Higher Education Supplement*, 23 November 1990.

Sherman, William H., *John Dee. The Politics of Reading and Writing in The English Renaissance*. Amherst: University of Massachusetts Press, 1995.

Skura, Meredith Anne, 'Discourse and The Individual: The Case of Colonialism in *The Tempest*', *Shakespeare Quarterly* 40 (1989), 42–69.

Smith, Margery, H., 'Some Humanist Libraries in Early Tudor Cambridge', *Sixteenth Century Journal* 5 (1974), 15–34.

Spargo, J. W., *Virgil the Necromancer: Studies in Virgilian Legends*, Cambridge, Mass.: Harvard University Press, 1934.

Srigley, Michael, *Images of Regeneration: A Study of Shakespeare's 'The Tempest' and its Cultural Background*, Studia Anglistica Upsaliensia 58, University of Uppsala Press, 1985.

Stahel, T. H., 'Cristoforo Landino's Allegorization of the *Aeneid*: Books III and IV of the Camoldese Disputations', PhD dissertation, Johns Hopkins University, 1968.

Starnes, T. DeWitt and Talbert, E. W., *Classical Myth and Legend in Renaissance Dictionaries*, reprint, Westport, Conn.: Greenwood Press, 1973.

Stern, V. F., *Gabriel Harvey: His Life, Marginalia and Library*, Oxford: Clarendon Press, 1979.

Still, Colin, *Shakespeare's Mystery Play: A Study of 'The Tempest'*, London: Cecil Palmer, 1921.

  The Timeless Theme. A Critical Theory Formulated and Applied, London: Ivor Nicholson and Watson, 1936.

Stok, Fabio, 'Virgil between the Middle Ages and the Renaissance', *International Journal of the Classical Tradition* 1:2 (1994), 15–22.

Stone, Lawrence, 'The Educational Revolution in England, 1560–1640', *Past and Present* 28 (1964), 41–80.

The Crisis of the Aristocracy 1558–1641, Oxford: Clarendon Press, 1965.

'Social Mobility in England, 1500–1700', *Past and Present* 33 (1966), 16–55.

Talbert, Ernest, 'The Purpose and Technique of Jonson's *Poetaster*', *Studies in Philology* 42 (1945), 225–51.

Taylor, Charles, *Sources of the Self: The Making of The Modern Identity*, Cambridge University Press, 1989.

Taylor, Gary, 'Licit and Illicit Quests', *Times Literary Supplement*, 16 August 1985.

Thorndike, Lynn, *A History of Magic and Experimental Science*, 8 vols., New York and London: MacMillan, 1923–58.

Trimpi, Wesley, *Ben Jonson's Poems. A Study of the Plain Style*, Stanford University Press, 1962.

Tudeau-Clayton, Margaret, 'Competing for Virgil: From the Courtroom to the Marketplace', *International Journal of the Classical Tradition* 4:4 (Spring 1998).

'Supplementing the *Aeneid* in Early Modern England: Translation, Imitation, Commentary'. *International Journal of the Classical Tradition*, forthcoming.

'"I do not know my selfe": The Topography and Politics of Self-Knowledge in *Bartholomew Fair*', forthcoming in P. Berry and M. Tudeau-Clayton (eds.), *The Texture of Renaissance Knowledge: Cultural Difference and Critical Method*.

Turk, E., '*Les Saturnales* de Macrobe: Source de Servius Danielis', *Revue des études latines* 41 (1963), 327–49.

Waith, Eugene, 'The Poet's Morals in *Poetaster*', *Modern Language Quarterly* 12 (1951), 13–19.

Walker, D. P., *Spiritual and Demonic Magic from Ficino to Campanella*, Studies of the Warburg Institute 22, London: Warburg Institute, 1958.

Waswo, Richard, *Language and Meaning in The Renaissance*, Princeton University Press, 1987.

'The History That Literature Makes', *New Literary History* 19 (1988), 541–64.

The Founding Legend of Western Civilization: From Virgil to Vietnam, Hanover, N. H. and London: New England/Wesleyan University Press, 1997.

Wayne, Don E., *Penshurst: The Semiotics of Place and the Poetics of History*, London: Methuen, 1984.

'Power, Politics, and the Shakespearean Text: Recent Criticism in England and the United States', in Jean H. Howard, and Marion F. O'Connor (eds.), *Shakespeare Reproduced: The Text in History and Ideology*, New York and London: Methuen, 1987.

Welsford, Enid, *The Court Masque*, Cambridge University Press, 1927.

Wilkinson, L. P., *The Georgics of Virgil. A Critical Survey*, Cambridge University Press, 1969.

Williams, Raymond, *The Country and The City*, London: Granada, 1975.

Wills, Jeffrey, 'Virgil's *cuium*', *Vergilius* 39 (1993), 3–11.

Wilson, Edmund, 'Morose Ben Jonson' (1948), in *The Triple Thinkers: Twelve Essays on Literary Subjects*, reprint, Harmondsworth: Penguin, 1962.

Wiltenburg, Robert, 'The *Aeneid* in *The Tempest*', *Shakespeare Survey* 39 (1987), 159–68.

Womack, Peter, *Ben Jonson*, Oxford: Basil Blackwell, 1986.

Wykes, David, 'Ben Jonson's "Chast Booke" – *The Epigrammes*', *Renaissance and Modern Studies* 13 (1969), 76–87.

Yates, Francis, *Giordano Bruno and the Hermetic Tradition*, London: Routledge and Kegan Paul, 1964.

Zabughin, Vladimiro, *Vergilio nel rinascimento italiano*, 2 vols., Bologna: Zanichelli, 1923.

Ziolkowski, Theodore, 'Vergil's *Nachleben*; From Monograph to Mélange', *International Journal of the Classical Tradition* 4:1 (Summer 1997).

Zukofsky, Louis, *Bottom: On Shakespeare*, University of California Press, 1987.

Index

Adelman, Janet, 192
air,
  agency of, 84–5, 91, 93–4
  Ariel as spirit of, 84, 106
  Juno as figure of, 87, 146–8, 152, 163, 216
Allen, Don Cameron, 25
analogy, 142–9, 211, 224, 225–8, 230, 235, 238
Appelt, T. C., 74
archaisms, Virgil's use of, 41–2, 68, 123, 177, 179–83
Ascham, Roger, 102–3
Attridge, Derek, 57, 62, 102–3, 104, 107
'author function', 155–9, 171, 206, 244

Bacon, Francis, 161, 198, 231, 233
Baldwin, T. W., 44, 72, 75, 81, 214–5
Barber, Charles, 64
Barclay, John, 225–8, 238
Barish, Jonas, 156
Barker, Francis, 197
Barthes, Roland, 62
Barton, Anne, 142–3, 161
Bassnett-McGuire, Susan, 63, 64
Baswell, Christopher C., 1, 7–8, 15, 27, 78, 79, 80, 83, 87, 190, 193, 216, 237
Bate, Jonathan, 4, 139, 151, 158
Bawcutt, Priscilla, 50–1, 81, 161
Belyea, Barbara, 64
Bennington, Geoffrey, 137
Berg, Sara van den, 156
Birch, David, 43
Bloom, Harold, 15
Boehrer, Bruce Thomas, 166, 167, 188
Bolgar, Robert, 32
Bono, Barbara J., 3, 194
Bourcier, Paul, 220
Brant, Sebastian, 22–4, 25, 88–9, 208, 216
  illustration to the tempest in *Aeneid* 1, *24*
  illustration to *Georgics* 1, lines 231–51, *88*
Brinsley, John, 33–4, 36–7, 44–7, 51–7, 72, 75, 76–7, 81, 107

translation of *Eclogue* 1, *52*
Brinton, Anna Cox, 23, 25, 210
Brissenden, Alan, 220
Brisson, Barnaby, 82, 146–7
Bristol, Michael, 156
Britain, construction of, 5, 6, 82–3, 120–2, 123–4, 128–9
Browne, Robert, 36, 71
Bruno, Giordano, 86, 104
Bullough, Geoffrey, 144
Bulman, James C., 4, 75
Burt, Richard, 136, 155–6

Cain, Tom, 1, 150, 151, 161, 162
Calder, I. R. F., 101
Camden, William, 121, 122, 123–4
Cameron, A., 78, 80
canonicity,
  of authors, 2–3, 196
  of early Virgilian commentaries, 26–31
  see also Macrobius; Servius
Cartelli, Thomas, 138
Cascardi, Anthony, 11
Caspari, F., 31
'castitas', as defining term of Virgilian character, 42–3, 133, 159, 166, 169–72, 176, 178–83, 188–9
Catholic,
  Dryden as, 13
  Jonson as, 12, 31–2, 79, 118
  structure of hermeneutic authority, 8, 12, 30, 31–2, 78–80, 118
  translation of Bible, 12, 123, 127
Cave, Terence, 15, 33
Céard, Jean, 95, 96, 97, 105
Charlton, K., 31
civil war, 13, 110, 225, 240, 241, 243
Clarke, M. L., 44
Columbus, Christopher, 23–4, 38, 208
Comes, N., 127, 128, 146, 196
commentary, 25–6, 28–31, 51–3, 59–60, 78–9

Printed in the United Kingdom
by Lightning Source UK Ltd.
119004UK00001B/214